WORK WITHOUT END

*Abandoning Shorter Hours
for the Right to Work*

LABOR AND SOCIAL CHANGE

A series edited by Paula Rayman and Carmen Sirianni

WORK WITHOUT END

Abandoning Shorter Hours for the Right to Work

BENJAMIN KLINE HUNNICUTT

Temple University Press
Philadelphia

Temple University Press, Philadelphia 19122
Copyright © 1988 by Temple University. All rights reserved
Published 1988
Printed in the United States of America

∞ The paper used in this publication meets the minimum
requirements of American National Standard for Information
Sciences—Permanence of Paper for Printed Library Materials,
ANSI Z39.48-1984

Library of Congress Cataloging-in-Publication Data
Hunnicutt, Benjamin Kline.
Work without end.
(Labor and social change)
Bibliography: p.
Includes index.
1. Hours of labor—United States—History.
2. Leisure—United States—History.   I. Title.
II. Series.
HD5124.H86   1988   331.25'7'0973   87-13966
ISBN 0-87722-520-6 (alk. paper)

For the memory of my father,
Robert Ayden Hunnicutt, Sr.

Works and days were offered us, and we took Works.

—Ralph Waldo Emerson, 1870

CONTENTS

ACKNOWLEDGMENTS

I am indebted to a number of individuals and institutions for help in writing this book. The University of Iowa has been a constant source of support for my work, providing me with free time, among the most precious of life's gifts, to write. Individuals at this fine institution, Ellis Hawley and John Schacht, have offered support and suggestions that have been valuable. My debts have mounted up for years and extend back to my days as a student at the University of North Carolina and to my teachers there, especially George Mowry, who started me on the topic of leisure, Douglas Sessoms, Frank Ryan, Joel Williamson, and Peter Walker.

Others have appeared in my life and lent support at just the right times. David Montgomery saw value in my work when I had about given up hope that anyone was interested in the "end of shorter hours." Even though a journal had lost one of my manuscripts, as one of its reviewers, he remembered my work and encouraged me to keep struggling with the question that is the central focus of this book. Carmen Sirianni, seeing the results of this persistence, also gave me a needed boost at the right time, encouraging me to finish the manuscript that has become *Work Without End*. He, along with Michael Ames, read the early drafts and offered suggestions that have given the book a focus and, I trust, a clarity that my first attempts sorely lacked. I would also like to thank Gary Cross for all the time we spent discussing shorter hours. His perspective as a European historian has given me an appreciation that the questions addressed here about American work have international dimensions.

Libraries provide the raw material for all history. Without them, the past would be lost, and the historian would have nothing to occupy his time. The library at the University of Iowa has been generous to me, giving me, among other things, permission to publish the charming "Ding" Darling cartoons. People in this library, Keith Rageth and Bob McCown, have always been there to help solve hard problems. The Hoover Library at West Branch, the University of Wisconsin Library, the University of Illinois Library, and the University of North Carolina

Library opened their doors to me and assisted me in my research. The Library of Congress collection of Hugo Black's papers has been critically important for this book.

I acknowledge my debt to my family—my wife, Francine, and sons Ben and Chris—for their support and encouragement. In addition I thank my mother, Cassie, for her lifetime of help and for her gift, the love of learning. I also appreciate the challenge of the younger generation, my students, who have with their questions and perpetual doubt kept me unsure of my own conclusions and always willing to change my mind. Finally, in turn, I offer this book as a challenge to my nephew, Daniel Deans, who has just begun as a historian; a challenge to find the joy that history can provide. History, done right, is its own reward. It should be more leisure than work, more art than science.

WORK WITHOUT END

*Abandoning Shorter Hours
for the Right to Work*

INTRODUCTION

S HORTER HOURS of labor were an important part of American history for over a century before World War II. Beginning in the early years of the industrial revolution, the shorter-hour process continued slowly but steadily until the turn of the century, at which time it accelerated rapidly. During the two decades after 1900, working hours fell sharply from just under 60 hours a week to just under 50. During the 1920s, the process slowed, but accelerated again during the Great Depression as weekly hours fell below 35.[1]

Moreover, shorter hours became a vital issue in the formation of the labor movement in the early nineteenth century and continued to be important for unions until the end of the Great Depression. Some of the most dramatic and significant events in the history of labor, such as the strikes of 1886, the Haymarket riots, and the steel strike of 1919, and some of labor's most notable achievements, for example, the 10-hour and 8-hour day, were part of this century-long struggle for shorter hours. On the one hand, organized labor recognized the widespread interest in shorter hours that existed among American workers and used the issue to gain members and support. But unions also led the way for all American workers, forcing reductions in hours for their members that acted as beacons for unorganized workers and spurs to nonunion shops and accelerated the existing tendencies of workers in the labor market to press for fewer hours.[2]

In addition, the issue of shorter hours was political almost as long as it was a labor cause. It was part of reform politics from before the Civil War through Franklin Delano Roosevelt's second term. It was endorsed by the idealistic, antebellum reformers. It had a prominent place in the Populists' Omaha platform and the Bull Moose platform, and appeared in both the Democratic and Republican platforms as late as 1932. Shorter hours also raised important constitutional issues in the early twentieth century, leading to the writing of some of the most progressive legal opinions of that time. Federal and state legislation and executive actions began before the Civil War and continued until the Fair Labor Standards Act of 1938. State hours legislation for the period fills a good-size book. Federal action, beginning with Martin Van Buren's 10-hour executive order of 1840, proceeded step-by-step to reduce working hours for government employees until World War II. Like labor's efforts, much of the politics of shorter hours was generated in response to widespread public interest. But, again similar to labor's influence, political achievements did have some impact in the sense that they augmented and speeded a process already under way in American society.[3]

Finally, influential writers and social critics had a lot to say about the process. Some welcomed and promoted shorter hours, believing that they were as natural and good a result of industrial advance as higher wages. Others supported the process for work's sake, believing that by reducing the hours of labor and hence fatigue, work could be perfected and made a thoroughly joyous experience—rendering the hard task of convincing workers of the ethical worth and intrinsic value of work a bit easier. At the close of the shorter-hour era, a few intellectuals even promoted shorter hours as an alternative to work, as an avenue for human progress leading the common man to exercise his higher faculties—body, mind, and spirit—in a democratic culture. Some of the most idealistic and "romantic" rhetoric of a generation of "Progressives" centered on the promise of increased leisure during the 1920s and 1930s.

But the shorter-hour process stopped after the Great Depression. After World War II, the workweek stabilized at around 40 hours. A broadly based economic and social trend that had existed for over a century reached some sort of historical plateau nearly fifty years ago. Some economists have made the claim that there has been *no* increase in leisure time since World War II and have written dissertations and books with such titles as "The Age of the Constant Workweek" and *An Investigation of the Stability of Hours of Work per week in Manufacturing*.[4]

In fact, if anything, a good case may be made that Americans have increased their work time. Since World War II, the percentage of Americans in the labor force has grown as more women have gotten jobs. As a percentage of the total population, more people are at work today than ever before—the percentage increase occurring largely during the recent period of work-hour stability. So, in aggregate percentage terms, figuring the percentage of total work time in terms of the total population's total hours, work time has increased. Retirement, from a cursory examination, may seem to have added more leisure to the worker's life. But Americans have more retirement years today primarily because they live longer. Seen in the context of a longer life span, the leisure time of retirement is only one part of an equation that includes more work time as well. The years added to the life span in this century have been divided between work and leisure; and most of those extra years have been devoted to work. Americans today have more free time in retirement, but they also have much longer average work lives than workers in previous times. Added to these trends, the last few years of Reaganomics have seen weekly hours of work increase to above 40, and some observers, with a degree of satisfaction, see this as a process that is likely to continue.[5]

In addition to these statistics, the various historical facets of the shorter-hour process have undergone a similar transformation. Organized labor, for instance, has turned its attention to higher wages, collective bargaining rights, and fringe benefits. These issues have virtually eclipsed any new calls for shorter hours. For over forty-five years, labor has done nothing comparable to its nineteenth- and early-twentieth-century initiatives and successes. Moreover, since the depression, no major party has made shorter hours a political issue; no resolutions have been passed, and no convention platform has been constructed with a reference to this traditional reform. In addition, state and federal legislators have ignored the issue, which earlier had occupied so much of their time, attention, and rhetoric. They have modified and corrected the 1938 Fair Labor Standards Act, but they have not altered its 40-hour-week provision. During this time, neither Washington nor the states have passed new laws substantially lowering working hours. Hours of labor, when they are mentioned by governmental officials, are most frequently included as one of the list of "leading economic indicators"—shorter hours being defined as a *negative* indicator. Indeed, the issue of shorter hours has ceased to be an important part of public discourse. The dreams of the utopian writers and the hopes of those who believed that progress involved leisure as much as it involved economic growth have largely evaporated, and labor's old call for "the progressive shortening of the hours of labor" has been forgotten. The study of "leisure," the word now appearing often in pejorative quotes, has been relegated to obscure scholars out of the mainstream of intellectual life by those busy with more important and serious matters, such as jobs and how to make more of them.[6]

Historians have not yet come to grips with these facts. They have not even begun to formulate appropriate questions, much less construct hypotheses. By contrast, economists have been asking, "Why have working hours stabilized in America since World War II?" and have come up with some valuable explanations—most of which, of course, are economic ones. Among economists' explanations are the reduction of fatigue, the availability of consumer credit, advertising and better marketing, patterns of family work and work at home, the "price of recreation," easier work, and stability of employment. But since the shorter-hour process was more than an economic event, and since its ending involved political, social, and cultural dimensions, historians need to pose their own questions, a few of which are suggested here.[7]

Why did such a broad-scale social and economic trend, which involved the mass of American workers for over a century and concerned vitally important parts of their everyday existence, suddenly stop? Why did organized labor abandon its long struggle for shorter hours almost overnight? Why have intellectual and public debates about the importance of the reduction of work practically ceased? Why did this one part of the nineteenth- and early-twentieth-century liberal/progressive tradition end, and by ending, disrupt reform's continuum? Why did the workweek and workday shrink when the United States was relatively poor and then stop shrinking when the nation became the richest one in history? How could Americans afford so much free time when they were poor and not be able to afford it when they have become so much better off? Why did the American concept of progress change from dreams about the growth of wages, which would improve material welfare, *and* the growth of leisure, which would free the individual from material concerns in order to accomplish finer and higher things?

Answers to these questions are at the heart of this book. The most obvious way to answer is to account for the long success of the shorter-hour process, to identify and outline the historical forces and events that supported it for so long and then identify those that have ended or weakened. In addition, a presentation and analysis of the historical factors that worked against the reduction of hours, when those factors emerged and when they overcame the earlier forces, would advance such an argument. A full explanation for the end of shorter hours would include a complete account of both kinds of forces and events.

This is a formidable task that is made more awesome because historians have done comparatively little work in this area. Even though scholars such as Gary Cross and David Brody are currently engaged in the necessary basic research, the body of knowledge that exists on this subject is woefully sparse and inadequate for such a synthesis. This first attempt at explanation, then, can hardly be comprehensive.

Nevertheless, the first step is at least to pose the right questions. If this study does nothing more than ask, "Why have shorter hours ended?" it will have served a worthwhile function.

The second step is to do what history does best. Tell the story. This initial task does not require a full account of long-term historical forces or a fullblown synthesis. The study's principal claim to explanation, then, is the claim that history itself makes for interpretive originality—the narrative—a description of events as they unfolded in logical and/or historical sequence. Telling the story, the historian provides a basic reason why things happened the way they did and not a great number of other possible ways. Hence, most of the book is devoted to the period from 1920 to 1940 and to describing the series of events that led up to and surrounded the end of shorter hours. Implicit in the chronicle of the debates, politics, labor struggles, sallies of businessmen and advertisers, and inarticulate choices of workers in the labor market are antagonistic historical forces that might be detected and seen to have met and conflicted: those supporting shorter hours opposed by those discouraging the process. But it is in the concrete of historical detail that these broader issues are contained. In the political, intellectual, and social dialogues about the importance of work as against the importance of work reduction, which formed and developed during these years, larger and longer issues and forces worked themselves out. And while the narrative might suggest such larger forces, it cannot make them fully explicit. That task must await further research and analysis.

Although the last twenty years of the shorter-hour movement is critical, for it stands at the juncture of two long and opposite historical trends, a brief description of the previous, century-long shorter-hour movement is useful to set the stage for the central narrative and at least begin to suggest some of the forces that supported the movement for so long and whose ending may have helped end shorter hours. Of special importance as prologue are the years from 1900 to 1920 when hours were reducing at their most rapid rate, work as a cultural value was challenged as never before, and governmental regulation and political involvement with the issue were widespread. In addition, an account of the years since the end of shorter hours (since 1940) may suggest how cultural values, intellectual positions, labor policies, political decisions, and governmental measures that began during the depression to counter shorter hours and redeem work have continued to discourage the increase of leisure time until the present.

Such a history is limited in several ways, many of which may be more obvious to the reader than the writer. But the ones that are evident should be confessed at the start. The focus is primarily on manufacturing workers, mostly male, living mainly in the industrial Northeast and North Central regions. Most of the people who wrote about shorter hours were also from these regions; they were part of the infamous Yankee bourgeoisie, even though groups such as the Twelve Southerners also contributed to the dialogue. In addition, statistical records from the period are notoriously unreliable, and even though they have been filtered through the best scholarly nets of the economic academicians, errors almost certainly remain, for which the user of these records must take the blame.

Finally, this study is limited by the ongoing interpretive controversy between economists and historians. It is very tempting to plunge into these troubled waters because important issues are involved. For instance, it is tempting to try to claim, with many economists, that since the shorter-hour process took place in the free labor market, the history of shorter hours represents a record of workers' free choices in, and responses to, that changing market. In the ideal free labor market, workers have a clear choice between work and wages or shorter hours. The choice is mutually exclusive; to the extent that workers choose leisure, they must give up work and wages. And, obviously, to the extent they choose to work more for more money, they must sacrifice free time. If one could substantiate such claims to everyone's satisfaction, then broad and sweeping conclusions could be made about workers' behavior and attitudes concerning the relative importance of work and wages as against nonwork activities and nonpecuniary values. This would open up important new ways to explore what Herbert Gutman and the new labor historians have been attempting: to understand how "the behavior [and values] of working people affected the development of the larger culture and society in which they lived."[8] One might suggest, with the Chicago economist Frank Knight:

> In so far as men act rationally—i.e., from fixed motives subject to the law of diminishing utility—they will at a higher [income] rate divide their time between wage-earning and non-industrial uses in such a way as to earn *more money,* indeed, but to work *fewer hours.* Just where the balance will be struck depends upon the shape of the curve of comparison between money (representing the group of things purchasable with money) and leisure (representing all non-pecuniary, alternative uses of time).[9]

Such suggestions—money representing purchasable things and leisure representing all nonpecuniary uses of time—tempt one to speculate on a classic historical debate: "Are economic motives or nonpecuniary considerations the salient historical force?" One might hope, however briefly, that a study of workers' hours and wages would shed new light on this perennial object of sophomore wonder. Then, with the suspicion that workers have economized the time of their lives, jointly dividing it between work and leisure "rationally" (as the economists say), the historian would have reason to look for parallel and equally large-scale changes in American opinion about such things as work, leisure, wages, play, recreation, and consumption that may have correlated with the dramatic ending of the shorter-hour process and the beginning of the current age of work and wages. And in so doing, the historian could make claims to new explanations.

But this requires accepting the economists' two assumptions: (1) that workers were aware that they had a mutually exclusive choice between leisure and work for wages, and (2) that they were able to act on that choice.

Historians, for the most part, are not willing to make such concessions. These assumptions differ from the conventional historical wisdom. Opposed to this "two goods" model and its possible interpretations of the record of wage–hour changes stands the traditional historian's understanding that sees workers' desire for shorter hours as a means to an end, as part of a calculated economic strategy rather than one element in a "rational" choice in the marketplace. From this point of view, what the workers "knew" was not shorter hours *or* higher wages but shorter hours *for* higher wages. From this perspective, the principal factor in the relationship between hours and wages was that workers wanted both, for many of the same reasons. They did not have to choose between them and between two different sets of motives since the relationship was conditional, not disjunctive. According to the nineteenth-century doggerel:

> Whether you work by the piece or
>   by the day
> Decreasing the hours increases the
>   pay.

In addition, historians have emphasized work-hour legislation and, curiously enough, employer decisions and labor demand more than economists have. Historians have not seen workers as having enough freedom in the labor market to set their own hours because workers were largely subject to the dictates of employers or to market forces beyond their control.

Since issues about workers' freedom in the market and their understanding of the wage–hour relationship have not been resolved, it makes sense to avoid this controversial area as much as possible. But a synthesis that would explain the ending of shorter hours depends on some resolution of this academic conflict. For no other reason, this is true because economists see increased wages as a central reason that work hours have declined, whereas historians see the reverse. Doubtless, both points of view have merit. The extent to which both can help explain the history of shorter hours needs to be worked out; com-promises and some meeting of minds need to occur. But until such time as these things are accomplished, the historical narrative may still make a beginning, limited though it is in its general conclusions and implications by these as yet unresolved differences.

CHAPTER 1

The Century of Shorter Hours and Work Reduction

OF THE MANY nineteenth-century industrial causes, crusades, and reforms, shorter hours of labor emerged as the issue of the working classes. At the start of the industrial process, workers were concerned about the portion of their lives and energy taken by their jobs and resisted the imposition of new forms of work discipline such as strict scheduling and long hours. This resistance took the forms of absenteeism, irregular work habits, and celebration of a long list of traditional holidays and special occasions, all of which plagued industrial managers. But as industrialization and the supporting social order were able to achieve more regular work schedules and more disciplined routines, such resistance—what E. P. Thompson called the "struggle against time"—diminished. Instead, workers expressed their concern and dissatisfaction another way—as "the struggle for time." Accepting work's new forms, workers turned to shorter hours to combat the drudgery and physical toll of their jobs and to find the time and energy for a life outside the factory. In the process, they initiated a century-long campaign.[1]

The story of the campaign has been told before. Indeed, it has become a central feature of both labor and worker history. Although there are disputes about the facts of this history—about major events, leaders, timing, and relevance to other labor–worker concerns—there are few disagreements about its importance or its most obvious feature: Workers wanted shorter hours and took action to get them for over a century. Moreover, there is general agreement as to why this happened. Traditional labor histories and more recent studies confirm that desires for leisure, higher wages, secure employment, and better working conditions were the main reasons workers struggled for shorter hours. Disagreement has arisen only about the timing and relative importance of these four constituent motives.

Originally, John R. Commons and the labor economists at the University of Wisconsin showed that organized labor supported shorter hours as one of the more practical ways to reduce the supply of labor and thus force wages higher and counter technological unemployment. This was a key part of labor's overall economic strategy during most of the nineteenth century and well into the twentieth. Leisure was in a different category. The labor economists conceded that the workers' desire for more leisure time for their families and communities, and for culture, religion, and traditional activities, constituted one of the few noneconomic motives that resulted in direct action and helped spur the organizational process.[2]

According to Commons and his associates, leisure was labor's earliest motive—the "cause of the awakening" of the American wage earner. In the 1820s and 1830s, the "most frequent cause of complaint among the workers was the lack of leisure."[3] At first, the reason workers most often gave for desiring more free time related to citizenship. They expressed the need for time to study and understand the democratic process, to discuss issues, to organize politically, and simply to vote. The citizenship argument was rapidly followed by other justifications: that the new machines made work harder, more stressful, and less rewarding; that the new pace of work caused accidents, sickness, chronic fatigue, premature aging; and that long hours in the factory disrupted the family and the community, in the process causing immorality, social instability, spiritual decay, and loss of tradition. Consequently, workers said they needed more leisure time in order to make their jobs bearable and allow time for living.

But the labor economists were careful to note that while the first demand was for leisure, this was only the prelude to the economic movement.[4] The leisure issue faded rapidly as soon as a few modest reductions in working hours had been made. By 1852, labor had fully recognized the economic importance of shorter hours and subsequently emphasized increased employment and higher wages. After the 1918 publication of the first two volumes of their classic work, Commons and his associates rarely mentioned leisure again. Leisure as an important labor motive was emphasized only in Helen Sumner's chapter, "Causes of the Awakening," in the first volume, which dealt with the period before 1850.[5]

Several writers have followed this line of interpretation. Harry Millis and Royal Montgomery, for example, showed that even though one may find in the origins of the shorter-hour movement "an interest in leisure, rest and recreation, more family life, social opportunities and self-advancement; in all these connections there is a vast difference between the ten and eight or six hour day." The difference was that these interests were "increasingly overshadowed . . . by the argument that shorter hours are necessary to avoid unemployment and increase real income." Millis and Montgomery concluded that in the late nineteenth and early twentieth centuries, "most of all . . . insistence upon the shorter work day is to be accounted for by the general feelings among the workers that shortening the work period both increased wages and contributed toward a solution of the problem of unemployment."[6] Irving Bernstein agreed. He observed that by the time of the Great Depression, "the economic argument crowded out the others."[7]

Emphasizing the economic motives behind shorter hours, the labor economists focused their descriptions on work and issues related to the job. David Brody praised this "steady focus on men and women at work" as having provided the field of labor history with a "comprehensive framework" that has been lost.[8] But the traditional focus on work did determine to some degree the kinds of findings made about shorter hours. For the labor economists, the issue of shorter hours was first and foremost a work issue. They saw it as one of a number of causes, among them job safety and worker education, that served to improve work, not offer an alternative to it. Moreover, these more traditional descriptions have centered on obvious public events such as strikes, walkouts, negotiations, and laws and have not explored the private part of workers' lives that had to do with the use or the value placed on the logical consequence of shorter hours: increased leisure.

Historians such as Herbert Gutman, writing more about unorganized workers and less about unions, have questioned this focus on work and labor organizations and the interpretations based on economic motivations. As David Montgomery noted:

> The question was not simply that Commons had taught us to study workers through the behavior of their unions in the labor market while Gutman scrutinized their activities in a broadened social context. It was rather that Commons had analyzed the worker as economic man, whereas Gutman showed that the basic thrust of the 19th century workers' struggles entailed a rejection of economic man.[9]

What has been written about the working classes has a direct relevance to the history of shorter hours. In effect, the "new labor historians" have changed the historical focus from "men and women at work" to workers' lives away from their jobs and have thereby altered the description of shorter hours. Older analyses of the public forms of the shorter-hour campaigns (analyses of strikes, union positions, etc.) have been replaced by analyses of the content or use of those hours won from work. Leisure, in the newer studies, has been understood less as a way for workers to perfect their work or gain economic advantages and more of a cultural necessity or asset. Leisure seems to have permitted the expression of traditional values and customs; the formation of class consciousness; and the maintenance of institutions such as family, church, and community. Thus leisure has been seen as important because it was necessary for the expression of a whole category of nonpecuniary motives that the new labor historians have emphasized. In addition, several historians have shown that many workers did not fully accept the dominant work ethic, and in their time away from the job they found alternative social contexts in which to express alternative values. As a result of this descriptive shift, historians have recently given leisure a greater emphasis.

For example, Steven Ross and John Cumbler have demonstrated the significance of leisure for worker culture. Ross claimed rather broadly that "although work was a central focus of daily life, it did not produce a single working class experience" for workers in nineteenth-century Cincinnati. Instead, it was during the time spent in saloons and churches, and as members of benevolent associations, or ethnic societies, that workers gave expression to their traditional cultures and came to "fashion their understanding and response to the problems of industrial life." [10] Cumbler drew similar conclusions from his study of workers in the towns of Lynn and Fall River, Massachusetts. There, workers' experiences in lunchrooms, poolrooms, bowling alleys, clubs, and social centers were the basis for the formation of a working-class ideology. [11]

The historians Virginia McLaughlin and Elizabeth Peck, among others, have written about the family and have shown that women, having to divide their time between jobs and homes, often tried to find part-time work or alter their work schedules in order to preserve traditional family arrangements. Buffalo's southern Italians, for example, were caught between the demands of work and family and tried to deal with the resultant tension by taking time off from their jobs. A direct link between workers' traditional culture and religion and interest in specific shorter-hour events has been found among Jewish garment workers in New York City, who initiated the five-day-week campaign in the 1920s in order to preserve Saturday as their Sabbath. [12]

Roy Rosenzweig assumed that an understanding of workers' leisure was a prerequisite for understanding working-class cultures—"the basic values, beliefs, and traditions"—the character of class relations and the evolution of these cultures into the "commercialized leisure world of the twentieth century." Moreover, Rosenzweig showed that workers in Worcester, Massachusetts, were able in their free time to create new and distinctive social institutions, such as the saloon, that symbolized both a rejection of the dominant cultural values of sobriety, thrift, and competition and the acceptance of "alternative public modes of mutuality, conviviality, and collectivity."[13] Rosenzweig agreed with Herbert Gutman that workers did not accept or participate fully in the dominant social and cultural values of the late nineteenth century. In particular, workers stopped short of endorsing the *sine qua non* of the era, the Protestant work ethic. Instead of looking to work as the source of value, or even to the eventual perfection of work, they rebelled first against work discipline and then turned away from the job to find their own cultures, building, on traditional and ethnic foundations, new and alternative institutions and values.

The newer studies, then, have shown that while organized labor may have tended to emphasize the economic and job-improvement benefits of shorter hours and to downplay leisure benefits as the nineteenth century wore on, unorganized workers continued to value their leisure well into the twentieth century, for a variety of nonpecuniary reasons. Because of the focus on workers and their cultures, these studies have not directly challenged the conclusions of Commons and his followers that economic issues dominated all others by the early twentieth century. But they have presented a *prima facie* case for leisure's importance as a shorter-hour motive, explaining the workers' behavior in seeking work and changing jobs, if not the positions and justifications of the unions.

But at most this is a simple change in emphasis, not a major reinterpretation. The point at issue is the importance of leisure relative to the importance of higher wages, unemployment, and job improvement. No claim has been made that any of these four major motives were not involved in the history of shorter hours. Because of the earlier historical focus on unions and the later focus on unorganized workers, even the differing stress on leisure may be reconciled.

Instead of overturning Commons's original findings, the newer studies have refined and added to the historical understanding. There may yet be disagreement about timing and the strength of motives among certain groups, but the groundwork has been prepared for a synthetic history of shorter hours based on Commons's original four motives.

The nonpecuniary concerns of workers described by the newer labor historians may be understood as having combined with the economic motives that were so important for the unions and thus to have added strength to the shorter-hour campaign. Workers who accepted the Protestant work ethic and tried to improve their jobs by reducing their hours joined in common cause with immigrants and others who rejected work as the center of life and turned to leisure to escape from their jobs into subcultures and institutions alternative to the dominant values of the "gilded age." The shorter-hour issue brought together workers and unions with different and even contradictory values and motives. Thus a coalition may have formed around this issue, one that may help to explain the beginnings, strength, and duration of the movement.

This review of historical interpretations lays the groundwork for some speculations about possible reasons for the end of the shorter-hour process. If, for example, the unions' economic and job-perfection arguments became less important for organized labor coincidentally with the end of shorter hours, one may suspect that this correlation is important and may serve as one explanation. Similarly, if the weakening influence of workers' subcultures, brought on by the assimilation of ethnic groups or the end of immigration or internal migration, coincided with the end of shorter hours, another possible explanation presents itself.

Clearly, workers wanted shorter hours for the four reasons outlined above and took actions in the marketplace and in their organizations to get them. But they did not struggle for shorter hours in a vacuum. Other economic and social factors contributed to the process and were in some cases essential to it. Economists agree that without increases in productivity, brought on by technological advances in the nineteenth century, neither shorter hours nor higher wages would have been possible. But increased efficiency was a necessary cause, not a sufficient one; this is made clear by the eventual ending of the shorter-hour process. Given the background of gradual improvement in the methods of production accomplished by both labor and capital, changes in the attitudes of workers and their unions, described above, and changes in the supporting social, political, and intellectual climate take on greater importance for the historian seeking reasons for the end of shorter hours.

Workers found widespread support for their shorter-hour campaign in the nineteenth century. This support was an important factor in the history of shorter hours; it reinforced workers' desires and helped sustain their initiative. It was crucial in the passage of shorter-hour legislation and part of the climate of opinion that allowed workers to bargain successfully with their employers. Although not as clear cut as the labor–worker four motives, that support had several dimensions and brought people with different ideas and values together in coalition.

The major reasons that politicians, intellectuals, and social critics supported the reduction of work hours in the nineteenth century have been described by historians and may be presented in summary fashion. Again, as in the existing histories of labor and workers, obvious features appear. By far the most important reasons were practical. People outside the labor movement endorsed the reform primarily because they believed that it would improve work performance and increase production—free time was to benefit work. Second, free time was seen as acceptable because of serious social concerns: health, citizenship, morality, family and religious duties. Of somewhat less importance were ideas about the eventual results of progress. Writers who speculated about the future often suggested that material progress, higher wages, and increased production were important because they would lead not only to a better standard of living but also to progress in the nonmaterial realms of culture, the mind, and the spirit. Such things would require more time than money. Others, looking back to the Declaration of Independence, saw shorter hours leading eventually to the consummation of America's third guaranteed freedom–the pursuit of happiness.[14]

To be sure, there was considerable opposition. Businessmen, conservative religious spokesmen and politicians, and industrial managers strenuously objected to specific shorter-hour proposals, seeing them as leading in the short term to immorality, social disorder, and poverty. Some even objected to shorter hours categorically, thus rejecting the idea that the common man would ever benefit from less rather than more work. The task at hand was, after all, inculcating the work ethic in order to overcome workers' too-ready attraction to ease and dissipation. More common, however, were ideas that work discipline prepared workers to be good stewards of their time and money and that material progress would eventually lead to more wealth and more freedom from work for more and more Americans. Hence, the point of debate was usually about the timing of higher wages and shorter hours, although the timing sometimes extended to the infinite. A popular hymn's verse, "Work for the night is coming when man works no more," summed up the somewhat paradoxical belief that work, as a prayer ascending to God, was life's beatitude: the means of salvation and the attainment of heaven's eternal Sabbath blessing of not having to work anymore. Leisure, as the singing of eternal psalms, may have been far off indeed. But the widespread belief in progress and human perfectibility in the nineteenth century involved the acceptance of both higher wages and shorter hours in the long term, reflecting the belief that work and even material progress were, at least in part, means to nonmaterial ends. Thus shorter hours, as a practical labor reform and political issue, figured prominently in nineteenth-century discussions about progress and the values and purposes of work and wealth.[15]

As a labor cause and a political issue, shorter hours grew in importance and involved many individuals and groups. A large number of influential writers—utopian novelists, socialists, Populists, mugwumps, intellectuals, and social critics—welcomed and promoted the issue of shorter hours, believing it was as natural and as good a result of technological advances as higher wages.

Partly because of a general climate of support, hours of labor were reduced gradually and steadily throughout the nineteenth century. Then, during the first two decades of the twentieth century, working hours declined rapidly—four times as fast as before and at a rate approached only twice since, during the first years of the Great Depression and for a brief period just after World War II. Coincident with this precipitous reduction, interest in shorter hours increased. Some social and economic factors that historians have associated with shorter hours in the nineteenth century also intensified, and new reasons for work reductions emerged. Yet other important forces and influences were weaker or were simply not present. The period from 1900 to 1920 presents a complex mixture of historical factors that have yet to be untangled in regard to their influence on the acceleration of shorter hours. But as a prologue to the end of shorter hours, the period is vital, and so a brief description is in order, even though it is not possible to judge authoritatively the relative importance of all factors.[16]

Historians have tended to look to labor demand as one determinant of work hours, reasoning that the lack of available employment increases unemployment and reduces available weekly working hours. For example, workers in occupations troubled by seasonal layoffs were interested in shorter hours during this period as a way to "rationalize" their industries (e.g., clothing) by spreading the work over the year. Unemployment from 1900 to 1914 did average a bit higher than in previous decades and in the years following, before the Great Depression. Thus there is a case to be made that lack of labor demand (represented by unemployment figures) was one factor in the acceleration of the shorter-hour process. Existing statistics from the period are far from convincing, however. Cross-sectional analysis of the 1900 census data, the Bureau of Labor Statistics' unemployment and wage–hour figures for 1914–1915, and longitudinal analysis of 1900 to 1914 figures showed no significant correlation between total unemployment rates and working hours.[17]

Nevertheless, a more detailed analysis of these figures reveals some effect of unemployment on working hours. Even though in the 1900 census data, unemployment, considered as a combination of all categories used by the Bureau of the Census, was not correlated in cross-section with hours worked per week, when unemployment was considered separately by the three census categories, there was a significant ($p < .001$) simple negative correlation ($-.468$) between hours worked and the percentage of workers unemployed 7 to 12 months. In categories "1 to 3 months" and "4 to 6 months," no significant correlation appeared. Similarly, analysis of the Bureau of Labor Statistics unemployment and wage–hour figures for 1914–1915 showed unemployment in categories "91 to 120 days," "121 to 180 days," and "over 181 days" significantly ($p < .01$) and negatively correlated ($-.356$, $-.197$, $-.177$) with hours, whereas in categories "31 to 60 days" and "61 to 90 days" there was significant ($p < .01$) *positive* correlation (.401 and .359). Categories "1 to 7 days," "8 to 13 days," and "14 to 30 days" showed no significance, although a slight positive correlation appeared.[18]

These figures indicate that unemployment's effect on hours worked may have been more complicated than historians have suspected. Short-term unemployment (e.g., seasonal layoffs) seems either to have had no impact on hours worked or to have encouraged longer hours during months employed. This, of course, does not discount the fact that workers in seasonal industries were interested in shorter hours, only that the problem was unresolved at this time. Only longer terms of unemployment were associated with shorter hours in occupations covered by the Labor Department and census studies—and they support the traditional interpretation. But even in the strongest and most significant correlations (census unemployment category "7 to 12 months" for 1900), unemployment considered as part of a multiple regression along with factors such as wages, race, age, nativity, and marital status accounted for less than 4 percent of the total variation in hours of labor and hourly wages from 1900 to 1914. So, at best, unemployment accounts for very little of the acceleration of the movement toward shorter hours. Moreover, the even more rapid reductions of hours during World War I occurred when labor demand was at one of its highest levels, a fact that raises additional questions about this kind of interpretation.[19]

Economists, in contrast, look to higher wages to account for such changes. But, here again, a traditional explanation breaks down for the period. The years just before World War I were unique in the history of the American worker, not only because of the unparalleled drop in the workweek, but also because they were the years of slowest increases in real wages. Albert Rees began his book *Real Wages in Manufacturing: 1890–1914* with the following: "The economic history of the United States has been marked by a strong and persistent rise in real wages. Only one period has seemed to stand out as an exception to this trend—the twenty-five years before World War I." Rees concluded that wage increases, although they did occur, were at an all-time low: "slightly lower than [before] . . . and considerably lower than the rate of increase . . . since."[20] Before Rees's study, economists Douglas, Long, and Ratner, Soltow, and Sylla concluded that there were no improvements in wages during the period.[21] In any event, this was the most that shorter hours have ever overshadowed wage advances during a period of moderate unemployment and increasing productivity.

Therefore, the contention that wage increases caused the shorter-hour acceleration is questionable, at least before 1914. During the war, wages increased much more, and the correlation between reduced hours and higher wages, which economists expect, appeared, so in the war years this argument may be more convincing.

Several other possibilities present themselves as likely candidates for explanation. Unions, for instance, although still committed to shorter hours, were comparatively quiet about the issue in these years. The big labor initiatives occurred in the late nineteenth century, for the 8-hour day; in the 1920s, for the five-day week; and in the 1930s, for the 30-hour week. The historian Marion Cahill observed that "at no time was the policy of uncertainty and lack of leadership . . . to reduce hours more evident than . . . in 1900–1914."[22] The five American Federation of Labor (AFL) conventions after 1901 made no mention of shorter hours, a fact that underlines the contention that unions were drifting into inactivity that lasted until the war.

Rank-and-file unions continued to present shorter-hour resolutions to the AFL, none of which were favorably received. Local unions also kept pressure on management on their own, without national leadership. In 1904, for example, the Typographical Union tried to inaugurate a national drive for the 8-hour day for their workers. But even though local unions pressed for both higher wages and shorter hours in the period, they showed no inclination to favor leisure. Quite the opposite. The overwhelming majority of strikes and issues pressed in negotiating sessions were about wages, not hours. Certainly unions saw shorter hours as a kind of wage benefit (i.e., higher hourly wages). But insofar as wages were concerned, shorter hours were still considered an indirect benefit, a means to an end. When the choice was between this indirect benefit and a solid weekly wage boost, unions stood squarely on the side of the bigger paycheck.[23]

Moreover as Ethel Jones pointed out, the most heavily unionized industries showed no exceptional movement toward shorter hours.

She made a convincing statistical case to back up her point, showing that industries that were more than 30 percent unionized experienced about the same level of reduction in hours as those less than 10 percent unionized, and that neither group deviated more than 1.5 percentage points from the average. All of which led Jones to conclude that there was little "evidence that union action explains the movements in either scheduled or actual hours over the time span 1899 through 1929."[24]

Jones questioned another mainstay for explaining shorter hours in the period: legislation. Few workers—fewer than 20 percent, mostly women and children—were affected by state legislation. For those workers, regulation came too late; reductions in actual hours outpaced the fall of legal maximums in all except two years. Moreover, Jones showed that "over the entire period from 1899 to 1929, full-time hours for the high female employment group industries fell more slowly than in all manufacturing."[25] If state regulation had any effect, the opposite should have occurred.

But these findings do not totally discount the role of unions and legislation. Although they raise questions about how important these two factors were in the acceleration of the shorter-hour process, they do not eliminate them from consideration as ongoing factors in the movement. Unions did not stop working for shorter hours; they simply did not make any exceptional efforts. Unions continued to work for the 8-hour day with success: Six heavily unionized industries were able to reduce hours from just under 54 a week at the turn of the century to around 48 (the 8-hour day) by 1914.[26]

Moreover, some important developments in organized labor occurred. Under the leadership of Samuel Gompers, unions became more consistent in their justifications for work reductions—stressing economic and practical reasons for reform. As usual, higher wages and concerns about unemployment, health, safety, and morality were emphasized. But particular interest was given to increasing productivity, for labor found businessmen and industrial managers more interested in this shorter-hour benefit and responsive to the idea that reduced hours increased overall efficiency. More elaborate economic arguments, such as nineteenth-century labor leader Ira Steward's belief that shorter hours increased total consumption, faded somewhat, and rhetoric about the social and cultural benefits of increased leisure was rarely heard.

Although state legislation regarding hours may not have been very effective in reducing the workweek, the passage of many such laws signaled increased public and political support for labor's efforts in this area. These laws also show some of the reasons why support intensified at this time.

In many ways, interest in shorter hours was part of a larger public concern with job safety and working conditions. Between 1907 and 1914, leading American corporations such as U.S. Steel, International Harvester, and the Chicago and North Western Railroad conducted industrial safety campaigns. The Triangle Shirtwaist Factory fire in 1911, which killed 148 women, raised a public outcry and focused national attention on unsafe working conditions. Interest in controlling occupational illnesses also increased, with groups such as the American Association for Labor Legislation exposing the problem and calling for reform. Interest in protecting women and children from overwork and exploitation also increased, and important reform legislation was passed during this period.[27]

The shorter-hour movement benefited from each of these developments. Safety, health, welfare, and working conditions were the dominant justifications for state and federal legislation regulating hours and were the reasons that these laws were finally ruled constitutional by the U.S. Supreme Court.

During this period, more state labor laws and regulations were adopted than ever before, or since. Twelve states passed general 8- or 10-hour laws (most of which had nullifying provisions that made exceptions for hours worked under contract, which rendered them impotent); thirty states passed laws limiting work hours for women; eighteen states regulated hours of labor for men in hazardous occupations or industries; and nineteen states established regulations for state workers either by constitutional provision, statute, or code revision.[28]

The aristocracy of organized labor, the railroad brotherhoods (conductors, engineers, firemen, trainmen), used very practical arguments to get their 8-hour day with the passage of the Adamson Act in 1916—the first federal shorter-hour legislation for a major industry not under government contract. The support necessary for passage of the bill centered on public and worker safety; exhausted railroad workers were dangerous. The U.S. Supreme Court, in *Wilson* v. *New*, narrowly sustained the Adamson Act, using the interstate commerce justification.[29]

By contrast, state regulations of workers' hours were founded on the constitutional provision that reserved police power to the states to protect public safety and welfare. Nearly all the state laws regarding hours were passed specifically for this purpose. As early as 1898, the U.S. Supreme Court, in *Holden* v. *Hardy*, upheld a Utah statute limiting miners to an 8-hour day. The Court found that such a law was a constitutional use of state police power; it protected workers' health and safety and was not an infringement of the freedom of contract. Nevertheless, presented with the same issues of safety and health in a

New York law in 1905, the Court reversed itself (*Lochner* v. *New York*); it reversed itself again in 1917, accepting such use of police power in an Oregon 10-hour law for men in industry (*Bunting* v. *Oregon*). Thus, from 1905 to 1917, the constitutionality of state regulation of hours for men was in question. Consequently, these laws had nullifying provision for exceptions when contracts were involved.[30]

Nevertheless, in 1908, in one of the most famous of the Court's decisions (*Muller* v. *Oregon*), the justices found that an earlier Oregon law limiting women to 10 hours of work a day was constitutional. This case became a *cause célèbre;* leaders of the social justice movement such as Florence Kelly and Josephine Goldmark became involved and employed Louis D. Brandeis to argue the case. The result was the "Brandeis brief," which made legal history. Brandeis presented a successful defense to the Court based on sociological and economic arguments rather than purely legal considerations. Aside from its significance as a first in jurisprudence, the Brandeis brief underscored the importance of shorter hours as a health, safety, and social welfare measure and gave some indication of the reasons social reformers had to support such legislation. Brandeis, in more than a hundred pages of social and economic argument, stressed that long hours were dangerous and unhealthy. He also emphasized the bad impact long hours had on the morals of a community and the social benefits of a reasonable working day, benefits that included strong families and responsible citizens.[31]

Politicians and reformers in the Progressive era used the same kinds of justifications. Walter Lippmann remembered that the reformers of his generation, those who "stood at Armageddon with Theodore Roosevelt" and struggled alongside labor for shorter hours, never worried about "leisure"; they never attempted to gain support by talking about the cultural or "idealistic" benefits of the reform. According to Lippmann, the Progressive reformers fought for shorter hours when the need was clear: The pain of overwork and fatigue cried out to be healed; the need for safety, health, rest, and some family life was manifest.[32] With Lippmann, the reformers assumed that with the cessation of drudgery, workers would do good and even noble things automatically. The prospect of the increased freedom of leisure did not bother them in the least.

Lippmann's observations are borne out by the political rhetoric that accompanied the 1912 Bull Moose platform plank for shorter hours and Woodrow Wilson's consistent support for an 8-hour day. The word leisure was seldom mentioned, and the few times it did appear it was used sarcastically, as a reference to how the rich lived in ease on the backs of productive workers. Wilson and Theodore Roosevelt, together with their supporters, consistently took a no-nonsense approach to shorter hours, stressing the practical benefits Lippmann outlined.[33]

For example, during World War I, Wilson established various administrative boards to regulate labor; among them were the Cantonment Adjustment Commission, the Board of Control of Labor Standards, and most important, the National War Labor Board. Organized labor flourished under wartime regulations; membership in unions increased, and the unions were protected somewhat in their organization efforts and collective bargaining. The Wilson administration virtually compelled industries to institute the 8-hour day in production for war—a policy that resulted in the reduction of average manufacturing hours to around 50 a week by the war's conclusion. As in the Adamson Act and the state laws regulating hours, practical justifications, centering on health, safety, welfare, were used by the war boards. In addition, the boards placed importance on the efficiency of the 8-hour day.[34]

These were happy days for the unions. Labor leaders, of course, continued to talk about the value of shorter hours in terms of increased wages and technological unemployment. But they were quite willing to take advantage of the widespread interest in safety, health, welfare, and efficiency, and to use these issues to cultivate support for their efforts.

Again, it is hard to judge the indirect influence such a climate of support had on the acceleration of the shorter-hour process. And since Jones and others have questioned the importance of what unions and state legislatures were doing, it makes sense to consider other reasons.

During this period, a number of employers tried out shorter schedules. Scientific managers and industrial psychologists conducted experiments and found that fatigue increased and productivity declined sharply after 8 hours of work. Journal articles reported these experiments and generated a good deal of interest among industrial managers. Many employers reduced their workday to 8 hours (reducing wages accordingly), and others tried different short working schedules. These measures had the additional benefit of being inexpensive. If workers responded to a shorter schedule by working harder, then a very attractive alternative to higher wages existed to motivate workers. Again, the actual impact that these experiments had in the acceleration of shorter hours has not yet been measured or even estimated, and so it is impossible to judge the extent to which employers were following suggestions of scientific managers rather than the drift of the labor market. Nevertheless, business interest in shorter hours as a productive alternative to higher wages has been seen as a factor during this period and should be included in a multifaceted analysis.

Moreover, unions used the new employer interest to their advantage in negotiations and even adjusted their rhetoric somewhat, from talk of wages and unemployment to emphasizing efficiency.[35]

Businessmen responded to shorter hours in another way. They recognized the new interest in, and reality of, increased free time and began investing in leisure goods and services. During this time, they developed many forms of recreation that have become common-place—amusement halls and parks such as Coney Island, sports equip-ment, games, bicycles, resort hotels, excursion packages, and so forth. The American response to this new recreation was enthusiastic. The economist John Owen noted that between 1901 and 1913, yearly per capita demand for recreation increased in constant dollars from $18.1 to $30.3. A period of "very rapid relative growth . . . took place from 1909 to 1929, when recreational spending as a percentage of total expenditures rose from 3.2 to 4.7 percent."[36] Since that time, such spending has remained nearly constant in percentage terms. Of spe-cial importance were the phonograph and recording industries, which by 1919 had grown sixty times larger than in 1899, and the motion picture industry, which began with a nickelodeon in New York on June 19, 1905, but drew 10 million people a week to "the movies" by 1910.

Business had an increasing stake in Americans' free time. The profits in recreational products may have been a good enough rea-son for some businessmen and managers to support shorter hours. This justification for more leisure time was not widely publicized until Henry Ford used it in 1926, but others had an economic reason much earlier to be concerned that workers had enough leisure to buy and use their products.

Rosenzweig places great importance on the development of com-mercial recreation as a major factor in changing the leisure patterns of native and immigrant workers. It was a change that resulted in the erosion of worker and ethnic cultures and more rapid assimilation into the mainstream.[37]

However, workers may have been more than passive consumers of the new commercial recreation. Asserting the importance of their subcultures, they may well have influenced the acceleration of shorter hours. One of the most interesting and most controversial ways to account for the acceleration in the shorter-hour process is to note the changes that were occurring in the American labor force because of immigration and internal migration.

Arguments of this sort have been made for other historical de-velopments. Beginning in the first decade of this century, observers noticed that the sluggishness of wages closely coincided with the all-time-high immigration numbers and the wave of "new immigrants" from southern and eastern Europe, and concluded that there was a connection.[38] Since then, the idea has appeared regularly as a historical interpretation. For example, Rees suggests that "this period . . . differs from both the earlier and the later period in the volume and composition of immigrants. Many more immigrants came to the United States in this period than in any other of equal length, and more came from places where levels of skill and education were low. These forces could have worked to lower the income of wage earners."[39] A variation on this explanation also is common: that because of racial and ethnic prejudice, the new immigrants were exploited and received lower wages than would have been paid to native workers or immigrants from northern and western Europe.[40]

Isaac Hourwich, however, defended the new immigrants against the charge that they were a totally bad influence on American labor. He argued that while they may not have been as skilled as native workers, and thus were not paid as much, they improved working conditions in this country by providing leadership in the shortening of the hours of labor. He maintained that "the length of the working day offers a fair measure of the effects of immigration on labor conditions" and attempted to prove this by showing correlations between immigration patterns and improvements in working hours. In the first place, claiming to demonstrate a longitudinal relationship, he argued that "since the beginning of the new immigration," hours had been reducing. "The decade of heaviest immigration from Southern and Eastern Europe was marked by a gradual reduction of hours of labor in the state of New York."[41] He also claimed that a cross-sectional relationship existed. Comparing New York City with the rest of the state, he found a negative correlation between the percentage of new immigrants and the hours of labor.

Hourwich's case is strengthened somewhat by the importance that the "new labor historians" have assigned to leisure as a basis of worker culture. Since so much of the recent discussions about working-class subcultures has revolved around the new workers' dissatisfaction with industrial work and American material values, on the one hand, and the importance of their lives away from the job, on the other, a *prima facie* case exists to link these attitudes directly to the shorter-hour process in American history. Given that more new immigrants were arriving than ever before, and given their "preindustrial" distaste for work and their interest in leisure, it is reasonable to conclude that changes in the American labor force may have been a factor in what Rees called "the strong unexplained shift of preferences toward leisure" that occurred in the period.[42]

Because of what economists have been doing in this area, this con-

TABLE 1. *Pearson Correlation Coefficients*

Variable	Hours per week	Hourly wages
1. Hours per week	1.0000	−.6927**
2. Hourly wages	−.6927**	1.0000
3. % of German immigrants	.0434	−.0824
4. % of British immigrants	.0986	−.0040
5. % of Irish immigrants	−.0537	.1286
6. % of all foreign born	−.1856*	−.1374
7. % of "new immigrants" from Italy, Russia and Poland	−.2586**	.0042
8. % with foreign born parents	−.0472	.0637
9. % under 30 years old	.2253**	−.2649**
10. % over 30 years old	.0850	−.0792
11. Total number unemployed	−.0555	.0494
12. % unemployed 1–3 months	.0102	−.0010
13. % unemployed 4–6 months	−.0724	.0743
14. % unemployed 7–12 months	−.4687**	.042**
15. % of Black workers	.0656	−.0035
16. % single	.0764	−.0531
17. % married	.0694	−.0524
18. % divorced	.0440	−.0202
19. % widowed/widower	.0289	−.0038

* Significant < .01.
** Significant < .001.

tention may be supported empirically, at least in principle. Given the right hour-and-wage data, it is possible to test whether immigrants' work–leisure behavior matched their historical attitudes. An impressive body of literature already exists in the economic study of labor supply, analyzing economic and demographic factors related to variations in the hours of labor.[43] So a methodology is in place.

Using Commissioner of Labor Carroll Wright's hour-and-wage data and Census Bureau demographic records for 1900, a composite analysis of ten selected occupations in twenty-three cites was performed to determine what factors were associated with variations in hours of labor in national cross-section.[44] The factors tested as independent variables against hours worked per week (the dependent variable) were average hourly wages, worker nativity (the percentage native or foreign born), nativity of parents, country of birth, age, race, marital status, and level of unemployment (number of weeks unemployed).

As shown in Table 1, there was significant simple correlation

TABLE 2. *Multiple Regression*

Step	Variable	Multiple correlate	Adjusted R^2	F(Eqn)
1	Hourly wages	.6888	.4724	224.83
2	New immigrants—total %			
	from Italy, Poland, Russia	.7149	.5072	129.66
3	unemployed 7–12 months	.7311	.5072	94.56

($-.259$, $p < .001$) between the percentage of immigrants in the work force from Italy, Poland, and Russia and the average number of hours worked, but no relationship between the percentage of immigrants from Britain, Germany, Scandinavia, and Ireland and number of work hours.

In multiple regression, it is clear from Table 2 that in order of importance, the percentage of workers from the three less industrially developed countries was second only to hourly wages as a determinate of hours worked per week.

Controlling for variation in the hours of labor associated with all other factors (e.g., hourly wages, unemployment) and thus isolating the effect of percentage of new immigrants on hours, one notices a slight increase in the coefficient of correlation, which remained significant ($p < .001$) in partial equations. Hence, in the occupations selected, those occupations with more immigrants from Italy, Poland, and Russia averaged fewer hours. Eliminating the effect of wages on hours by partial equations shows that this correlation is strengthened. This indicates that in occupations with more new immigrants, wages tended to be lower or the same.

Thus, new immigrants' attitudes seem to match their behavior in a straightforward manner in these cases. Valuing leisure more and work–wages less than other workers, they worked relatively fewer hours for lower or the same hourly wages.

This whole project is clouded by the ongoing controversy between economists and historians concerning how much workers were able to select or influence their work hours in the "free" labor market or on the job. Historians tend to disparage the notion that a Slovak worker in the Pittsburgh steel mills had any say about how long he worked. Economists respond by pointing out that these workers changed jobs so frequently that they had a choice about wage-and-hour levels and, in the aggregate, might very well have influenced elements of the labor market by "voting with their feet." But even if one concedes that these new workers were able to make a difference in the labor

Signif-icance	R^2 Change	FCh	Signif of R CH	BetaIn	Simple correlation
.000	.4745	224.830	.000	−.6888	−.6888
.000	.0367	18.600	.000	−.1923	−.2553
.000	.0234	12.432	.001	−.1733	−.4686

market, their impact was small. Judging from the 1900 cross-section study presented here, they accounted for less than 4 percent of the total variation in the hours of labor, or about the same percentage as unemployment. Much needs to be done to analyze the influence new immigrants had on the economy. Nevertheless, in the search for all possible reasons for the acceleration of shorter hours, the wave of immigration and the strengthening of workers' subcultures, which developed simultaneously, at least suggest one kind of historical factor.

There is also some evidence that at this time native workers became increasingly dissatisfied with their jobs and more interested in time off from work. The statistics about increased spending on commercial recreation, travel, sports events, and outdoor activities hint that a new appreciation for the rewards of leisure was emerging. This positive response to amusements may be contrasted with what was happening on the job: job turnovers and absenteeism. Paul Brissenden and Emil Frankel concluded that from 1910 to 1919, "the number of persons who quit, were laid off, or discharged, as well as the number who had to be hired, was much larger than the total number of workers on the force at any one time. . . . This is as if during one year all the employees had left their jobs and a complete new set of people had taken their places." Within this generally mobile labor force, a core of compulsively restless employees, amounting to perhaps one in seven workers, changed jobs even more frequently.[45] Absenteeism rates were also high enough to trouble employers, causing many to take extreme measures.

Intellectuals and social critics of the period add to this statistical evidence. According to many accounts, because of the changes in work (e.g., the assembly line, the loss of crafts, the rise in unskilled positions, efficiency and "speed up" programs), workers were dissatisfied with their jobs as never before and were, in increasing numbers, turning to leisure as a way to express themselves and find the fulfillment no longer available at work. Writers of the day tended to find such attitudes represented in a broad range of occupations and among the middle class as well as manufacturing workers. Questions may be raised about how workers translated their new attitudes about work and leisure into shorter hours. Still, the coincidence of such attitude changes with the acceleration of the shorter-hour process is at least suggestive of an explanation that deserves some attention.

While the writers' reports about workers are valuable, in their discussions they reveal much about themselves and their own struggles with work and leisure. Historians have paid a good deal more attention to these writings on their own merits than for what they reveal about workers—understandably so because of the difficulties involved with investigating workers. What many have found is that intellectuals and "social statisticians," reformers, academicians, and social critics, were questioning the work ethic as never before.

For example, James Gilbert devoted a book to exploring the "social crisis . . . that typified the late part of the [nineteenth] century up to the First World War . . . the intensified feeling that work, the sacred myth of mobility and individualism, was undergoing a rapid and crucial degeneration," which "by the turn of the century . . . had become . . . unavoidable."[46] Intellectuals outlined and social statisticians detailed workers' discontent about the ways that work had changed and concluded that the alterations boded ill for society. Gilbert and others noted that the nineteenth-century work ethic, the galaxy of beliefs that assigned to work such functions as creativity, expression, self-reliance, and community, was undercut by the reality of industrial work, which had become anything but ennobling. Work was now repetitive, dull, unskilled, tightly controlled and regimented; there was neither workmanship nor fellowship. And, declared Gilbert, in the "growing discontinuity between the ideal and the reality . . . work . . . seemed to be the key to a condition of alienation" for American workers. Moreover, "psychological and moral problems," deviancy, vagabondage, and violence were seen to be brought on by new forms of labor and its "specialization and ennui." A completely new disease, neurasthenia, was discovered, which, according to Gilbert, was "the name given by psychologists to the breakdown of the structure of the personality when it proved incapable of adjusting to the regime of modern industrialism."[47]

Various individuals and groups tried to deal with these problems by reforming work and shoring up its ethical supports. Reform efforts included the arts and crafts movement, vocational education, and manual training in the schools. Intellectuals such as William James tried to reconcile individualism with modern work, while behaviorists such as Gustave Le Bon and John Watson tried to adjust the worker to the workplace by testing and placement, discarding the out-of-date notions about work's ethical function. But the "crisis of work" continued from the turn of the century until World War I.

The historian Daniel Rodgers agreed that "the transformation of work undercut virtually all the mid-nineteenth-century assumptions about the moral preeminence of work" and noted the further complication of "excess productive capacity." "If the industrial cornucopia could spew out far more goods than the nation was able to buy, what then was the place of work?" While industrialization's "transforming effects on work" were gradual, the sense of crisis came just after the turn of the century when, for example, "the discovery of industrial monotony came with a rush."[48]

Rodgers found a response to this crisis that Gilbert overlooked. Rodgers concluded that "most critics of industrial monotony came to a far simpler answer: if modern industrial work was soulless, then men should do less of it. . . ." By the early twentieth century, "a sizable number of Northern Protestant moralists had begun to argue that it was not in self-discipline that a man's spiritual essence was revealed but in the free, spontaneous activity of play."[49] While some intellectuals and moralists were documenting the bad effects of industrial work on workers and talking about "alienation" and "neurasthenia," others were devising a new leisure ethic, looking more to leisure and play as the foundation for progress and individual achievement and less to work. In the process, they found in the alienated worker a new, parallel interest in free time, which, said Rodgers, did not spring from "all the complex intellectual rationale behind the eight-hour campaign" but from an "essential . . . obvious appeal: the promise of the relief from toil."[50]

Gary Cross found the "new leisure ethic" to be a phenomenon that transcended the musing of moralists and intellectuals in America. Reaching international proportions, it was widespread in the transatlantic region. Cross concluded that "new [positive] attitudes toward leisure and family time" had emerged from 1880 to 1920.[51]

This leisure ethic was a "new" development because it was different from most nineteenth-century justifications for work reductions, which stressed the importance of shorter hours as a way to perfect work. Instead of the older "work ethic" concept, "leisure for work," a new interest in free time for itself and as a positive alternative to work, emerged. This idea included a critical assessment of most modern jobs as boring and repetitive, together with an expectation that leisure could be used to give expression to things that work used to provide. Since work was no longer creative, leisure would provide creative opportunities. Since work was increasingly impersonal, leisure could be the place for individual freedom. The craftsmanship, social mobility, pride in achievement, inventiveness, and self-discipline lost at work could be regained in leisure.

But difficulties present themselves when one attempts to use the emergence of this leisure ethic to explain the acceleration of shorter hours—even more difficulties than in trying to find a reason for the changes in worker attitudes. At best, these scholarly goings-on played a minor role in the political developments and labor struggles of the period. The practical ideas of practical reformers and union leaders were far and away more important. Safety, health, and welfare were heard often in public debates; ennui, neurasthenia, and alienation were seldom mentioned. Rhetoric about the need for free time to relieve fatigue and improve productivity drowned out discussions about a new leisure ethic, self-expression, and spiritual essentials. All that one is able to say is that perhaps such ideas were part of a general climate of opinion that nurtured the shorter-hour movement, however indirectly. Nevertheless, these developments in intellectual history were to become important in the 1920s and 1930s. Such discussions emerged then as practical and exceedingly important parts of very real developments in America's political, cultural, and economic life. As such, the earlier discussions may be seen as preparing the ground for what was to come—as prologue, setting the stage for the debates that surrounded the end of shorter hours and the American recommitment to work.

The emergence of the new leisure ethic had other dimensions, both theoretical and practical. For instance, another prologue occurred in the field of economics. During this period, economists had their own ideas about why the workweek was decreasing and what was to become of work and leisure in the future. These were the days when neoclassical marginalists were influential, and they spoke often and long about "declining utility." For example, W. S. Jevons speculated that even though most work was a combination of pleasure and pain, overall it had a net pain sum. Work, in the final analysis, was a cost incurred. This "cost" though, was balanced by the utility gained through working: the right to consume. But this utility tended to become less the more income was received, because workers could buy more things they truly needed and even a few things they did not really need. With increasing per capita real wages, workers could satisfy wants in addition to needs. But these new goods and services were ever less urgent; utility declined ever more, to the point where marginal utility was small or even negligible.[52] And as John Kenneth Galbraith put it, under such a theory, "the effect of increasing affluence is to minimize the importance of economic goals."[53] This was true in part because as wages continued to increase, workers took more time off from work because the unpleasantness of working long hours outweighed the attractiveness of the new goods and services that were coming into their financial reach. A worker would stay at work from dawn to dusk when he was starving, but would see the point in taking off early when he was assured of a big supper.[54]

Other neoclassical writers added leisure to these ideas, assuming that leisure itself was attractive—a "normal good" or a "utility gained." The tendency for workers to desire shorter hours under the condition of increasing wages seemed to be the result of both the carrot of leisure and the stick of work's unpleasantness. In his famous *Principles of Economics*, Alfred Marshall pointed out that history was full of "stories of people who in a sudden burst of prosperity, had contented themselves with wages to be earned with very little work."[55] While Marshall made no grand statement about this tendency, he hinted that prosperity created a condition that would lead relentlessly to work's reduction, leisure's increase, and production–consumption stabilization.

Another neoclassical economist, Frank Knight, expounded on Marshall's views:

> Suppose that at a higher rate per hour . . . a man . . . worked as before and earns a proportionately larger income. When, now, he goes to spend the extra money, he will naturally want to increase his expenditures for commodities consumed and to take some new ones. To divide his resources in such a way as to preserve equal expenditures in all fields he must evidently lay out part of his new funds for increased leisure: i.e., buy back some of his working time or spend some of his money by the process of not earning it.[56]

Knight gave as examples of this phenomenon the behavior of "native workers in backward countries" and certain highly paid occupations during World War I. In simplest terms, Knight believed that as prosperity increased in the United States, hours would get shorter as wages got higher; just as they had done for a century before he wrote. The upshot of all these theories was that as workers took more of their time and energy from work and devoted them to leisure, the economy would level off and cease to grow. In Galbraith's terms, "the effect of increasing affluence is to minimize the importance of economic goals."[57]

The notorious "backward-bending supply curve of labor," the oldest of the economists' models, dating back to the days of mercantilism, was refurbished and used to show that the relationship between wages and hours was such that after a certain wage level was reached, work would decline and would eventually become infinitesimally small.

This was enough to worry some economists and spur them to look around for ways to avoid the prospect. But there remained the question whether it was such a bad thing.

Many writers of the time objected to the materialism and obsession with economic matters they observed around them. William Wordsworth's famous observation that "getting and spending we lay waste our powers" was quoted often, and the thought behind the phrase was elaborated by such writers as Sidney Lanier. Coupled with the criticism of "philistine" materialism was a dream of a better world where people would at last be freed from the preoccupation with economic matters and be able to grow morally, spiritually, and aesthetically. Utopian novelists, almost without exception, looked forward to the bright future time when only 4 hours a day would be required for work; people would spend the remainder of their energies, not on consumption or worrying about money, but on more important things.

Apart from literature, these ideas began to show up in the writings of late-nineteenth-century economists, who, observing the economic progress around them, were optimistic about the future. The British economist John Stuart Mill, for example, had a large American following and proposed that a "stationary state" of the economy was inevitable because the "increase of wealth is not boundless." At the end of economic growth lay a "stagnant sea" toward which the "stream of human industry" irresistibly flowed. But this was not such a bad thing, since human progress was more than economic progress. In fact, Mill was more than a little disillusioned with the prevailing idea that "the mere increase of production and accumulation" constituted progress:

> I know not why it should be a matter of congratulations that persons who are already richer than anyone needs to be, should have doubled their means of consuming things which give little or no pleasure except as representative of wealth; or that numbers of individuals should pass over, every year, from the middle classes into a richer class. . . . It is only in the backward countries of the world that increased production is still an important object.[58]

In fact, wrote Mill, the best economic state for human nature would be stationary, one in which "no one is poor, no one desires to be richer." In this condition, laborers would be paid enough to meet their needs, and no enormous fortunes would exist to excite envy. People would then have "sufficient leisure, both physical and mental . . . to cultivate freely the graces of life." In such a stationary state, people would also be able to enjoy nature and its solitude, which too much economic development would destroy. They could "contemplate the world," and in doing so, constitute a "happier population."[59]

Mill concluded with the hope that "for the sake of posterity," people would be content with a stationary state long before they were forced by necessity to accept limits. This hope was based on Mill's belief that progress would not cease with the stationary state of the economy.

> It is scarcely necessary to remark that a stationary condition of capital and population implies no stationary state of human improvement. There would be as much scope as ever for all kinds of mental culture, and moral and social progress; as much room for improving the Art of Living, and much more likelihood of its being improved, when minds cease to be engrossed with the art of getting on. Even the industrial arts might be as earnestly and successfully cultivated, with this sole difference, that instead of serving no purpose but the increase of wealth, industrial improvements would produce their legitimate effect, *that of abridging labor.*[60]

Mill's moral argument may be abstracted as follows: Excessive attention to economic growth for its own sake gets in the way of real human needs and potential and corrupts life; human material needs are finite and can be met; once these needs are taken care of, other human needs—the extraeconomic "graces of life" such as culture and learning—should be cultivated; leisure represents the way to reduce unnecessary production and unnecessary work and make progress possible in other valuable human areas; hence leisure ("abridging labor") ought to increase as productivity improves and as human material needs are met.

This sort of reasoning appeared regularly in Europe and America among economists and others after Mill wrote. The actual trace of ideas is complex, but a few representative samples can show that Mill's train of moral logic was not an aberration but was in fact the beginning of an important "current of thought" that continued to question assumptions about the absolute value of work and economic growth, and to offer an alternative vision of human progress based on work reduction.

Certain threads of Mill's logic ran through the writing of America's prophet of abundance, Simon Patten. Patten suggested as early as the 1880s that industrial productivity and technological advance were ushering in a new economic age, radically altering the demands previously made on individuals by the "age of scarcity." Since the beginning of human history, workers had developed values and habits that were appropriate for economic survival in the constant condition of want and deprivation. But the advent of abundance made these values and habits lose their usefulness. The overriding problem in the "age of abundance" was to adapt old customs and concepts and find more appropriate economic values. The chief danger of abundance was that behavior, conditioned by ages of scarcity, would survive unchanged. This economic maladaptation could result in a generation of "gluttons" who worked more and harder to consume ever more fantastic luxuries when they were already satiated with too many things.[61]

Patten suggested that proper guidance was needed to direct the masses into more appropriate and human activities. He thought that "noneconomic pleasures" had to be sought in the condition of plenty, otherwise the sensual debauch in material goods would destroy the more human desires for aesthetic, cultural, and religious pursuits. These more worthwhile things had to replace the fascination with economic growth for its own sake in order to avoid economic chaos.[62]

Patten's writings were so vague that they could be interpreted in at least two ways. At first, associates such as Edward Ross, Walter Weyl, Stuart Chase, and Frances Perkins applied Patten's ideas to work reduction and tended to see free time as the opportunity to begin to use increased wealth in human ways. For example, Weyl (as editor of the *New Republic*) wrote in his influential book *Tired Radicals*: "Above all, pleasure is limited by the time to enjoy it. In enjoyment, time is more than money." He suggested that wealth should be used wisely, not for the constant "squirrel-cage existence" of making and spending, but for a better quality of life, "improved recreation and larger pleasures."[63] In *The New Democracy*, published in 1912, Weyl proposed that "the article of consumption most often neglected is leisure. Leisure is an indispensable element to all enjoyment. It is the thing in which the American, despite his overflowing wealth, is poorest."[64] Edward Ross was to write an introduction to one of the most important books supporting shorter hours to be published during the Great Depression: A. O. Dahlberg's *Jobs, Machines, and Capitalism*.[65] But several of Patten's followers, such as Rexford Tugwell and Edward R. A. Seligman, although influenced by Patten's ideas about economic abundance, later came to other conclusions: that work had to be reformed and saved from too much leisure. But at least before World War I, Weyl's interpretation was dominant.

The rapid reduction in hours of work that took place from 1900 to 1920 was accompanied by a bewildering array of social, economic, and intellectual developments each of which might have had a role in causing the phenomenon. One has the feeling, though, that if these could be adequately judged as to their importance, then all the historians would have to do to explain the end of shorter hours would be to unravel the puzzle and trace each strand of influence out through time, until it ended or frayed enough so that it could no longer support the process. But, without exception, each factor explored in this chapter is controversial. Moreover, so little work has been done on each individual strand that any hope of considering them together, judging their relative importance and their influence on one another, is remote.

Nevertheless, these factors may at least offer some clues about where to look for reasons for the end of shorter hours. Changes in unemployment rates, wages, labor's position, immigration, workers' subcultures, commercial recreation, and business opinion might be worth considering as they occurred and were related to shorter hours from 1920 to 1940.

Moreover, most of these factors have at least one obvious feature in common: They point to the fact that many Americans were exhibiting and developing more positive views about free time during the acceleration of shorter hours. One may characterize this view in additional ways. In the main, it was based on practical considerations ranging from the new interest among Progressives in safety, health, and welfare to the fascination among businessmen about how production could be improved by shorter hours to labor's acceptance of both issues because they strengthened practical arguments about higher wages and unemployment. By and large, the new outlook on leisure was not based on a rejection of work. Support came most often from those interested in improving jobs, reducing stress and strain, and making the workplace more attractive. Changes in these points of view can be valuable indeed in explaining the end of shorter hours.

Other ideas that were emerging as part of the positive view about increased leisure questioned the value of work and proposed a future in which progress would transcend work. The more abstract nineteenth-century notion that work was a preparation for the finer and higher things began to be heard more frequently, but applied to the here-and-now rather than the eternal Sabbath. Another nineteenth-century notion, that work was good and noble in itself, life's beatitude preparing for eternal leisure, was increasingly challenged. More intellectuals began to believe that earthly progress would come in two stages: taking care of necessities and then going beyond necessary work to the freedom to think, create, love, pray, and even work outside the constraints of necessity. But it is very questionable that intellectuals who talked about a "new leisure ethic" or a two-stage progress had much to do with the acceleration of the shorter-hour process at this time. They may have been influenced by it as much as they influenced it. Still, changes in the way in which such ideas were received by the public and applied to practical political, economic, and social concerns will, like changes in safety–health–efficiency justifications, be of great value in explaining the end of shorter hours from 1920 to 1940.

CHAPTER 2

The New Economic Gospel of Consumption

THE TWENTIES OPENED with a depression. Lasting almost two years, this downturn raised questions about the future of American economic growth and the place of work in the new industrial state.

In 1922 Garet Garrett pointed out that "American business is despairing at overproduction," believing that "we are equipped to produce more of the goods that satisfy human wants than we can use." John Hobson wrote that "experienced businessmen all over the world realize that the market does not expand rapidly enough to keep up with demand" and that American business, and industry in particular, "testifies by quite undersigned coincidence of theory and practice, ca'canny, trusts, protection, and imperialism to the belief in a limited market." Similarly, Francis J. Boland, reviewing the depression of 1921–1922 in a dissertation for the Catholic University, concluded that business cycles had recently been made more severe because of the firmly held conviction that markets were limited and that in an increasingly wealthy economy, demand could be saturated by too much production.[1]

Examples of bullish investors and pessimistic businessmen who expressed these sorts of fears may be found throughout the decade. The *New York Times*, in its annual assessment of "the financial outlook," reported periodically that business experts believed that the great prosperity of the decade was ephemeral and that industrial reactions threatened, since the "saturation point" in traditional markets such as textiles had been reached, and it was near in newer industries such as automobiles.[2]

But most of this rhetoric occurred during and just after the 1921–

1922 depression. During this time the press was full of expressions such as "buyers' strike," "psychological reactions," the "dominance of the buyers' market," "overproduction," and "limited markets."[3] Otto Kahn, speaking before the Pittsburgh Traffic Club, took note of the "inflation of production" that had occurred during the war and had disrupted business afterward.[4] The U.S. Chamber of Commerce conducted a survey of two thousand business leaders in 1921 and found that there was widespread concern about sales resistance among consumers.[5] The National Association of Manufacturers (NAM) appealed to the public to "end the buyers' strike," which had caused such widespread unemployment. J. Philips Bird, general manager of NAM, saw consumers buying "only the necessities of life," cutting down on "comforts . . . and other purchases."[6] Businessmen in New York organized a Prosperity Bureau to counter this "buyers' strike," using as its slogans "Buy Now," "Put the Money Back to Work," and "Your Purchases Keep America Employed." According to the *New York Times*, this movement grew to national proportions, being endorsed by chambers of commerce and bankers throughout the country.[7]

S. W. Straus, president of his own banking firm, found that the saturation point in building construction had been reached and that New York and other large cities were in grave danger of being overbuilt. He went on to explain his reason for stopping loans for new apartments and hotels by pointing out that "boom times in construction" set the stage for "eventual busts"—there was "the grave danger of overproduction."[8] Lee Thompson Smith, president of the National Association of Building Managers and Owners, agreed that "there is no doubt that we have reached a point of overproduction. . . . Buildings may be erected without number . . . but tenants cannot be manufactured."[9]

Victor Cutter, president of the United Fruit Company, summed up the gloomy views of the prophets of overproduction and limited markets. Assuming that "history . . . shows that visits of prosperity are never prolonged beyond a few years at a time . . . then come periods of depression," Cutter suggested that "we have reached a point where we are faced with the specter of overproduction . . . and accumulated surpluses." "Sufficient consuming power" was no longer guaranteed by higher wages alone. It was "demand saturation" in industries such as automobiles that complicated the problem of marketing surpluses. For Cutter, "the greatest economic problem" facing the nation was the fact that production was outpacing demand and "consuming power" was limited not only by wages but by "human nature."[10]

Ignoring economists who tried to assure the nation that motives to buy were not limited to some set of specific human needs and would expand readily when wages increased, businessmen as well as labor leaders feared that Americans were working themselves out of their jobs by producing more than they would consume. To many observers, production appeared to have outrun human needs. Chronic unemployment and depression seemed to be a likely result of this "need saturation." [11]

Throughout the decade and into the 1930s, economists and more optimistic business leaders made efforts to put this idea to rest. The fact that so much was written to disprove what the Brookings Institution called "the prevalent business view" about "universal consumptive indigestion"—the "outright satiation of human wants"—gives some indication of the wide coinage of the idea.[12]

Not only did prosperity and "need saturation" seem to invite economic disaster—unemployment and depression—they also created a condition in which workers might choose to work less. This was a reasonable conclusion given that the workweek had been decreasing so rapidly since the turn of the century and that unions had become even more active in the 1920s, initiating a drive for the five-day week.

But in contrast to their more positive attitudes about shorter hours in the previous two decades, most businessmen who recognized this possibility in the 1920s despised it. They no longer saw the increase of leisure as a positive development, assisting productivity and making work better. Linked with "need saturation," shorter hours represented a clear threat to future economic growth.

Labor and other supporters of the five-day week tried to use the argument of increased productivity again. But it had lost its appeal; how having Saturdays off could increase work effort and efficiency was not nearly as clear as how 8 hours could do so. Fatigue was the key difference. While scientific studies and experience confirmed that tired workers were less productive at the end of 8 hours, the same simply could not be said for the five-day week. The few businessmen who supported the reduction talked more about worker morale and less about fatigue. The shorter-hour movement had outrun its practical appeal for most employers and managers.[13]

But of more importance than the missing fatigue factor, the business fear of chronic overproduction made the shorter week seem a threat to economic growth. If basic needs were being met by industry, and if workers chose to devote less and less time to their work, then extended periods of general unemployment would not be necessary to halt progress. Free time in the form of leisure could create the same conditions as free time in the form of unemployment: reduced production and consumption, idle productive capacity, limited investment opportunities, and even a mature and stable economy.[14]

Businessmen's increasing fears about the threat that shorter hours posed to economic growth were expressed throughout the decade. The most elaborate and thoroughgoing expression may be found in NAM's *Pocket Bulletin* of October 1926. The association questioned thirty-two prominent business leaders about the five-day workweek unions were demanding and Henry Ford had already instituted in some of his automobile plants. All but two of these businessmen were opposed to it. Some equated increased leisure—"the extra holidays on Saturday"—with crime, vice, the waste of man's natural capacity, corruption, radicalism, debt, decay, degeneration, and decline. John E. Edgerton, president of NAM, declared that

> it is time for America to awake from its dream that an eternal holiday is a natural fruit of material prosperity, and to reaffirm its devotion to those principles and laws of life to the conformity with which we owe all of our national greatness. I am for everything that will make work happier but against everything that will further subordinate its importance . . . the emphasis should be put on work—more work and better work, instead of upon leisure—more leisure and worse leisure . . . the working masses . . . have been protected in their natural growth by the absence of excessive leisure and have been fortunate . . . in their American made opportunities to work.[15]

George L. Markland, chairman of the board of the Philadelphia Gear Works, declared that "any man demanding the forty hour week should be ashamed to claim citizenship in this great country," warning that "the men of our country are becoming a race of softies and mollycoddles."[16] Adequate rest after a hard day's work was just as necessary as enough to eat, just as important in rebuilding energy for the next workday. But having Saturdays off was different. This free time was not for work; it was for idleness and pleasure, and it took the wage earner's mind off his job. Markland saw the five-day week as "a gradual sinking into decay," a trend toward the dissipation and frivolity that had caused Rome's downfall.

Similarly, George F. Reynolds did not believe "that the average working man cares to have too much time on his hands, and he is much happier and more contented to be working, earning money, than he is to be loafing."[17] James C. Martien opined that "mankind does not thrive on holidays. Idle hours breed mischief. The days are too short for the worthwhile men of the world to accomplish the tasks which they set for themselves. No man has ever attained success in industry, in science, or in any other worthwhile activity by limiting his hours of labor."[18] James F. Dewey, a Vermont executive, wrote that "nothing to my mind could be worse . . . than the five-day week."[19] Edgerton concluded that "nothing breeds radicalism more quickly than unhappiness unless it is leisure. As long as the people are kept profitably and happily employed there is little danger from radicalism. . . . Study the sources of radicalism today and you will find them for the most part in the discontented houses of leisure and the leaky tents of the unemployed."[20]

All these businessmen saw increased free time as a natural result of improved production techniques. Nevertheless, they vehemently opposed the further reduction of work hours and searched about for alternatives such as "new foreign markets" and "*enforced* attention to business," which might deal with overproduction and stop the "erosion of work." They all agreed that shorter hours meant less production and limited growth. They also characterized labor's position on this issue as "un-American," since they felt that labor's bid for the 40-hour week was basically an attempt to limit production. But most of all, they feared the decline in the importance of work and the implications of this decline for future economic growth.

Another business spokesman, Walter Henderson Grimes, summed up the pessimism about increased leisure and its relationship to the economy. Looking about him at the rhetoric of businessmen, industrialists, and bankers, he saw "everywhere . . . the same story." It seemed to Grimes that everyone was agreeing that "there was too much of everything," "flooded markets," "overproduction," and "underconsumption"; all the products of "saturated demand" and increased productivity. To Grimes, "it is perfectly clear that the middle class American already buys more than he needs," but "unless we have a greater outlet for our goods . . . as manufacturing efficiency increases, there will be larger groups with too much leisure." Neither Henry Ford's humanitarianism nor labor unions' demands caused shorter hours. The curse of leisure was a natural result of prosperity. Since many Americans had achieved a standard of living above "need," economic growth was doomed. Increasingly less work would be required to produce life's necessities. For Grimes, excessive leisure was almost the same as unemployment. Both signaled the end of economic growth and created human suffering. Work was the basic human need, but in the new economic era, work was becoming critically scarce because, as so many observers agreed, human needs for work's products were being satisfied.[21]

Whereas before the 1920s many businessmen had endorsed shorter hours because they believed they increased productivity and improved work, in this decade they came to believe increasingly that the process had gone too far. Instead of accepting a shorter workweek as a practical asset, they saw shorter hours as a threat to future economic growth. Excessive free time was symptomatic of economic failure, of the inability to find markets for new products and the increasing burden of surpluses. In either form, unemployment or leisure, free time would mean slower growth or outright cessation of growth. Work was seen to be critically scarce and becoming more so as productivity improved. A virtual work famine was threatening.

But by mid-decade, these fears were evaporating. They were gradually replaced by a new and vigorous optimism, founded on what Edward S. Cowdrick, an industrial relations "counselor" to several of the largest American corporations, called the "new economic gospel of consumption." The good news was that increased consumption could save economic growth and redeem work.[22]

Responding to the threats of chronic overproduction and the decline of the need to work, businessmen began to concentrate on consumption. If existing markets were being saturated, then the reasonable response would be to find new markets and increase consumption, not reduce working hours. Businessmen became increasingly convinced that Americans could be persuaded to buy things produced by industry that they had never needed before and could consume goods and services, not in response to some out-of-date set of economic motives, but according to a standard of living that constantly improved. With this concern with consumption, the business community broke its long concentration on production, introduced the age of mass consumption, founded a new view of progress in an abundant society, and gave life to the advertising industry.[23]

For example, Charles Kettering, general director of General Motors Research Laboratories, emphasized the importance of keeping "the Consumer Dissatisfied." He believed that "there is no place anyone can sit and rest in an industrial situation. It is a question of change, change all the time—and it is always going to be that way. It must always be that way because the world only goes along one road, the road of progress." Successful effort was simply the prelude to more effort. The alternative to growth was not economic "maturity," a "steady state" of the economy where workers maintained a minimum standard of living; rather, the alternative was the stagnation of civilization and death of the economy.[24]

Some businessmen and economists, such as Henry Ford, went so far as to suggest that workers be paid enough to buy what they produced. But many businessmen were afraid that if wages increased too rapidly, workers would continue to leave their jobs for shorter hours, as they had been doing for twenty years. Growth in the "new era" of abundance seemed to be complicated by the fact that workers did not desire new goods and services—automobiles, chemicals, appliances, and amusements—as spontaneously as they did the old ones—food, clothing, and shelter. This lag in consumption had to be dealt with, and many businessmen looked to capital spending to provide the stop-gap. Capital investments could provide new outlets for surplus money and idle manpower and at the same time promote new inventions and better commodities. As capital spending kept the economy going, marketing experts and advertisers could gradually convince the American consumer to buy more. Then, as this evolution continued, wages could be increased, since it would be safe to trust workers to spend more rather than work less. Consumption was not guaranteed, but it could be promoted. It would be the hard work of investors, marketing experts, advertisers, and business leaders, as well as the spending examples set by the rich, that would promote consumption and help prevent workers from taking too much time off from work.[25]

Businessmen's new interest in consumption has been well documented, as has their optimism that demand could be stimulated. Herbert Hoover's Committee on Recent Economic Changes published one of the first and finest examples of this documentation in 1929. The committee criticized pessimistic predictions about "saturation points," calling these predictions "abstract" and the likelihood of market saturation "remote." They pointed both to economic theory and actual accomplishments to attack the notion that the economy had matured. On the one hand, "economists have long declared that consumption, the satisfaction of wants, would expand with little evidence of satiation if we could so adjust our economic processes as to make dormant demands effective." On the other hand, Americans had proven that this theory actually worked in the 1920s. The "almost insatiable appetite for goods and services, this abounding production of all things which almost any man can want, which is so striking a characteristic of the period covered by the survey" was the hard reality shattering false fears about overproduction.[26] The committee found

> from study of the fact finding survey on which this report is based, that as a people we have become steadily less concerned about the primary needs—food, clothing and shelter . . . the slogan of "full dinner pail," is obsolete . . . and we now demand a broad list of goods and services which come under the category of "optional purchases." . . . "Optional consumption"—optional in the sense that this portion of the income may be saved or spent, and if spent the manner of this spending may be determined by the tastes of the consumer or the nature of the appeals made to him by the industries competing for his patronage—

presents one of the marked characteristics of the recent economic situation . . . the survey has proved conclusively what has
long been held theoretically to be true, that wants are almost
insatiable; that one want satisfied makes way for another. The
conclusion is that economically we have a boundless field before us; that there are new wants which will make way endlessly
for newer wants, as fast as they are satisfied. . . . By advertising and other promotional devices, by scientific fact finding,
by carefully predeveloped consumption, a measurable pull on
production has been created which releases capital otherwise
tied up in immobile goods and furthers the organic balance of
economic forces . . . . it would seem that we can go on with increasing activity. . . . Our situation is fortunate, our momentum
is remarkable.[27]

Whereas the Hoover Committee on Recent Economic Changes described for the first time the widespread interest and faith in increased
consumption current in the 1920s, several historians who have written
since then have noted that this emphasis on increased consumption
was a central part of that decade, was new, and has characterized
economic thought to the present.

For example, in W. W. Rostow's view, during the "age of high
mass consumption," which "was pressed to . . . its logical conclusion"
in the 1920s, the American economy started to depend for the first
time more on increased consumption for growth than on the relatively
simple matter of increasing production.[28]

Other historians have agreed and noted that the new economic
problems of maintaining aggregate demand created new institutions,
new ways of looking at the economy, and new social patterns that
were untenable in the previous ages of "economic scarcity" but vital
to the new "economy of abundance." Joseph Dorfman found that during the 1920s a new subfield in economics ("consumption economics")
sprang up, reflecting the "general interest" in and "wide-spread discussion" of the "new aspects of consumer spending" and marked by
enthusiasm for installment buying and "almost complete . . . acceptance of the doctrine formerly considered radical, of the economy of
high wages."[29] Thomas Cochran pointed out that "the shift in business
activity toward marketing" that characterized the twentieth-century
economy ("the Age of Demand") and distinguished it from earlier
periods was "first noticeable in the 1920's," during which time "the
consumer had become the likely savior of private enterprise in America."[30] Herman Krooss mentioned a "new concept of distribution" and
a "new economy of consumption" prevalent in executive opinion in the

decade.[31] Charles E. Hession and Hyman Sardy stated that "gains in productivity . . . created a new concern about . . . marketing goods, as contrasted with their production," and concluded that the "20's was a period of transition between the values of an older capitalistic culture and the demands of the consumer society."[32] Frederick Lewis Allen remarked of the 1920s: "Business had learned as never before the importance of the ultimate consumer. Unless he could be persuaded to buy and buy lavishly, the whole stream of six-cylinder cars, super helerodynes, cigarettes, rouge compacts, and electric ice boxes would be dammed up at its outlets."[33] David Potter, discussing the growth of advertising, suggested that the industrial surplus of the 1920s made it necessary that "the culture . . . be reorientated to convert the producer's culture into the consumer's culture."[34] David Riesman considered the early decades of the twentieth century as the turning point, during which time "scarcity psychology" gave way to an "abundant psychology," a process typified by the rise of consumer-oriented values and behavior and the ascendancy of "the other-directed man."[35] William Leuchtenburg, interpreting Riesman, pinpointed this shift to the 1920s.[36] The dramatic growth in advertising, the creation of a new range of consumer goods, the decline of the importance of growth in agriculture and textiles, and the growth of trades and services were understood by these writers as indicators in the American economy of a new movement, from concern for production to consumption.

This shift in the focus of attention had several implications for shorter hours. Instead of being seen as a way to increase production and perfect work, leisure was pressed into the service of consumption. Business optimism about the possibility of increasing "optional consumption" soothed some of the concerns expressed by organizations such as NAM about the declining need to work and the threat of leisure. Optimistic businessmen such as Henry Dennison, president of a manufacturing company in Massachusetts and director of the Central Bureau of Planning and Statistics in Washington, D.C., saw the 40-hour week as an ally to growing consumption rather than a threat to production. Like the new "consumption economists," such as Teresa McMahon and Hazel Kyrk, Dennison believed that increased leisure would increase consumption. Spokesmen at the National Distribution Conference agreed and pointed out that increased leisure stimulated the growth of some of the most vital new industries, such as amusements, radio, phonographs, motion pictures, publishing, and hotels.[37] Henry Ford argued that "leisure [was] a cold business fact." He maintained that "where people work[ed] less they buy more," since "business is the exchange of goods. Goods are bought only as they meet needs. Needs are filled only as they are felt. They make themselves felt largely in the leisure hours."[38] E. S. Cowdrick agreed that the 40-hour week was good because "it promises more leisure to use up motors and golf balls and holiday clothes." He also suggested that advertising should be used to increase the consumption of leisure goods and services and to educate workers in the new skills of consumption, instilling in them the desires for those new things industry was producing.[39]

Examples of this reasoning were numerous in the decade, but the President's Committee on Recent Economic Changes again presented one of the best summaries:

> It was during the period covered by the survey (the 1920s) that the conception of leisure as "consumable" began to be realized upon in business in a practical way and on a broad scale. It began to be recognized, not only that leisure is "consumable" but that people cannot "consume" leisure without consuming goods and services, and that leisure that results from increasing man-hour productivity helps to create new needs and new broader markets. . . . The acceleration of technological shifts in production and consumption would have resulted in much more serious unemployment if workers had not been absorbed in the newly expanded service industries which both create and serve leisure.[40]

While recognizing leisure as an ally to consumption, businessmen such as Ford and Cowdrick, as well as the Hoover Committee, nevertheless reaffirmed their faith that work was, and should remain, the center of life. Ford, for example, while praising the economic significance of leisure, cautioned that "of course, there is a humanitarian side of the shorter day and the shorter week, but dwelling on that subject is likely to get one in trouble, for then leisure may be put before work rather than after work—where it belongs."[41] Agreeing with Ford, the Hoover Committee saw leisure, not as an alternative to work, but as creating new reasons to work.

Leisure's significance lay in the fact that "basic needs" were being met; hence the traditional motives for working were diminishing. New motives to consume had to be created. Free time could provide these new work motives. Hence leisure, within limits, was vital. Subordinate to work, leisure supported economic growth and thereby helped to save work.[42]

And because leisure entailed increased consumption, it was limited. The century-long shorter-hour process would taper off, since workers would need higher incomes in order to finance the leisure they already had. Together with the traditional pessimists, such as

Judge Gary and John Edgerton, who were calling "the thought of reducing the week's working time" a "blasphemy," most optimistic businessmen supposed that leisure had to have a limit. Even though the 40-hour week was reasonable because it stimulated consumption, they rejected shorter hours as a continuous, open-ended process.[43]

According to the optimistic business view, the shorter-hour process would either stop naturally or be controlled by the work of advertisers and marketing experts. Ford argued that since "more spare time would mean desire to spend more money," and "it is impossible to reduce income and the supply of goods and services (through reduced hours) and then have more money to spend," progressively shorter hours would eventually come into direct competition with new spending.[44] Then, what the economist Constance Southworth called "the infinite capacity of the common man to want things" would check workers' desire for increased leisure.[45] The desires for increased material wealth and a higher standard of living would overcome the desire for more leisure. The economy would not "mature" because of too much leisure; instead, it would be the desire for additional leisure that would run out of steam.

As Henry Dennison put it, prosperity offered society the chance to "take more leisure or to get more wealth, as it chooses." But he felt that leisure, as a form of wealth, was as subject to the laws of supply, demand, and value as any other product or service. Like all "items of wealth," the value of leisure was determined by a "free consumer's choice." "Luxuries or leisure" was the basic economic choice before American workers. But Dennison was confident that business could successfully compete with leisure, limiting it by linking it to new consumption.[46] *Existing* leisure time, and the new increment given leisure by the 40-hour week, was a national resource, a marketing bonanza. With no need to be replenished by additional reductions in work, this existing resource would be enough and could be exploited well into the future. Led by businessmen, Americans could be counted on to want more "luxuries" for their leisure, not the opposite.[47]

Businessmen also defended work against the threat of shorter hours by attacking the notion that work was unpleasant—some kind of trial or a negative part of living. They spoke of work as "a joy," a "critical factor of human evolution," a "wonder," a "dignity," "the American secret," a cure for "that tired feeling" and "mental fatigue," the "developer of character," an "adventure," a "form of play but better," a source of "spiritual inspiration," and the creator of "saints of the workshop." In contrast to the previous two decades, when work as a social value was undergoing a "crisis," in this decade few such doubts remained, at least in business and trade publications.[48]

In his best-selling book *The Man Nobody Knows*, Bruce Barton tried to clear up the confusion about work versus leisure. Barton portrayed Christ as having embodied business virtues; the Savior's life was exemplary because he lived it in a businesslike manner. Certainly Christ's work was that of salvation. But people misunderstood this example and made a distinction between ordinary occupations and spiritual expression. Barton felt that "great progress will be made in the world when we rid ourselves of the idea that there is a difference between *Work* and *religious work*."[49] Work, in its industrial and business forms, was as much a spiritual exercise as praying, going to church, or giving to the poor. Work in all its forms was precious. It was not a preparation for higher things outside the job because nothing could be more sublime.

People such as Ford and Ethelbert Stewart, chief of the Bureau of Labor Statistics, agreed that work was becoming easier and more noble as burdensome tasks were taken over by machines. As Stewart put it, the machine "has taken the load off the back of the workingman and has changed him from a beast of burden to a thinking animal." Ford proposed that no one benefited as much by the machine as did the worker it replaced, for the machine freed "the ditch digger" for nobler work and transformed him into a more productive, skilled worker—it could even elevate him as businessman or entrepreneur.[50] In contrast to the many critics of mechanical jobs, Ford and Stewart welcomed the machine as the great "humanizer" of work, a force that was redirecting work into new paths of progress.

Walter T. Pitkin, professor at the Columbia University Department of Journalism, declared in his book *The Twilight of the American Mind* that in the "era of leisure" a "job famine for the best minds" existed. He concluded, "Better a world less good and [more] busy. Better a sea of trouble than a desert of ease! Better the burning dust of tired men than the twilight of best minds." But with Ford and Stewart, Pitkin looked to the new frontiers of work to save America from ease and dissipation. He also felt that along with new products, new kinds of occupations would be discovered, and work, not leisure, would be made the place for individualism and self-expression, as he supposed it once had been.[51]

Dennison suggested that although "as the great number of highly specialized machines increases, there is less and less carry-over of skill from one job to another, and fewer places to which a worker can put to use any special skills he has managed to gain," nevertheless, "there are more places in which he can reach average ability in a very few days. . . . General opinion repeats that 'there are fewer highly skilled jobs but fewer really unskilled jobs' . . . all of the really skilled workers can find high places in the new schemes of things as foremen, tool makers, machines fixers, and the like."[52]

William Feather, a publishing executive and a frequent contributor to *Nation's Business*, orated in "A Fourth of July Speech—New Style," that the "100 per cent American realizes that he can unload all drudgery on the machine, and thereby achieve universal prosperity exceeding the dreams of the most moony Bolshevist." Not only would the American be richer with such an attitude, he would be free from "machinelike" work to become a businessman himself, creating and marketing his own products and thus providing employment and "real welfare" to struggling workers around him.[53]

The industry leader A. C. Bedford told a group of Standard Oil employees that "even admitting the beauty, the charm, the inspiration and the greatness of [love, learning, religion, and patriotism], none of them can be put into effective operation without work." Work strengthened the nation and so was the act of a patriot, not the empty words of a chauvinist. Work produced needed goods, while industry provided jobs, the cornerstone for all charity. Learning apart from application was sterile; learning for the purpose of more effective work and new kinds of occupations was fruitful. He concluded that "industry is the fundamental basis of civilization," since "the high office of civilization is to train men to productive effort."[54]

In addition, several businessmen and some educators contended that workers could be taught the "joy of work" and led by those who recognized work's vital social role to find jobs wherein happiness lay for them. Industrial psychologists, for example, assumed that proper evaluations of workers' interests and abilities could be used to direct them to jobs that were a source of satisfaction rather than a place for alienation. Vocational guidance, as well, developed as educators began to use the schools to assist in work's transformation.[55]

For these apologists, work could and should be reformed. Under the direction of enlightened employers and managers, jobs could be remade to become places for creativity and self-expression, as was supposed to have been true in the nineteenth century. With economic growth, new machines, and industrial techniques, new occupations would emerge that would give individuals a place to express their finest qualities. It was through new jobs, not new leisure, that the old virtues could be restored. It was in transformed work that the hope for progress lay. Civilization itself depended on such transformation, since its essence was "productive effort."

Notable for its absence in such discussions about work improvement was shorter hours; an issue that had been a primary means to work perfection in the nineteenth century was abandoned. The goal of work was no longer work reduction but the opposite: better, improved, and more work.

The historian James Prothro, reviewing the "dollar decade," assumed that the *summum bonum* for American businessmen was increased material wealth. He went on to show that work was the first and most logical corollary to the supreme good that businessmen defended against attack from radicals and promoted for those who did not readily recognize its value. It is difficult, however, to rank-order business values. Certainly increased material abundance and work were both vigorously defended and promoted. But they were so interrelated, the one supporting the other, that a distinction between means and ends is impossible.[56]

As Ford said, "Business was responsible for the welfare of people," the most important components of which were work and more material wealth.[57] The "new gospel of consumption" was designed specifically to ensure industrial advance and save work. If needs for traditional products were being met, then new needs could be discovered, promoted, and used to redeem industrial progress. According to Ford, industrial managers had the duty to see to it that new kinds of occupations were created that would keep people happy in their work and would thereby assure work its central position in American life.

The "new gospel of consumption" banished the threat of increased free time (leisure or unemployment) as businessmen found "a boundless field before us; that there are new wants that make way endlessly for newer wants; as fast as they are satisfied."[58]

Moreover, work was seen in new terms. It was based less on necessity and more on privilege. Work was seen more as an end in itself— an intrinsically rewarding experience that developed the personality and provided workers with a purpose in life and a place in the community. This new "work ethic" differed from the nineteenth-century version. It was not "Protestant" because it had few religious dimensions in the traditional sense. Words used in the 1920s, such as "saints of the workshop," and work's "spiritual inspiration," were secular versions of the nineteenth-century idea. The whole theological superstructure that had once supported work—ideas about vocation, being called by God to work, concepts about the purpose of work as meeting natural needs and progressing toward life that transcended material necessity—these were replaced by secular goals, the most important of which was economic growth. Leisure was seen to be valuable, not because it perfected work or led to higher things, but because it was helpful in promoting consumption and more employment. Productivity was valued, not because it reduced the burden of working, but because it allowed industry to progress to new frontiers of goods and services.

And work was without end. Work was for more work, but it was transformed and more fulfilling—noble work. It was not for the "singing of eternal psalms," not some fantastic transcending of necessity into some wonderland of freedom.

A similar set of events occurred in the field of economics; there was a similar dismissal of increased leisure and a reaffirmation of the importance of work and economic growth. Like businessmen, economists began to search for ways to save work from further erosion.

One of the most important developments in economics in the 1920s was the rejection of marginalism and the movement toward the increased use of empirical methods. Economists were discarding the *a priori* theories about prices and value and consumer motivation that were current at the turn of the century. According to Raymond T. Bye, no economic doctrine was subject to more rigorous attack than marginalism and its implications concerning welfare and work hours. Nevertheless, such theories were still enshrined in the textbooks of the day and continued to have supporters.[59]

Marginalists such as John Bates Clark and Stanley Jevons had maintained that utility or value in consumption was a function of the amount of goods and services an individual could purchase. The more income a person, or indeed a nation, had, the less desirable additional consumption would become. As John Kenneth Galbraith noted, marginalism "put economic ideas squarely on the side of the diminishing importance of production under the conditions of increasing affluence . . . the effect of increasing affluence is to minimize the importance of economic goals."[60] From the marginalist perspective, as wealth increased and each additional satisfaction gained by additional income diminished, economic progress would lose its momentum and its very reason for being. Production and growth would become ever less important.

Moreover, according to the marginalists, the importance of economic growth declined relative to alternative kinds of utility or values, those taken outside of work and the marketplace and those gained by the simple relief from toil. As the urgency to consume diminished with increased incomes, workers would work less and devote more of their time and attention to extraeconomic, nonpecuniary parts of their lives. The predictions made earlier by Jevons and other marginalists that work hours would become increasingly short as wages increased were still heard.[61]

For example, following Alfred Marshall, Frank Knight at the University of Chicago, and later A. C. Pigou, suggested that this "income effect" might be inevitable and universal in the richer industrial nations. Reacting to World War I and to the depression of 1921–1922, Knight restated the classical argument about the marginal relationship between money utility and labor disutility; he suggested that the point had already been reached and was "very conspicuous" in World War I when "wages for certain kinds of work rose to unprecedented heights," which caused "the anticipated effects" of "increased loafing and dissipation instead of increased production."[62]

While agreeing with Knight that the "quasi-commodity, leisure," would continue to be taken increasingly because of higher wages, Pigou felt that government taxation could prevent workers from taking so much time off from work that "the national dividend" would be threatened. In his own turgid way he wrote that "when the functions relating the quantity of income to satisfactions derived from it and to the dissatisfaction involved in obtaining are given, the aggregate sacrifice will be smaller the more the volume . . . of income is caused to increase." He suggested, however, that by using taxes to take away wages, the demand for income by the individual would increase, "since the margin of utility . . . of money . . . is raised but the marginal disutility of work unchanged. Hence [workers] will increase the amount of work done" and the national product would be protected.[63]

Moreover, in the first cross-sectional study done in this area, Paul Douglas found strong empirical evidence to support Knight's contentions about the strength of the "income effect." Based on the reports of the Bureau of the Census, Douglas's study covered fifteen industries (both unionized and payroll) over the years 1890 to 1926. Douglas concluded that

> Knight therefore seems to have been correct in his general interpretation of what would happen if incomes were increased.
> . . . Workers in the United States tend to divide an increase in hourly wages into two parts. The first is a higher material standard of living while the second is increased leisure. . . .
> Approximately two-thirds of the gain is devoted to the first and approximately one-third to one-quarter to the second. . . . The supply of hours of work is negatively inclined.

Douglas found that in 1890 a − .78 coefficient of correlation existed between average hourly earnings and the length of the full-time average workweek. In 1914 it was − .80 and in 1926 − .84. Douglas concluded that even though it was not an inevitable consequence of economic abundance, still the "backward bending supply curve of labor" was an empirical fact—an historical reality with profound implications.[64]

Moreover, Thomas Nixon Carver, the well-known Harvard economist, argued that the "new leisure" was a threat rather than a help because

> there is no reason for believing that more leisure would ever increase the desire for goods. It is quite possible that the leisure would be spent in the cultivation of the arts and graces of life; in visiting museums, libraries, and art galleries, or hikes, games and inexpensive amusements. If the cult of leisure should result in the cultivation of Gandhiism, humanism, or any of the highbrowisms, it would decrease the desire for material goods. If it should result in more gardening, more work about the home in making or repairing furniture, painting and repairing the house and other useful avocations, it would cut down the demand for the products of our wage-paying industries.[65]

Hence there was considerable concern among economists about the growth of leisure and the challenge this represented to economic expansion.

But marginalism had long been criticized as a price theory because of just these sorts of assumptions about consumer motivations. Economists pointed out that economic value was determined by social forces and individual motivations that changed from place to place and time to time, and was not set according to some natural hierarchy of utility needs. The relative pleasure-giving of one product against another could not be measured by the individual or by the impartial economist. The "last dollar's purchase" was not necessarily different from the "first dollar's" in the real world. Moreover, the buyer was not the rational "economic man," performing a mental calculus each time he made a purchase of one good instead of another. Because of irrational choice, motives such as the desire to imitate, foolish decisions, social customs, fads, and changing moods, individuals did not behave "rationally" in regard to the "economic facts" or even basic physical needs. Moreover, the idea that a psychological hedonism moved all people to behave in the market always to maximize pleasure and minimize pain was simply not provable by observed behavior. As John M. Clark pointed out, marginal utility did not explain consumer behavior but tended to be based on a logical tautology—the identification of pleasure with consumption and consumption with pleasure.[66]

In 1932 Paul T. Homan observed that most economists had concluded that "for the purposes of explanatory analysis, ethical hedonism was obviously irrelevant" and "the idea of a utility calculus" had "been reduced with the utilitarian theory to a minor and disputed status." Instead, a strong tendency existed to "develop the theory of economic consumption by the behavioristic method of inference from extensive observation."[67]

Economists who departed from marginalism rejected the old ideas about *a priori* motives to consume. They made no value distinctions based on whether a product was naturally more or less necessary. "Necessity" was such a vague idea, incapable of demonstration or measurement, that it was confusing. Instead, they concentrated on observable consumer behavior and discarded previous theories about human nature and values. As Joseph Dorfman observed, most economists of the 1920s agreed that questions about value theory were settled, since behavioral scientists and the "pragmatists" had disproven the bulk of previous *a priori* theories.[68]

Accordingly, most economists rejected the idea that an inverse relationship necessarily existed between high wages and work time. The conclusion that the urgency of wants did not diminish appreciably as the more basic or primary wants were met and the finding that motives to buy were indeterminate, based on social or psychological factors that changed, undermined the marginalists' predictions about increased leisure. Without declining utility, the backward-bending supply curve of labor lost its theoretical supports. If goods and services produced to satisfy desires for display, amusement, and pleasure were on the same utility level as desires for basic food and clothing, then increased leisure was not inevitable.

The marginalist case for increased leisure was based on the idea that the utility of wages decreased but the utility of working remained negative—had, as Jevons declared, a "net pain sum." According to this point of view, with more income, workers would at some point be bound to see the advantage of leaving work; leisure would emerge as more desirable than continuing to work to buy fewer desirable things. But according to economists Hazel Kyrk and Theresa McMahon, "leisure is itself a desirable good which must be paid for." Leisure or work reduction did not stand outside the arena of consumption as a kind of universal option not to consume. Instead, leisure, and all the "nonpecuniary pleasures associated with increased free time," had to be paid for by giving up wages and hence other kinds of specific goods and services. In this sense, leisure was no different from other kinds of consumption.[69]

These sorts of ideas were used by Lionel Robbins in 1930 in his seminal article, "The Elasticity of Income in Terms of Effort." The article overturned once and for all the marginalists' predictions about inevitable work reductions, and it stands today as a starting point for a modern analysis of the economics of leisure. Simply put, Robbins argued that when wages increase, workers are drawn in two directions at once. On the one hand, they want to take more time off; they want to spend their new income in the form of less work (the income effect). On the other hand, they realize that their time has become more valuable and are drawn to work even longer hours, trading more of their time for even more income (the substitution effect). Moreover, Robbins concluded that when the price of anything rises, "it is not clear that more will be bought even out of an increased real income." For example, if a worker's wages increased, the taking of an additional hour of leisure would be more expensive; he would have to give up more of the other goods and services that he could purchase with his potentially larger income. Hence the price of additional leisure had to be measured, like any other commodity, within the universe of potential consumption. Since all motives to consume were "indeterminate," set by changing social pressures and needs, "the attempt to narrow the limit of possible elasticity by *a priori* reasoning must be held to have broken down." The point was clear: Leisure was a commodity, like all others, the taking of which was relative to social customs and changing values. To use Robbins's language, with increased wages the "income effect" (workers' preference for more leisure) could be weaker or stronger than the "substitution effect" (workers' preference for more work and wages), or they could simply offset one another. Depending on how much they cared for leisure or for buying new goods and services, American workers could give expression to their choices in the marketplace in several ways.[70] Kyrk, in her *Theory of Consumption*, reasoned that increased productivity offered three possible choices: "increase in numbers" (population), "more leisure" or an "elaborate, expanded standard of living." Only time would tell if Americans would choose more leisure or choose a higher standard of living. From all indications, though, given what Constance Southworth had called "the limitless capacity of the common man to want things," and the fact that work in America was a value and not a liability, most economists concluded that leisure had little chance of replacing work in the more abundant American economy.[71]

Nevertheless, the new theories about consumption raised some other concerns at the same time they provided answers to the threat of increased leisure. If motives to consume were indeterminate, subject to change from time to time and place to place, then consumption was not necessarily automatic, as had been assumed in the classical theories. Consumption could lag behind production for a variety of reasons and cause severe economic dislocations. Hence economists began to consider the problem of overproduction and tried to find ways to make sure that consumption kept up with production in the free market.

According to Dorfman, concern with the problem of increasing consumption was a hallmark of economic theory in the 1920s; it was one of the "legacies" of that decade to the modern discipline. The widespread public concern over the problems of overproduction, or "underconsumption," were influential in the rise of a new "subfield," consumption economics. In addition, the problems of technological unemployment, the growth of families with incomes above subsistence level, the rise of installment purchasing and consumer debt, and the beginning of consumer organizations were other factors that caused economists to assign a new importance to the investigation of consumption patterns.[72]

In this subfield of consumption economics, the problems of sustaining economic growth in a condition of economic plenty were dealt with in detail. The new school presented theoretical solutions to the problems of chronic technological unemployment and cyclical depressions, and in so doing countered the pessimistic business view that general overproduction, periodic depressions, or increased free time were the natural results of prosperity.

Two of the most prominent consumption economists were Hazel Kyrk and Theresa McMahon. Both rejected the marginal utility explanation of value and turned to social explanations of consumer behavior; they reasoned that as social standards changed, consumer motives changed as well. Since economic values rested on no *a priori* theory, they suggested that only "by analysis of social standards, and how they came to be, and how they changed" can one "explain the concrete facts of consumption."[73]

But Kyrk noted that when surpluses did occur, as they had after the war, old habits and traditions of consuming and thrift, born of scarcity, could continue. They could easily result in the dangerous "oversaving" and "underconsumption," causing fluctuations in the economy and even depressions. Influenced by Thomas Hobson's theory of underconsumption, Kyrk suggested that if savings made possible in times of surplus were put "into the production of stable necessities," there may be "oversupply." "The poor cannot buy more and the rich will not." This presented Kyrk with a problem: "To the production of what new goods and services will it [savings] apply? Can producers invent new activities and new interests which will increase the will to spend of those who are able to do so? Unless they can, over-investment will arise."[74]

The way out of this dilemma was what Thorstein Veblen called "the emulative propensity of man." Reasoning that "a high standard of living must be dynamic, a progressive standard," Kyrk supposed that "one of the advantages of economic inequality" was that "it permits an experimentation with activities and modes of living which would be impossible if the surplus were scattered." Culture, as well as "our civilization as shown in consumption," were, according to Kyrk, "the products of the rich." The richer classes led the way to progress, consuming new luxuries, which, coveted by those in social situations just below them, turned the wheels of economic advance. Advertising and "producer activities in marketing" also had a role in this "dynamic growth of consumption," since they "augment and accelerate the changes in the standards of living." Kyrk suggested that economic growth required a dynamic standard of consumption that "necessitates expenditures upon luxuries"—luxuries for the well-off that eventually turned into "necessities" for the poorer classes. Chronic unemployment and periodic depression could be avoided if "dynamic consumption of luxuries" provided expanding domestic markets.[75]

McMahon agreed with the substance of Kyrk's ideas about the necessity of wealthier classes showing the way to economic growth by spending on luxuries. But she noted that "certain commodities whose significance was wholly sociable . . . implied decreased work efficiency." Although it was impossible to divide the market between more and less necessary products and services, still some workers seemed not to be as interested in the newer things being produced; they were not as spontaneous in their buying as before. This had resulted in a "productive loss . . . of national concern." New slack had developed in economic growth: the sluggishness of workers to consume new things and their regrettable tendency to take leisure rather than these new goods. But McMahon saw a way out of this problem in the "leadership of those who by virtue of their achievements are accepted as guides." The intelligent few, businessmen, the rich, economists, and even government officials could and should lead the masses to consume new products and attain "the common goal" of increased production and consumption, instead of leaving work for "unproductive reasons." Advertising and other aggressive methods of persuasion had become vital parts of the economy, necessary to sustain growth and adequate "levels of employment."[76]

The importance of new kinds of "socially motivated" consumption was demonstrated by what was already happening in the economy. Woodlief Thomas, head of the division of research and statistics of the Federal Reserve Board, noted that according to the Census Bureau's *The Growth of Manufacturers*, "the most striking increases [in growth] shown have occurred in those industries manufacturing goods which

are devoted to recreation and diversions or which have brought about
radical changes in manners of living—in many cases so called luxury
goods that have in fact become necessities." In addition to the new
class of goods—automobiles, silk, phonographs, photography, confec-
tionary products, cigarettes, rayon, radios, tires—the second group
showing "outstanding increases" were "producer's goods"—industrial
machines and other capital improvements. The economy was beginning to diversify. Demand for "the great staple products of agriculture
seems to have about reached the limit of expansion except as population increases. . . . The inability to explain the demand for these
products seems to be in part the result of general prosperity of all
people, permitting them all to consume such staple products as wheat,
potatoes, beef . . . up to their per capita capacity . . . as they increase
their prosperity they . . . spend their surplus upon a great variety
of cheap luxuries, ranging all the way from automobiles to chewing
gum."[77]

Wesley Mitchell observed that "scarcely less characteristic of our
period than unit-cost reductions is the rapid expansion in the production and sale of products little used or wholly unknown a generation or even a decade ago." Among consumer goods, the conspicuous
examples were "automobiles, radios and rayon. But the list includes
also oil-burning furnaces, gas stoves, household electrical appliances in
great variety, automobile accessories, antifreezing mixtures, cigarette
lighters, wrist watches, airplanes." The link between economic growth
and new consumption patterns, which had to be carefully developed,
was clear.[78]

Nevertheless, some economists were not sure that such developments and efforts in the private sector—new products, marketing,
advertising, and the spending examples of the rich—would guarantee
permanent prosperity and be enough to avoid periodic depressions.
In their book *Money*, published in 1923, William T. Foster and Wad-
dill Catchings cautiously advanced the economic heresy of general
overproduction. They proposed that the chief cause of industrial distress in the 1921–1922 depression was "underconsumption," the chief
remedy for which was adequate consumer income. This higher-wage
prescription was a radical departure from the orthodox position and
generated a flurry of responses.[79]

The editors of *World's Work* sponsored a contest with a $1,000 first
prize for the best answer to the Foster/Catchings thesis. The *Journal of
Political Economy* also ran a series on the question of general overproduction, as did the Pollak Foundation.[80]

Many of the economists who responded to these journals, and to the threat of overproduction, repeated the classical argument that equilibrium between wages and industrial production was assured by the market mechanics of supply and demand. If wages were too low, prices would fall in response to a softening of demand. Capital formation, profits, and savings would respond to a decrease in demand with a general cutback. More consumption would result because of lower prices, and the market would recover. Nevertheless, new kinds of concerns were expressed about the need to make adjustments in the economic system to avoid market cycles caused by periodic surpluses and overbuilt inventories.[81]

In the first place, economists such as Constance Southworth attempted to put the idea of "satisfied desire" to rest. Because so much was being written about "saturated markets" and the lack of willingness on the part of wage earners to consume enough new goods and services, Southworth pointed out that there never could be general overproduction in the sense that supply "exceeded desire." "This . . . situation [oversupplying desire] is yet more theoretical, and is based on hypotheses which are almost impossible of realization at any time on earth. It appears doubtful that the average worker . . . will ever admit that he has all he wants of everything."[82]

But serious concerns remained. Foster and Catchings had raised critical issues about overproduction that challenged the classical assumptions in other ways. One observer commented that the two had raised the overproduction problem "not in the crude and easily refuted form in which it has long been used as a socialist argument, but in a form which reckons with the spending of profits and capital funds, and hinges on the dynamic element of the timing of expenditures." Analyzing the "circuit velocity" of money (income flow), Foster and Catchings proposed that sustained production depended on sustained consumer expenditures. But these expenditures were variable and could be inadequate to support production, depending on the size of consumer income and the "circuit velocity" of money.

Moreover, oversaving was a real possibility. Money invested was used primarily to make more goods and services, more so than direct consumption. When too much was saved, a deficiency was created in purchasing power. That interest rates declined in this situation of oversaving did not guarantee that less would be saved and more spent on direct consumption. In fact, in 1921–1922 the opposite had occurred. The fall in prices during this depression had resulted in less rather than more consumption. Even in the best of times, if too many businesses paid off bank loans with their undistributed profits, then there was nothing to guarantee that new borrowers would show up to put "idle money" back into circulation. All these factors—"circuit velocity" of money, oversaving, and sluggish demand—could cause "underconsumption."[83]

Foster and Catchings went beyond Kyrk's and McMahon's remedies, which were based in the free market; Foster and Catchings suggested that government policies had to be established to make sure that consumption was kept up to the level of production. Monetary policy was the first line of action. By decreasing taxes and regulating the supply of money and the rediscount rate, the government could help to increase direct consumption. Moreover, even though installment buying could help counter underconsumption, as Kyrk and McMahon had pointed out, this would require an increasing debt level that would eventually become unmanageable—at least in the private sector. Foster and Catchings suggested instead that the government establish countercyclical spending policies through such things as public work projects (flood control and roads) to take up the slack in the economy—reemploying otherwise "idle" capital and labor, and using debt at the governmental level as a tool for increased economic activity. Decreased taxes could also be used in a countercyclical way to stimulate spending when demand faltered.

In short, anything that increased per capita purchasing power would help to stave off underconsumption. But in their several books published in this decade, Foster and Catchings never expressed concern that higher wages could cause increased leisure taking. Instead, they consistently defined all time and effort outside "useful" or "productive" employment as "idleness"—a disturbance in normal economic functioning that needed to be corrected by government action. They consistently stressed the overriding need to reemploy "idle" capital and labor, and simply assumed that more wages would mean more consumption. Foster and Catchings were not concerned that increased leisure could compete with economic growth. They simply assumed that "idle" labor and capital were undesirable by definition, always the same as unemployment, never the result of a free labor market choice. This tendency to ignore the possibility of voluntary free time and define all "idle" labor and capital as involuntary disturbances in the marketplace became more prevalent during the Great Depression.[84]

The logical corollary to the "underconsumption" thesis was that unemployment could become a chronic problem. Under classical theories, labor supply and demand would tend to stabilize at "full employment." According to this view, unemployed workers would take pay cuts in order to get a job, reducing the price of goods and services and thus increasing demand and employment. Alternatively, if demand slackened, workers could deal with that condition automatically by taking more time off from work—shortening the hours of labor and thus reducing surplus production. The way in which satisfied desires to consume would be expressed would be through less work and less production, not "underconsumption" of what the worker had already produced. Shorter hours and less pay were the ways that the market would function automatically to ensure "full employment."[85]

In the 1920s, however, new concerns were expressed about "technological unemployment." Given the new theories about indeterminate motivation in consumption and the rejection of marginalism and utility theory, economists had to struggle with the possibility that the workforce could stabilize at any level of unemployment—there was no reason to expect that "full employment" would be a natural outcome of the free market, since "full employment" was no longer seen in terms of a flexible and declining workweek. All work reductions were understood as "idleness."

Wesley Mitchell was typical of economists in the way that he dealt with "technological unemployment": He looked to economic growth to provide this new "full employment." Based on empirical studies, Mitchell observed that " 'labor-saving' machinery has turned out to be job-making machinery." Workers had been displaced, but not removed from work. They had left depressed sectors of the economy such as agriculture and textiles and had gone to better jobs in "public service, construction, transportation and communication, retailing, hotels, restaurants, garages, repair shops, moving picture places, barber shops, hospitals, insurance work, professional offices." Mitchell interpreted the U.S. Census of Occupations as showing that "American wage earners met 'technological unemployment' . . . mainly by turning to other ways of making a living. 71 per cent of workers displaced had attached themselves to new trades by 1927." Mitchell began a remarkable alteration of words, a rhetorical transformation of historic proportions. Defining "labor saving machines" as "job creating machines," he reversed the meaning that the first group of words had connoted for over a century, leading the way for modern economists.[86]

John M. Clark, reviewing "Recent Developments in Economics" in the 1920s, pointed out that the focus of attention had shifted from marginalism and its *a priori* speculations to "observable consumer behavior." He found that economists had recognized that consumption could no longer be explained by set ideas about necessity or utility and had at last realized that economic problems could not be "solved in the old sense of the finality resulting from discovering what 'natural law' demands and then fulfilling it." It was no longer possible to accept the idea that economic growth had some kind of finite goal, such as meeting "human needs." Instead, most economists of the period had

concluded that economic growth was important on its own terms; it
was its own reason for being. As a consequence, they had become
concerned mainly with promoting a dynamic economy, dealing with
the problems of maintaining adequate consumption and redefining
the role of government, business, and advertising to make sure that
consumption was kept up to the level of production.[87]

The question of "welfare" had been put in proper perspective.
The "welfare economists" of the old school, people like R. H. Tawney,
had talked about the need to provide "necessities" for the poor and to
redistribute wealth. They assumed that it was somehow not right for
the economy to provide luxuries for the rich when it was not producing necessities for everyone. Instead of talking about welfare in these
terms, the new empirical schools were concerned more with the problem of how to increase total production and hence total wealth. In a
growing economy, everyone's income would increase; the rich would
get richer, but so would the poor. This, as Galbraith pointed out,
provided an admirable detour around the rancor anciently associated
with efforts to redistribute wealth.[88]

In terms of welfare, Clark noted that economics had taken a
broader view about what a growing economy could provide for the
common worker. He pointed out that neither increased production
nor consumption were the "sole ends" of the economy. Instead,

> economics is taking a comprehensive view of man's interest in
> industry, in harmony with Ruskin's doctrine that "there is no
> wealth but life." Consumption is no longer the sole end nor
> production solely a means to that end. Work is an end in it-
> self and its character and surrounding conditions are among
> the most important elements determining ultimate welfare, ele-
> ments which the market does not adequately register or protect.

Clark observed that many economists had concluded that work was
not a negative or painful activity, to be entered on the debit side of
workers' ledgers, as the marginalists had maintained. Instead, it was
the center of individual welfare, a positive value to be served by the
rest of the economic machinery. And as far as Clark was concerned, if
the economy did not provide the "right to work," then governmental
action to assure that right was a reasonable policy. It was the provision
of steady work, not "basic needs," that was the economy's first moral
imperative.[89]

According to Clark, economic growth and steady employment had
replaced "necessity" and "utility" as the governing principles of the
new industrial state. Like many other economists, Clark divorced the
need for ever higher levels of production from essential human needs,

concluding that there would never be "enough." Work was not simply
for "basic needs" or some given "utility, " but was identical with social
well-being. Work was important not only in terms of what was produced but because it was the most important part of life—productive
effort was what it meant to be useful and valuable to others. To be at
work was to have purpose and meaning.

Paul Homan, assessing the progress of economic theories of consumption in the 1920s, came to the same conclusion. He observed
that "the recent prominence of consumption in economic analysis"
could be attributed in part to "a reconsideration of the problems of
economic welfare." In contrast to those who thought the welfare was
founded on "necessities," Homan noted that "recent discussions of
welfare have tended to emphasize . . . useful employment as an essential element in individual welfare." Welfare was more than having
enough to eat; it was having steady and gainful employment. Moreover, according to Homan, economists in the 1920s, realizing that work
was more a privilege than a burden, had turned to economic growth
as the foundation of that welfare. Without growth, work would be
steadily lost and unemployment or "idleness" steadily increased.[90]

Moreover, the "idea of maximum satisfaction," which was "dependent upon a quantitative comparison . . . of the satisfaction of consumption with the irksome labors of production," was not scientific;
such a relationship was incapable of being measured. Hence the "negative sloping" supply curve of labor was no longer an important concern. The clear-thinking economists of the 1920s had reduced "consumption to an auxiliary position in the theory of welfare." People
were well-off when they were working and achieving, progressing
toward a higher standard of living, not when they were merely having their "basic necessities" met and then being "forced" to work less.
Economists had found that the "uninterrupted productive efficiency
of the industrial system" and the sure provision of "useful employment" were "the most important elements" of human and economic
welfare. As Foster and Catchings put it, the "only insistent demand
which people make on organized society is steady work and gains in
real wages."[91]

During the 1920s, economists tended to depart from marginalism and reject its *a priori* assumptions about "necessity" and "utility."
Attempting to base consumption theory on objective standards and
behavioral principles, they nevertheless tended to display a bias about
what ought to be the major goals of the economy. In spite of their
claims to objectivity, they engaged a good deal in normative speculations. To them, welfare was not a given standard of living that
met definite needs. They assumed that two interrelated goals were

of major importance for the economy: economic growth and "useful employment." Work was the "essential element" of welfare, and economic growth served that value. Faced with neoclassical theories that predicted increased leisure instead of economic growth, and reacting to the problems of cyclical "oversupply," "underconsumption," and chronic unemployment, they looked to higher wages and new goods and services to support both economic growth and "useful employment," the authentic foundations for human welfare and progress.

All economists did not identify nonwork with "idleness" and unemployment. A few still believed that workers might freely choose less work because of increasing prosperity, and leisure might become a force to be reckoned with. For example, John M. Keynes, in *The Economic Consequences of the Peace*, a best-seller in the United States in 1920, declared that once enough comforts and necessities were produced and the economic trauma of war faded, Western man could proceed to exercise "his nobler faculties." Having created machines and expanded production enough, the industrial nations could usher in a new age of prosperity where effort would be redirected from work and the struggle for survival to leisure and the "graces of life."[92] This theme reappeared periodically in Keynes's writings and found full expression in his 1930 essay "Economic Possibilities of Our Grandchildren." He saw a process beginning after the war that would result inevitably in the condition of plenty. Keynes was hardly a marginalist, but he maintained that there was a categorical difference between goods and services "necessary for survival" and others that were only for display and status. Hence he still talked about a difference between "scarcity" and "plenty" in these terms. Moreover, like Simon Patten, Keynes feared that the habits and values acquired by centuries of want and hardship would make the transition to abundance difficult. Keynes reasoned that "we have been expressly evolved by nature with all our impulses and deepest instincts for the purpose of solving our economic problem. If the economic problem is solved, mankind will be deprived of its traditional purpose." Without work to provide meaning to life, people would be adrift in a sea of freedom, unsure of purpose and direction. They could well expect a "nervous breakdown" when suddenly exposed to the reality of leisure and forced over a few decades to discard the traditional reasons for existence.[93]

Whereas the ordinary worker fantasized that nothing could be sweeter than to "do nothing for ever and ever" and dreamed of heaven as a place and time to sing "eternal psalms," Keynes pointed out that such a condition would be tolerable only for those who did the singing, adding, "how few of us can sing." The new challenges of leisure rivaled those of the traditional economic problem. "Thus for the first time since his creation man will be faced with his real, his permanent problem—how to use his freedom from pressing economic cares, how to occupy the leisure, which science and compound interest have won for him, to live wisely and agreeably and well."[94]

McMahon also speculated about such matters. She suggested:

> If we accept the evolutionary theory that the progress of peo-
> ples can be measured in terms of standard of living, material
> standards may be but one step in the evolutionary process of
> standards, which in their highest expression, as demonstrated
> by a superior few, become simplified. . . . In this sense high
> social standards of living will no longer be material standards
> of living but social standards demanding a higher spiritual life
> common at present only among the few.[95]

Even some businessmen felt this way. For example, Walter S. Gifford, president of American Telephone and Telegraph, concluded that technology was remaking the world and men's lives. Led by the business elite, industry and the American people were at last conquering nature and establishing the foundation for a "new civilization." This new civilization, by "taking the load off men's shoulders," would give "every man the chance to do what he will . . . both materially and spiritually." Gifford thought that leisure was the just reward for the centuries of hard work. He believed that "leisure will give us the time to cultivate the art of living, give us better opportunity for the development of the arts, enlarge the comforts and satisfactions of mind and spirit as material well-being feeds the comforts of the body."[96]

But only a few examples of this sort of speculation can be found in the decade. For the most part, economists and businessmen had discarded the idea that progress was the outgrowing or transcending of material necessity. For the majority, economic progress prepared the way for more economic growth; it did not result in the transcendence of "economic concerns." Labor-saving machines had become job-creating tools. In the main, the dream now was for more work, not less. Progress was new jobs, new products, and an ever higher standard of living; it was not some resolution of the economic problem in favor of the "satisfactions of the mind and spirit." Economic freedom was not release from work, but the "climax" into new and better kinds of "productive effort." Abundance was not simply enough goods and services; it was, above all, enough work. Scarcity now had more to do with the lack of "productive employment" and less with the absence of the "necessities" of life. The word *famine* was now used to discuss work and jobs, not food.[97]

CHAPTER 3

Leisure for Labor

A T THE SAME TIME that businessmen and economists were reaffirming their belief in steady work and industrial growth, elevating these tenets to the center of discussions of social progress and individual welfare, and looking to increased "optional consumption" to undergird them, labor spokesmen, religious leaders, reformers, intellectuals, educators, and social critics were turning to a more traditional solution to unemployment. Sharing the widespread pessimism about "saturated" demand and limited markets in the early 1920s, these groups promoted labor's alternative solution to general overproduction: shorter work hours.

From 1920 to 1925, the "shorter hour cure for overproduction and unemployment" (what came to be known as the share-the-work plan during the Great Depression) was nearly as influential in America as the gospel of consumption. Those who supported the continuation of the shorter-hour movement believed that the measure would be more effective than increased consumption in stabilizing the economy. The critical debate about unemployment that developed in the early 1920s was not, as it has been since the Great Depression, how to stimulate demand (even though supporters of economic growth argued whether capital spending, advertising, business leadership, higher wages, government spending, or foreign markets was the better method). Instead, it involved the question of whether work time would continue to decrease, limiting unnecessary production and distributing necessary employment, or whether new markets would be established. Both views had in common the belief that the economy had reached a critical juncture, a point where productivity presented new kinds of challenges.[1]

Immediately after World War I, organized labor attempted to consolidate the gains made in securing the 8-hour day. Whereas the

8-hour day had received considerable public support and advanced rapidly during Wilson's administration—one observer noted that "it seemed quite literally to sweep the country"—pockets of "long hour resistance" remained in major unorganized industries.[2] Labor set the goal of standardizing the 8-hour day as one of its top priorities. In support of 8 hours in the 1920s, labor continued to emphasize the same kinds of benefits they had championed for twenty years. For example, in the steel strike of 1919 for the 8-hour day, unions dwelt on issues of health, safety, and fatigue. Even though the efforts of the American Federation of Labor (AFL) to organize the steel industry were thwarted by the "Red Scare," public support for the steelworkers was strong. As before, this support centered more on labor's practical concerns and less on unemployment and leisure. The Commission of Inquiry of the Interchurch World Movement found in 1921 that "the Americanization of the worker is a farce . . . night schools are worthless . . . Carnegie libraries are a jest . . . church welfare agencies are ironic," since steelworkers were required to work as many as 72 hours a week. Such overwork did not leave time "even for their families."[3] What steelworkers wanted, above all, was time to rest and at least some family life. Based on its survey, the commission reported that public opinion was overwhelmingly in favor of the 8-hour day in steel primarily because of the demonstrably unhealthy effects of overwork. Following Wilson's example, President Warren Harding used these traditional arguments to coerce Judge Gary and other heads of the industry to abandon the 12-hour-shift system and institute a three-shift, 8-hour day in 1923.

Some data are available about the attitudes of workers outside the steel industry toward the 8-hour day during this time. These tend to confirm what the Interchurch Commission and labor leaders were saying about workers' need for shorter hours.

Over a three-month period in 1925, the Consumer League of New York conducted a questionnaire and interview survey of 500 women in New York State about their feelings concerning a pending New York law setting the workweek at 48 hours for women. The league made an ambitious attempt to question a random but "representative cross section" of women in the state by contacting workers in 11 cities and 19 industries. Since only 36 responses came from members of trade unions, the league claimed that their report represented "the sentiments of unorganized women in factories and stores . . . the more inarticulate and poorly paid" workers. Attempting to analyze the "overwhelmingly affirmative vote" (81 percent said they were for the law, 8 percent were for it with qualifications), the league conducted interviews with 380 of the workers to find out why they supported the law. The league concluded that "with the older women, the necessity of doing housework or helping at home and the effect . . . of long hours upon their health were the determining factors in back of their decision for shorter hours. . . . Among the younger workers the need for rest and health was the dominant concern." But workers also mentioned such things as "recreation and real living," a "life worth living," "grandchildren," "church," "culture," "spiritual things," "time to enjoy the extra money," "decent conditions," "an enjoyable life," "Y classes," and "time to live." The league listed only 8 positive or qualified responses having to do with unemployment and none having to do with higher wages. The league also asked, "Would you rather work longer hours regularly if you could make a little more money by doing so?" Seventy-three women said yes, 343 said no, and 80 gave qualified answers. While not exact, this is at least an approximate indication of relative wage and leisure preferences. Of these women, 209 opposed any kind of overtime, even with time-and-a-half pay.[4]

A much less precise survey was taken by the Women's Bureau of the U.S. Department of Labor in the same year. Investigating the hours of work of 230,000 women in 2600 establishments in eighteen states, the Women's Bureau concluded that "from the workers' standpoint . . . the noise and speed of machinery . . . the complexity or the monotony of the job . . . undue fatigue . . . participation in community life . . . citizenship . . . interest in the home . . . home responsibilities . . . and leisure—and all that is implied [by leisure]" were the important reasons for a preference for shorter hours. No mention was made in this investigation (or in the Women's Bureau's 1928 report) of higher wages or unemployment.[5]

By contrast, concerns that were so important in the issue of the 8-hour day were less in evidence during labor's shorter-hour initiative in the 1920s. Most of organized labor had won the 8-hour day before the decade began, and observers were predicting the "doom" of the 12-hour day and the "triumph" of the 8-hour day nationwide by 1923. Fairly confident that the 8-hour day was becoming universal, labor leaders began to turn their attention to a shorter workweek, a five-and-a-half day or five-day week, at this time not for health, safety, and fatigue reasons but increasingly as a way to deal with unemployment and provide more leisure time.[6]

During the early 1920s, union leaders, like businessmen, argued that technological unemployment and periodic depressions resulted naturally from increased productivity and limited markets, especially in the "new era" of economic abundance. Whereas during the previous twenty years they had been content to follow the popular idea that shorter hours in the form of the 8-hour day improved production and made work safer and workers more moral, initially they turned to the 40-hour week primarily as a way to counter the threat of technological unemployment that seemed to have intensified after the war. Agreeing that shorter hours were a reasonable response to the new era's increased productivity and economic surpluses, labor raised again Samuel Gompers's famous rallying cry of the 1880s: "So long as there is one who seeks employment and cannot find it, the hours of labor are too long."[7]

Before the end of the war, fewer than twenty manufacturing establishments had adopted the five-day week. Most of these few firms were Jewish establishments, managed and staffed by Jews who considered it a religious obligation to observe the Sabbath. But during the 1920s, more than 240 manufacturers adopted the plan. By 1929, approximately 400,000 to 500,000 employees were working a five-day week. Moreover, the average workweek in industry during the 1920s was virtually stable at around 49 hours per week. Hence this new initiative was not very successful. Nevertheless, it was important enough to spark a lively debate about increased leisure and alter organized labor's position on the shorter-hour issue.[8]

At the end of the war, labor leaders throughout the nation were afraid that mass unemployment would occur with demobilization and the cessation of wartime production. Four days after the Armistice, a wave of strikes occurred nationwide; strikers included the Amalgamated Clothing Workers in New York and Chicago, who struck for a five-and-a-half-day week and a 15 percent increase in wages and workers in the textile industry in New England and New Jersey. Strikes were also called by the printer's union, longshoremen in New York, and telegraph operators. Some 2600 strikes involving 4 million workers occurred in 1919. Wages and collective bargaining rights were the most important issues in these strikes. Nevertheless, the shorter workweek had become an issue for the first time.[9]

Painters' and plasterers' unions, and other building trade unions such as plumbers and carpenters, printing and publishing unions, and especially unions in the clothing industry, initiated and led the way in the five-day-week movement. And in their support for this reform, unemployment and the cultural benefits of leisure dominated. Few workers outside these trades were successful in this initiative during the decade. Analyzing the "prevalence of the five-day week in American industry" in 1926, the Bureau of Labor Statistics reported that it was common in three industries: clothing (with 33 percent of workers so employed), printing and publishing (6 percent) and the building trades (6 percent). Foreign-born workers were the majority in the clothing and printing and publishing industries involved. And the worker group making the most rapid gains in the five-day week from 1918 to 1929 was heavily composed of first-generation Middle European and Russian Jews in the clothing industries of the Northeast and Chicago.[10]

The first major union to propose a five-day week was the Amalgamated Clothing Workers of America, which passed resolutions at their biennial conventions, beginning in 1920. Led by Sidney Hillman, the national union worked with local unions, especially in New York, during the decade to incorporate 40-hour clauses in trade agreements, or a clause that committed manufacturers to institute this reform "as soon as possible." But for several local Jewish unions, progress through trade agreements and resolutions was too slow. Strikes were called by the needle trade, the New York City clothing workers, the Paterson, New Jersey, silk workers, and several other local unions between 1920 and 1924, which included demands for either a five-and-a-half-day or a five-day week. These early strikes were settled for the most part by compromise, the workers agreeing to give up hours' benefits for higher wages. But beginning in 1924, a series of major successful strikes was called by 50,000 New York City Ladies' Garment Workers Union members (the largest strike in the nation that year), 40,000 clothing workers in New York City in 1926, 5000 fur workers in New York and 3000 in Boston (both in 1926), and all members of the New York and Philadelphia Cloth Hat and Cap Workers' Union in 1927, as well as other smaller unions working in children's dresses, bathrobes, and kimonos. In these strikes, the 40-hour, five-day week was the major issue. When coupled with demands for higher wages, the issue dominated. For example, observers of the seventeen-week strike of the New York furriers concluded that "the main difficulty [prolonging the strike] seems to have been what points the union should barter away in order to gain the forty-hour week." These strikes were successful, so much so that by 1927, the Bureau of Labor Statistics concluded that the five-day work week was "practically the rule in trade agreements in the clothing industry."[11]

In these events, the workers' overriding concern was unemployment. The high level of joblessness in the industry, the return of soldiers from the war, and the depressed nature of the clothing business after the loss of army contracts troubled workers much more than issues of fatigue, health, or safety. Moreover, clothing was notoriously a seasonal industry, and workers had long believed that shorter hours would help spread the work from the fall and early spring busy seasons over the year, providing at least some employment in summer and winter months. From the beginning of the five-day-week movement, union journals in the clothing industry (such as the *Ad-*

vance, Clothing Worker, and *Lady Garment Worker*), as well as publications such as the *New York Times* and *Women's Wear Daily*, reported that workers were quite concerned about temporary and long-term unemployment. Worker interest in the unemployment issue ebbed and flowed throughout the decade with changes in the industry's fortunes. Periods of unemployment prompted a rash of articles and letters dealing with the need to "spread the work" and "rationalize the industry" through shorter hours.[12]

But in the clothing unions, new kinds of concerns emerged, having to do with cultural and religious benefits of Saturday holidays.

The religious concern was most evident. Some attempts were made at the time to explain the clothing workers' exceptional interest in the five-day week. The National Industrial Conference Board, reporting that the clothing industry encompassed 60 percent of the 270 establishments in the nation that had adopted the five-day week, observed that since workers in these clothing establishments were predominantly immigrant Jews, the "main" or "most potent" reason for their interest was the "Hebrew Sabbath." Another contemporary observer, Frank De Vyver, agreed with this assessment.[13]

One of the main difficulties that Jews faced in America during the nineteenth and early twentieth centuries was the loss of Saturday as the historical Sabbath. Although the Jewish concern for keeping the Sabbath was as keen as the Christian, Jews were in effect prohibited this religious freedom and forced by society and their jobs to observe Sunday as what amounted to a national religious holiday.[14]

Throughout the nineteenth and early twentieth centuries, Jews faced this problem but never resolved it. Orthodox spokesmen were afraid that the Sabbath as a unique part of their religion was dying out—being observed more in the breach than in the keeping. Often they would predict that the Sabbath was doomed because of the constraints of American culture. They saw in the death of the Sabbath one more force that would speed the assimilation and even the conversion of the Jewish people. For example, Rabbi Israel Herbert Levinthal argued that "if we see Jewish life crumbling before our very eyes in America it is mainly due to the fact that we have lost our Sabbath."[15] That this view was widely held was demonstrated by a joint statement issued by the Union of Orthodox Rabbis of the United States and Canada, the Rabbinical Assembly of America, the Union of Orthodox Jewish Congregations of America, and the United Synagogue of America: "This violation of the Sabbath, if continued indefinitely, must inevitably lead to the gradual disintegration of our people."[16] For the Orthodox and for a number of Conservatives, the preservation of the Sabbath was a precondition to the preservation of American

Judaism. The Sabbath also contained ideals and values central to the Jewish religion. It was the special, holy time for ritual matters, for community, for family, for tradition, and for the individual and his God, set aside from the busy, materialistic, and profane world. A strict observance of that day preserved the forms and institutions of Judaism to be sure, but it also contained central truths that were timeless.

As early as 1910, Rabbi Bernard Drachman, president of the Jewish Sabbath Alliance, told the group that the problem of the Sabbath was so interwoven with American conditions that the issue could be resolved only if both Saturday and Sunday were observed as days of rest by "Christians and Jews alike." As efforts to exempt Jews from Saturday work failed and attempts to open up Sunday work proved fruitless and generated hard feelings among Christian Sabbatarians, more people came to appreciate the wisdom of Drachman's original vision.[17]

Beginning in 1919, the Sabbath Alliance supported local unions in New York, Boston, Philadelphia, and other large cities that were launching campaigns for the five-and-a-half-day week, a campaign that worked directly toward the institution of Saturday holidays. "Sabbath patrols" were organized in New York City (they were constituted both to stamp out competition and encourage Sabbath keeping), and mass rallies were held in support of Saturday holidays. In addition, several Jewish groups joined together to fight the passage of new "blue laws" in the early part of the decade. As a direct result of these grassroots efforts, in February 1924 the convention of Orthodox Rabbis of New York, New Jersey, and Connecticut met in New York City to "further the establishment of the five-day-week system." Several speakers (among them Bernard Drachman) noted that since their opposition to blue laws had not been successful and was bringing "protests from Christians," the five-day week offered a compromise. The convention concluded: "So, to please both Jews and Christians, the plan for two days of rest each week was adopted."[18]

The idea gained ground rapidly, among Jews and others. In 1925, the Sabbath Alliance formed an interdenominational committee, composed of such men as Drachman, Carlyle B. Haynes, Cyrus Adler, and N. Taylor Phillips, to promote the cause. Spokesmen for this group agreed that "this great public reform . . . will . . . tend to remove the greatest causes of friction and religious intolerances existing in America today."[19] Also in 1925, representatives of several rabbinic bodies (Orthodox, Reform, and Conservative) met in New York to "further the five-day week in American industry." They launched what they called "a vigorous campaign in publications, lobbying, and promotion." Leaders in these efforts included M. Z. Margolies, Chaim Block, and A. B. Burak of the Union of Orthodox Rabbis, Samuel Schulman and Nathan Stern of the Central Conference of American Rabbis, and "lay organizations" such as the Union of Orthodox Jewish Congregations of America, the Sabbath Alliance, and Young Israel.[20] In addition, beginning in 1924, the United Synagogue of America planned a series of conferences between employers and labor unions "with a view to the establishing of a five-day week in as many industries as possible." By 1927, the Union of Orthodox Jewish Congregations, the Central Conference of American Rabbis, the Rabbinical Assembly, the United Synagogue, and the Union of Orthodox Rabbis of the United States and Canada had endorsed this cause as a general labor reform and in several instances had encouraged the efforts of local unions, such as the needle trade and the Ladies' Garment Workers.

The primary concern of all these groups and individuals was, of course, the revitalization of Sabbath observances on Saturday. But Jewish leaders who supported the five-day week also endorsed the other justification of the union leaders. For example, Drachman stressed the importance of Saturday holidays to deal with unemployment among clothing workers.

It is hard to judge religion's influence on the five-day week and measure its importance compared with the unemployment issue. But since the unions that first pressed for the five-day week were composed mostly of Jews, the desire to revive Saturday observance was very prevalent in Jewish groups, and national Jewish organizations, as well as local congregations, endorsed the five-day week, a *prima facie* case can be made that religion was a critical factor.[21]

Along with this "religious sanction," interest in leisure for "culture," family, community, and learning was also an important part of clothing workers' concerns with shorter hours. At the onset of the five-day-week movement, union journals in the clothing industry reported that workers were interested in the five-day week for its "humane" benefits: "rest and life." Occasionally these journals, as well as the *Monthly Labor Review*, observed that workers were willing to give up wages or postpone wage demands for progress toward the 40-hour week. Letters from workers and statements by local and national union leaders published in the journals were full of praise for leisure and observations that workers were interested in increased free time for spiritual, cultural, family, and community matters.[22]

For example, leaders of the International Ladies' Garment Workers (ILGW) Education Committee saw in the "dramatic" increases in the popularity of worker education programs, union social centers, and public recreation facilities "clear evidence" of workers' desire for increased free time to "improve the mind and spirit." Juliet Stuart Poyntz, national education director of the ILGW, observed that

> the great movement for the limitation of hours that is sweeping over the trades employing hundreds of thousands of women will bring working women the great boon of Time—time for rest, time to play, time to be human. . . . It is a new day indeed. Workers have declared that their lives are not to be bartered at any price, that no wage, no matter how high can induce them to sell their birthright. [The worker] is not the slave of fifty years ago. He has something to live for. He is not a machine. He is a person. He reads . . . goes to the theater . . . [and] has established his own libraries, his own educational institutions. . . . And he wants time, time, time, for all these things. Time to eat, time to live, time to be happy, time to be a person . . . more education, more recreation, more pleasure, more rest, more time for himself. The great struggle for shorter hours is therefore based on the revolutionary principle of equality.[23]

Some of this may have been mere rhetoric—a cover-up for other purposes. But according to historical accounts, workers in the clothing industry were especially concerned with tradition and culture. Many Jewish immigrants in the clothing trade were well educated, with a deep and abiding interest in literature, philosophy, politics, and music.

There is also some evidence that the "flowering of Yiddish culture," which Irvine Howe has described as occurring at this time, had links to the 40-hour movement. Marcus Ravage, writing about the popularity among clothing workers of the "sweatshop writers" and the political and academic lectures in New York City, described worker interest in having at least a half-day holiday on Saturday to attend these lectures and be involved with the various discussion groups, political and social clubs, and other organizations that sprang up in the early 1920s.[24]

In addition, the autobiographical works of Morris Rosenfield and Elizabeth Hasanovitz describe in detail, and from the workers' point of view, the problems that long work hours presented for those who valued more time at home, reading, with friends, and for the theater and education. One of the strongest themes in Hasanovitz's books was her desperation at long work hours and her yearning to escape work "to live," "to walk in Central Park," to attend lectures and the opera, and to go to the libraries and museums in New York City. Pauline Newman, another clothing worker, remembering those days, remarked: "We fought hard for those free hours. . . . We used to read Tolstoy, Dickens, Shelley."[25]

Taken together, these examples indicate that some workers did indeed see a connection between the shorter workweek and the importance of leisure for religion, community, family, education, rest, tradition, and culture. But in the clothing industry, leisure, while a prominent motive, did not stand alone. Unemployment was almost certainly the key concern. But the combination of leisure and unemployment motives particular to workers in the clothing industry, plagued by seasonal and cyclical unemployment and heavily composed of immigrant Jews keenly interested in cultural things, the family, community, and Saturday religious holidays, help explain why they were so far ahead of the nation in the five-day-week movement.

From 1920 to 1924, however, the clothing, printing, and building trades were mostly on their own. The AFL felt it had its hands full mopping up "pockets of long hour resistance" in these years. Even though the 8-hour day, six-day week had become the norm by the early 1920s, enough unions were still struggling to catch up with this standard to occupy the AFL's attention. Although it had endorsed the Amalgamated Clothing Worker's shorter-week drive in 1920, it was not until 1924–1926 that the AFL was ready to turn its attention to this cause as the next logical step in the century-long process of shorter hours.

In the winter of 1925–1926, in preparation for the next convention, the AFL executive council began to publicize its support for the shorter working week. Whereas during the previous twenty years labor had been content to follow the popular idea that shorter hours in the form of the 8-hour day improved production and made work safer and workers more moral, initially the AFL turned to the 40-hour week primarily as a way to counter the threat of technological unemployment.[26]

William Green, president of the AFL, Matthew Woll, vice-president of the AFL, Sidney Hillman, founder and president of the Amalgamated Clothing Worker's Union, A. O. Wharton, president of the International Association of Machinists, and other labor leaders argued that the continuous and gradual reduction of work hours, matching the increased efficiency of industry, was vital in order to improve the workers' bargaining position and deal with the problem of technological unemployment. They understood technological unemployment as a natural result of increased efficiency, economic surpluses, and limited markets. With the gradual meeting of basic needs, the available work to be done was decreasing.

In order to deal with the threats of a "standing army of the unemployed" and periodic depressions (which would naturally force worker time to equalize to increase productivity over the long term), these labor leaders called for the 40-hour week. Green, for example, explained that free time was a natural result of the industrial process. That time could be forced on workers in the form of chronic unemployment or acute depression, or it could be rationally apportioned for workers' benefit through decreased hours.[27]

Wharton agreed that "increased production accentuates the problem of overproduction or underconsumption. Increased wages and reduced hours go hand in hand with increased production." Economic balance could be maintained only if "wages advance and leisure hours increase. If some sort of balance is not maintained, we are headed straight for disaster."[28]

Woll observed that although one of the reasons "unions have supported shorter hours" was that "labor might enjoy the gifts of God freely," their overriding concerns were unemployment and low wages. Since limited markets and surpluses existed, and "production is overlapping our ability to consume" shorter hours acted as a "restraining influence" to limit production to "rational levels" and to the production of cheap necessities. He supposed that shorter hours could be a way to improve wages and limit production, control surpluses, increase the consumption of necessities, and avoid business cycles.[29]

These leaders also argued that wages had to be increased before overproduction ceased to be a problem. But in their initial statements about the five-day week, they claimed that shorter hours would help that process, resurrecting briefly the old "eight hour theory of wages." They claimed that shorter working hours would solve not only the problem of overproduction of goods by limiting production but would also solve the problem of oversupply of workers. Initially, many labor leaders supported the five-day week in the belief that it would create a scarcity of labor in relation to business demand and thus raise wages and improve labor's bargaining position. By "deflating labor," production could be limited to basic needs, prices reduced, and wages improved to the point of assuring a minimum standard of living for everyone. Labor maintained that in a condition of "forced labor scarcity," the rich would not buy more luxuries, but the poor could buy more necessities. Shorter hours were seen by unions as an efficient and democratic way to redistribute wealth. In the face of business views about welfare being based not on the redistribution of wealth but on increasing total wealth, such a position was precarious.[30]

Green took labor's case to Calvin Coolidge, and at a White House luncheon in the summer of 1926, remarked, "Labor must have shorter working hours in order to meet this condition of overproduction." Later, in an August 1926 speech in Philadelphia, Green said, "We can only readjust our economic life to the constant increase in production of manufactured articles through a reduction in the hours of labor," thus limiting "overproduction" and the resultant unemployment.[31]

Green's remarks at the White House and in Philadelphia were met with an onslaught of editorial and business protest. The *Washington Post* argued that "instead of reducing production, the aim should be to increase consumption. This can be accomplished only through the medium of high wages." In fact, "the production of wealth is never a calamity. To arbitrarily reduce the hours of work in order to reduce production and give work for more laborers is bad for everybody." The *Boston Post*, meanwhile, held that "overproduction . . . is regarded today as pretty much of a fallacy." And the *Louisville Herald Post* informed its readers that "the belief that the remedy for overproduction is for labor to work shorter hours . . . is one of those economic fallacies that even the wisest of the labor leaders are unable to rid themselves of."[32]

For years, the AFL had courted business support for shorter hours by stressing the fact that reductions in hours increased productivity and aided total production. When labor shifted its position in 1924–1926, emphasizing again the shorter-hour cure for overproduction on the national level, the business and editorial outcry was overwhelming. The idea of limiting production ran against the tide of optimism that had begun to flow in America; it was the very antithesis of the gospel of consumption and the new faith in economic growth through new work and new, "optional" consumption. Moreover, this was a period of generally high employment and economic growth, so much so that public support for having Saturdays off as an unemployment measure found very few supporters outside labor.

In the face of stiff opposition, the AFL backed away from the overproduction–unemployment issue during and after the 1926 convention. Subsequently, the shorter-hour cure for unemployment was downplayed until the Great Depression.

This process began in 1926 when the AFL Committee on a Shorter Work Day, drafting the "progressive shortening of the hours of labor" resolution, struck from the original resolution submitted by several affiliate unions all mention of "overproduction" and unemployment, substituting instead language highly critical of modern work. Subsequently, when affiliated unions offered resolutions concerning unemployment to the Committee on a Shorter Work Day, the members routinely buried such resolutions and deferred to the Executive Committee, which by 1929 had come to justify shorter hours mainly by criticizing work and praising leisure.[33]

After October 1926, the editors of the *American Federationist* published articles specifically rejecting the argument that "overproduction" caused unemployment and that shorter hours would, by reducing production, help solve the problem. In addition, articles were published that criticized all schemes to limit production. Unemployment was still frequently discussed in the *American Federationist* between 1926 and 1930. But shorter hours were seldom mentioned.[34]

Instead, the AFL largely adopted the businessmen's and economists' solutions to unemployment. Following the new interest in higher wages, current among some economists, the AFL stressed the importance of keeping wages high enough to absorb the new levels of industrial production. Other remedies economists were suggesting appeared in the *Federationist*, such as public works, unemployment insurance, central work exchanges, and even guaranteed employment. And these sorts of things were featured to the exclusion of shorter hours.[35]

In addition, the AFL abandoned the argument that shorter hours would force wages higher and act to redistribute wealth. Instead, in convention and speeches, and in the *Federationist*, union leaders stressed the importance of economic growth and the increase in both productivity and total production as the means to higher wages as well as shorter hours.

As the historian Jene Trepp McKelvey pointed out, the AFL's attitudes toward production were changing even before 1926. McKelvey showed that up to 1900 the "eight hour theory of wages . . . furnished the intellectual driving force behind the AF of L." But increasingly, the AFL leadership after Gompers abandoned the idea that shorter hours would, by making labor scarce, drive up wages and redistribute wealth and help deal with unemployment. It came to accept the view that the road to higher wages lay in increasing total production and improving productivity. Leaders such as Green and Woll, and even Gompers in his last years, stressed industrial cooperation and advised their followers that "higher wages could best be secured by increasing output." Hence, the brief endorsement of the "eight hour theory" in 1925–1926 was in some ways an anomaly, the result of the AFL's responding to local and affiliated unions' pressure and the period of pessimism about the economy that was widespread immediately after World War I.[36]

The AFL's commitment to economic growth entailed changes in its position on shorter hours. After 1925, the AFL developed what one might term "the productivity theory of shorter hours," since it evolved directly from what McKelvey termed the AFL's "productivity theory of wages." The *New York Times* observed in October 1926:

> Labor is making this latest demand [for wages and hours] on entirely new grounds. It maintains that the workers are entitled

to an increasing share of the benefits derived from the amazing industrial increases . . . benefits in higher wages as well as
shorter hours. . . .

The new labor theories . . . are an elaboration of the stand
taken a year ago when, for the first time, the AF of L accepted
joint responsibility for production and officially announced it
was willing to cooperate with employers for greater output in
return for a share of the accrued profits. . . .

. . . the federation has made a definite concession in its
philosophy between the efficiency of industry and the shorter
working week. There has been [since 1925] a definite acceptance of the fact that a shorter work week with the same wages
can now come only by increasing the output per worker.[37]

Official statements in AFL conventions and labor leaders' public comments in the *American Federationist* and other publications confirmed
this piece of reporting.[38]

This sort of argument was new and in marked contrast to previous
discussions about shorter hours and increased productivity. Before the
1920s, labor had stressed the fact that shorter hours increased production. After 1925, leaders spoke more in terms of shorter hours as
the workers' just reward for increased productivity. The timing of the
two was reversed, as was their causal relationship. After 1925, labor
leaders tended to stress that workers should share increases in wealth
brought on by productivity by both working fewer hours and receiving higher wages. Between 1925 and 1930, labor was busy, as Green
observed, trying to "trade" productivity advances for both wages and
hours.

Having given up on the idea that shorter hours caused higher
wages and downplaying the shorter-hour solution to unemployment,
the AFL faced the problem of finding ways to justify new advances in
shorter hours. But the 8-hour standbys, fatigue and efficiency, had lost
some of their appeal; businessmen were much less interested, and public support, once so spontaneous and powerful for the 8-hour day, was
simply absent. Moreover, increased productivity no longer provided
the rationale for shorter hours; it simply established the opportunity—
it was indeed possible to argue, as many businessmen were doing, that
increased productivity could provide higher wages *or* shorter hours,
but not both at the same time. The choice was a mutually exclusive
one.

Nevertheless, the AFL endorsed shorter hours in the 1926 convention and showed more interest in this reform for the next ten years
than they had over the previous twenty-five years. In its resolution

adopted in the 46th Annual Meeting in October 1926, the AFL supported the doctrine of gradually reducing work hours (the 40-hour week was understood as just one step in the continuous long-term reduction of work that began before the Civil War) for some interesting reasons:

> Whereas under present methods of modern machine industry the workers are continually subject to the strain of mechanized processes which sap their vitality; and
>
> Whereas if compelled to work for long hours under modern processes of production, the vitality, health, and very life of workers is [*sic*] put in serious jeopardy;
>
> *Resolved,* that this convention place itself on record as favoring a progressive shortening of the hours of labor and the days per week and that the Executive Council be requested to inaugurate a campaign of education and organization to that end.[39]

This resolution appeared to emphasize the same kinds of practical concerns expressed during the push for the 8-hour day. In subsequent statements, however, a clear difference emerged. Whereas earlier labor had stressed the *physical* toll that workers paid for long hours, increasingly labor leaders talked in more abstract terms about the psychological, social, cultural, intellectual, and spiritual price of "devitalized" jobs. Increasingly, labor leaders used the same rhetoric that intellectuals and social critics had used around 1900. The "crisis of work" and the "new leisure ethic" had finally become more than parts of an intellectual debate; they had emerged as primary reasons for the AFL to continue to support "the progressive shortening of the hours of labor."

Following the attacks by newspaper editors on labor's shorter-hour proposals in 1926, Green wrote in the *American Federationist*: "The human values of leisure are even greater than its economic significance." This statement set the tone for labor's rhetoric about shorter hours, which became increasingly "romantic" until the Great Depression. Labor leaders linked leisure directly to worker culture, both broadly and narrowly conceived, and to workers' dissatisfaction with their work in general.[40]

For example, Green talked about modern work as being "meaningless, repetitive, boring," without "creative expression," offering "no satisfaction of intellectual needs," and increasingly stressful—leading to "nervous disorders" and mental health problems. He contrasted the worker's lot in the 1920s with that of "our ancestors," who "were at liberty to rest during the day, to take moments of refreshment."

The modern worker, surrounded by the "grinding roar and noise of modern plants" and forced to keep pace with the machine, "if he is to live at all . . . must reduce the number of hours."[41] Thomas Lewis, an officer of the International Typographical Union, agreed that "the conveyor system is the nearest approach to a mechanical slave drive that has ever been installed in a factory." Hillman concurred that "the speed and strain of industry are always greater."[42]

Green argued that in order that "our social and human values may not be overwhelmed in the general mechanizing process and the lives of workers may not be merged with the machine until they, too, become mechanical . . . there must be a progressive shortening of the hours of labor . . . to safeguard our human nature . . . and thereby [lay] the foundation . . . for the higher development of spiritual and intellectual powers." He spoke of "the dawn of a new era—leisure for all" and a "revolution of living." "The leisured proletariat" could at last have access to "good music, the fine arts, literature, travel, and beauty in all guises." The family, the community, and traditional cultures would be revitalized. Things that work used to provide, such as craftsmanship, creativity, worker control, and even "meaning," could be regained in hobbies and individually chosen work in the freedom of leisure. Shorter hours were necessary for "increased knowledge of technological principles," and for "recreation and recuperation . . . necessary to sustain vigor." For Green, gradually increasing leisure could redeem traditional values that had been lost at work, as well as open up new democratic and human vistas for the masses.[43]

Green and other leaders of the worker education movement spoke of leisure as providing both a new opportunity for learning and a vast "new expanse of time" to apply learning to life away from the job.[44]

On one occasion, Green remarked: "Two fundamental factors determining the life of any person are income and work hours. Income furnishes the key to [economic] opportunity. Work hours conditions physical well-being as well as personal contributions to community life."[45]

Woll and Hillman defended the "leisured proletariat" by criticizing the "devitalized nature of modern work." Like Green, both saw increased leisure as a way to regain traditional values that had been lost in modern occupations. But Woll noted that "unfortunately, our industrial life is dominated by the materialistic spirit of production, of work and more work, giving little attention to the development of the human body, the human mind, or the spirit of life. . . . All the finer qualities of life are entirely ignored." The dehumanized nature of modern jobs was complicated by the "materialistic spirit" of the business community. For Woll, leisure was a "restraining influence";

it was a way to control the material values rampant in the "gospel of consumption." For Woll, "constructive recreation" for physical, social, aesthetic, and spiritual purposes could provide a foil to devitalized work, as well as counter the new demands to consume more and more goods and services that were less and less needed.[46]

The AFL's 1929 convention at Ontario, Canada, was one of the best illustrations of these points. Two affiliated unions, the International Association of Machinists and the Bookbinders, Stenographers, and Local Union 12646 of New York, brought resolutions to the convention that included unemployment as a prominent justification for the 40- and 44-hour weeks. Referred to the Committee on a Shorter Work Day, these resolutions, while accepted as written, were buried in committee. Rather than deal publicly with the unemployment issue, the committee responded to the Executive Council's report on leisure and worded its own report by quoting the council's language. The Committee on a Shorter Work Day "heartily approved" the Executive Council's paean to leisure and observed that labor's recent national efforts to achieve "social acceptance" of the idea that "every individual needs leisure . . . not only the leisure class" had made "definite progress." The Executive Council's report on shorter hours made no mention of unemployment or higher wages, presenting instead a lengthy praise of worker leisure, describing it as necessary for "rounded development of the body, mind, and spirit . . . , the richness of life . . . , social progress . . . , and civilization itself." Furthermore, in discussions about unemployment, the Executive Council made no mention of shorter working hours but emphasized higher wages. At the 1929 convention, as well as at the three previous conventions, leisure stood virtually alone as the reason given by the AFL to continue its shorter-hour campaign.[47]

Leisure emerged from 1925 to 1930 as the major reason for the AFL to continue its shorter-hour drive; the higher-wage argument was eclipsed and the unemployment justification overshadowed. Trying to "trade" productivity for both wages and hours, labor emphasized leisure and the nonpecuniary benefits of shorter hours more than economic benefits.

Even though they accepted the "productivity theory of wages and hours," the unions did not accept the businessmen's and economists' idea that work was a primary element of human welfare or was getting easier or somehow more creative, enriching, and noble. For the unions, and for their leaders, high wages and reduced hours were more important than the abstract ideal "work." Higher wages made a minimum standard of living possible for the masses, shorter hours reduced the drudgery of work that had grown worse, not better in the machine age. For labor, higher wages and shorter hours were two sides of the same coin, mutually supportive of the workers' welfare.

The unions' position on shorter hours and higher wages was in clear contrast to the businessmen's gospel of consumption. Even though they shared the idea that basic needs were beginning to be met and traditional markets were limited, they concentrated their attention on cheap necessities and not "optional consumption" as the prime direction for the economy. They also supported the "progressive reduction of work hours" instead of expecting the end of the century-long process of shorter hours. In so doing, they looked to higher wages instead of stimulated demand to stabilize the economy. In the last place, they saw work as an increasingly great burden and looked to secure jobs with shorter hours and higher wages as the primary elements of welfare and not to newly idealized "work" or "full employment." Certainly they did not share the economists' or the modern idea that "full employment" had something to do with a stable workweek and that fewer hours a week constituted "idle manpower."

Bernstein may have been right in his observation about shorter hours that during the depression, "the economic argument crowded out the others."[48] But from 1926 to 1930, both the high wage and the unemployment justification were crowded out by labor's commitment to increased production, its reliance on higher wages to combat unemployment, and its willingness to respond to public criticism. Leisure for nonpecuniary purposes emerged more than ever as labor's primary justification.

Labor's five-day-week initiatives and commitment to the "progressive shortening of the hours of labor" were met by exceptionally strong business opposition. But they were also supported by an unusually large and varied group of people ranging from James Truslow Adams to Stuart Chase, from Orthodox Jewish groups to "progressive" educators. This was true because, more than at any time before, labor's shorter-hour cause involved basic questions about the purpose of work and economic growth, the future of capitalism, and the course of progress. This widespread public interest took the form of a debate, with one side supporting labor and the other rejecting the open-ended increase in leisure time and steady reduction of work.

During the time businessmen were reaffirming their belief in work and industrial growth, others were disturbed by this new economic gospel of consumption. Some people became convinced that it was beginning to exploit workers. By producing new goods and new demands for these goods, industry was keeping people at work longer than necessary. Americans were working more to serve the interests of the capitalist profit system and less to take care of their material necessities or meet their individually felt needs. A large number of Americans questioned perpetual industrial growth, believing that it would continue to exploit workers by convincing them to produce unnecessary "luxuries." Workers had lost control of production. Now they were losing control of consumption and the ability to shape their future and culture. They were facing a new definition of progress: economic growth for the sake of economic growth. Growth toward obtainable goals, such as the meeting of basic needs, still made sense. But long hours of work in the new "squirrel cage" that capitalism had set up did not. These people continued to feel that higher wages and shorter hours *together* constituted "genuine progress" and accused the disciples of the new economic gospel of consumption of breaking tradition and setting up a false idol to resemble real progress.

In addition, the "crisis of work" that Daniel Rodgers and James Gilbert described as occurring at the turn of the century continued during the 1920s. Specialization increased in skilled occupations, and many jobs were lost to the machine. Moreover, the assembly line was now a prominent part of the unskilled worker's life. Scientific managers such as Frederick Taylor wielded their influence on jobs, which became ever more standardized and impersonal. As the "organizational revolution" continued, industrial psychologists began to be influential, looking to planning and testing to adjust workers to their jobs instead of seeing individuals as agents of choice and of their own salvation at work. Indeed, as industrial efficiency grew at its most rapid rate, the crisis of work grew apace. Many observers were as disturbed by alienation, boredom, loss of individualism, the end of creativity and craftsmanship, and the lack of personal control, fellowship, and social mobility on the job in the 1920s as they had been in earlier years. Even though the new gospel of consumption reaffirmed the importance of work, and many of its adherents hoped to see work expand and evolve as an intrinsically rewarding activity, others shared labor's jaundiced view of "the glory of work."[49]

But a change for the worse occurred in the decade. Not only was the job changing, becoming less a vehicle for the expression of traditional skills and values, but the very purpose of work was being undercut by increased production. Before the 1920s, few writers suspected that increased production and work were not linked to definite objectives: the necessities of life. As long as production had definite purposes, work had firm and traditional ethical supports.

In the 1920s, however, in the light of unprecedented prosperity, the purpose of increased production and thereby the purpose of work were questioned. If machines could provide more than enough for everyone, generating huge surpluses, what, then, was the future of work?

According to the gospel of consumption, this was an idle question, since work was important on its own, apart from any connection with "necessities." A job was the center of life. At their workplaces, people found meaning and community with others; they were able to contribute to society. The great purpose of an economy, the very definition of *welfare*, was, in Foster and Catchings's words, the "steady provision of work" and a higher standard of living.[50]

But reformers, intellectuals, sociologists, educators, religious leaders, labor spokesmen, psychologists, humanist scholars, and displaced aristocrats were disturbed by the new gospel of consumption and the elevation of work to an intrinsically important, self-justifying activity. Such critics saw the erosion of the last firm ethical foundation of work in business's new ideas about "optional" consumption and in the assumption that motives to buy, and hence to produce and work, were thoroughly relative. They felt less need to support the tradition of work. Instead, they turned to shorter hours to save what they thought were more important values that were no longer a part of work. They believed that perpetual industrial growth would continue to make work inhuman and unsatisfying, and would exploit workers by convincing them to produce things they did not need or want—in fact, had to be persuaded to buy. Individualism, among other things, was the price Americans paid for what Stewart Chase called the "new consumer wonderland."[51]

But some of these people shared the pessimism of those who thought that "saturated" demand limited markets. Like businessmen, they feared and wished to avert the unemployment, chronic or acute, threatened by industrial productivity. But, in contrast to businessmen and economists, they promoted labor's alternative solution to general overproduction and unemployment that was current before 1926: limited production through shorter work hours.

Their arguments may be abstracted as follows: Modern work was an increasing burden; the "crisis of work" had grown worse. Economic abundance threatened overproduction and unemployment. Shorter hours could decrease work, raise wages, spread employment, reduce unnecessary production and surpluses, and ensure a minimum standard of life for everyone. Therefore, leisure was as practical in the "new economic era" as were new markets, and leisure was preferable. It was preferable in the first place because leisure could be used to revive the benefits and values that work had lost to the machine. Craftsmanship, creativity, and worker control and initiative could take

place during sports, hobbies, volunteer projects, and other constructive recreations. Leisure was preferable also because it would help
keep alive institutions and traditions threatened by mass society, standardization, and mass consumption. Individualism, the community of
workers, the family, and the church would be strengthened as people
had more free time to devote to these things. In addition, increased
leisure would keep open the possibility of what Edward Sapir called
"genuine progress." The dreams of utopian writers, socialists, and reformers that had been around for over a century—dreams of a democratic culture, worker education, the universal pursuit of happiness,
and humane and moral freedom—were reasonable possibilities given
increased leisure. Lastly, shorter hours would counter the new economic gospel of consumption that had begun to define progress solely
in terms of economic growth and expanded work, abandoning hope
for a nonmaterial, "higher" progress.

As Daniel Rodgers pointed out, some of these concerns had been
raised before.[52] But in the 1920s they were increasingly important
as a direct justification for shorter hours, since labor ceased to use
much of its 8-hour rhetoric after 1926. Moreover, never before had
such interest in leisure been in evidence in the popular press and
among professional groups. And never before had these concerns had
to confront the new definition of progress contained in the gospel of
consumption.[53]

In addition to labor leaders, a number of reformers from the Progressive era became active in support of "the progressive shortening
of the hours of labor."

Arthur Link suggested that the "progressive coalition" formed by
Woodrow Wilson in 1916 was shattered by World War I and afterward by the rise of economic prosperity. The critical defection from
that coalition was the "middle classes—the middling businessmen,
bankers, manufacturers, and the professional people," most of whom
"found a new economic and social status as a consequence of the
flowering of American enterprise under the impact of the technological, financial, and other resolutions of the 1920's." The goals of Progressivism seemed outdated; economic security was being provided,
not by government or reformers, but by the ability of business and
industry to produce the necessities of life. "Mass production and consumption, . . . high wages, full employment, and welfare capitalism"
were the things that made for a good life, and business and industry, not government, were making these things possible.[54] The middle classes that Link described were extremely optimistic and at times
exuberant. Free enterprise had actually created what the Progressive
movement had promised.

Confronted by the "new era's" optimism and success, the reform coalition broke into many groups, each with its own particular agenda. The "farm bloc," "alienated intellectuals," labor unions, and other groups went their separate ways in disjointed efforts at reform that included such things as agricultural parity, immigration restriction, Prohibition, and tariff reform.[55] One example of the diverse reform directions taken during the decade was increased support for labor and the shorter-hour issue.

A number of old Progressive reformers tended to agree that industry and business were doing the job of providing for the social and economic welfare of the people. Like most businessmen and economists, these reformers were impressed with industry's efficiency and the new spirit of welfare capitalism. But they remembered that old reform ideals included more than material and economic welfare; individualism, culture, morality, and "nonmaterial values" had traditionally been parts of reformers' programs. Whereas business and industry might have coopted the material welfare reforms suggested first by the Progressive movement, they were not providing the more human improvements America needed. And shorter hours offered an opportunity for this kind of progress.

An excellent example of this kind of reformer was Monsignor John A. Ryan, one of labor's strongest and most influential supporters and a foremost proponent of shorter hours. Ryan was a leader of the social reform wing of the Catholic church; he drafted the "Economic and Social Objectives" of the Administrative Committee of the National Catholic War Council (later known as the National Catholic Welfare Council), which, according to Joseph Dorfman, "reads like a blueprint for the New Deal legislation enacted in the 1930's."[56] Ryan was one of the main forces popularizing the papal encyclical *Rerum Novarum*, which embodied the major Catholic tenants of social reform. He also established and edited the *Catholic Charities Review*, a leading voice for Christian social reform.[57]

Ryan's contributions to the shorter-hour movement were exceptional, since he presented a systematic attack on the Hoover Committee and the gospel of consumption, as well as outlining an alternative way for the economy to progress by continuing to reduce work. And he did this, not only as a churchman, but also as a respected economist; Ryan had received a doctorate in economics from Catholic University early in the century and had written extensively in the area.[58]

When Ryan wrote in the 1920s and 1930s, it was against the backdrop of the spread of the gospel of consumption and the shift of business and economic interests from production to stimulating consumption. Ryan voiced his objections to this general economic development by criticizing the Hoover Committee and its findings. He pointed out that "by suggestion and implication they [the Committee on Recent Economic Changes] convey the idea that national prosperity and national welfare are dependent upon the indefinite expansion of human wants and the indefinite multiplication of luxuries."[59] He objected to the idea that "wants are insatiable and one want satisfied makes room for another" and rejected the committee's conclusion "that material prosperity is largely based on the limitless desire of humanity for pleasure and luxury, that no great prosperity can be based merely upon the satisfaction of the primary needs of food, clothing and shelter." Such assumptions were the opposite of "industrial sanity, social well being, and desirable human life." Ryan called the committee's talk about insatiable wants "loose" and its optimism about the "boundless fields" for economic growth opened by "extravagant luxuries" misinformed and misplaced. He declared that the creation of new, unneeded goods and services and the stimulation of new kinds of demand for these luxuries were "not a moral foundation for progress." As a general solution to unemployment and "underconsumption," this viewpoint was also impractical. It had "two vital defects," one moral and one practical.

> In the first place it is quite unlikely that the requisite new commodities will be invented. More fundamental is the objection that this would be an undesirable industrial society. People of our age, even the wealthy, would not be benefited by new luxuries, and the masses ought not to be required to provide superfluous goods for the few, while they themselves are unable to obtain a reasonable amount of necessaries [*sic*] and comforts.[60]

Yet Ryan did not believe that this "new gospel of consumption" was as new as the Hoover Committee and many other people thought. He claimed that the prevailing materialistic ethic, the wrongheaded "conception of a wider and fuller life," was the direct result of the separation of ethics and theology from economic life that began during the Reformation and had continued to grow during the "Puritan movement." The dominant view among English Puritans "that economic activities constituted a separate department of life with which religion and ethical rules had little or nothing to do" was "deeply imbedded and widely distributed in American society and ethical theory." This idea countenanced not only excessive poverty and the exploitation of the poor by the rich but also created a materialistic culture in which economic virtues became dominant, replacing all other ethical principles and moral insights and leading to the "absurd tenet of capitalism that production for its own sake is the end of industrial society." Ryan thought that "the members of the Committee (on Recent Economic Change) are in line with our baneful tradition of puritan industrial ethics . . . in their preoccupation with the conception of prosperity which logically implies a belief in production for its own sake." Quoting R. H. Tawney, Ryan concluded that "the urge for production and even greater production" was "squirrel-cage" progress, unenlightened by considerations of the other ethical and human claims of the individual or the church. It produced a culture sunk in materialism without a transcendent vision.[61]

The separation of ethics from economics had produced a catalogue of practical problems. Prominent among them were "underconsumption" and unemployment. The consumption of luxuries by the richer classes was not reliable; it was problematic and fickle. It was neither a moral nor a realistic way to promote enough consumption to match increased production. Ryan reasoned that the propensity to consume declined as people became more wealthy, as they were able to assure themselves of "a reasonable degree of comfort" and yet had a surplus of income to spend. Like the consumption of luxuries, investment in new capital goods by the rich was also limited in practice. He consistently maintained that available savings had become "excessive" in that no matching development of new capital goods had been forthcoming. Reviewing the causes of the Great Depression, Ryan made the same point about the results of "excessive savings" that he had made often since his dissertation in economics at the Catholic University of America in 1905. "But industry did not need more money. It was already oversupplied. Not lack of money or credit for productive operations but lack of demand for goods already produced was the cause of the Depression."[62]

In the condition of chronic "underconsumption" caused by the rich having too much of society's wealth, not enough people were buying the products made possible by increased investments and savings. It had created a situation in which "the poor cannot buy more and the rich will not"—a time of poverty in the midst of abundance and unemployment, when people were desperate to work to feed themselves and their families. The basic reason for unemployment and "underconsumption" was in "the last analysis bad distribution."

> What do I mean by "bad distribution"? Simply that the actual distribution of the product among our industrial groups prevents our industrial plant from operating continuously. The actual distribution gives to one group of income receivers more than they can spend for goods of any sort, and to other groups less than they could and would spend if they had the money.

The first group does not want to spend more for consumption goods and cannot spend all of their savings for capital goods, that is, in the form of business investments. The second and third groups would like to buy more consumption goods but cannot do so because they have not the requisite purchasing power. The first group is composed of those who receive interest, rents and profits; the second and third groups comprised, respectively, of wage earners and farmers. Speaking generally . . . , we may say that capital received too much purchasing power and labor too little.[63]

The problems of unemployment, "underconsumption," and bad distribution were the results of ignoring the fundamental natural law that would have provided parameters for reasonable standards of living within minimum and maximum limits. Ryan thought that the ethical teachings of the church, based in the "natural law," could counter both the immoral directions of the economy that produced luxuries before necessities and the Puritan view that progress was found only in work and increased production. They were also the basis on which to establish reforms to solve these practical economic problems. One of the beauties of the church's moral teachings was that they were exceedingly practical—they could be used as a realistic guide to action. Ryan based his solution to the "bad distribution" of society's wealth on Pope Leo XIII's encyclical *Rerum Novarum*, believing that the pope had made it clear that

> the right of the laborers to get from the joint product the means of satisfying their essential and fundamental needs is morally superior to the right of the employer to the means of indulging in luxurious living or of making new investments. To deny this proposition is to assert that the claims of the laborer on the common bounty of nature are morally inferior to those of the employer, and that they are but instruments to his welfare, not morally equal and independent persons.[64]

With these ethical principles in mind, Ryan consistently stressed higher wages for workers as both morally sound and eminently practical. He felt that if workers were paid more, were given enough to meet their "minimum requirements," the problem of "underconsumption" would be largely solved. In order to keep industry going "it is necessary that the consuming power of those who would like to buy more should be increased." By redistributing wealth and providing workers with enough to live on, the situation in which the rich were slow to buy luxuries that they did not need and industry was "already oversupplied with capital" would be obviated.[65]

Ryan's theories about the solution to "underconsumption" and unemployment, based on higher wages and the redistribution of "the social surplus," have been thoroughly documented and discussed. But when discussing the practical reforms that Ryan supported to achieve the better distribution of wealth, historians have emphasized minimum-wage legislation, public-works projects, and unemployment insurance. Certainly Ryan supported these things and thought they would go a long way toward dealing with unemployment. But what Ryan considered on several occasions to be "the most rapidly effective means of securing and maintaining high wage rates" has been generally overlooked: "a shorter working day, or a shorter working week, or both."[66]

Ryan supported all of labor's initiatives for shorter hours. He reasoned: "Reductions of working time would create a larger demand for labor (by reducing labor supply) and automatically bring about higher rates of remuneration."[67] Earlier he had argued that shorter hours, by creating a

> greater demand for labor would keep wage rates above what they would have been in the absence of increased employment. The increased wages would provide increased purchasing power for the product of many industries, thereby extending further the demand for labor. The order of events would be directly contrary to that set in motion when men are thrown out of work.[68]

Acting to redistribute wealth, shorter hours would also help to redirect the economy away from the production of luxuries and toward the creation of necessities. In so doing, shorter hours would help solve the immoral and irrational condition in which the poor were unable to buy what they needed and the rich were able but slow to buy products they did not need. As Ryan put it: "The shorter work period would check and retard the production of new luxuries because workers' increased demands for necessities and comforts would tend to keep capital fully employed in industries that are already established . . . . (and which were producing reasonable necessities)."[69]

Shorter hours would also be an immediate solution to unemployment. Ryan stated: "With a shorter work day or work week a given demand for goods would require more laborers, thus decreasing unemployment."[70] Shorter hours would force industries to hire more people to maintain existing production levels and hence be a way for workers to share existing, necessary work. Of course, he maintained that wages should not be decreased as hours were reduced. But he also thought that wages would naturally increase as a result of the "enforced labor scarcity" brought on by uniformly short hours. In this he was thoroughly in accord with labor's position in the early 1920s.[71]

Briefly put, Ryan believed that the introduction of shorter hours was a practical reform; it was one of the best ways to increase absolute wage rates, redirect the economy from unnecessary production to the "basic needs" of the workers, and solve unemployment by redistributing available work. But as important to Ryan were the more general social and ethical benefits of this reform. Shorter hours "would reinforce higher wages," to be sure, but shorter hours would also "promote a better social order than that which results from the development of new wants."

Ryan directly contrasted the shorter-hour solution to unemployment and "underconsumption" with the Hoover Committee's findings both before and during the depression. Ryan consistently believed that shorter hours, by providing workers with increased leisure, would "make possible the development of higher intellectual and moral life." At the same time, they would tend "to retard the invention of new luxuries." Not only was it possible to argue from the church's teachings, and specifically from *Rerum Novarum*, that necessities ought to be created before luxuries, but it was also evident that increased leisure was morally superior to unnecessary production.

> Since production is justified only as a means to rational and beneficial consumption, it ought to be so organized as to yield a maximum good life for all. The elementary necessities and comforts and the conditions of reasonable leisure and progressive mental and moral development ought to be placed within the reach of all people, while the supply of useful [*sic*] and harmful luxuries should be kept down to a minimum.[72]

To Ryan, it was clear that *Rerum Novarum* directly implied the abolition of "excessive labor"—of work devoted to producing things not directly required for the reasonable comfort of all people.

Contrasting his ideas with the Hoover Committee's findings and with the prevailing materialistic ethic, Ryan pointed out that the "primary needs for food, clothing and shelter," which could be defined and met, could indeed provide the basis for "a great prosperity." Once wealth was properly redistributed and industry rechanneled to the production of "necessaries," work hours would continue to get shorter, as they had for over a century, if productivity increased at its accustomed 2 percent annual level. As leisure for everyone increased, real progress would be possible in this growing freedom. Workers could be taught by church and school to "learn to use it [leisure] wisely," for the human ends of religion, culture, individualism, mutual understanding, and sharing. Leisure opened up the "higher goods of life," focused attention on things that were ultimately important, and promised to promote a civilization based on morality and learning rather than production for its own sake.

Ryan expressed his vision of authentic progress based on wealth redistribution and increased leisure on several occasions, each time contrasting his vision of progress with the prevailing materialistic ethic. In 1931 he argued:

> Finally, we must notice the objection that the lessened amount of products which might result from the shorter working time would be an obstacle to progress. It all depends on what we mean by progress. Just why a people should spend its time in turning out and consuming a hundred kinds of luxuries which minister only to material wants, instead of obtaining leisure for the enjoyment of the higher goods of life is not easily perceptible. After all, neither production nor consumption is an end in itself. The former is only a means to the latter and the latter is beneficial only in so far as it is exercised upon goods which promote genuine human welfare.[73]

Another time, he stated:

> Even if all our workers were receiving living wages, the productive capacity of our industries might still be so great that all the goods could not be sold nor all our labor continuously employed. We could cross that bridge when we came to it. Nevertheless, the manner of crossing is obvious. It is by way of a shorter work-day or a shorter work-week. One of the most baneful assumptions of our materialistic industrial society is that all men should spend at least one-third of the twenty-four hour day in some productive occupation. If all their efforts are not needed to turn out the necessaries and reasonable comforts of life, they should be utilized in the production of luxuries. If men still have leisure, new luxuries must be invented to keep them busy and new wants must be stimulated in the consumers to take the luxuries off the market and keep the industries going. Of course, the true and rational doctrine is that when men have produced sufficient necessaries and reasonable comforts and conveniences to supply all the population, they should spend what time is left in the cultivation of their intellects and wills, in the pursuit of the higher life. If American industries

can make the requisite leisure possible, they will have provided at least the opportunity for a more rational society than any people has yet enjoyed. Moreover, a shorter work-day or work-week would reinforce the movement for higher wages and more general employment; for it would require more workers to produce the same amount of goods and thus make labor scarcer and dearer. Indeed, this is the most practical method available for increasing the remuneration and the consuming power of the masses, short of minimum wage legislation.[74]

Ryan was certainly for limited production. But the production he had in mind to limit was of "unnecessary goods"—what he called luxuries. He was also for limited production (a stable economy) after everyone had received a "living wage." The time for this was in fact close at hand, since "the general fact of the situation is that our industries produced sufficient necessaries [*sic*] and comforts to provide more than a decent livelihood for all our people, and in addition are capable of turning out a vast amount of luxuries."[75] Once the primary needs were met by industry, a finite and imminent possibility given wealth redistribution, America and its workers should then turn their attention away from material concerns and toward more important things. Increased leisure made this kind of social reconstruction a practical possibility and thereby a moral obligation.

Ryan's vision of "genuine progress" based on increased free time for the "higher activities" was firmly set in church doctrine. In abstract form, Ryan reasoned that the church had established parameters for "reasonable material comfort" within minimum and maximum limits. Moreover, the church's teachings and doctrine recognized the hierarchy of humanly valuable things. Necessary, but lowest on the scale, were material goods that supported a life of "reasonable, frugal comfort." More important, and just as necessary, were things such as learning, marriage, children, and human associations outside the economic sphere (community, family, and state). Highest in the scale of valuable things and determining by its place of ultimate importance the whole ethical hierarchy was "the primacy of the individual soul" in relation to the divine. Ultimately, the only things worth doing for their own sakes were those spiritual and ritual matters that offered union with the supreme good. Everything else was proximate, a means to that end. But because of God's design, the means to that end were moral, good, necessary, and set according to their relative importance. Ryan conceived of social reconstruction as progressing along the hierarchy of valuable and necessary things: (1) making provisions for material welfare; (2) developing the rational faculties; (3) enriching and expanding human, brotherly contacts; and (4) leading on to what was really important for itself.[76]

The doctrine of a living wage or a minimum standard of living had been explicitly spelled out in *Rerum Novarum*. Pope Leo XIII stated that "a workman's wage ought to be sufficient to maintain him in reasonable and frugal comfort" and that this proposition was "a dictate of natural justice."[77] Ryan elaborated on this "reasonable minimum" doctrine by pointing out that human material needs were finite, that they could be found out and met. Not only could they be determined, but they also had a primary moral claim on the state and the economy. They were based in the natural law and as such were reasonable and had the force of "natural right." Ryan assumed that this "reasonable minimum" was readily apparent to all persons who used their God-given ability to think. The fact that there was "substantial uniformity" among social scientists and others about what was necessary to live "proves that 'reasonable comfort' is not only a practical, tangible conception, but one that springs from the deepest intuitions of reason and morality."[78]

Ryan's and Leo XIII's point that human material needs were finite was completely out of step with the economic theory and political practice of the 1920s and 1930s, and indeed of later decades. This point also led him to the church's traditional position that too much material wealth was bad for a person and a country, a position completely opposite to the new economic gospel of consumption and the economic and political developments since the depression.

Ryan assumed, as did St. Thomas Aquinas and generations of church leaders, that the natural law also determined a "reasonable maximum" standard of living. Just as having too little was in conflict with reason and God's laws, too much was dangerous to morality and right living. Both the maximum and the minimum were parts of natural law and equally subject to being determined by reason and the moral intuition that everyone shared. Ryan stated that "it is not desirable that any class of people expand living standards indefinitely." But "after the demand for reasonable comforts has been met," people tend to desire more and more things, out of all proportion to reason and temperate living. Desires for new and luxurious things, "for richer, exotic foods, expensive entertainment, ornate decorations for the home, showy and fashionable apparel" were all capable of "indefinite expansion."[79]

The rich exhibited this regrettable human failing and paid for it. The passion for higher and higher levels of material possessions and consumption involved "a great waste of time, thought, energy, and money, an increase in the passion of envy, a desire to out-do one's neighbor in the splendor of material possessions, and in outward show generally, a lessening of sincerity in social relations, a weaker consciousness of Christian brotherhood, and finally such an emergence in the things of matter that the higher realities of life are increasingly forgotten or ignored." These higher realities—the religious and the altruistic sense, the "mental powers and activities," art, culture, learning, serving, giving, loving—all were "choked by the cares and riches of life." In short, "the things of God are crowded out" by ignorance or willful contravening of the "reasonable maximum."[80]

Although this was not a pressing problem for most people at the time, it could easily become one. The unfortunate lot of the rich could easily become a general problem, since "how ever much a person pays for the meeting of these [new and excessive] wants, he can still maintain, in accordance with the language of the standards of the day, that he is merely 'improving his social position': and this theory of welfare is held not only by the rich and well-to-do, but in some degree by substantially all classes." Ryan claimed that the "indefinite striving for indefinite amounts of material satisfaction" was part and parcel of a modern malaise and "prevailing theory of life." Such a theory produced a culture ignorant of authentic living and could corrupt all classes.[81] According to Ryan:

> The contradiction between this theory and the Christian concept is obvious. Christ declared that "a man's life consists not in the abundance of things that he possesses." In many places and under many forms, the Founder of Christianity insists that material possessions are unimportant to His followers; and that those who have much wealth will find it almost impossible to get into His Kingdom.
>
> According to the Christian principle, it is not the number but the kind of wants that is important. Right human life is primarily *qualitative*. It consists in thinking, knowing, communing, loving, serving, and giving, rather than in having or enjoying. Its supreme demand is that we should know more and love more, and that we should strive to know the best that is to be known and to love the best that is to be loved. It demands that we satisfy the cravings of our senses only to the extent that is compatible with a reasonable attention to the things of the mind and the spirit. The senses are not on the same moral level as the soul. Their true function is that of instruments.[82]

Ryan believed that increasing leisure would free people from excessive concerns with material things and open up the "higher goods of life" for everyone. He also believed that the depression had confirmed the "bankruptcy of materialistic civilization." Progress could not be based on "production for its own sake." This was not practical because it was not moral. Genuine progress lay in living within reasonable material limits and engaging in more important things than getting and spending. The challenge of the future lay in using the time freed by industrial advance for moral and more valuable activities and achievements. The church could offer guidance in the matter, but as a practical and social problem, increased leisure would require the best of the individual's and society's efforts. But this new reality, this freedom in time, promised a new, qualitatively different progress, one more genuine and more practical than that based on the separation of ethics and religion from economics—than that based in capitalism's "absurd tenet that production for its own sake is the end of industrial civilization." [83]

Prominent supporters of the five-day week in the clothing industry used arguments similar to Ryan's, expanding and altering Jewish Sabbatarianism in the process. As it did with Ryan, the five-day-week issue led Jewish intellectuals to investigate larger concerns: broad-scale labor reforms and general questions about economic development and cultural progress. The five-day week served the practical purpose of Jewish Sabbatarianism, to be sure, but Jewish Sabbatarianism, as expanded by the issue, served in turn to justify the broader labor reform of the "progressive shortening of the hours of labor" and to inform the cultural, social, and economic debate about the decreasing importance of work and the increasing importance of free time.

Rabbi Israel Herbert Levinthal expressed the logical broadening of the argument for the Sabbath in this way:

> I can see but one way to save the Sabbath for the Jew, and that is through the establishment of the five-day week. . . . I would favor the five-day week even if I were not interested in the preservation of the Jewish Sabbath. I would favor it because it would add health and strength to the American people. It would promote the home and home life, giving the father an added opportunity to become more intimately acquainted with . . . his children. [84]

In a like manner, other prominent Jews who supported the five-day week agreed with the AFL endorsement of increased leisure. Jews active in the Sabbath movement agreed that work was becoming less rewarding and meaningful and that leisure offered the opportunity to recover some of the old values work once had. Felix Cohen, for example, offered a parable of the modern economy that was able to provide the necessities of life and still supported work as a prime virtue.

"Adam's children inherited the [curse of work] and soon learned to make a virtue of necessity. Idleness came to be regarded as a sin rather than source of love, art, inspiration, and wisdom." Offered a chance by "God's messenger" (represented by machines) to slip the bonds of toil, men chose instead to "sing new hymns in praise of the sweetness of chains" and hold on to work because "they had so long praised each other . . . for their industriousness. . . . The message of the machine is that we shall have *work without end.*"[85]

According to Cohen, much of that work was useless. It no longer had the firm sanction of "necessity." Work was being channeled in absurd directions: the production of useless or shoddy articles, advertising, and a new industry—war. If useless work were abolished, then the workweek could be reduced to "thirty hours immediately" and a "general working week of ten hours is then a fairly immediate possibility," given the rate of increased productivity.[86] For Cohen, work's new forms—specialization, mechanization, and impersonal organization—destroyed the old nineteenth-century ideals about work's value, such as creativity, craftsmanship, self-fulfillment. In this he agreed with the union leaders. But he also suggested that work's purpose—its product—had been undercut by the machine. Much of modern work was without a firm purpose because there was "no natural" use for its product. Consequently, work had been made a demigod—a thing worshipped for its own sake. It mattered little if its products were useless. One consumed them out of respect for this supreme virtue, like it or not.

Abba Hillel Silver, later president of the Central Conference of American Rabbis, believed that the Sabbath movement contained a justification for the "progressive shortening of the hours of labor" and as such rejected what he called the "false" gospel of consumption. He described the Sabbath as representing "the day of rest, the consecrated covenant between God and man." It was "much more than mere relaxation from labor. It is a sign and symbol of man's higher destiny." The Sabbath was a model for shorter hours; it was a way that labor could open up a new field of human progress. Increased leisure could provide a time for culture, for learning, for individual creativity and freedom, for the appreciation of life and creation, for spiritual exercise, and for essential rituals—just as the Sabbath had for centuries been the "universal humanizing factor." Silver suggested, "We must say to ourselves . . . so far shall I go in my pursuit of the things of life and no further. Beyond that I am a free man, a child of God. Beyond that I have a soul and I must give to it time, energy, and interest."[87]

He saw in the gospel of consumption a new way in which "our population has been victimized." Just when the opportunity for real human development had been opened through technology and increased free time, it had been closed again by businessmen intent on selling the "golden fleece" of useless luxuries and "excessive wealth." For Silver, human needs for industrial products could still be defined—they were not infinite. Increased productivity and job specialization had created two potential avenues of progress, one spurious and one genuine. If Americans chose to pursue "success," defined in terms of the piling up of useless luxuries, they would turn their backs on the more human form of progress offered by reduced working hours.[88]

The job of preparing individuals for "worthy use of leisure" was great. But Silver saw the new wealth of free time as a force revitalizing the church, the family, and the school. As people were able to spend more of their time and energy in these more human institutions, they would naturally learn how to use their time to develop their higher potentials and humane interests.

Moreover, according to Silver, it was no longer possible to assume that all work was valuable because of its products. The relationship between work and the necessities of life was becoming increasingly tenuous. Businessmen and economists ignored this problem. Instead, they had begun to understand work and increased wealth as indeterminate values, relative to no set of given, basic, or higher standards. Yet they continued to support and cherish these values. In this way, work, increased production, and consumption had been redefined as ends in themselves, values to be used to judge other economic, social, and human concerns. Losing extrinsic justification, work and economic growth had taken on intrinsic values during the decade. For Silver, these ideas were a corruption of what was truly valuable in itself—what Ben Eliezer described as "the highest religious and ethical sentiments."[89] For Silver, the Sabbath was the only true "telos" in its "self-contained spiritual world," the model for a qualitatively new kind of progress through increased leisure. Businessmen and economists had entered the realm of philosophy and theology in their "gospel of consumption," promoting the old virtue of work and economic growth by radical ethical arguments. Silver believed that work and increased productivity were still instrumental in that they could meet rational needs and then lead to real virtues through shorter hours—to human activities that were really worth doing for their own sakes.[90]

The Jewish Sabbath movement flourished in its support of the more general labor movement for the five-day week. Finding practical success in reform, individuals in the Sabbath movement then went on to engage in even larger economic and social debates about modern progress and work, using the Sabbath model as a philosophical base. Certainly many Jews were content with the practical accomplishments of the five-day week. It did, after all, satisfy their original purpose and constitute a significant social reform. But others, such as Drachman, Cohen, and Silver, supported the "progressive shortening of the hours of labor," reasoning that as human needs for industry's products were met, increased production should begin to free the worker from his job for other, "higher" pursuits. They understood the economy as beginning to offer two avenues for progress: increased wealth and luxuries or increased leisure. Rejecting the first option as a kind of "chasing after the phantom of insatiable desires," they supported the second as the way to authentic progress, humanistic rather than materialistic, individualistic rather than collective. They saw in the Sabbath the "symbol of man's higher destiny" and in increased leisure the practical opportunity to broaden and spread the Sabbath's values and truths.

In Ryan's writings, as well as in the works of Jewish intellectuals, a refinement of religion-based social reform is evident. Several Protestant churchmen also came to believe that shorter hours provided a new opportunity for the "social gospel of reform."[91] Whereas before most of the social gospel had to do with reforming society so that the physical welfare of the people was taken care of, writers such as Ryan and Silver were concerned also with "spiritual poverty." Certainly the state had an obligation to make sure that the material necessities of life were available to everyone. But there was more to religious reform than this. Ryan's term for the social gospel, "social reconstruction," reflected his and others' concern that religion play an increasingly large role in America. To the extent that the economic problem was solved, people needed to be freed from overconcern with material things—with production, commerce, and budgets. This freedom automatically forced people to confront religious questions: What is life for? What is worth doing for its own sake? Answering these questions by work and economic growth was a new heresy, a break with the Jewish as well as the Christian tradition. The "true and rational doctrine" was that economic abundance should be devoted not to creating more and more wealth and building larger storehouses to preserve that surplus; instead, progress should be in the realms of the mind and the spirit, cultivated in the time of life freed from the machine. This outgrowth of the social gospel, caused in some part by business success and optimism in the decade, focused attention on shorter hours as a practical reform that would at least present the opportunity to transcend work and move beyond material and economic matters, challenging people to go on to more important kinds of issues.

Other reformers, discouraged in some of their causes by the economic success of the "new era," followed these lines of reasoning in more secular terms. For example, George Alger had been very active in various reform efforts in New York. A lawyer, Alger drafted New York's employers' liability act in 1907 and a number of labor and child labor bills. He also was very active in that state's prison and parole reforms, serving on the Moreland Act Commission in the 1920s. His claim to be an old-fashioned progressive reformer was well founded. But during the 1920s Alger came to believe that social reform had more to do with the "growing social surplus . . . of time" than the "distribution of the social surplus of things." He described the industrial conquest of nature as a "miracle," one socially important product of which was leisure. He looked forward almost casually to the time when the 4-hour workday would become universal. But he pointed out that Americans had been mesmerized by economic success. They had been caught up in a "squirrel-cage conception of progress." Business and industry were doing the American people a disservice by creating artificial demands for useless products. All human values had been subordinated to "material production." In this situation the "radical minds" in America were concerned with controlling the spread of "material values" and the dominance of the mass, "consumer wonderland." [92]

Alger thought there was "no doubt that any theory of the use of leisure which should make it something else than principally an expression of buying-power might be considered an alarming heresy because of its possible effect on sales." But he believed that the charge of heretic would be a small price to pay in order to convince people that the business idea of progress was in reality a "new slavery." Leisure for consumption, under the sway of business and advertising values, was passive, expensive, commercial, impersonal, and worst of all boring. He reasoned that "a civilization that bores its beneficiaries is perhaps even worse than one that overworks its slaves." [93]

Alger concluded that a change of attitude was needed so that America could produce a "civilization that does not degenerate under leisure." Two of the old Progressive ideals excited Alger's imagination: the spread of culture to the masses, and the importance of the individual. Through a proper understanding of leisure's potential, Americans could "enlarge the field of self expression," "become active and in control of their freedom, recover lost arts of conversation, renew spiritual resources, gain appreciation of the needs and problems of other people," and come to grips with "the greatest practical problem before us on which depends the future of western civilization. . . . the reapplication of love to life." [94] Leisure could "lift us . . . in the great world of intangibles, the world not of material but spiritual values." [95]

In Alger's writing one can detect some of the most idealistic dreams of earlier social reformers. But in Alger's hands these dreams were given a practicality they had not had before. The new industrial reality, increased leisure, seemed to Alger to give substance to reform ideals and dreams for the first time.

Another influential work on the subject of social welfare through increased leisure was written by a Canadian. Stephen Leacock's popularity as a humorist had given him a wide audience in America when he wrote a serious book on *The Unsolved Riddle of Social Justice*. The book was very well received in this country and reviewed favorably by most major American newspapers and periodicals, both popular and professional. As a professor of political economy at McGill University, Leacock commented at length on the impact of industrial growth on social values. Like Alger, Leacock thought that industry's needs to grow, to promote more consumption, and to create new markets for luxuries were socially destructive. He believed that the concept of progress was changing. Progress as a chasing after the "phantom of insatiable desires" had little to do with the old Progressive dreams of good life. Industry and business were not interested in "producing plenty." They were attempting to "produce values" that had little relation to real human needs. These values only served the cause of more unnecessary industrial growth and frayed the "nerves of our industrial civilization."[96]

According to Leacock, the satisfaction of human needs through industrial production had reached the point of diminishing returns. The relation between "production and the satisfaction of human wants" had always been clear when workers had been struggling to meet the elemental needs to feed, clothe, and house themselves. Economic abundance, however, was an entirely different situation. Needs that had to be discovered and desires that had to be stimulated could never be met in the same way that basic needs were met. The satisfaction of these new needs (the need to be amused, diverted, or stimulated, and the need for social display, pride of possession and enjoyment) was of a different kind. They were never complete. One knew, within reason, when the need for food had been satisfied; one never knew for sure that he had been properly amused. The ability of industry to satisfy the needs it was creating was decreasing. It would continue to decrease because industrial and capital growth was being established on the foundation of "luxuries and superfluities." These new needs did not mean new satisfactions. They added up to a "gigantic misdirection of human energy."[97]

The creation of "luxuries and superfluities" was a perversion of progress. "Real human needs" were being ignored. Leacock suggested that "the shortening of the hours of work with the corresponding changes in the direction of production was really the central problem of social reform."[98] In leisure time, authentic human needs could be given attention only if workers were not distracted by artificial desires, created by advertising, to consume. Leacock thought that Edward Bellamy's utopian dreams of a 4-hour workday was a perfectly reasonable objective for modern reforms. He urged that society recognize the fact that "a working day of eight hours is too long for the full and proper development of human capacities and for the rational enjoyment of life."[99]

As they achieved the goal of the shorter working week, American workers could begin to satisfy their real needs. In free time, they could become more self-reliant; individualism would flourish in the new expanse of time just as it had on the frontier, that old "expanse of free land." Workers could begin to enjoy life "rationally." They could be as creative as ever they had been in their work, but in new ways, in hobbies, crafts, or household projects; they could recover the craftsman instinct that had been lost at work. They could begin to guide their own lives, deciding what was important for their personal growth and then demanding these things from industry. In this way, the individual could direct production and the machine, rather than the other way around. Workers could also have time to appreciate spiritual and moral values instead of having the values of the "gospel of consumption" forced on them. In the last place, they could experience the finer things of life, such as "culture, music, friends," and the day-to-day human and simple pleasures that were so often taken for granted but were really vitally important; the whole point of industrial progress might very well be enough time to watch the sun set.

A number of other individuals shared some of these views. Even the conservative Elihu Root saw leisure as the "most serious educational and social problem" of the 1920s. Suggesting that "the only consequential thing that machinery does for the world is to give us more spare time," Root thought that leisure could be put to valuable use by the individual in activities that allowed for self-expression, creativity, and culture. Leisure was a modern form of freedom and, like all forms of freedom, was good. For Root, leisure represented freedom from materialism and freedom for individualism.[100]

Alfred Lloyd, a sociologist at the University of Michigan, thought that leisure was essentially a way to democratic culture. He also believed that overvaluing work, creating new forms of it as new professions and new occupations, was silly: "To take interest today only in quantity production and traditional accumulation, to value only the professional and occupational, only technique and efficiency, is to be merely a conservative . . . in politics or economics or social life or religion."[101]

The old Progressive reforms that dealt with these matters were out of date. Reforms for the quality of life and for the final realization of freedom for "the pursuit of happiness" formed the new Progressive agenda.

Joseph Hart, the associate editor of the *Survey*, and Samuel Strauss, the editor of the *New York Globe*, agreed that individual freedom and real human values could be the fruits of leisure time if it were well used. They also agreed that the materialism implicit in the "new economic gospel of consumption" had to be countered and the way to do this was by giving people access to the finer human, spiritual, and cultural experiences of life through leisure.[102]

Furthermore, concern with the new leisure came from some surprising quarters—from groups and individuals not concerned as much with social reform as what leisure could mean for some older, more conservative values.

As Clark Chambers pointed out, the twentieth-century belief in progress was changing during the 1920s; it was being attacked by many intellectuals. Certainly the war had much to do with the doubts expressed about human perfectibility. But the new understanding of progress that the prophets of the gospel of consumption promoted was also a factor that raised doubts about the "simplistic belief in progress."[103] Intellectuals such as Edward Sapir, the linguist and anthropologist, agreed that technology would continue to grow but, in growing, would stifle "genuine" progress. Industrial growth for its own sake and for the artificial reasons of created demand was "spurious" progress. The human standards of the "harmonious, balanced, and self-satisfactory" society and the "spiritual primacy of the individual soul" were the bases of "genuine" progress but were being ignored, since "part of the time we are dray horses: the rest of the time we are listless consumers of goods which receive not the least impression of our personalities."[104] The gospel of consumption had redefined progress in terms of the machine, of collective control and material values. In so doing, this "spurious" progress had lost its ethical underpinning. Before the advent of this gospel, industrial progress made sense. It could be understood as a reasonable way to meet basic material needs. But in the 1920s "spurious" progress was destroying "genuine" progress. Not only had the war confused the "simplistic belief in progress" but the consumerist direction taken by the economy had perverted what was once a reasonable avenue to perfectibility.

According to the displaced aristocrat James Truslow Adams, busi-

nessmen had become the *arbiters* of American culture, a culture that
was inevitably cheap and materialistic. It seemed to Adams that businessmen were intent on selling the "golden fleece" of material values
to Americans and propagating the doctrine that acquisitiveness was
the final end of human existence. Overproduction was symptomatic,
not of progress, but of the growing materialism of mass culture. The
"orgy of material well-being" blotted out the real culture and human
concerns.[105]

Adams thought that leisure was the victim of this orgy. True leisure
was "essential for human civilization." But businessmen had corrupted
leisure, "seeing it as a waste, except in so far as it promotes the individual's productive capacity" and his ability to consume. Adams declared:

> Having little use for sanely occupied leisure themselves, our
> business spokesmen try either to confuse it in the public mind
> with idleness or to make people utilize it for the satisfaction
> of more material wants. . . . The danger lurks in exactly that
> situation; for the one who needs most but least realizes the value
> of leisure and culture, of a full rounded personality, of what we
> may call humanism, is the one who has become the controller
> of the destiny of us all.[106]

Adams believed that the freedom of leisure was rapidly becoming
a lost opportunity. He thought that traditional culture and the "human
pursuits" had always depended on the leisure of the select few who
were free from the cares of economic necessity. But industry had freed
the ordinary citizen for leisure and then reenslaved him by advertising and social pressure. A glimmer of hope showed through Adams's
pessimism. If only the leisure being won daily by industry were rechanneled and directed by those who recognized the value of real culture,
if only institutions such as schools, colleges, churches, and the press
could counter the material business values, leisure might become for
the common man what it had been for the aristocrat, the basis for
real civilization, for culture, morality, and humanism. But those who
recognized and supported these finer human qualities were few, their
influence small, and their numbers steadily thinned by the domination
of the businessman. And Adams held little hope that leisure would
ever regenerate culture and make the finer things of life accessible to
large numbers of people.

Irving Babbitt agreed with Sapir and Adams:

> Both humanism and religion require introspection as a pre-
> requisite of inner life. With the disappearance of this activity

what is left is outer activity of the utilitarian . . . leading to the one sided cult of material efficiency and finally to standardization.[107]

For Babbitt, leisure was the goal of liberal education, founded on discipline in the humanities and not naturally acquired. Leisure was freedom through mastery. The "cult of material efficiency," which Adams so despised, threatened leisure to be sure:

The tendency of an industrial democracy that took joy in work alone would be to live in a perpetual devil's sabbath of whirling machinery, and call it progress. Progress, thus understood, will prove only a way of retrograding toward barbarism.[108]

But the glorification of work had reached even to academic leisure. "Baconian strenuousness" had invaded the colleges, making them resemble modern factories in the degree of strain and pressure. For Babbitt, this fact presented an anomaly, "the hustling scholar." The word "scholar," derived from the Greek word for leisure, could never reasonably be associated with words like "hustle," "go-getter," or even "hard worker." The humanist and the man of leisure were being elbowed aside by the scientific specialist and the "bustling" scholar intent on winning reputation.[109]

True leisure faced another danger than the modern glorification of work. The "Rousseauist," the romantic dreamer, and the "idler" were like the "southern aristocrat," unable to see the difference between "sessions of sweet silent thought and wise passiveness." Seeking refuge in the world of "luxurious dreams," the "aesthetic vagabond" attained nothing except a sort of "transcendental loafing." Romantics of the nineteenth century were incapable of true leisure, since their "wise passiveness" was revelry and not reflection. They ignored the classics and the humanists' contributions to civilization, retreating into an impotent solipsism.[110]

Babbitt recalled a mural in the reading room at the Sorbonne in Paris. Two female figures were pictured there. One, with a "strenuous aspect" and worried and rushed look, was entitled *Science*; the other, with flowing draperies and a "vague, far-away eye," was called *Rêve*. These figures symbolized for Babbitt the way in which "the scientific analyst and the romantic dreamer had divided up the nineteenth century and in their very opposition have been hostile to leisure." Between these two opposite historical tendencies, real leisure was to be found.

Leisure—the word from which our world "school" is derived—was for the Greek the expression of the highest moments of the mind. It was not labor; far less was it recreation. It was that employment of the mind in which by great thoughts, by art and poetry which lift us above ourselves, by the highest exertion of intelligence, as we should add, by religion, we obtain occasionally a sense of something that cannot be taken away from us, a real oneness and center in the universe; and which makes us feel that whatever happens to the present form of our little ephemeral personality, life is yet worth living because it has a real and sensible contact with something of eternal value.[111]

Babbitt supposed that the "serious advantage" of the modern industrial advance was that it reduced the drudgery of work and "opened up the opportunity of leisure to more people" than ever before. He cautioned that the success and prosperity offered Americans by their technology should not be seen only as a "point of departure for a still intense activity."

If we ourselves ventured on an exhortation to the American people, it would rather be that of Demosthenes to the Athenians: In God's name, I beg of you to think. Of action we shall have plenty in any case; but it is only by a more humane reflection that we can escape the penalties to be sure to be exacted from any country that tries to dispense in its national life with the principle of leisure.[112]

Adams and Babbitt insisted that morality and traditional culture were reasonable goals for industrial America, more worthwhile than the fantastic, material world of endless production proposed by the business community. Leisure, a product of industrial growth, could possibly be made an alternative to it. If only the custodians of culture could direct the masses when they were free from the necessity of work, then old virtues and traditional culture might be renewed; the dominant idea of industrial progress as work and consumption might be questioned. Leisure as the traditional foundation of formalist culture and as the basis for the humanist ideal could renew parts of the "genteel tradition" and make them reasonable in the modern world where progress was no longer tied to basic human utility or even to the welfare of the masses. These conservatives, these inheritors of the old genteel tradition, had their own agenda for progress then, the resurrection of the triptych of values, morality, culture, and old-fashioned progress in noneconomic realms.[113]

CHAPTER 4

Leisure for Culture and Progress

IN ADDITION TO labor leaders and reformers, several professional groups began to be concerned with leisure and the shorter-hour issue. One of the main organizations involved with these topics was the National Recreation Association.

The recreation movement began during the 1890s as one of many social welfare movements of the Progressive era. In response to urban problems of overcrowding, immigration, and juvenile delinquency, recreation leaders promoted playgrounds as an urban reform as basic as sanitation, fire protection, and efficient government. They reasoned that through public recreation facilities, immigrant children could be "Americanized," juvenile misbehavior controlled, and the natural childhood desire to play given a proper opportunity. The movement was a success, and in 1906 its leaders organized the Playground Association of America. The old recreation reform goals served the association well until 1910 when new goals were established through the leadership of social scientists, who began to dominate the national organization. Men such as Clark Hetherington (a follower of Lester Ward) and Henry Curtis believed that recreation should be planned scientifically and that the major value of recreation was its ability to educate and socialize children. They were convinced that play was a major way through which children adjusted to the environment and that planned and structured recreation facilities and programs could make that adjustment efficient and rapid.[1]

Before 1915, the Playground Association, which had changed its name to the National Recreation Association, led the recreation movement. Other groups, among them primary and secondary school teachers, Boy Scouts, YMCA, YWCA, and camping directors, were active in the field but followed the ideological and organizational initiatives of the National Recreation Association in this area.

From 1915 to 1925, two economic and social changes altered the recreation movement's direction. In the first place, commercial recreation and amusements grew at a rapid rate. G. T. W. Patrick guessed that the typical urban American purchased over 95 percent of his recreation and made use of public facilities seldom or not at all. Recreation leaders were increasingly alarmed by this during the 1920s, afraid that business and industry were taking over the recreation field, reducing the importance of public services. As Arthur Link suggests, economic abundance in the 1920s changed the direction of social reform, and the recreation movement is a good example.[2]

In the second place, the shorter-hour issue became more prominent, and other groups and individuals became interested in leisure.

Commercial recreation and the leisure issue caused basic changes in the recreation movement's leadership and ideology. First, recreation leaders shifted some of their attention from the child to the adult. This shift was a critical change in the recreation movement, one that greatly influenced the future of the profession. Second, a new kind of leader emerged in the movement. Reacting against the social scientists' domination of the movement and against the growth of commercial recreation, men such as Joseph Lee and Howard Braucher looked back to some older and more idealistic recreation ideology for new direction.

In the 1920s, recreation leaders downplayed some of their previous reform goals, which tended to be paternalistic and intrusive, such as immigrant assimilation, crime prevention, and social adjustment through play. Instead, they renewed portions of the earliest ideology. In the 1890s, recreation leaders had supposed that play was a natural and individual expression of childhood. The city, because it was overcrowded, prevented expression of this natural desire. The function of recreation reform was to allow the individual child the chance to be free from social and environmental constraints to express his or her natural play instinct. The idea that a child could be socialized, educated, and changed for the better through recreation was not totally accepted by playground reformers for the first few years. The main point of the early movement was play, and play had to be free; "controlled play" seemed a contradiction in terms. In the 1920s, recreation leaders again called for individual self-determination in play and freedom through recreation. But the appeal now was directed at the adult instead of the child.[3]

Recreation leaders attacked commercial amusements because they destroyed individualism, encouraged passivity, ignored natural needs, prevented creativity, obscured real culture, and encouraged immorality. Just as the child had been boxed-in by overcrowded cities in 1890, the adult in 1920 was boxed-in by commercial pressures and mass culture. His freedom in leisure to be himself had been lost. In this situation, recreation's major function was to liberate the individual. Through public recreation facilities, adults could have access to their community's culture and not lose their individuality, subjected to mass culture forms such as tabloid newspapers and movies. Through hobbies, they could have the opportunity to express themselves, an opportunity denied them by standard and routine jobs. Public recreation could allow the individual to be actively involved in sports and games, thereby improving his physical well-being and health. It could also give him the opportunity to experience nature firsthand.[4]

One of the most important functions of public recreation was to provide an opportunity for expression of the "community spirit." Most recreation leaders from 1915 to 1925 were concerned that the small, intimate community was being overrun and destroyed by mass culture. They believed the value of the small social organization lay in providing important kinds of human relationships that were impossible in large, impersonal groups. Moreover, the democratic spirit had been the product of the small town and the farm community in America's past; this spirit was in danger of being lost in modern mass society. Morton Grodzins called these kinds of complaints the "gemeinschaft grouse" and characterized the early reformers in America as too much concerned with them.[5] But as late as the 1920s, these same complaints were being expressed by recreation leaders.

During the 1920s, recreation leaders were moved by a much wider vision of their role in American society than ever before. They were impressed with the fact that shorter hours had become a national issue. They were moved by the old utopian visions of the future in which leisure was the central reality of life and work merely an adjunct. If leisure was going to be a central part of American society, then the role of a profession designed to deal with problems of play was a critical one. They also were able to see historical precedents for America's concern with leisure. For example, they saw a parallel between Greek civilization and the urban technological world. Whereas slaves had freed a few fortunate Greeks to devote their lives to leisure and the pursuit of art, philosophy, and science, the "machine slaves" of the twentieth century were freeing every man for a good portion of his life for the higher human pursuits. Leisure, as the modern equivalent of the Greek ideal of *Skola,* was for everyone, and recreation leaders fully expected a cultural renaissance with a democratic base that would overshadow all previous cultures based on privilege.[6]

They also compared the American frontier experience with the new leisure time. The American West had provided the free space in which the common man could be himself and could escape from the artificial demands of the city. But in the twentieth century, technology had opened up a new time expanse that could provide the individual with the same fine things. Free time, like free land, would result in democratic virtues, provide a "safety valve" for worker discontent, instill self-reliance, and most of all allow the individual freedom for self-expression and "self-realization."[7]

A few leaders such as Howard Braucher, secretary of the National Recreation Association, began to see how increased leisure fit into the total American economy, not as a new reason to spend money and expand the economy, but as an alternative to the consumer society. In late 1929 and 1930, he argued that "more and more people are being urged to buy what they do not need and to replace it before it is worn out. The more we learn to use up what we do not need, the greater our consumption; the greater our production, . . . the greater our prosperity." This new concept of progress and prosperity, which he called in one article the "Theory of the Economic Value of Waste," allowed production to be "doubled, tripled, quadrupled. . . . By this system business need never face the saturation point. For, though there is a limit to what a man can use, there is no limit whatever to what he can waste." Under this business theory, maximum consumption was founded on maximum waste, while the "economic support for happy and worthwhile living" was forgotten. The recreation profession had the responsibility to provide an alternative: "the promotion of wise, sane [recreation] for a community" that would bring a "very much larger measure of happiness, without the expenditure of large sums of money."[8]

Braucher pointed out that even though "skill and ingenuity and advertising . . . can force upon people new wants," in the long run "happiness does not lie in making men want more things, be dependent upon more things." Additional leisure would be a

> boon to the world if men's hopes can be shifted from the possessing of more things to desiring to live more richly. Will not men and women in the long run have greater happiness if, while enabled to have the absolutely essential things as a result of shorter number of hours of work, they are free in their spare time to engage in such activities as come from inner desires

and which give spiritual satisfactions? Is it not likely that in music, art, handcraft, familiarity with nature, understanding and comprehension of the world, comradeship in wholesome, inexpensive activities, there lies a pathway to greater human satisfaction than is to be found in longer hours of work to clutter homes with more furniture, more clothing, more things? . . . We are . . . in the midst of a revolution in work, leisure, life, thought, brought about by the machine we have created. We can keep from becoming slaves to the machine by exalting Time, Leisure and Life.[9]

Moreover, responding to Owen Young's assertion that "new inventions must put displaced men at work and new fields of skills must be developed," Braucher argued that machines should free men for increased leisure, not merely provide the opportunity for new kinds of work.[10] Braucher was an early advocate of the shorter-hour solution to unemployment, suggesting that it was better to "decrease the number of working days and of working hours and leave less work but steady work for all." Since "machines now turn out goods faster than the public can consume them," leisure was bound to increase.[11] Like William Green, Braucher thought that the choice before the worker was a simple one: unemployment for a growing few or leisure for everyone.[12] For Braucher, play, not work, was the wave of the future, the new "social progress." Work was becoming less and less valuable. From now on, play would be the vehicle of progress. Play was not "a preparation for more work, but is itself life." Braucher envisioned a new Golden Age:

> The Golden Age in Grecian history was possible because there was leisure for play. The modern Golden Age is being ushered in when there shall also be opportunity for play; this time in a democracy where there shall be no slaves. . . . Except as a people gain . . . the play spirit which is natural to children, they do not enter into the possibility of social progress.[13]

The Playground and Recreation Association of America's annual congresses and its publication, *Playground*, expanded in the 1920s and early 1930s. The journal was full of reprints from the American press, reflecting the widespread interest in shorter hours and the leisure issue. At the 17th Annual Congress, speakers such as Rabbi Abba Silver addressed problems of work and leisure as centrally important issues of the day.[14] Letters from such notables as George Eastman and E. R. A. Seligman, president of the American Association of University Presidents, and reports from Elihu Root and John

Finley enlivened the journal's pages.[15] Future national leaders of the share-the-work movement, such as Governor John Winant, addressed the congresses.[16] Never before or since was the organization so involved with issues of central political and intellectual importance on a national level. After the depression, the organization subscribed to the belief that leisure makes better work, provides professionals with jobs, and helps stimulate the economy. Braucher's vision of leisure and play as an alternative to mass culture and consumerism, like Ryan's dreams, was largely submerged by the depression.

In addition to ideological developments, the recreation movement achieved a number of practical goals during the 1920s, reflecting the national passion for recreation and fascination with increased leisure. Municipalities, with the help of the National Recreation Association, pressured state legislature to pass laws enabling cities in twenty-two states to spend tax and bond money on recreation. Before this time, only two states had passed these vital laws, and until 1940 only three more were to do so. In addition, between 1920 and 1927, thirty-two states passed laws that permitted townships to use school buildings as community and recreation centers. In the 1920s, cities expanded recreation and community service programs. Over half of the cities with more than 30,000 population that provided recreational facilities began to include recreational programs in music, drama, nature study, arts and crafts, hobbies, and adult education.[17]

All facets of the recreation movement showed increases during the 1920s comparable to the growth in the municipal programs. For example, during these years, organized camping grew more than ever before. The Boy Scouts increased their membership from 250,000 to over 800,000, and the Camp Director Association doubled its membership and expanded its programs. Other private organizations, such as the YMCA and YWCA, the Knights of Columbus, and the Jewish Community Centers, grew during the decade, and their leaders began to talk of teaching young people to use their leisure time wisely, a skill they believed invaluable in the new industrial world. The YWCA and the Knights of Columbus both broadened their services beyond welfare work and recreational programs for the underprivileged to include educational programs and recreational facilities for all the community.[18]

The recreation movement developed in the cities and in private organizations apart from the national parks and forests movement until 1924 when Calvin Coolidge realized that both shared similar aims. Before 1924, the parks movement was part of the conservation drive to protect natural resources. Not until that year did the federal government begin to emphasize the recreational potential of the parks system and to redevelop the national forests and parks with this end in mind. In 1924, President Coolidge called a Conference on Outdoor Recreation and established the Committee on National Outdoor Recreation to replace Theodore Roosevelt's County Life Commission.[19] Coolidge declared that every American should have a "reasonable" amount of leisure time and that government facilities should be provided for the "proper" use of this time. It was Coolidge's opinion that since "all those engaged in our industries needed an opportunity for outdoor life and recreation no less than they needed the opportunity for employment," the federal government should use its parks system to provide for this need.[20] Coolidge reasoned that since the parks system was already established, the only thing he, as President, had to do was to take inventory of the existing facilities and promote the system's recreational potential. But he was not willing to embark on any program to convert the parks to recreational uses that would involve heavy federal expenditures. This was consistent with the conventional wisdom of the time; outdoor recreation was best left to the individual, not planned and manipulated by overdevelopment and concessionaires.

During this same conference, Coolidge called on all cities to cooperate with the national Recreation Association and Federal Parks System by setting aside 10 percent of their land for parks, playgrounds, and community centers. The members of the Conference on Outdoor Recreation agreed with Coolidge and recognized that it was the duty of every community to provide space for play and recreation and thus promote "physical health, love of nature, self-control, endurance under hardships, reliance on self, and teamwork."[21] Conference members argued that the new urban environment was such that many human needs were being denied, such as those for physical culture and communion with nature. Hence they concluded that city governments and the federal government, under its power to protect the health of its citizens, had the responsibility of providing facilities that would promote the wise use of leisure time. Again, the emphasis was on free public space, not the development of land or recreational programs that needed the guidance of many professionals.[22]

Recreation professionals also began working with groups involved with the shorter-hour movement. Problems of providing public facilities for workers with increased free time occupied the attention of the American Federation of Labor in 1923 at the Portland convention. Endorsing the efforts of the Playground and Recreation Association of America to establish recreational facilities and community centers in American cities, the convention concluded that the "strain and rush of modern life and . . . the evil effects of present day machine industry" had to be alleviated by providing the worker with proper facilities "to recreate his physical, social and intellectual being."[23] This need was underlined in 1924 at El Paso when the union's Executive Council called for the active participation of all local unions in beginning municipal recreation and social centers and adult education projects.[24]

Unions began to offer their own adult education courses and recreation programs. For example, the Brookwood Labor College was established in 1927 by the Workers Educational Association, a body composed of various industrial unions attempting to organize worker educational opportunities. Most unions, if they did not actively participate in adult education schemes, endorsed the university extension programs and public night schools.[25]

Observers of the shorter workweek began to comment on the ways that workers were in reality using their free time. Failing to see the masses, once given a little free time, rushing to cultural centers, people such as George Cutten, president of Cornell University, and Rose Field, a Pennsylvania sociologist, realized that workers used their leisure by spending more time with their families and in creative and practical home-improvement tasks. Field made a study of leisure time among workers in Pennsylvania steel towns just after the 12-hour day was replaced by the 8-hour day throughout the steel industry. She concluded that, since the long workweek in steel mills made activities other than sleeping, eating, and working either impossible or unrewarding, workers used the time freed by the 8-hour day to reestablish family ties. Workers with the 8-hour day naturally turned their attention to the most basic of social institutions, the family. In addition, workers followed their "creative instincts" by beginning "do-it-yourself" projects at home; gardens, garages, and workshops sprang up all over the state. Second jobs were also common when the 8-hour day was still a novelty, but rapidly decreased as workers adjusted themselves to the new leisure. Amusements, primarily commercial ones, were increasingly popular.[26]

In 1924, the International Labor Union made a study of American urban workers' leisure time and concluded that such commercial amusements as movies, radios, tabloid newspapers, spectator sports, the automobile, poolrooms, and roadhouses occupied more of a worker's time than did any other activity (time spent with the family was excluded).[27] That mass culture pervaded workers' free time distressed some union officials, as it did the recreation professionals.

Paralleling the increasing interest in leisure among labor and recreation leaders, educators began to focus on the issue.

The historian Lawrence Cremin believed that the history of progressive education in America was formed by two major currents.

On the one hand, progressive educators believed that reform of the schools was a lever for reform in society. They felt that the evils of capitalism could be partially controlled by educating children to deal with and change the political system and become skillful in the practical business of making a living. Social melioration through education consisted of teaching individuals to become economically secure with practical work skills and politically aware with the ideals of "social reconstruction." On the other hand, progressive educators valued "child-centered pedagogy." G. Stanley Hall's injunction to "keep out of nature's way" in the schools was observed by liberal educators, who stressed creativity, self-expression, exploration, and individual freedom. Since a child learned naturally, and since learning was best done in the pleasurable activity of play, children should be given great freedom in school and could benefit from that freedom.[28]

But Cremin saw World War I as "a great divide" in the history of the progressive education movement. He opines: "Like Progressivism writ large," the movement changed, and "social reform was virtually eclipsed by the rhetoric of child-centered pedagogy" during the 1920s. The "play school" dominated the movement during these years as the Progressive vision of training for work, social melioration, and reconstruction became somewhat less important. Cremin views this situation with distaste, pointing to the excesses of the child-centered pedagogues with their unstructured classrooms, uncontrolled children, bohemian values, and romantic and unrealistic visions. These educators, like most Progressives, were "tired of moral indignation"; in their fragmentation and confusion they wanted "only to be amused," and asked for nothing better than amusement for the children under their care.[29]

But the progressive educators' vision of social reform and reconstruction was not rendered impotent as much as it was transformed by the "new era." Like so many reformers, progressive educators had their faith in reform shaken by the facts of industrial production and business success. The spirit of welfare capitalism tended to make many of the old appeals of progressive education seem out of date. Why should an economic system that was providing for economic and social welfare be fundamentally altered? An even more disturbing question presented itself. What could the schools offer Americans that was not already being provided by the beneficent economic order? It had become clear to some that even training for work was being taken over by industry; most jobs could be learned in a matter of weeks on the job.

The progressive educators' reform vision was transformed by the new direction taken by the economy in the "new era." Like other old reformers, many educators believed that industry and business had taken a new tack after they had accomplished the miracle of economic abundance. Instead of concerning themselves with the practical matters of increased production, businessmen were busy in the 1920s producing values and redefining progress. The new danger of capitalism was inherent in the "gospel of consumption," which ignored all human values other than acquisitiveness, greed, envy, and vain display. Needs invented to support unnecessary capital growth and the mass culture were beginning to destroy elements of the progressive vision. Social melioration in this situation did not consist merely in teaching vocational skills or in education for change in the political system. Instead, it consisted of vigorously promoting human values through education to counter the artificial values of the "gospel of consumption."

In the 1920s, the advent of the shorter-hour and leisure issue influenced educators more than any other group in America with the exception of professional recreational workers. With this one issue, educators saw a practical way to promote traditional educational values and stem the flood of mass culture and consumer luxuries. Educators actively competed with business and industry for control of the time freed by economic abundance. They reasoned that Americans could be prepared for the "worthy" use of leisure through proper education and could be prevented from converting to the gospel of consumption. Many educators saw a clear choice to be made between luxuries and businessmen's artificial values, on the one hand, and leisure and human educational values, on the other. They set about to assure that the proper choice was made.[30]

The tone of the educators' program was set in 1917 when the National Education Association (NEA) drew up the Seven Cardinal Principles of Secondary Education, one of which was "education for the worthy use of leisure." The Commission on the Reorganization of Secondary Education, which set the seven principles, developed what they believed to be a new philosophy of education, a philosophy that "aimed to reconcile the needs of the individual with those of society."[31] Leisure was a prime tool to effect this reconciliation. The story told by Eric Goldman about Herbert Croly, who, when the "new era" began, retreated to his home for three days, speaking to no one, and then called his friends together and declared that the Progressive era was at an end and that "from now on we must work for the redemption of the individual," may be apocryphal, but American educators practically acted out this scenario.[32]

The cardinal objective of the "worthy use of leisure" received wide support throughout the 1920s.[33] This objective had never been seriously entertained by educators, and it came to be one of the most important of their responses to the realities of industrialization.

Many prominent members of the education profession supported this one objective and practically ignored the other six.[34] For example, William J. Cooper, as head of the Federal Education Commission, stressed the value that education for the "proper use of leisure" had in the fight against commercialism and the standardization of life.[35] John J. Loftus, president of the New York Principals' Association, supposed that the "N.E.A.'s program for the desirable use of leisure time was the most important development in modern education" because it provided a reasonable method to "counteract the influences" of advertising and consumerism and a powerful incentive for teachers to "inspire and control" the new wealth of free time.[36] Dr. John H. Finley, editor of the *New York Times*, vice-president of the National Playground and Recreation Association, and influential spokesman for educational reform, supposed that the educational "training for personal leisure was the dominant call of the age" for teachers and students alike.[37] Dr. E. R. A. Seligman of Columbia University was president of the American Association of University Professors when he stated: "The most important of the fundamental rights which the members of the National Association have been attempting to emphasize is the right to leisure." He felt that the shorter workday could be a new form of human "wealth for the community and welfare for the laborer" if Americans were properly prepared in school and at the university for leisure.[38] President Baker of the Carnegie Institute of Technology stressed the importance education for leisure had for liberal education. He supposed that as "vocations became more specialized and easily learned," liberal education would become necessary for avocational and leisure pursuits.[39] Henry Suzzallo, president of Washington University and an influential member of Hoover's National Advisory Committee on Education, considered "every American who is not yet a social rebel is afraid to be a man of leisure." He considered every teacher responsible for the education of children for the right use of leisure. Such an education would make children rebel against cheap commercial values and the standard of materialism.[40] A. H. Reeve, president of the National Congress of Parents and Teachers, believed that the cardinal objective of the "worthy use of leisure" was vital for the well-being of the family. He may have been one of the first Americans to suggest that "the family that plays together stays together."[41] J. W. Dorey, executive secretary of the Progressive Education Association, was bold enough to say that "all education programs for the past ten years (since 1922) deal with how to educate for leisure" and that "all education programs and periodicals suggest taking the agencies which science and society have created—the movies, radio, press, dance halls and clubs and insisting through law or by an appeal

to conscience that they shall reform" and cease exploiting the leisure
of the people.[42] Henry T. Bailey, editor of the *School Arts Magazine*, believed "if the products of industry were properly divided . . . nobody in
America would have to work over four hours a day." In this situation,
education for "leisure centered living" was the prime responsibility of
the schools.[43]

Supporters and teachers of liberal arts courses, fine arts courses,
and traditional courses such as Latin and Greek on the secondary
school level were among the first to seize on the leisure issue in the
schools. They reasoned that they could at last demonstrate the practical and even pressing need for the study of Latin, music, English literature, and world history. They proclaimed that the curriculum needs
of the 1920s were the reverse of those of ten years earlier, when the
drive for practical and vocational courses was in full swing. Most jobs
in industry had become so repetitive and simple that they required
only a few weeks of on-the-job training. Vocational training in school
had lost its reason for being.[44] The new reality that teachers had to
deal with was training for leisure, not work. They were convinced that
the time freed by American industry had created a cultural vacuum
in which "millions of people with money in their pockets and time at
their disposal had no rational notion of what to do with the one or the
other."[45] Nevertheless, they were aware that this cultural vacuum was
rapidly being filled by consumer goods and mass amusements.

From its inception, progressive education had "implied the radical
faith that culture could be democratized without being vulgarized."[46]
This faith was renewed by the issue of leisure. Supporters and teachers
of liberal arts courses and traditional curriculum offerings thought
that by making the masses proficient in the humanities, in those regions of the intellect and imagination that made life full, they could
transform the barren time space in workers' lives into a fertile ground
for democratic culture and creative individuals. Like other reformers,
they predicted that a cultural renaissance was in the offing, a renaissance with a democratic base made possible by leisure and midwifed
by enlightened educators.[47]

In addition, the possibility of democratic culture through leisure
had proponents among educators concerned with the sciences and
with some of the newer mechanical arts courses. Charles Proteus Steinmetz, one of the leaders of what Henry Elsner called the "technocrats,"
had strong views on education and leisure. Steinmetz spoke for many
educators in the sciences when he declared that the greatest value of
science education was its intrinsic pleasure. The major achievement
of the application of science to technology was freedom to enjoy the
pleasure of pure scientific exploration and discovery. Although he was

ready to admit that not everyone would see the joy of science as a leisure activity, he did feel that everyone should at least be given a chance to partake of such pleasures. He reasoned:

> When I say that the workers will labor but four hours a day and two hundred days a year, I do not mean that they will be idle non-producers the balance of their time. Leisure will be occupied in productive diversions satisfying the particular instinct of the individual. We will be more collective in the operation of our essential productive life and individualistic in the pursuit of personal happiness and contentment.[48]

Personal happiness and contentment, for Steinmetz, consisted of contemplating the beauty and order of nature. Here was the chief value of education in the sciences.

Some teachers of the mechanical arts were disturbed by the trend in modern occupations away from craftsmanship and toward specialization. For example, Emmanuel Erickson believed that the NEA's cardinal objective concerning leisure had great significance for all mechanical arts teachers. He thought that the teaching of skilled craftsmen in the schools remained important, even though many of the skills learned in the schools' shops were no longer needed by industry. Leisure provided the opportunity for individuals to express their "need to make things by hand" and the spirit of true workmanship. This need and spirit may have been disappearing at work, but it could be given a new life through leisure.[49]

Librarians were impressed by the educational promise of leisure time. Such educators considered libraries to be "creative agencies in intellectual movements." According to one observer, "Librarians banded themselves together in lively craftsmanship organizations . . . and a veritable missionary spirit of progress" moved them.[50] The *Library Journal* published a number of articles by educators who saw leisure as the new opportunity for progress. Since "inarticulately, blindly, but inevitably the workers of the world reached out after beauty and adventure, for music, poetry, and romance," libraries could provide access to these things. Since leisure was increasing, the library would become the center for a "great intellectual movement," which would bring the best books and ideas to people who had at last found the opportunity to use them.[51]

Other educators interested in combating the values of the gospel of consumption focused their efforts on the actual beneficiaries of leisure: adults. The adult education effort was a primary thrust of educational reform in the 1920s, and the leisure issue figured prominently in discussions about this development. Public night schools, university extension courses, and commercial adult education enterprises grew more rapidly in the 1920s than ever before. Surely this growth resulted in large part from the great demand for vocational courses. Vocational adult education courses constituted nearly 75 percent of the total adult education effort.[52]

Even so, some adult educators insisted that this figure indicated the extent to which business values were coming to dominate American culture and was not a true indication of adults' real needs. Instead of letting adult education become the "purveyors of businessmen's standard of monetary success," leaders of the adult education movement promoted courses in the fine arts and liberal arts, and tried to redirect scientific and mechanical courses to emphasize the avocational values of amateur science and home workshops.[53]

Like other educators concerned with the leisure issue, leaders of the adult education movement believed that individualism, creativity, culture, self-expression, and imaginative exploration were primary goals. In addition, like the recreation professionals, these educators thought that the traditional community spirit could be resurrected through proper use of leisure time. Advocates of progressive education, such as John Dewey, had long thought that the schools should be a microcosm of the democratic community, teaching students the values of direct democratic decision making and group responsibility. Leaders of the adult education movement stressed this point of view, supposing that since the trend in industry, business, and government was toward large, impersonal organizations, adults needed to be taught the value of community and democracy in schools that were themselves communities. This information in turn could be used outside the classrooms in leisure time through public recreation organizations, community centers, and churches.[54]

During the 1920s, vocational courses in the regular school curriculum and adult education classes were not the only ones under attack. Professional preparation in colleges was also questioned. Some educators thought that higher education, like most jobs, was becoming increasingly specialized. The "danger of the doctorate" lay in the fact that much of higher education was becoming so specialized and geared to a particular profession that the whole concept of a liberal education was being forgotten. Professionals, more than most people, needed education in liberal studies not only for their own increasing leisure but also for their roles as leaders of communities. Traditionally, through such things as the sabbatical, colleges and universities had stressed the importance of leisurely scholarship and humanistic endeavor. These institutions were now in a position to educate students in a proper appreciation and use of leisure. Leisure as a new social problem needed to be dealt with by those with an appreciation of its values. Leisure, growing daily, made training in the liberal arts a social responsibility for which institutions of higher learning were uniquely suited. Instead, these institutions were abandoning their responsibility by offering more specialized, professional education and ignoring the new importance of the liberal arts and humanities. The emphasis on finding new occupations and discovering new forms of work had damaged the colleges, leading to an overemphasis on the "practical arts." According to critics, the colleges, by returning to their origins in the liberal arts and to learning that was important in itself, could meet the leisure challenge and counter the consumer values that threatened higher education.[55]

In the bewildering array of writings concerning education for leisure, one stands out both as a personal statement and as representative of the widespread interest. Althea Payne taught English literature in the Oak Park and River Forest Township High School in Oak Park, Illinois. In 1918 she took a course given by "one of our foremost advocates of vocational training" at Columbia University, but left the course still distrusting business and commercial English. She distrusted the "narrow objectives" of such courses and insisted, in the face of the "educational experts," that students who did not intend to go to college should nevertheless be taught traditional English Literature. She reasoned that the "second great industrial revolution" that was going on was creating more and more leisure; that the "movement to cut the number of working hours per week to forty-two" made "education for leisure a timely theme." In fact, industrial growth and financial success made such education a "direct and urgent problem." She insisted that "the safety of our democracy" and the future of progress were at stake.[56] Rebelling against education only for work and the commercial values, she wrote: "Believing then that in this commercial age it is the privilege and the obvious duty of every English teacher . . . to stand for something higher and better than mere material and financial standards . . . we must face the question, How shall we English teachers educate for leisure?"[57]

For Payne, the love of reading and good books could help counter the modern preoccupation with work and financial success. "What do they do?" she asked, if workers are not able to read or are not shown how to gain access to their culture, their birthright? A world of only work and material concerns was a poor world indeed. But leisure presented a new challenge, a new opportunity to offer all high school students something better than mass culture; it was a new frontier for learning, a new way in which everyone could give birth to the life of the mind. She remembered that over one of Harvard's old halls was the inscription "He shall never earn a dollar more who enters here." But she observed that what was earned in a liberal education was much more important: "breadth of view; sensitive response to the beautiful; innocent . . . recreation; love of books; aspirations; ideals."[58] What was good for the Harvard aristocrat should now be offered to each high school student.

The third major professional group concerned with leisure was American psychologists. Before 1916, serious discussions about the value of play were carried on in America mainly by people concerned with children. Psychologists were among the few who considered play seriously enough to develop a body of work about the subject. In spite of their differences, psychologists who studied play concentrated almost exclusively on children. Although European theorists such as Lazarus Guts Muths, Karl Groos, and Wilhelm Wundt considered adult play and proposed explanations for it, American theorists who studied under these men or were influenced by them neglected this field. Beginning with the publication of Patrick's *Psychology of Relaxation* in 1916, American psychologists finally began to focus attention on adult play.[59]

Patrick pointed out that "many books have been written about play, but it is the play of children that they usually deal with. But little or no study has been made of the psychology of the play of adults."[60] He used the word "suddenly" to describe a "new and unique public interest" in America about adult play. He predicted that the new topic would involve "questions of great social importance" and that within a few years, psychologists would have the task of explaining the nature of adult play and defining its role in the modern world.[61]

Having studied with G. Stanley Hall in America and W. Wundt in Leipzig, Patrick was in a position to draw on the best American and European developments in play psychology.[62] Beginning with the assumption, respectable because of its long usage among psychologists, that the repression of primitive impulses was necessary, was indeed the fundamental law of both human society and progress, Patrick pointed out that in recent years this repression had increased enormously because of the demands of industry.[63] But recent forms of repression were "excessive." "The everlasting urge to progress," without reference to the basic needs of the individual, created a dangerous situation. Work specialization, monotonous jobs, and the loss of craftsmanship and creativity were the prices the typical worker paid for the spurious pleasure of buying things he really did not want. Nervous disorders, psychotic and neurotic behavior, and chronic and acute fatigue were increasing among American workers. These maladies were the result of excessive and unnecessary demands made on the individual by his "progressing" world. Patrick proposed that a "psychological and physiological adjustment" be made to economic and social advance in the form of intelligent and guided "relaxation."[64]

Patrick gave as an example of the need for relaxation the nature of most modern jobs. Many jobs in industry, business, and management put a premium on abstract reasoning and the exercise of small muscles. The intricate coordination of fingers and eyes overtaxed and overdeveloped a few muscles and left the rest of the body tense and neglected.[65] This unnatural situation created a "constant subconscious rebellion" and a "desire to escape" within the individual.[66]

One of adult play's major values was that it could relax those components of the human being that were overused or neglected by modern occupations. Patrick reasoned that men could escape their oppressive jobs by enjoying "age old" activities in their leisure. Recreation provided a contrast to specialized jobs and a unique form of relaxation based on activity. For example, the exercise of large muscles relaxed the body in ways that immobility could not. Patrick believed that play allowed the tension-ridden adult to "return to nature," to recover the ability to use his body in healthy and constructive ways, and to return to natural places such as forests, lakes, streams, and oceans.[67] Leisure provided an opportunity, for the first time in human history, for "temporary reversions to simpler and more primitive forms of behavior," at just the time they were most needed.[68]

These temporary reversions to primitive habits were essential for the well-being of the individual. But they were also vital for the maintenance of human society. Such reversions were the "actual condition to renewed progress." Without planned forms of relaxation, tensions brought on by excessive change and repression built up to the breaking point in individuals and societies. "After great tension, there must be great relaxation" was both an individual need and a social rule.[69] Unless the return to nature and the primitive was planned and was counted a positive good by a society, outbursts of uncontrolled savagery would inevitably occur, as witnessed by the European war. The progress of a society that was made possible by the repression of primitive and "racially older forms of behavior" could be suddenly destroyed by such outbursts.[70] Social and economic progress, if they were to continue, had to provide the leisure necessary for the common man to exercise his primitive nature. Society had the responsibility to provide recreation and allow controlled forms of "primitive" activities.[71]

Adult play held two other potential advantages. First, primitive behavior in the form of constructive play kept alive instinctual options that would deteriorate if not used. Future civilizations might require abilities such as physical endurance and strength in order to survive; one never knew for sure. Second, adult play was a characteristic human trait. It was fun, a healthy expression of irrationality that was an important foil to the typical, overstressed existence of modern man. Play provided a special, bodily way of being-in-the-world, a way of living and even knowing neglected by modern rationalism.[72]

In the conclusion to *Psychology of Relaxation*, Patrick discussed general historical trends:

> It is characteristic of our times to be expansive, centrifugal, iconoclastic, self-conscious, and nervous. It is a time of labor, of endeavor, of effort, of expenditure, of adaptation, and of change. These are all masculine motives, and their tendency is not toward peace or freedom or rest or balance or beauty or of attractiveness or reserve of power or conservation of forces. Dionysius is the god of this century; Apollo we have forgotten. The Dionysian motive, the motive of the strenuous life, is not tempered, as it was among the Greeks, by the Apollonian motive of balance, harmony, and repose.[73]

For Patrick, psychologists had a chance to change this situation and, through structured recreation, to temper work and the "dionysian motive" with relaxation and play.

G. Stanley Hall reacted to the leisure issue in a similar manner. In the 1920s Hall, then in his eighties, was enjoying the reputation of one of America's foremost psychologists, having established his place in the profession with his work on adolescence, his role as founder and editor of *Pedagogical Seminary*, and his introduction of Sigmund Freud to America in 1909.[74]

In "Notes on the Psychology of Recreation," *Recreations of a Psychologist*, and his autobiography, *Life and Confessions of a Psychologist*, Hall expressed some second thoughts about his earlier ideas about the importance and function of play.[75] He declared that he was not at all satisfied with the direction that evolution had taken in the modern industrial world.[76] Industry required great specialization and thus the increased "subordination of the individual to the welfare of the group." This process, while it resulted in the "mastery" of nature and production of life's essentials, required an "unnatural docility" of the individual and made his dependence on others and on authority nearly absolute.[77] This submergence of the individual was the "chief cause of the present (industrial) unrest and the chief peril of democracy."[78]

Hall thought that "we cannot avoid the necessity of harder and ever more specialized work." But as work became harder and more intense, it would be more "potent" and productive, hence less of it would be required. Thus he believed that Americans "can and must, at times, turn away from work and find not only diversion but recreation in so doing." Like Patrick, Hall suggested that the modern worker could find compensation for the loss of craftsmanship, pride, and creativity in his job during leisure time. Leisure offered the worker the opportunity to "exercise unused muscles and psychic powers and appetencies, which the conditions of modern life tend to relegate to innocuous desuetude." Flights from the "exaction and drudgery of occupational life to the more primitive states and attitudes characteristic of childhood and youth of the world and of man" were more than just a "safety valve," a form of escapism.[79] Recreation and leisure pursuits allowed the individual to adjust to his changing and increasingly repressive work, providing an "elasticity," a "recuperative sanity," and a "regenerative charge" from the "primeval source of energy." Adult play and leisure could "limber and mobilize the soul and . . . pick up lapsing functons and thereby reanimate and rejuvenate" the individual as well as the culture.[80]

Like Patrick, Hall believed that the renewal of "decadent and ancestral mechanisms" in recreation was a delicate social undertaking. The process had to be planned rationally. Danger would arise if men were allowed total freedom without guidance when they ventured into the dim world of the primitive within them or if they were prohibited by a spurious brand of progress from renewing themselves by the experience of the "primal source of energy." Like Patrick, Hall thought that delight in the primitive had to be a "conscious delight," which presupposed the ability to reconcile and compromise the primitive experience with the modern world.[81]

Hall believed that the time was right for this reconciling of the two "antithetical worlds," the primitive within and the civilized without. Technological progress and efficiency had created a wealth of free time that could make the renewal of natural and instinctional behavior forms practical. Because people had long subordinated their natural selves to the demands of the machine and the industrial state, they had at last been freed from economic necessity for at least part of their lives. They were free to express that part of themselves that was being increasingly repressed at work.[82]

But Hall noted a curious phenomenon. Just when the external reasons for servitude—the need to feed, clothe, and house the body— were less pressing, men were choosing a form of voluntary servitude. Americans were choosing to continue instinctual repression for a variety of illegitimate reasons, such as consumerism and faith in unlimited industrial progress.

Ancestral and decadent psychic mechanisms and rudiments are awakened and rejuvenated with intense conscious delight because they add to the present powers of man what he had in the past but had well nigh lost, and this revival would be impossible save in an atmosphere of freedom, not to say license. Again if the world grows somber as it grows free, it is because as external restrictions are destroyed, as all admit they are in the progress of history, they are replaced by self-imposed ones, so that our servitude though now voluntary is no less severe than when it was constrained. Only if and in so far as this self-enthrallment has supervened on the world is joy abated, and how far this has gone is the question. Man has been proper, decent, judicial, and scientific but a very short time compared with the long history of his race, and he is very prone to slip in thought, word, if not in deed, the leash of conventionalities and be all himself again if only in a flitting moment, and to revert to the prelogical stage of wild fancy and the prelinguistic stage of cachination. He is like a potted house plant in the north that dreams of its native tropical jungle, like a domesticated stabled animal that longs to cavort, frisk and snort in the old unfenced pastures of ancient feral days. . . . He is weary of being stable fed and wants to nibble and browse and taste again the old gamy flavor of the wildwood and the prairie, to woo folly and "cut up" as madly as he can. Alas for him who does not and cannot thus at times renew the youth of the race in him, for cadaveric rigidity has begun.[83]

Hall viewed play for the adult as a way to recapture the youthful vitality of the race, resurrecting the body and the outmoded instinctual reservoir. Leisure could provide an opportunity to lessen the pressures of work and cope with the "chief danger of democracy," the loss of individualism. But in America, this chance was slipping away as more people chose "self-imposed" restrictions even as "natural" restrictions were being reduced.

In the first decades of this century, William James had talked about "the fear of the emancipation from the fear-regime."[84] Hall, in his discussion of work and recreation, saw a similar fear, an escape from the freedom of leisure into new, chosen forms of work and continued repression. Simon Patten also was puzzled by such developments. Patten's works had always tended to be theoretical and wide ranging, and he was willing to discuss psychological matters if they had relevance to his economic theories. He thought Freud's idea that instinctual sublimation was biologically necessary for survival was historically relative and not an absolute fact of human existence. The "reality principle" changed from place to place and time to time. Claiming that industrial productivity was solving many of the old economic problems, Patten concluded that the reasons for instinctual sublimation were less pressing. But repressive forms in abundant industrial societies were as prevalent—indeed, they were even more prominent—as they were in the economy of scarcity. And Patten echoed Hall's question: Why did people continue to work hard and repress their individuality and instinctual needs when the reasons to do so were diminishing?[85]

The themes of instinctual release and compensation through play and leisure, surfaced by Hall and Patrick, were repeated throughout the 1920s by prominent psychologists and by writers from other disciplines who were interested in psychological topics. For example, William Ogburn, president of the American Sociological Society from 1925 to 1929, often speculated about psychological matters that had bearing on his work in sociology and occasionally published in journals that dealt mainly with psychology.[86] He reasoned that recreation "may be defined as that activity which exercises the dynamic traits and tendencies of man to function which underfunction during his life work." He felt that the playground or the national forests or even the theater and the movies could be substituted for "hunting the hairy elephant" and "marriage by club." Through recreation and adult play, the drives in man that made primitive forms of behavior attractive could be expressed in other ways and thus made compatible with current social demands.[87]

George Cutten, author of *The Psychology of Alcoholism, The Psychological Phenomena of Christianity*, and several other books dealing with the history and theory of psychology, was the president of Colgate University when he wrote *The Threat of Leisure* in 1926. Although Cutten did not do any experimental work and had little influence on the emerging profession of psychologists, he was able to synthesize and popularize the works of more important psychologists. His book on leisure was a popular one in the 1920s, and most writers concerned with the topic were familiar with Cutten's work.

Cutten thought that Prohibition had come along just at the right time, accompanying the rapid increase in leisure.[88] Workers were at least not liable to misuse their leisure through escape in alcohol.[89] But Cutten predicted that the workday would decrease below 8 hours. If efficiency increased in industry, the 4-hour day would be possible for everyone, Cutten thought, because the modern economy was rapidly reaching a state of "consumption equilibrium." Like Patten, Cutten believed that a new and "second industrial revolution" was at hand. This second industrial revolution would produce leisure instead of industrial products, since the need to consume goods would decline as basic needs were met.[90]

But, like Patten, Cutten was afraid that instead of realizing freedom and individualism through leisure, the industrial world would begin to "overconsume." Already the needs of business and capital expansion were beginning to subvert the gains of individual workers. Mass culture forms, such as movies and sporting events, were already expropriating the worker's free time, making what should have been an experience of individualism and self-expression a mindless and expensive commercial product.[91]

The major theme throughout Cutten's book was creativity. Above all things, he valued the active and creative individual.[92] He reasoned that the repression of primary sexual drives had always been necessary. But, earlier, this repression had its rewards. By sublimating libidinal drives to the needs of the family and society through work, the individual had the opportunity to express himself in creative ways. This sublimating of primary sex drives into creative channels made craftsmanship, invention, art, and culture itself possible. But modern means of factory and assembly-line production had taken away the creative rewards long associated with work. Society had to provide individuals with the opportunity to be creative and to find a practical way to redirect sex drives into creative forms. Leisure offered that opportunity.

> Attention has already been called to the fact that instincts have at least two forms of expression, a direct form which in most animals is the only form, and a secondary form most common in human beings and which is the result of sublimation in them. The sex instinct may show itself in its natural or primary form or it may be sublimated and result in any creative work. . . . Now the question comes, if recognized creative work is not supplied in the factory system, and if leisure does not furnish the opportunity for self-expression in creative work, may we not expect an expression of sexual looseness?[93]

But several influential and prominent psychologists in America were not at all optimistic about the prospect that, through play and leisure, instinctual inhibitions could be reduced. According to such writers, the "fear of emancipation from the fear-regime" was not a baseless fear but was founded on the needs of civilization and the realities of man's psychic makeup. For example, Sigmund Freud had a great influence on the discussion of instinctual release through the play impulse in adults. Yet Freud never considered the merits of adult play without pointing to several mitigating factors. Freud had long thought that the extended childhood of humans allowed a critical expression of pleasure-seeking behavior. Free from the demands of economic necessity and sexual maturity, the child expressed erotic energy in a multitude of forms involving his entire body. Play as erotic experimentation explained why human sexuality was qualitatively different from that of other animals and why the processes of repression and sublimation were so severe for the human child. This expression of erotic gratification through the "polymorphously perverse" body took the form of play. Play in childhood was under the rule of the "pleasure principle," and as such, established an erotic heritage for the adult with which he had to cope.[94]

As the protection afforded the child by his parents was lost, the child's "polymorphously perverse" play activity suffered strict curtailment. The social needs for procreation in the context of the human family and productive work gradually channeled erotic energy into specific body parts and approved activity. In Freud's terms, "genital organization" of erotic behavior replaced the disorganized and random eroticism of child play.[95] Just as activity under the rule of the "pleasure principle" was play, activity controlled by the reality of economic necessity and family responsibilities was work.

But within the adult who had to sublimate and organize his erotic energies, the playful child remained in memory as a constant reminder of the earlier and more complete erotic career. The serious business of making a living and raising a family never obscured that memory or the desire to return to the free play of eros. Expression of disorganized eroticism by the adult, because it was forbidden by society, most often took the form of an escape from reality or neurotic and psychotic activity. But sometimes the adult was able to give free play to the erotic energies and express them in socially acceptable and even highly valued forms.[96]

For example, the artist could experience and express free eroticism for all men to enjoy. Art was a form of adult play. But all adult play had to be reconciled to the needs of culture. The expression of the "polymorphously perverse" heritage by the adult had to be a conscious expression. It had to be reconciled and made compatible with the real world. It had to take definite cultural forms, given the outward form of work by the serious artist or the professional musician. Although childhood and free erotic play remained the goal for all men, the return to those things was not feasible except through the arduous process of making erotic play harmonious with cultural demands.[97]

In both *The Future of an Illusion* and *Civilization and Its Discontents*, Freud spoke directly to the issue of work in an age of abundance and the contention that because of economic abundance instinctual release was reasonable. Although Freud never used the term "leisure," he discussed in depth the possibility that the importance of, and rationale for, traditional forms of work was diminishing.[98] He supposed that this process was the result of the increased ability of society to control nature and meet the economic needs of its members. Apparently he was referring to himself when he used the pronoun "one" in the following statement: "One thought at first that the essence of culture lay in the conquest of nature for the means of supporting life . . . , but now the emphasis seems to have shifted away from the material plane on to the psychical."[99] This shift raised the "critical question" whether or to what extent one can "succeed in diminishing the burden of instinctual sacrifices imposed on men" through work.[100]

Attempts to answer this question took the form of what Freud called a "great cultural experiment that is at present in progress in the vast country that stretches between Europe and Asia."[101] He believed that the psychical and cultural reasons for continued instinctual sacrifices through work had to take precedence in this experiment. Without repression and sublimation, civilization would begin to crumble as the destructive desires of its members were let loose. Incest, cannibalism, and murder were instinctually desirable, and no society could tolerate open expression of these things. Without repressive forms, one of which was certainly work, life in society would cease, and the rule of nature would result.[102] Moreover, the "heritage of ideas, morality and artistic creations" would be destroyed, as would the sublime satisfaction these things afforded civilized man. Nature was not banished by the simple "conquest of nature for the means of production."[103] Human nature and the values of culture still made instinctual control necessary.

But the masses of men were "not naturally fond of work." In an age of economic abundance, they could be expected to crave increased release from work's demands. The masses, being lazy and unintelligent, "would have to be coerced" either by the social *illusion* that work and continued repression was as necessary as ever before or controlled by their leaders. They would have to be made "to submit to their labors and renunciations on which the existence of culture depends."[104]

During the 1920s, Freud was in the process of redefining his reality principle, so he no longer thought of reality solely as a function of society's claims on the individual. Instead, he was beginning to believe that the reality principle was a result of competing forces within the individual: life and death.[105] Not only did individual organisms seek to avoid pain and seek pleasure, but they tended to strive for the elimination of stimulation altogether and seek a "nirvana" state in which no demands were made on them. Within the individual, the desire for the end of all stimulation competed with the seeking after pleasurable experiences. Thus reality for the individual was composed of the life force of gratification seeking and the death wish of stimulus avoidance.[106] If, as several psychologists had agreed, this was the case, then the reduction of repression would be accompanied by the increase of stimulus avoidance. Play and release from the need to work in this situation would not be a simple experience of erotic release and creativity. It would necessarily be accompanied by a rise in expressions of the "death wish," as indeed the modern phenomenon of boredom demonstrated.

"Sunday neurosis," a term coined by S. Ferenczi, [107] was given wide circulation during the 1920s. Several writers had noticed that there was an apparent increase in antisocial behavior and suicide on Sunday. They speculated that boredom was the culprit. Weekends were not only the opportunity for leisure but also provided an emptiness, a distressing boredom to many people. The result of this boredom was often a desperate need to find something to do. Often, that "something" was crime or an attempt to achieve total emptiness through self-destruction.[108]

Even though Carl Jung was enthusiastic about the possibility of uncovering the unconscious self and thereby discovering new and potentially "spiritual" modes of living, he still shared Freud's fears about general erotic release: "We cannot possibly get beyond our present level of culture unless we receive a powerful impetus from our primitive roots. But we shall receive it only if we go behind our cultural level thus giving the repressed primitive man in ourselves a chance to develop." [109] But Jung, in his influential *Psychological Types*, was frightened by the prospect of the general liberation of the play impulse. Reacting against the radical implications of Friedrich Schiller's formulation of "liberating play," Jung supposed that the rule of the play instinct would accomplish a "release of repression" that would bring about the "deprecation of the hitherto highest values." The result would be a "catastrophe of culture" and "barbarism." Even though a "powerful impetus from our primitive roots" could revitalize culture, that impetus had to be controlled, and only the elite few, guided by the precepts of psychoanalysis, could possibly benefit. The "general release of the play impulse" was impossible, since most men could not handle instinctual freedom.[110] Moreover, Jung was ready to identify repressive culture with culture per se. Without repressive forms, culture and the highest achievements of individuals would cease. The play impulse could never achieve the seriousness and the history-making purpose that repressive culture made possible. The return to the primitive was a serious business, reserved for the brave few who could fashion new culture in the midst of repression.

The identification of instinctual repression with culture creation and culture itself was widespread among psychologists, as were fears regarding the "play impulse." It seemed clear to these men that culture resulted from the confrontation of the individual's desires with the demands of civilization. If the "play impulse" were given free rein, then a general dissipation of psychic energy would follow. Psychic energy had to be focused and made useful by cultural forms if civilization was to continue. The radical implications of Schiller's ideas had become clear. If, as Schiller had foreseen, the "play impulse" functioned by "abolishing time in time," "reconciling being with becoming," and "reconciling change with identity," then history would lose its motive force.[111] According to Henry Adams, history would run down.[112] Others, such as Patrick and Hall, took the opposite view and, looking to increased leisure, expected that the play impulse could be introduced gradually and thus strengthen culture.[113] The problem of industrialization was not too little repression but too much; "excessive repression" had dried up the wellsprings of human creativity and made people increasingly passive and idle consumers of life. In this situation, increased leisure was necessary for mental health.

The fourth professional group concerned with increased leisure, social scientists, tended to be optimistic about America's future and the future of their profession during the 1920s. Even though technological advance had thrown the social order into some disarray, they were confident that, through the use of "social intelligence," the future could be ordered rationally and growth planned.[114]

Discussions of leisure time figured prominently in many social scientists' works during the 1920s. A number of sociologists and anthropologists thought that through an objective analysis of leisure patterns, a great deal of information could be gained about cultural values, changing mores, and social structure that could be used to predict trends and facilitate social planning. Other sociologists, who concentrated on industrialization, concluded that leisure behavior played a vital role in a society's adaptation to industrial change and was important in solving the problem of "cultural lag."[115]

Analysis of leisure-time patterns as a way to understand social structure and processes began in the 1920s. This new interest in leisure is partly explained by the increasing use of scientific methods and the preference for concrete empirical research among social scientists. Leisure was one of many social elements not investigated before 1920 and thus was attractive. But, equally important, anthropologists such as Margaret Mead, W. H. R. Rivers, and Clark Wissler had paved the way in their works on the play of adolescents, children, and adults in primitive societies.[116] They had concluded that play was an integral part of the social structure and that in the societies they investigated, it was difficult to distinguish clearly work from play. Play and nonwork behavior were governed by the needs of the group and by tradition, and were most often done in the context of rituals and celebrations that were structured and culturally functional. Children's games in primitive cultures tended to be imitations of serious adult behavior such as hunting, food preparation, and family living. Through games, children prepared themselves for adult roles. But adult "games" were serious business. Rituals, festivals, celebrations, feasts, and dances were the very things that held society together. Through them, cultural exchanges with other groups were made, and social rules and structures reenforced.

But social scientists who concentrated on modern industrial societies were able to see a clear division between work and adult free time. Sociologists such as George Lundberg, Robert Lynd, and Helen Lynd stressed that leisure was a modern phenomenon, the social dynamics of which were not yet known. But they were sure that leisure time held one of the keys to understanding modern societies. Moreover, they believed that the measurement and study of modern leisure developments would serve to uncover changing social forces. Leisure was the time in which people were free to experiment with their social lives and develop new ways to live together. As such, it was a dynamic force in modern societies.

For example, Herbert Hoover's Committee on Recent Social Trends considered leisure and recreation in America to be critical areas for study.[117] The committee was composed of some of the best-known sociologists in the United States. In preparation for the committee's work, William Ogburn and Howard Odum, in their respective capacities as director and assistant director of research for the committee, were concerned that recreation and leisure be investigated adequately and that a competent person be chosen for this study.[118] They agreed that leisure was a vital issue of modern society and that finding ways to use leisure to solve social problems was a pressing need.[119]

Odum had been interested in these matters for some time.[120] He had been instrumental in bringing Harold Meyer to the University of North Carolina's Sociology Department during the 1920s as one of the first teachers of recreation on a university level. Ogburn considered leisure an important part of his study of inventions, a natural result of technological innovations.[121] Hence, in line with their interests, they pressed for a detailed study of leisure and recreation, and found J. F. Steiner of the University of Washington to do the job for the committee.[122]

Steiner reasoned that the trend in America toward more leisure time and recreation was, as the committee suggested, one of the most significant social developments of modern times. But the largest part of Steiner's study for *Recent Social Trends* was devoted to the simple measurement of increased leisure services and recreational facilities. The only explanation he offered for the increase was the fact that work time was being reduced. Furthermore, he had little interest in interpreting what this advance meant for society or how it could be used to help social planning.[123]

Steiner saw gains in all kinds of recreation in the United States, including governmental, philanthropic, educational, religious, and, most of all, private and commercial forms. According to Steiner, the growth in recreation and leisure activity had been most notable in the 1920s. For example, the number of municipal public playgrounds increased 74.9 percent in the decade, while the number of cities reporting municipal recreation facilities increased 62.3 percent. State and federal recreation facilities had grown almost as much. The number of visitors to national and state parks had grown fourfold. The number of visits to parks was partly attributable to the rise of the automobile as a common means of transportation. But Steiner considered car trips to the parks as much a recreation form as the park itself. In fact, Steiner suspected that the automobile was used mostly for recreation and should therefore be included in any measurement of the nation's expenditure for leisure activity.[124]

The growth of professional and collegiate sports was dramatic, capturing the public's attention and imagination. Baseball and football had become spectator events and by the end of the decade were multimillion-dollar concerns. For example, attendance at major league baseball games grew from 9 million in 1920 to 10 million in 1930. Class AA baseball games had nearly a 20 percent growth in attendance. Collegiate football earned only $2.5 million for the schools in 1920; by 1930, games brought in $8 million in gate receipts.[125]

Steiner was suspicious of the increased interest in mass spectator sports. These forms of leisure activity were both expensive and passive. He saw a more healthy trend in the increase in active participation in sports. Golfers, for example, became so numerous from 1923 to 1930 that 3953 new golf courses were built, an increase of

207.7 percent. Interest in tennis, hunting, and winter sports also grew rapidly during the decade. Clubs and associations devoted to recreation showed an increase in dues from $6 million in 1921 to $12.5 million in 1930.[126]

Steiner reasoned that fraternal clubs were largely devoted to recreation and leisure pursuits. He therefore gave figures to show the rapid growth of the Masons, Rotary International, Kiwanis, and Lions, each of which enrolled two or three times as many members at the end of the decade than they had at the beginning.[127]

But commercial forms of recreation and amusement had experienced the greatest growth. Traditional amusements—vaudeville, burlesque, stage shows, cabarets and nightclubs, dancehalls, poolrooms, and amusement parks—had of course grown in receipts and numbers. But the newer amusements had increased more dramatically. For example, motion picture attendance doubled between 1925 and 1930. By 1930, over 100 million Americans went to the movies every week, spending more than $1.5 billion in that year. Radio broadcasting began on a regular basis with one station in Pittsburgh in 1920 and ended the decade with 600 stations all over the country and two national networks, the Columbia Broadcasting System and the National Broadcasting Company. In 1930, 40 percent of all American families had a radio, a rare possession in 1920.[128]

Steiner estimated that the total annual "cost of recreation and leisure activities" was just under $10.25 billion. A nation that earned $681 per capita, or $82 billion in aggregate, each year, spent nearly 13 percent of its earnings on recreation, according to Steiner. A critical group of figures in Steiner's estimate related to "automobile touring" and "automobile costs." He thought the $4.5 billion spent on these things constituted a leisure expense.[129]

Steiner concluded that recreation planning and the public provision of recreational services were the pressing needs uncovered by his study. The high cost of recreation had put amusement out of the reach of a number of Americans. In addition, public recreation needed more funding and careful planning to counter the commercial trends. He advocated more stringent legal controls of commercial amusements to curtail what he saw as an increase in vice and in passive amusements. The term "spectatoritis," coined in 1917 and given circulation by Jay Nash in the 1920s, summed up what Steiner disliked about commercial amusements. The passive "fans" at movies and sports events had given up their right to be active and in control of their recreation. They improved neither mind nor body by looking at spectacles; instead, they became puppets in the hands of professionals and moneymakers in the business of selling mass amusements. Planned and public recreation could reform this situation, making leisure time an active and positive experience.[130]

Steiner was content to recommend modest recreation reforms based on rational planning for active participation, but other members of the Hoover Committee believed that recreation and leisure could be used in social planning for more important ends.

In contrast to Hoover's earlier Committee on Recent Economic Changes, the Committee on Recent Social Trends did not believe society's problems could be solved by the simple expedient of stimulating consumption.[131] Instead, the committee considered the problem of the "coordination of the factors of our evolving society" a complex and multifaceted one. A common theme running through the committee's works and made explicit in *Recent Social Trends*'s introductory summary, "Committee Findings," was the problem of "cultural lag." The members reasoned that of the "great social organizations, two, the economic and governmental," were growing most rapidly; the other two "historic organizations," the family and the church, had declined in relative social significance. Effective coordination of these four social institutions required the "slowing up of the changes that occur too rapidly and the speeding up of the changes which lag." The committee denied that it wanted a "moratorium upon research in the physical sciences and invention." Instead, it emphasized the importance of growth in the "nonpecuniary," social institutions to keep pace with industrial and economic progress.[132]

But the committee concluded that industrial growth had begun to compete with family life, spiritual values, moral values, educational goals, and cultural life. Industry and the importance of work had come to dominate American life and to be given effort and attention disproportionate to their actual social worth.[133]

The way to correct this situation, according to the committee, was through the application of scientific social planning through public policy. The Committee proposed that a National Advisory Council be set up that would represent the scientific, governmental, economic (industrial, agricultural, and labor), and educational communities and be responsible for social policies designed to coordinate the advance of society.[134] Even though the "immense structure of human culture exists to serve human needs and values are not always measurable," still it was important to try to help institutions such as the family and church "to promote and expand human happiness, to enable men to live more richly and abundantly."[135]

Leisure would be useful in this endeavor. This uniquely modern form of freedom could be utilized by individuals and government to recover social and cultural values that had been sacrificed to economic ends. The time freed by industrial efficiency could be redirected from economic concerns and utilized to advance nonmaterial values and strengthen institutions that served these values. In this way, the disproportionate growth of industry could be countered and the "social inventions," necessary to solve the problem of cultural lag, made.

For example, adult education was one practical way through which the time freed by industry could be directed to educational ends. The arts—music, painting, literature—could be given a new life. Time was at last available to make participation in amateur art and crafts a realistic option for more people.[136]

The family and the church were both potential beneficiaries of the new leisure. The family could be made more stable if people chose to spend more time in that institution. The church also required time more than any other of its members' resources.

But the committee saw a danger in this situation. Choices that were being made in leisure were being influenced too much by business pressures. Advertising and mass amusements were exerting an unfair pressure. As a result, time that should have been spent strengthening the weaker elements of the society was being diverted to consumption because of industry's appetite for growth.

> Business, with its advertising and high pressure salesmanship, can exert powerful stimuli on the responding human organism. How can the appeals made by churches, libraries, concerts, museums and adult education for a goodly share in our growing leisure be made to compete effectively with the appeals of commercialized recreation? Choice is hardly free when one set of influences is active and the other set quiescent. From one and a half to two billion dollars were spent in 1929 on advertising— how much of it in appealing for use of leisure we do not venture to guess. Whether or not the future brings pronounced irritation with the increasing intrusions upon our psychological freedom by advertisements, the problem of effecting some kind of equality in opportunity and appeal as between the various types of leisure time occupations, both commercial and noncommercial, as between those most vigorously promoted and those without special backing, needs further consideration.[137]

Other sociologists dealt with these themes. Helen and Robert Lynd had explored the social use of leisure in their study *Middletown*. After investigating a "typical midwestern city" in 1924, the Lynds found that six general areas of activity were characteristic of that city's everyday life. Most of Middletown's residents divided their time between making a living, keeping house, training young people, engaging in leisure activities, participating in community activities, and engaging in religious pursuits. Like the Hoover Committee, the Lynds supposed that the major problem facing the society under study was the "ragged, unsynchronized movement of social institutions."[138] The Lynds also recognized that most of this social imbalance had to do with the fact that making a living and consuming products were the dominant concerns of Middltown's residents. The "long arm of the job" extended into all activities and was especially felt in leisure.[139]

Typical of a "pecuniary society," Middletown "spent" its leisure. This "precious time" was absorbed by commercial amusements, mass culture, organizations, and the all-consuming wish to buy things. Free leisure was practically impossible because "both businessmen and working men seem to be running for dear life in this business of making money earned keep pace with the ever more rapid growth of their subjective wants."[140] The Lynds recognized that the "gospel of consumption" had been accepted as dogma and that "the American Citizen's first importance to his country is no longer that of a citizen but that of a consumer." Pressured by advertising and by neighbors, the Middletown citizen spent his leisure consuming goods and services or worrying about what he ought to buy.[141]

As a result of industry's pressure and advertising, leisure was a poor experience. Entertainment no longer involved good books and conversations; it was dished out by mass media in the form of cheap books and cheaper radio programs. These mass amusements encouraged escape, not education and enjoyment. Passive and effortless amusements ruled leisure in this situation, making creativity and active enjoyment things of the past.[142]

Other pressures also were remaking Middletown's leisure. Inventions were changing long-established patterns. The automobile, motion pictures, and radio were contributing to the "increasing standardization of leisure."[143] The passive and collective features of mass culture extended even to local organizations. One of the most notable features of Middletown's leisure was that it was thoroughly organized. Voluntary associations were proliferating. No longer did the family or the individual govern leisure. The club or lodge absorbed much of the free time that had recently been achieved. All these trends added up to a dramatic increase in mass culture and a loss of individualism.[144]

Nevertheless, according to the Lynds, leisure still provided an opportunity for the individual to be active and creative. It was also a time in which the worker could "seek compensation" for the "sense of craftsmanship and group solidarity" lost in work. But because of the great influence of industry and mass culture, these opportunities were being rapidly lost.[145]

Weaver Pangburn, Alfred Lloyd, and Simon Patten's student Edward Ross were also concerned that individualism be recovered through leisure and recreation. According to Pangburn, the days when work provided self-expression, creativity, and "inspiration" were over. Specialization and mass production had made most jobs repetitive and dull. He told of the "derisive laughter" that swept an audience of manual laborers when they were told of a university president's address about the "joys of work."[146] But the shortened workday left the worker with a "surplus of energy" that could be used to meet his "spiritual needs and to work out his own destiny."[147] Although the "chief responsibility for fulfilling his purpose in life rests on the individual," society could at last give each person "his chance" to realize his full potential. Given access to things such as adult education, public recreation workers could effectively utilize leisure. The "community's responsibility" was to provide opportunities for the worker's "self-expression." He concluded that "although industry denies the natural instinct for self development, we have not learned to so order our ways and institutions that what industry prevents leisure may adequately provide."[148]

Edward Ross, president of the American Sociological Society, saw America experiencing the stress of transition from "a pain economy to a pleasure economy." The nature of work in the "pleasure economy" had changed. It appealed "less and less to man's native tendencies" and was becoming "ascetic." As work became more "monotonous, meaningless, fragmented, dreary, and irksome," leisure became more important as a way through which the individual could "feed his famishing instincts." Ross thought that natural needs and desires were being forfeited in the job and that leisure could compensate the individual for this loss.

Ross concluded that "it is the rehearsal of activities of body and state of mind belonging to the childhood of our race that rests the overtaxed, higher cerebral portions of the brain." For Ross, one solution to industry's problems—boredom, collectivization, alienation—was play and the active expression of the individual's "native tendencies." The unequal advance of society's various elements was not nearly as destructive as the increasing alienation of the individual. Society had to provide ways through which "natural" needs and desires could be expressed so that the individual was not submerged and neglected. Leisure provided that opportunity.[149]

Alfred Lloyd, president of the University of Michigan, believed that the time had come when a "new culture" was made possible by the "new leisure." Since the beginning of time, only the elite few had had the freedom from work to make and enjoy culture. The arrival of the "iron man," in the form of industrial automation, had put the enjoyment of cultural things and the creation of a new culture within the reach of every individual. He looked for a new Golden Age, a "cultural renaissance," in which every man could transcend economic concerns and experience the joys of education, imaginative expression, and "progressive adventure." Leisure had given life to the Declaration of Independence's promise of the "pursuit of happiness." [150]

By the 1920s, the old justifications for the shorter workweek, based on practical values such as efficient production, health, safety, and morality, were no longer sufficient or persuasive enough to support additional reductions. Unlike the 8-hour day, having Saturdays off was seen to offer the worker leisure—the opportunity to become increasingly free from the job to do other things. The implications of the precipitous drop in the workweek became clear. Free time was as natural a corollary to increased production as new products and better wages, and free time in an economy of abundance was leisure. In contrast to previous discussions, which had emphasized that shorter hours improved work, in the 1920s that connection was broken. Free time was justified or attacked on its own, as an alternative to work.

During the 1920s, indexers of books, periodicals, and newspapers found that not only was the word *leisure* used more often (at an approximate tenfold increase) but that it was being used in different ways. For the first time, they found it necessary to use *leisure* in cross-reference with words such as *play, amusements, hours of work, adult education, religious instruction, community centers,* and *commercial entertainments.* The word was used differently and more often, reflecting a widespread concern.[151]

As the 1920s advanced, the word leisure became increasingly useful as leisure become a major social and economic issue. Like the "gospel of consumption," the leisure issue was new, and it seemed to threaten, or at least require changes in, traditional values and concepts. If people were to be freed from their jobs and the discipline of work, what would take their places? To some people, the social order seemed threatened. They feared that progress would slow down and civilization decline in proportion to the decrease in the importance of work. Others believed that the new freedom from the job could bless the masses with the benefits of democratic culture, allowing for the first time the exploration of "nonpecuniary" activities and values on a broad scale.

During the 1920s, a dialogue formed in America about the use of abundance and direction for progress. This dialogue was also a response to the threats of general overproduction, saturated demand, and the declining need to work. On the one hand, businessmen and economists solved the problems to their satisfaction by their new faith in "optional consumption" and a "dynamic economy." Supporters of the shorter-hour cure for unemployment had a contrasting view. They saw the "progressive shortening of work hours" as the way to limit production to basic necessities and avoid acute periodic depressions and chronic technological unemployment.

These responses to abundance included divergent views of work, its value and purpose. Businessmen and economists reaffirmed the central importance of work for human welfare. They understood that their ability to stimulate and promote new consumption saved work as well as economic progress. But a large number of old Progressives, economists, intellectuals, educators, sociologists, psychologists, displaced aristocrats, humanist scholars, religious leaders, and labor union leaders believed that leisure, like higher wages, was a basic element of social reform. They were convinced that leisure made a number of traditional humanitarian reforms practical for the first time in American history. Culture, morality, spiritual values, and, most of all, individualism were at last capable of being enjoyed by the majority of the American people. In fact, in the face of chronic overproduction, they were pressing needs, not idle dreams. Some people were also in arms against the new "gospel of consumption" and mass culture, which represented to them the newest form of "American Philistinism." They criticized work in its new forms and new purposes, seeing leisure as a new alternative.

In the dialogue, each group attacked the other for its deviation from tradition. Both, however, offered new directions for progress, the one economic and collective, and the other more cultural, "idealistic," and individualistic. Both agreed that even though prosperity was perilous, it still offered new technological or human frontiers—"boundless fields," according to the Committee on Recent Economic Changes.

The dialogue had other points of agreement. Labor, for instance, was eager for both higher standards of living and shorter hours. But it was polarized to the extent that businessmen and economists hoped to see an end to the century-long process of shorter work hours, while others looked forward to "the progressive shortening of work hours." It was polarized because work time, if continually shortened, could impose a limit to industrial growth that businessmen and economists would not accept. Time was short, but industry's products and its need to grow were long.

Nevertheless, this dialogue took place at a time when working hours for the average worker stabilized. Paradoxically, interest in shorter hours increased most as actual hours declined least. Much of the interest in the issue, then, was a response to the previous twenty-years' rapid reduction in hours, which led to the expectation that the trend was strong enough to continue, an expectation strengthened by labor's new five-day-week initiative.

For the historian, the questions remain: Why did hours stabilize in the 1920s? What changed from the period of rapid reductions, from 1900 to 1920? The most obvious difference was business and employer support. Interest in an 8-hour day for practical reasons, increased efficiency above all the rest, was replaced by strong opposition to a Saturday holiday. When shorter hours were for work, business managers were supportive; when for leisure—an alternative to work—opposition arose. Moreover, followers of the new economic gospel of consumption actively opposed additional decreases in work time. Offering a new alternative, what supporters called "optional consumption" and opponents called "luxuries," the gospel of consumption presented new reasons to keep working for the fine things industry and invention were discovering. Instead of accepting leisure as an alternative to work, the gospel of consumption commercialized free time, transforming it into a new reason to work. And great effort was expended to sell new products for amusement, display, and enjoyment, as more attention was paid to the problem of increasing consumption than ever before.

Economists have noted that a historical correlation exists between advertising and the reduction of work hours; it is a negative correlation in which the more that has been spent on advertising and marketing, the fewer hours that have been lost from work. Such studies support the contention that business and advertising were effective in competing with increased leisure during the decade.[152]

Labor's changed position may have played a part. Abandoning arguments for safety, health, morality, and productivity in the first years of the decade and then moving away from the unemployment issue after 1926, labor was left with supporting the five-day week primarily for leisure. With the fading of these traditional supports, shorter hours may have lost some of its appeal among the rank and file. Moreover, accepting the productivity theory of wages and shorter hours, labor tried to trade productivity for both of these. But in so doing, union officials outlined a choice between the two: the more hours were short-ened, the less wages. Business managers had long argued this in negotiations, stressing the choice between the two and the need to give up one to the extent that the other was taken. By abandoning the 8-hour theory after 1926, the AFL may have lost contact with workers, who were certainly still interested in both hours and wages, but much more concerned with the size of their paychecks.

For the most part, the 1920s saw high labor demand and low unemployment. With such steady demand for workers, interest in the shorter-hour solution to unemployment may have weakened among unorganized workers.

Immigration restriction may also have played a role. The decline in the number of immigrants from nonindustrialized countries after 1912, together with the limitations on immigration in the 1920s, resulted in far fewer immigrants in the workforce than before. Since the leaders of the five-day week were mostly immigrants in the clothing and printing trades (over 60 percent of workers with the five-day week were in these two industries, and it was confined to firms with heavy immigrant concentrations), Hourwich's contention that immigrants were more interested in shorter hours than were native workers is strengthened. Fewer immigrants may have weakened one component cause for the decline of working hours between 1910 and 1914.

But there is one puzzling development. Wages increased in the 1920s more than they had from the turn of the century until World War I. According to economic theories, this spurt in wages should have done what it did during the war: encourage leisure taking. But this decade was the opposite of the first years of the century in terms of the relationship between hours and wages. Although during the Progressive era, hours were shortened at a record level, wages were nearly stable. By contrast, during the 1920s, hours were virtually stable as wages increased. Both developments raise questions about theories that explain the historical changes in working hours in terms of wages. The pattern that economists expect, higher wages and shorter hours, has been the exception rather than the rule in this century. The historical record seems to indicate that there have been changes in "leisure preferences" as expressed in the labor market. This casts some doubt on the economists' assumption that such preference has been a constant.

The widespread discussion of increased leisure had little or no real impact on actual hours worked. The new gospel of consumption seemed to have ruled the 1920s. But this support prepared the way for a series of dramatic political events that took place during the Great Depression.

CHAPTER 5

*Shorter Hours in
the Early Depression*

WITH THE ONSET of the Great Depression, shorter hours became more than a topic for public debate. It took center stage as a political issue for most of the 1930s. The different opinions expressed in the 1920s about the social and economic potentials of increased leisure, on the one hand, and the benefits of the new economic gospel of consumption and the need to create jobs, on the other, became political positions and surrounded concrete proposals such as the Black–Perkins bill and key components of Franklin Roosevelt's New Deal. What had been a cultural dialogue became a political contest.

Because of the depression, the shorter-hour cure for unemployment resurfaced and received more support than ever. During the last two years of Hoover's administration and the first of Roosevelt's, this solution was one of the most prominent political responses to the depression.

Labor abandoned its reliance on increased productivity and with a vengeance set out for the universal five-day week and then the 30-hour week. Strong support for these reductions came from groups interested in increased leisure in the 1920s. And groups that had not been so interested, or had actually opposed the five-day week, offered support. The movement for shorter hours as a depression measure built a seemingly irresistible momentum in these years, so much so that by 1933 observers were predicting that the 30-hour week was within a month of becoming federal law and that the "progressive shortening of the hours of labor" was an inescapable economic fact of life and the dominant political trend.

Even businessmen, industrialists, and conservative politicians, the traditional champions of long hours, seemed to have come around to support the cause, albeit reluctantly and with conditions (e.g., that wages would be reduced proportionately, that the measure would be temporary and only for the duration of the depression, and that it would be voluntary). Even with their conditions, they had taken the first positive steps of the depression, abandoning, at least for the time being, their faith in expanded consumption and the creation of new work. Hoover's secretary of labor, William Doak, went so far as to observe that "industry, in general, favored" shorter hours.[1]

Several major industrial firms voluntarily cut weekly hours to 40 and then to 30 in 1930 and 1931. For example, Kellogg's of Battle Creek, Sears Roebuck, General Motors at Tarrytown, Standard Oil of New Jersey, Hudson Motors, and several cotton manufacturers took these measures as alternatives to laying off workers. The American Cotton Manufacturers endorsed plans to curtail working hours in its industries. The Baltimore and Ohio Railroad adopted a share-the-work scheme for shopmen in August 1932; and on October 8, Remington Rand adopted the four-day week, a move praised by William Green.[2] The Industrial Conference Board (ICB) surveyed 1718 business executives late in the year, on the basis of which it estimated that 50 percent of American industry had shortened hours to save jobs. Typical of reasons given by executives to the ICB were that more workers could be employed and relief provided at once, whereas wages, even though lower per capita, would be more widespread and thus would promote confidence and consumer spending.[3]

H. I. Harriman, president of the National Chamber of Commerce, addressing the nation over the CBS radio network, advocated the "application of spread work to all classes of workers . . . to white collar workers, commercial firms, banking, municipal and state government," concluding somewhat awkwardly that "it is better for all of us to be at work some of the time than for some of us to be at work all of the time while others are not at work at all."[4]

Even such a bastion of conservatism as the American Legion took its stand and organized for action. Beginning on August 24, 1932, its own work-sharing drive, what it called its "war against Depression," it claimed that 3300 of its posts nationwide had been working to lead their communities in the effort.[5]

Herbert Hoover began to favor these voluntary efforts to share the work in 1932. With his support of the chemical industry's program, Hoover incorporated shorter hours into his administration's depression policies and declared that the issue was part of his "nine point economic program," a step that Secretary Doak, the Emergency Committee for Employment, and the Organizations on Unemployment Relief had encouraged for over a year.[6]

Some activity had already begun in Congress. The Senate passed a bill for a 44-hour week for postal employees in February 1931. On January 11, 1932, Representative Lewis offered a bill for the equal partition of available hours among workers nationally. Governor Pinchot endorsed a 30-hour week on May 16; and New York Mayor Fiorello La Guardia observed in June 1932 that unless a 6-hour day, five-day week was passed by Congress, the U.S. Constitution would have to be rewritten within three years.[7]

From Hoover's early support, the political story unfolded rapidly during the election year. In June 1932 Hoover was pressed by the AFL to call a national convention on shorter hours. He chose to meet instead with a group of New England politicians and businessmen organized by Governor John Winant of New Hampshire. Disapproving of labor's move to shorter-hour legislation, Hoover joined with business and supported their voluntary efforts based in trade associations. In July Hoover instructed the Departments of Commerce and Labor to survey industry on the institution of the shorter-hour week. Secretaries Doak and Lamont met again with the New England politicians on August 1, tentatively approving the New Hampshire plan, which called for cuts of 10 percent in the working week. And in a speech to the National Conference of Business and Industrial Committees in late August, Hoover called shorter hours the quickest way to create more jobs.

These efforts came to fruition in August when the National Conference of Business and Industrial Committees, with Hoover's blessing, created the Teagle Commission for work sharing.[8]

The "share-the-work" drive opened in September and grew immediately into a national force with strong business support. Even though the National Association of Manufacturers (NAM) supported the drive primarily as a hedge against labor's push for national legislation, public response to the idea and business cooperation were impressive. Assessing the movement, the U.S. Department of Labor estimated that 25 percent of all employees "held jobs on the plan."[9] On the basis of this report, Teagle claimed that 3 million to 5 million jobs had been created.[10]

The movement gained momentum in the 1932 campaign. Both major parties included a shorter-hour plank in their platforms. During the campaign, one of the most important unemployment issues was shorter hours. A strong case may be made that it was *the* most important issue, since other methods to deal with unemployment and create jobs were vague suggestions or mentioned as possibilities. The issue of shorter hours was a specific measure, already in place, tried out by Hoover and by Roosevelt in New York State, and had attracted a considerable political constituency.

Hoover and Roosevelt vied with each other in their support of the share-the-work drive. Roosevelt pointed with pride to his efforts in New York State to pass legislation lowering hours and setting minimum wages; Hoover countered with a rehearsal of his support for the national share-the-work drive. Prominent supporters were to be found along the entire range of the political spectrum, including John Ryan, Gifford Pinchot, Fiorello H. La Guardia, Frances Perkins, Henry Ford, Senators Wagner and Walsh, E. A. Filene, and Vincent Astor. For example, on October 5, Wagner recommended the permanent adoption of share the work as a basis for reducing the competition for jobs.[11]

The shorter-hour momentum continued after the election. But with the change in the political climate in Washington, public and congressional interest shifted from voluntary business efforts to national legislation.

After a few halfhearted overtures to the Teagle Commission in September 1932, and a lukewarm endorsement in October, the AFL leadership in Executive Council rejected the Teagle campaign with its pay cutting and drafted a bill that limited hours per week to 30. The AFL had considered a constitutional amendment for the regulation of hours in their November convention, but settled on legislation suggested to the organization by such groups as the National Citizens' League for Industrial Recovery and the National Grange. In December, Hugo Black introduced the AFL bill to the 72nd Congress, to prohibit, in interstate or foreign commerce, all goods produced by establishments where workers were employed more than five days a week or 6 hours a day.[12]

Several affiliated unions had argued that provisions for a minimum wage should be included in the bill. The AFL, however, concluded that such a piece of legislation would have less political support and would almost certainly be ruled unconstitutional. Moreover, most labor leaders opposed minimum-wage provisions, reasoning that a minimum wage could easily become a maximum wage. The best course of action would be to enforce a nationwide reduction in the supply of labor. This would provide immediate "work relief." Then, as more people were put back to work at 30 hours, buyer confidence would return, purchasing power would expand, and the economy would recover. Once the economy improved, labor could bargain effectively for higher wages in a condition of continued labor scarcity. Because of the excess of work supply—in the form of excess hours—reductions in hours seemed to be the necessary first step to higher wages. This was a historic break from tradition for the unions, which had always opposed such legislation in favor of collective bargaining.[13]

The hearings held in Congress and the public debate on the bill attracted a good deal of attention and prompted numerous individuals to lend their support for a variety of reasons. Old-fashioned reformers, hearing the echoes of their Progressive past, farm groups, intellectuals, educators, religious leaders, and sociologists were persuaded by labor's argument about the employment benefits of shorter hours. In addition to these practical discussions, some of the most idealistic and "romantic" reformers' rhetoric, which had surfaced during the 1920s, was heard again. Like labor leaders, supporters of the legislation felt obliged to defend the leisure time that would result from a 30-hour week. In so doing, they revived an older vision of a nonmaterial progress hotly debated in the previous business decade; others offered new ideas about leisure's potential for individual freedom and democratic culture in a modern and collective world.[14]

Throughout these hearings, Roosevelt was conducting his own negotiations. During the interregnum, he had remained active on the issue. He suggested at a meeting with businessmen in Washington, D.C., in mid-February that he would be willing to consider relaxing antitrust laws in return for a voluntary 6-hour-day, five-day-week agreement; this would be put in operation through the trade associations. He was reported as having said that the strong trust-busting Progressives in the Senate, such as Norris, were ready to compromise with "Big Business" in order to get the shorter workweek.[15]

With such congressional activity and with Roosevelt beating the bushes for the issue, speculations about the bright possibilities of a leisured future filled the press, as incongruous in the depression as the plowing up of fields of corn and the burning of food for fuel in the Midwest. But such incongruities were commonplace in days when poverty was born of abundance.[16]

Just as in 1921–1922, the rhetorical climate of the early depression, the clouds of words and phrases, repeated enough that they seemed to take on a life of their own, gave more and more indication that less and less work would be needed in the future.

Teagle's trademark phrase, "share the work," was accompanied by "technological unemployment," "economic maturity," "market gluts," "overproduction" "the shorter-hour cure for overproduction," "limited production," "secular stagnation," and Hugh Johnson's famous "Saturnalia of Destruction." All pointed to a widespread feeling that economic growth had come at long last to a turning point. These phrases reflected the general belief that the depression had been caused by overproduction. So much had been produced that the business world had been turned upside down. Problems of economic distress stemmed, not from a lack of industrial growth and production, but from too much. Growth had destabilized the economy. To some, this was an unmitigated disaster. To others, such as Monsignor Ryan, overproduction proved that the economy had grown to a point where human needs could be largely met and "a life of reasonable and frugal comfort" was available to all workers if only the problems of redistribution, both of work and of wealth, were solved.[17]

As in the early 1920s, the two obvious solutions to overproduction, producing less and selling more, were offered. But the latter seemed to have been discredited, even in the minds of some business people. The president of the AFL, William Green, along with most other Americans, had heard the "new business gospel of consumption" throughout the 1920s. Its prophets had preached that enough new markets could be found, enough "luxuries" transformed into necessities by advertising and the spending example of the rich, that overproduction could be averted, and workers, finding new horizons of work, could escape the scourge of unemployment. But for Green and many others, the depression had shown this gospel and its prophets to have been false and had proved that Green had been right all along. He, like most others in the labor movement, never fully accepted the idea that industrial growth could go on indefinitely and new work found to replace jobs taken over by the machine. Labor's counterargument was that free time was the natural result of technological advances and the satisfaction of basic, "reasonable" human needs. The depression had shown that technological displacement was a reality and that workers had a choice only as to the forms the new free time would take. They could have either increased unemployment or more leisure time. All the advertising and business hype about new markets and perpetual economic growth could not change that hard fact.[18]

The shorter-hour cure for unemployment, proposed by labor in the early 1920s to counter the gospel of consumption, represented the other common-sense approach to too much production and ruled the day in the early depression. The "cure" provided that if production had become excessive and had resulted in pools of copper and other commodities and glutted inventories of retail traders, then the best course of action would be simply to work fewer hours and produce less. Necessary work would be spread around naturally by the market, and workers would have the blessing of leisure, not the curse of unemployment. Industry would have to change direction, turning to the creation of sufficient necessities, effectively demanded by workers. Useless work, "makework," and the multiplication of occupations and profession would cease, and people once so employed would be put back to "productive" work at shorter hours. Economic balance required that wages be increased enough so that workers could buy what they produced, to be sure. But the counterweight, shorter hours, was essential to deal with existing surpluses and act as a governor on future runaway overproduction. Such had been the reasoning behind the share-the-work movement and behind the 30-hour legislation that had started to build a seemingly irresistible momentum in the U.S. Congress.

By April 1933, Roosevelt had ignored the shorter-hour "thunder from the left" as long as he could. After the Senate passed the 30-hour bill without major modification on April 6, reports were widely circulated that should the House version of the bill (introduced by William Connery of Massachusetts) reach the floor, it would pass with little opposition.[19] Ernest K. Lindley characterized these developments as a "revolution boiling up from the bottom."[20]

Roosevelt, prodded to action, directed Secretary of Labor Frances Perkins to draft an administration response. In the meantime, Speaker of the House Henry T. Rainey vowed that the House would hold back the "hotheads" in the Senate and "wait till all of the president's reconstruction legislation [was] passed" before the 30-hour proposal was taken up.[21] At the same time, Senator Trammell introduced a motion in the Senate to reconsider the bill's import bans, further stalling the bill.[22]

With a few days' leeway, Perkins prepared the administration's position. After a Cabinet meeting on April 12, Perkins and Secretary of Commerce Daniel C. Roper announced the administration's support of the 30-hour legislation with some adjustments: "to make it flexible and workable."[23] Perkins proposed that provisions for a minimum wage should be included, as well as stronger production controls, over and above simple reduction of hours. Perkins and Roper also reported that Roosevelt opposed the import-ban provision and would try to have it removed. But, bowing to political realities, the administration accepted the basic purpose of the Black bill: to reduce unemployment by reducing work hours "across the board" for as many workers as possible.

On April 13, Perkins appeared before the House Labor Committee to endorse the 30-hour principle and present the administration's modifications and additions. Afterward, she announced that the committee and the administration were largely in agreement and that she would "clear the way for passage." The main point of controversy was the import ban, which the House committee steadfastly supported.[24] These developments prompted the *New York Times* and other newspapers to predict prompt passage of the bill by the House and Roosevelt's signature within the month. William Green, after his visit with Perkins and Roper, was quoted as saying that passage and signing were sure things and that the nation was days away from a 30-hour week.[25]

This series of events, labor's legislative initiative, the building political support for work sharing, the passage of the Black bill in the Senate, and Roosevelt's endorsement, persuaded observers that shorter hours had become inevitable. For example, among the technocrats' most confident predictions in 1933 were that hours of work would continue to decline, as they had for over a hundred years, and that before this century was half over, less than 660 hours per year would be required of the average worker—fewer than 14 hours a week. But Technocracy Inc.'s chief, Howard Scott, and his lieutenants M. King Hubbert and Harold Loeb, were hardly alone in this expectation, and it is understandable that they would predict what many others assumed at the time was simple common sense. Such figures as George Bernard Shaw and Julian Huxley had made similar predictions.[26] In comparison with Huxley's view that a 2-hour day was in the offing, the technocrats seemed restrained and conservative. Few other historical trends were as clear in the early years of the depression as the trend toward shorter hours in American industry, and even in the world economy. Few indeed were those prescient enough to foresee that the century-long movement had reached a turning point in 1933 and that the process would suddenly reverse, with hours of work getting longer for a decade and then remaining stable.[27]

If what technocrats and engineers saw from their point of view was convincing, from the perspective of a professional historian of the 1930s, a Charles Beard or a Marion Cahill, the shorter-hour movement was even more impressive, and its prospects surer.[28] Predictions that on the surface seemed obvious, in greater, historical depth proved founded on solid fact. Looking back, the historians saw in the statistical record the steady decline of work hours throughout the nineteenth century. This decline had accelerated during the first dozen years of this century and then had plummeted a record 8 percent from 1913 to 1920. Even though hours had stabilized for the first time in the 1920s, at 49 per week, that brief hiatus had ended with the stock market crash, and hours had started to drop again at their fastest rate—down to an average of less than 33 by 1933. From the statistical record, the obvious conclusion was not merely that the shortening of hours of labor was a continual process, but that the process was accelerating. Record decline in hours worked had been following record decline.[29]

But more than numbers were involved. Historians in the 1930s knew full well that shorter hours had been the central concern of organized labor during its formative years (the 1820s and 1830s), and had remained one of labor's two most important goals. The other, higher wages, had been more frequently mentioned in conjunction with shorter hours by union leaders. The two had become a team and had gone together, the one supporting the other, like horse and carriage. And in the depression years, when labor was beginning to emerge as a national force to be reckoned with, its interest in shorter hours had intensified. Labor was now taking a militant stand for national 30-hour legislation as a necessary depression measure; it was a stand accompanied by dramatic threats of a "universal strike" if legislation was not passed and passed soon.

The issue of shorter hours, then, for years a centerpiece of American reform, ignored by the Republicans in the 1920s, now, in the dawn of the New Deal, in the "rendezvous with destiny," seemed bound to come more fully into its own. Historians had seldom had stronger reasons to risk predicting the future from the perspective of the past.

This, then, was the series of events that historians in 1933 witnessed. These events were what led prominent men and women to expect as reasonable what utopian writers in the nineteenth century had contemplated only in a fantasy world: progressively shorter hours, the withering away of work, and the birth of a new kind of progress in the free realm of humane leisure. Rhetorical climates, historical trend lines, and political realities—all pointed to shorter hours. Those who once tried to save work from leisure's erosion— businessmen and conservative politicians—seemed to have realized their error, put away their gospel of consumption (which in fact had been one of the causes of too much production), and come to serve the cause. Finally, weekly work time had decreased 15 hours in less than four years, and prospects were great for another, immediate 3-hour legislated reduction. Surely the prediction of the 14-hour week was reasonable; even Julian Huxley's 2-hour day seemed not too extreme.

Why were these people so wrong in their predictions? Why, just at the moment when the shorter-hour process seemed irresistible and to be gaining strength, in the spring of 1933, did hours of labor reach their lowest point and begin to increase? Why does the technocrats' augury seem strange now when, even in retrospect, the historical case for their claim appears strong? What might have given away the events to come—the end of shorter hours and the resurrection of work?

There were, in fact, hazards in the shorter-hour issue's open waters and clear sailing, reefs that might have foretold things to come to the gifted seer. Among these hazards were Roosevelt's lukewarm endorsement of 30 hours, his behind-the-scenes manipulation of the bill in Senate committees and on the House floor, his firm opposition to import limitations, and finally the opposition building within the administration and in the business world. These were the surface tips of submerged political and public opposition that was to emerge, challenge the shorter-hour process, topple it from prominence, and set in its place rival solutions to the depression and a new definition of progress: the American's "right to work" a "full-time job."

A careful reader of business periodicals could have detected business's growing alarm. Even though most businessmen and industrialists supported the Teagle campaign in September and October, they began to draw back by December 1932, after which their support for shorter hours was more apparent than real. Teagle found himself defending his campaign against business charges that it was "communist inspired," especially when he began to suggest that the voluntary establishment of 30 hours might be a long-term but necessary response to the depression. Because he alienated a number of business supporters, and because of the Black bill's momentum, the National Chamber of Commerce shelved Teagle's program early in 1933.[30]

Thereupon, the Chamber of Commerce and the National Association of Manufacturers conducted what amounted to a rhetorical share-the-work movement, designed more to castigate "cutthroat" competition by firms, especially in the South, that worked their employees more than 40 hours. A Chamber of Commerce committee headed by P. W. Litchfield, president of Goodyear Tire, issued a call in early April for a maximum workweek of not less than 40 hours and warned that trying to legislate for fewer hours might have disastrous results (e.g., such an emergency measure might become permanent).[31] Since the National Industrial Conference Board had already reported that the average workweek was 32.2 hours and somewhat sarcastically pointed out that "reducing" the workweek to 40 hours would have little impact on unemployment, observers concluded that the Chamber of Commerce had turned to the regulation of hours as a method to regulate competition, not as a means to create jobs. Other journalists felt that such rhetoric was a ruse to deflect political support from 30-hour legislation.[32]

But many businessmen, and people whom the *New York Times* called "trade association executives," simply ignored political realities and blithely assumed that the Black bill was too radical to have any chance in Congress or with the President. Even after Senate passage, many businessmen thought that Congress was bluffing—trying to force Roosevelt to act and reveal his recovery program. Others, more realistic and more fearful, took some comfort in the fact that the Supreme Court would very likely find the law unconstitutional if it ever was signed by the President.[33]

Just before Senate passage of the Black bill, a North American Newspaper Alliance survey showed industry divided on the bill but with an increasing majority in opposition to it. Representative opinions were expressed by Alvan McCauley, president of Packard Motors and chairman of the Detroit Chamber of Commerce, who argued that because overhead and capital costs were fixed, any plan that would reduce production–overhead ratios presented grave dangers to industry. Others, such as the National Council of American Importers, maintained that the bills's import restrictions constituted a new and ruinous obstacle to commerce and were bound to set off new international trade wars. Still others pointed out that seasonal and farm occupations—canning, the dairy industry, and cotton ginning—could not operate under the 30-hour constraint. This sort of down-to-earth reasoning appealed to Roosevelt, who stated: "There have to be hours adapted to the rhythm of the cow."[34]

But the overriding concern reported by this survey was that this piece of legislation might result in hours of work stabilizing permanently at then current levels or below. Numerous business people who were fully content to support a voluntary and temporary share-the-work movement were horrified by the prospect that the workweek might never recover from the depression, that the Black bill might set shorter hours rigidly in place. Instead of looking at the increase in leisure as inevitable or as potentially beneficial, business people tended to equate recovery with the restoration of work and work hours—if not to the pre-1929 level of 49 hours, then at least to a standard 8-hour day, five days a week. Nevertheless, some continued to support share the work and to look the other way as the Black bill built support.[35]

After the Senate passed the Black bill, the House gave every indication that it would follow suit and Roosevelt, through Perkins, endorsed the 30-hour principle, business opposition solidified so much that Hugh S. Johnson observed that economists, businessmen, and industrialists "would turn back-hand somersaults against the thirty hour week."[36]

Businessmen held emergency meetings in Philadelphia, Chicago, and other cities. Talk of "chaos and disaster" filled the air.[37] James Emery, counsel for the NAM, testified that the bill "excites anxiety throughout American Industry as a rigid and highly centralized regulation not of commerce but of production."[38] Perkins reported that after she had testified before the Labor committee, "a flood" of objections and requests for exemptions inundated her office.[39] The *New York Times* bristled with indignant letters and sarcastic editorials. *Newsweek* announced: "Thirty Hour Week Startles Nation."[40]

CHAPTER 6

FDR Counters
Shorter Hours

THERE WAS surprise and some consternation within the administration at the vehement opposition to shorter-hour legislation. Raymond Moley remembered that "the Perkins substitute proved almost
as great a shock to employers as the Black bill itself. Perkins and FDR
were aghast at the commotion it caused."[1]

Understandably, Roosevelt and his advisers had misjudged the
political opposition to the Black–Connery bills. Roosevelt had made
attempts to deal with the issue earlier and to lay the groundwork for
legislated shorter hours. For example, at Perkins's and Felix Frankfurter's prompting, he had tried to get individual states to pass laws
limiting hours of work to 35 a week. At the Governors Conference on
March 6, 1933, the matter was brought up, and on April 11 Roosevelt
sent a message to the governors of major industrial states pressing
them to regulate hours and wages on the state level as a constitutionally
more legitimate measure than national legislation. Moreover, Perkins
was a staunch advocate of limits on hours and wages and made such a
policy a precondition to agreeing to be secretary of labor.[2]

In addition, Roosevelt had tried to come to grips politically with
the Black bill behind the scenes. He had instructed Senate Majority
Leader Robinson of Arkansas to attempt to substitute a 36-hour provision for the 30 hours. The consensus at the White House, even
among shorter-hour supporters, was that 30 hours was too extreme.
Although the 36-hour amendment failed, Roosevelt's other contribution, an amendment limiting the law to a two-year trial period,
was successful. Roosevelt expected that this amendment would satisfy most business critics, even if the legislation retained the 30-hour

baseline. After all, business opinion had been divided until the eve of Perkins's endorsement. Even though the tide was flowing against the bill, prominent industrialists such as Fred Chapin and Frederick Rentschler, chairman of Pratt and Whitney, still supported it as "the most constructive plan yet advanced . . . a great aid to recovery," and influential groups such as the Associated Grocery Manufacturers were willing to compromise and give it a try.[3]

Moreover, it had been businessmen who suggested and promoted some of the more creative ways to share the work. For example, Edward A. Filene, a member of the influential Paul Raushenbush group, had argued that the $500 million being considered for public works by Congress should be diverted to indemnify employers for possible losses resulting from a 30-hour law, a course that would, in his estimation, "reduce unemployment faster than public works" and by itself help "start up" the economy. Other businessmen had promoted Nobel Laureate Irving Langmuir's plan to tax work time over 30 hours a week, a constitutional use of federal taxing power that would get around the legal objections concerning direct hours legislation.[4]

Hence the great outcry after the Perkins endorsement put Roosevelt on the defensive and set him and his advisers looking for ways to placate the opposition. At first, Perkins tried to work out some compromise within the framework of the Black and Connery bills. In addition to the minimum-wage and regulation-of-production amendments, she floated proposals for greater executive control of hours and wages in order to reduce the 30-hour bill's rigid provisions; control would be administered through her office with operations delegated to a three-person board. These proposals set off new protests and accusations that Perkins wanted to control all of American business out of Washington. Perkins, "amused and astonished" that her efforts to reconcile factions and make the Black bill "flexible and workable" had been so misunderstood, tried to explain that she only wanted to make it possible to set hours over 30 and up to 40; she added, somewhat apologetically, "Please remember that the Black Bill is limited to two years."[5]

But a change in the administration position was evident in the emphasis Perkins began to place on minimum wages and flexible regulation of hours by federal boards. A week after she endorsed the 30-hour principle, she downplayed it as an unemployment remedy in itself, referring to it, with disapproval, as "compulsory share-the-work." Instead, using the same words and phrases businessmen had used to distance themselves from the Teagle proposals, she began to stress the necessity of preventing "cutthroat" competition by firms that set hours above "reasonable levels." By stopping "chiselers" from engaging in unfair practices, some new jobs would be created, especially in such "sweatshop" industries as cotton textiles. But job creation through work sharing "across the board," the major rationale for labor's bill, was given less emphasis.[6]

At the same time, Perkins stressed the importance of minimum wages. She pointed out that minimum wages would help stop the erosion of incomes and contribute an immediate boost to the economy. She also suggested that as the economy rebounded, hours should return to "normal." Minimum wages would then act as a long-term economic stimulant, an advantage impossible under the inflexible Black bill as originally proposed. The administration had begun to understand shorter hours primarily as a way to stabilize industry and to look for other measures for industrial recovery.

But by mid-April, Roosevelt's administration had managed to tie itself firmly to the 30-hour bill, so much so that the press was referring to it as the Black–Perkins proposal. Roosevelt and Perkins found it increasingly difficult to explain to business why their backing for the Black bill was not support of "compulsory work sharing," and to argue simultaneously to labor that their many modifications of the strict 30-hour provision would create enough new jobs.[7]

Meanwhile, Roosevelt and his advisers were struggling to put together a comprehensive recovery program. Immediately following the Perkins endorsement of the Black bill, opposition to 30 hours and the principle of work sharing built strength within the administration. Several members of the so-called Wagner group objected to it. Harold Moulton of the Brookings Institution, more than any other, was opposed and devoted more time to discounting the "shorter hour solution to unemployment."[8] Donald Richberg and Alexander Sachs, using the same phrase, described the bill as "sharing the poverty . . . and fundamentally unsound," and Richberg reported that "many in the administration" agreed with his point of view.[9] Rexford Tugwell, while conceding that shorter hours might have to be used to limit production in "extreme cases," observed that if "we shall have to resort permanently to limitation of hours . . . [this] would not be progress . . . it would be an admission that we have created a Frankenstein which we are unable to master."[10] Raymond Moley was careful to distance himself from the Perkins substitute, recalling that he had "had nothing to do with it." He thought the whole idea "utterly impractical."[11]

As assistant secretary of state, Moley began work on proposals that had been accumulating in his office and contacted business leaders to find out what could be done to minimize the Black bill's potential damage. Alternative suggestions soon began to emerge from Moley's office in the form of a remarkably early and accurate *New York Times* report by Louis Stark. On April 14, Stark reported that the "administration's plans for changes in the Black bill" constituted a "mobilization of industry." Senator Wagner had told Stark that the administration was considering federal regulatory agencies, similar to the old war boards, that would help "stabilize industry, . . . quicken and regulate it, . . . protect it against losses, . . . and rebuild, not just hold the line." Stark also reported that Roosevelt was considering an enlarged public works program as "a key to revival and industrial expansion" to be added as an amendment to the Black bill.[12]

Through April, pressure mounted in the Senate among Roosevelt's strongest supporters for passage of such a public works program. Led by Senators Wagner, La Follette, and Costigan, and supported by members of the Cabinet and Brain Trust, backers of a public works program vied with supporters of 30-hour legislation in Congress, trying to turn the Black bill, its momentum and support, to their own purposes. At a White House conference held on April 15, these senators met with Cabinet officers and issued a statement to the press. They asserted that together with a $2 billion public works program, the minimum-wage provision added to the Black bill would eliminate the necessity for 30 hours or any general reduction of working hours. The senators agreed with administration representatives at the conference that all the "essential features" and "major goals" of the Black bill could be "effectively embodied" in public works legislation, increases in the Reconstruction Finance Corporation (RFC), and the expanded relief efforts provided by the Wagner bill.[13]

The conference concluded that 30-hour legislation was impractical and observed further that even the flexible regulation of hours between 30 and 40 could not stand by itself. Such regulation had to be part of an overall strategy for recovery in order to make any sense. To be sure, the President's efforts to "prime the economic pump and add the necessary stimulus for recovery" included stabilization of the economy, one aspect of which was control of hours and production. But, as Wagner observed, "domestic programs," public works, and aggressive "negotiations with foreign nations" to "restore foreign trade . . . [were] necessary for complete economic recovery." And this complete recovery program included not only the curtailment of unemployment but also involved the restoration of "normal working hours." Newspapers quoted administration officials, who called these conference proposals a new "national work program."[14]

Added to the opposition mounting in the Senate and within the White House, and to the pressure to amend 30 hours out of existence in the House of Representatives, the State Department began rumblings on its own. The unwillingness of Representative Connery, chairman of the House Labor Committee, and other committee members to compromise on the Black bill's import limitations alienated a number of people, including Cordell Hull, who looked forward to a reduction of trade barriers and freeing and expanding foreign trade to help end the American and world depression.[15]

Hence, within two weeks of Perkins's endorsement of 30 hours, the skeleton of Roosevelt's recovery program emerged as suggested additions and amendments to the Black bill. Moley described these as "a hodgepodge of provisions [to] stimulate industry and [for] business-government planning . . . to satisfy the forces behind the Black bill." Included in the list were public works, stimulation of spending through wage minimums, regulation of industry by federal boards, and more liberal commercial policies.[16]

Through mid-April, Perkins tried to work with the House committee to restructure the Black bill, struggling on her own, increasingly without the aid of administration leaders, who would have nothing to do with 30 hours. Led by Connery and Welch from California, the committee resisted her efforts. They were willing to accept a three-person board in the Department of Labor, regulating maximum hours up to and even over 40 hours a week and a minimum wage, but they would do so only if the administration would "withdraw its objections to the inclusion of foreign products" in import bans. This was something Roosevelt and the State Department would not do.[17]

Trouble also arose for Perkins from labor, which continued to oppose the addition of minimum wages. Matthew Woll, for example, accused Roosevelt of trying to make "serfs" out of American workers by telling them how much they could make and what kind of work they should be doing.[18] Labor leaders also held steadfast to the 30-hour principle and opposed making the proposed legislation flexible, reasoning, as they had always done, that the only way to control overproduction and reduce unemployment was to limit hours by law—to reduce work time for the majority of workers, not just regulate hours for the relatively few who were "overworked."[19]

Finally, in response to Perkins's attempts to turn the Black bill into an administration vehicle and blunt the 30-hour provision, the House committee suggested that the administration gather together all the amendments they were offering the committee and present them to Congress as a separate administration bill—let the Black and Connery bills stand on their own, on the 30-hour principle.[20]

Roosevelt, his advisers and Cabinet, then broke with the 30-hour bill and its share-the-work rationale and began work on a National Industrial Recovery Act (NIRA) to replace the Black and Connery bills and Perkins's revisions of them. On May 1, Senate Majority Leader

"Ding" Darling was a popular and influential newspaper cartoonist during the time that the issue of shorter hours was at the center of American public and political attention, from just before World War I until after World War II. Drawing for the *New York Herald Tribune* and the *Des Moines Register*, Jay Norwood Darling left behind a thirty-year record of the issue. Although he was generally opposed to shorter hours, his cartoons still have some of the flavor of the vanished debates concerning work reduction. The original captions and year of publication appear with each of those reprinted here. The author gratefully acknowledges permission granted by The University of Iowa Libraries, Iowa City, Iowa, to reproduce these cartoons.

What Again?
1916

Speaking
of Working
Overtime!
1919

*The Business
Manager's
Nightmare,
1919*

*When the
Eight Hour
Day Meets
Work on
the Home
Grounds,
1922*

*The New
Command-
ment, 1926*

*Hi Ho for
the Six Hour
Day, 1933*

*A Great Day
for Labor,
1933*

*Never Quite
Catches Up,
1937*

*Wages and
Hours and
Hours and
Hours, 1938*

*Quitting
Time, 1940*

Unlimited Emergency —With Reservations, 1941

The U.S. Census Is a Great Disappointment, 1941

Robinson reported that the Black bill was no longer "part of the President's program," a report that Connery attacked the next day as misleading.[21] But Hugo Black, aware of the change in administration policy, countered in the Senate by introducing an amendment to a Washington, D.C., appropriations bill to prohibit government purchases from industries that worked their employees more than 30 hours (the amendment died in committee).[22] The same day, Speaker of the House Henry Rainey confirmed that Roosevelt had withdrawn his support, and Robinson reiterated that the Black–Perkins bill was "not now on the administration's schedule."[23] Rainey, after having blocked the bill's progress for four weeks, then expressed his willingness to allow the bill to reach the floor, confident that House members would wait for the Roosevelt replacement before moving on the 30-hour bill. By May 12, Connery was reported to have given up, conceding his bill to Roosevelt's.[24]

But Roosevelt attempted to hold the political forces behind the Black bill together and marshall their support behind his bill. The AFL's support was among the most problematic. Roosevelt met with Green on April 29 and May 2, and laid out parts of the NIRA for him. Gradually, Green and other labor officials were persuaded, lured by Section 7a's provisions guaranteeing union organization and collective bargaining and outlawing yellow-dog contracts. The addition of public works sweetened the deal. Green speculated that the $5 billion figure mentioned for public works would reemploy millions. With these concessions, the AFL was willing to accept vague provisions in Section 7a of the bill about reductions in hours that would come eventually when industrial and labor leaders worked with the new federal boards to write industrial codes. Labor also withdrew its veto of the minimum wage, having Roosevelt's assurance that this regulation would not replace collective bargaining (and even though labor was not successful in having "union scale" wages used as the baseline to set industry minimums). Thus labor, succumbing to Roosevelt's political charm and acumen, fell in line behind the NIRA and temporarily withdrew pressure for the 30-hour legislation. But Green and other union leaders took a wait-and-see attitude, holding 30 hours in reserve, ready to employ it again if the NIRA did not live up to expectations. Even while praising Section 7a and public works, Green insisted that "thirty hours [was] imperatively necessary."[25]

Business, with the threat of 30 hours hanging over its head, fell raggedly into line as well. With the notable exception of the NAM, which remained opposed, the business community supported the NIRA. On May 3, Moley, Hugh Johnson, and Tugwell met with representatives of the national Chamber of Commerce in Washington and worked out an acceptable compromise. The chamber's original proposal, which had been submitted to Moley in April, envisioned, as Harriman put it, "an appropriate government agency . . . empowered to approve agreements entered into voluntarily by the majority within an industry."[26] In other words, Harriman had proposed industrial self-government backed up by federal law. But the chamber was ready to compromise and accept the principle of federal partnership. The chamber also was willing to accept Section 7a with its concessions to labor as the only workable compromise with labor—the only way to turn the tide behind the Black–Connery bills. Harriman, relieved at escaping the 30-hour threat, was moved to eloquence, calling Roosevelt's program the *"Magna Carta* for American industry and labor."[27]

With his political house in some degree of order, Roosevelt presented the National Industrial Recovery Act (NIRA) to Congress on May 15, 1933. The bill was in two parts. The first part was designed to "promote the organization of industry for the purpose of cooperative action among trade groups," to control what Roosevelt called "unfair . . . cut-throat competition by selfish competitors." By the establishment of industrywide codes, "unfair competition [which had led to] disastrous overproduction" would be replaced by industrial cooperation under the supervision and, if need be, the threat of new government agencies.[28] Section 7a, the labor section, contained provisions for union organization and collective bargaining, the prohibition of yellow-dog contracts, and the setting of minimum wages and maximum hours. The second part of the bill provided for public works projects funded at $3.3 billion and designed to provide work relief and act as a stimulant to industrial activity. The stimulation would take effect as industry, stabilized under codes, was readied for recovery.[29]

The NIRA was a compromise. As such, it represented a collection of approaches to industrial stabilization, relief, and recovery. The issue of shorter hours was included, but competing programs had been formulated and set in place. These programs were to grow and finally replace the use of shorter hours as an employment strategy. To be sure, shorter hours remained an important part of the National Recovery Administration (NRA) until its end in 1935, largely because labor kept constant pressure on the administration. Moreover, traces of the political effectiveness of this measure may be found in Social Security, the National Youth Administration, and the Fair Labor Standards Act. But this solution to unemployment reached its high-water mark in the NRA during the winter of 1934–1935; from there, its fortunes receded along with the decline of the NRA and the belief within the administration in the Berl–Johnson doctrine of economic maturity.

Shorter hours faced competition from at least three kinds of programs represented by the NIRA. First, within Title I of the NIRA, and in the NRA as it was administered, various programs vied with reductions in hours: the "buy now" consumer campaign, the regulation of production–consumption by codes, limits placed on times that machines could be run and times of factory operation, and stabilization of industry by administered wages and prices. Each measure represented an alternative way to regulate production and jobs in a "mature" economy. In addition, public works grew to become a more effective competitor, as did its principle of creating new work by direct government spending and federal programs. Finally, alternatives to the notion of limited production in a "managed" economy, represented in their initial stage as Roosevelt's efforts to use the NRA to "restore the domestic market" (promoting production and consumption instead of limiting them), increasingly challenged shorter hours, branding the issue as a regressive limit to progress. With the coming of the "second New Deal," policies designed to stimulate economic growth overshadowed this century-long reform.

Presenting the NIRA to Congress on May 17, Roosevelt's opening words were: "My first request is that Congress provide for the machinery necessary for a great cooperative movement throughout all industry in order to obtain wide reemployment, to shorten the working week, to pay a decent wage for the shorter week and prevent unfair competition and disastrous overproduction." [30] This and similar statements appeared to support work sharing. But in reality, reacting against the widespread public and political enthusiasm the measure had aroused, the Roosevelt administration began to deemphasize share the work from the start of the NRA. Even though Roosevelt spoke of shorter hours and reemployment together, and while he used the rhetorical forms of the 30-hour forces, his emphasis was different and his meaning altered. After his May 17 recommendation, he appended a note to his statement, pointing out what he really intended. He admitted that in May he had agreed that "if the hours of labor for the individual could be shortened . . . more people could be employed," and he recognized that "this was in line with the plank in the Democratic National Platform of 1932 which advocated 'the spread of employment by a substantial reduction in the hours of labor.'" Nevertheless, he contrasted the "previous administration's" efforts to share the work with his own, which he called an "effort to increase and spread the work." As the NRA moved forward, his meaning became clear. He expected to deal with unemployment by creating new jobs: "I also aim to provide further purchasing power by a large program of direct employment by means of $3,300,000,000 of public works" and by stimulating additional hirings in industry. Simply redistributing a stable amount of work would have been sharing the poverty, something Hoover had been guilty of.[31]

Moreover, Roosevelt, in masterful style, began to talk about something else when he used the same words as the share-the-work forces. Like Frances Perkins, he changed the emphasis from shorter hours for everyone to shorter hours for the few: the "overworked," those in "sweatshops," who worked longer than 48 hours a week and 12 hours a day. "Slackers and chiselers" who worked their employees such ridiculously long hours to gain an unfair, competitive advantage had to be brought to heel. Preventing such practices would create some jobs. But such regulations would have the more important advantage of stabilizing industry in preparation for recovery.[32]

Commenting further on the purposes of the NRA, Roosevelt observed on June 16: "The act gives employment through a vast program of public works. We should be able to hire many men at once and be able to step up to about a million new jobs by October 1st and a much greater number later. . . . *Our first purpose is to create employment as fast as we can.*"[33] In this "To Put People Back to Work" speech, Roosevelt did mention the shorter-hour strategy: "the idea . . . for employees to hire more men to do the existing work by reducing the working hours of each man's week."[34] But he was clearly more interested in public works and business expansion. He stressed that "the aim of this whole effort is to restore our rich domestic market by raising its vast consuming capacity . . . the pent-up demand of this people is very great and if we can release it on so broad a front, we need not fear a lagging recovery."[35]

This trend toward deemphasizing share the work continued during the initial stages of the NRA and the creation of the first industrial codes. In theory, the code-making authority was divided between labor, industry, and "consumers." In practice, trade associations, led mostly by their largest members, dominated the code-writing process. Consequently, industrywide reductions in working hours with the same weekly pay were seen as liabilities from the start, even more unacceptable than the minimum wage and sure to drive up production costs and inflate prices. The issue of shorter hours was circumvented, ignored, or used more for industrial regulation than to create jobs.

The first code was written for cotton textiles and submitted to Johnson in July. It was one of the more effective codes of the NRA and actually had a temporary impact in an industry where long hours were common. Southern textile mills in particular were given to low wages, to requiring workers to put in 58 or more hours a week, and to child labor. Large firms in the Northeast felt the competitive pressure and were quite happy to limit these practices, especially since the code provisions had little impact on their businesses. Hence the first NRA code "reduced" weekly hours in textiles to 40, setting what turned out to be the standard for the NRA.[36]

Meanwhile, businessmen and trade associations were continuing to oppose industrywide reductions in hours, turning a deaf ear to Johnson's radio plea in June for a standard 32-hour maximum and $14.40 weekly minimum wage for unskilled industrial workers. Since the interregnum, businessmen such as Harriman had held fast to the 40-hour "minimum maximum," even when Roosevelt was trying to get the trade associations to give in to 30 hours in exchange for suspension of antitrust laws. Thus most of the other codes coming into Johnson's office by mid-July were patterned after textiles' 40-hour week.[37]

Labor realized that if trade associations continued to control the code-making process as they had in textiles, 40 hours would prevail. Apprehensive about this and trying to improve on their poor showing in textiles, labor leaders launched a counteroffensive for 30 hours in mid-July. The AFL and William Green chose the public hearings being held concerning the bituminous coal industry to begin a "drive by all the unions in the federation in support of the miners' demand for the thirty-hour week." Green insisted that even though labor had reluctantly "acceded" to the textile code of 40 hours, this should not be seen as a precedent. For Green and the AFL, the "primary purpose of the Industrial Recovery Act is to overcome unemployment through a reduction in the number of hours and through an increase in wages. The slack of unemployment cannot be taken up until hours are reduced." For Green, "the time had arrived . . . when the six-hour day and five-day-week should be included in all codes." Accordingly, the AFL planned to dominate the public hearing on soft-coal codes so that the recovery administration would have no choice but to grant 30 hours. *Newsweek* reported: "Labor Opens War for Its 30-Hour Week."[38]

This new initiative was a major factor in stalling the code-making process in July; industrial representatives were not about to give in to such demands. With the bituminous coal industry codes deadlocked and no progress made on other major industrial fronts, Johnson tried to set things moving again, turning to blanket codes. Following labor's 30-hour offensive, a meeting was held in Washington by the Industrial, Labor and Consumer Advisory committee that Johnson had recently set up. This group worked out a plan for a blanket wage-and-hour code, which Johnson unveiled on July 21.[39] Within days, 5 million copies of the President's Re-employment Agreement (PRA) were sent out. To make sure of distribution, postmen were instructed to hand out copies to everyone on their route who employed more than two people. Johnson had convinced Roosevelt to moderate his position on work sharing, arguing that since the code-making process had stalled and labor was up in arms about the likelihood of a 40-hour standard, the time had arrived to launch the PRA with a "wartime publicity campaign to induce employees to subscribe voluntarily."[40]

The PRA included provisions for 35 hours and a $14 weekly wage, and was the high-water mark for shorter hours. Accompanied by the ballyhoo of the "Blue Eagle," the effort to share the work through the NRA came nearest to being realized.[41] For a while, concern grew about the management of the new leisure time that would result. Some reasoned that since the NRA was responsible for creating a vast amount of free time, it should take responsibility for the provision of necessary recreational facilities and services. This concern reached its zenith in the autumn and winter with a series of meetings in New York City called by the NRA's state offices in New York, which had organized a Committee on the Use of Leisure Time. The meetings received national attention in the press, partly because they brought together such well-known people as Raymond B. Fosdick (president of the committee), Nicholas Murray Butler, Alfred Smith, and Matthew Woll, and partly because of the seeming incongruity of such concern with leisure, play, and recreation in the midst of the financial distress of New York City.[42]

But the Blue Eagle did more than arouse interest in the problem of leisure. In fact, the PRA seemed for a time to be a rousing success. Thousands of responses were returned to Washington, and the campaign to get the codes accepted from the bottom up, from small employers to large, seemed to be working. Johnson, with some new leverage, was able to get the code-making process back on track for major industries, at least for a while. Shipyards signed a 36-minimum-hour and 35- to 45-cent-minimum-wage code; this was followed in less than six weeks by the automobile industry. Talking bluntly to auto representatives in early August, Johnson hammered out a code with 35 maximum hours and a 40-cent minimum wage (which Henry Ford refused to sign). Thus the influence of the PRA on shorter-hour code provisions was felt at least into the first two weeks of August. Administration officials also claimed that the Blue Eagle had a direct impact on hours and wages. Since thousands had signed the PRA pledge to limit weekly hours to 35, Johnson reasoned that the share-the-work principle was operating nationwide on this voluntary basis, serving as a sterling example for major industries that were slow to reach code agreements.[43]

But by late August, the momentum the PRA had built up for the NRA's version of share the work had dissipated. Codes drawn up for the lumber, steel, and oil industries reverted to textile's 40-hour standard. Subsequently, of the 557 basic and 208 supplementary codes written from September 1933 to February 1934, most had (Section 7a) provisions for 40 or more hours per week.[44]

Notwithstanding the PRA's voluntary standard of 35 hours maximum and $14 weekly minimum, NRA codes for major industries reduced actual working hours in only a few cases (e.g., cotton textiles and mining) where hours were extremely long—over 48 a week. Even though these few codes were important and highly visible, the vast majority of major industrial codes set maximum hours well above then-current averages. Typically, industrial associations used wages as an excuse; they pointed out that wages and hours were mutually exclusive: The more of one that an industry had to give up to its workers, the less of the other was possible. Providing both at the same time was sure to inflate prices on all goods and services. In order to keep wages from falling farther and allow for noninflationary increases in weekly wages, industrialists argued that the 40-hour maximum was essential.[45]

Over 90 percent of the NRA codes set hours at 40 a week or longer at a time when the actual average workweek in American industry was well under 36 hours. A case-by-case evaluation shows that the average workweek in particular industries was longer than the code maximum only 14 percent of the time in the early months of the NRA, ranging to a high of 18 percent at its end. Moreover, during the life of the NRA, actual hours (seasonally adjusted) in industries covered by the codes increased in most cases, up an average of 3 percent from 1933 to 1935. In those few industries that experienced a decline in work hours, most had average workweeks below 37 hours with a code maximum of 40 or more, so the codes could hardly be said to have been a major factor in these declines.[46]

Labor was well aware of the trend toward a 40-hour standard and was troubled by the NRA's obvious inability or unwillingness to reduce work hours substantially, and by the failure of the PRA. The AFL's July offensive for 30 hours having run out of steam by September, the union began to demand immediate code revisions. In a speech before the building trades unions, Green pointed out that "after we have gone through with the preliminary codes we will have to go through them again in order to bring about a reduction in the hours of every code . . . so that these codes will square with the spirit of the Industrial Recovery Act," adding, "we can't put people back to work on a forty hour week."[47]

Green pointed out that unless things changed in the NRA and such code revisions were undertaken, labor would be forced to renew its push for 30-hour legislation. In a speech before the Metal Trades

Department of the AFL in September, Green issued what news reporters called "a virtual ultimatum to the recovery administration" in a strongly worded attack on the NRA and a call for reintroduction of the Black–Connery bills.[48]

The AFL convention in Washington, D.C., in October and November repeated Greens demands. This convention was marked by a new sense within labor of its political power. Delegates resolved to "abandon [labor's] non-partisan political policy" and work to elect candidates who would support labor's interests, regardless of party affiliation. Some AFL members even called for the establishment of an "independent labor party"; the first items on the agenda of such a party would be 30 hours, followed by Social Security legislation and unemployment insurance. Although suggestions about a third party were forgotten, this list of issues survived through 1935 as labor's political program and was used as a test for candidates in both the 1934 congressional elections and the 1936 presidential contest.[49]

By January 1934, labor had contacted its supporters in Congress and had begun to organize its legislative forces. William P. Connery issued a call for code revisions, and some of labor's other congressional backers attacked the way that business and industry dominated the code-making process. Hugh Johnson was forced to admit that the codes' standards on hours would have to be revised across the board in order to deal with unemployment.[50] But neither labor nor William Connery was impressed by Johnson's assurances. On January 24, Connery introduced a bill in the House of Representatives to set the NRA code hours at 30 a week.[51]

At first, because of labor's growing political power and the support behind this new version of Connery's bill in the House, the Roosevelt administration was somewhat receptive to labor's renewed share-the-work effort. Following discussions with Perkins and Connery in early February, Hugh Johnson released a trial balloon, suggesting that Roosevelt would promote *voluntary* reductions to 32 hours per week (four 8-hour days) under the codes.[52] Subsequently, Perkins actually endorsed Connery's bill and the 30-hour rule, in the process going well beyond Roosevelt's position on the issue.[53] Harry Hopkins, head of the Federal Relief Administration, testifying before the House committee on the Connery bill, was forced to agree that the codes were inadequate and that further reductions were advisable.[54] Similarly, Johnson's testimony that hours needed to be reduced reflected the administration's continued interest in the measure and willingness to try to amend the codes in labor's favor.[55]

Less than a week after the Perkins endorsement, however, the administration, through Johnson, issued a statement opposing the new Connery bill, arguing that it would hurt industry and stall the recent economic upturn.[56] This confusion within the administration had resulted from continuing divisions about how best to solve the unemployment problem. The Perkins and Johnson faction still believed that hours had to be reduced to relieve industrial surpluses and spread the available work. These were the administration forces that had supported the PRA and code revisions that actually reduced average working hours. But advisers such as Moulton, Henderson, and Leon Blaisdell were adamant that more production, not less, was needed and that only through economic growth could industry reabsorb the bulk of the unemployed. This faction in the administration was willing to accept a cap on hours that affected relatively few workers, but was dead set against any industrywide reductions.[57]

As the new Connery bill made its way through the House Labor Committee, opposition by business grew along with the administration's. By the time the bill was reported favorably out of committee in late May, Roosevelt had been convinced by his more conservative advisers to oppose the measure and put his trust in industrial growth and the continuing economic upturn. Opposing the Connery measure, the Chamber of Commerce and other businessmen reassured Roosevelt that industry would make every effort to find jobs for the unemployed and that the volume of business necessary for that goal was within reach. As the chamber pointed out, the economy was experiencing an "brisk upturn."[58] Indeed, in some of the more healthy industries, hours were getting longer as unemployment declined. Several business spokesmen equated the return of predepression wages with a return to predepression hours and viewed this as a sign of industrial recovery. Hugh Johnson was inclined to agree, pointing out that hourly wages were the multiplier and hours the multiplicand. According to George McNeir of Mohawk Carpet Mills, the only "serious cloud on the business horizon was the evident purpose of labor to continue agitation for the thirty-hour week."[59]

Without administration support, the new Connery bill was defeated on June 19, 1934. But with his opposition to the bill, Roosevelt placed himself in the position of siding with business and depending on continued and expanded growth of economic activity to reduce unemployment levels. Through the summer, however, unemployment remained high, and labor kept up the pressure. By mid-August 1934, shorter hours emerged as a key issue in the off-year congressional elections.[60]

In late August, business leaders tried to blunt the political forces building up for 30- and 32-hour weeks by mounting a campaign for the voluntary establishment of a 36-hour week in the NRA codes—

what amounted to a modified version of Roosevelt's February trial balloon. A number of key industrial association representatives met in Washington and agreed that the administration would be forced to grant broad concessions to labor after the election because "labor would be able to prove conclusively that it was responsible for any victories accruing to the Roosevelt candidates."[61] Realizing that they had left Roosevelt in a politically difficult position with their assurances in the spring that the economic upturn would reduce unemployment significantly by fall, these executives agreed that it was prudent to compromise at 36 hours before the election rather than be forced to endure 30 hours afterward.

These trade association representatives also thought that Roosevelt's recent executive order, cutting hours and raising wages in the cotton garment industry over the protests of the code authority, represented the beginning of a trend in the NRA toward "curtailment of hours in all industry." The Chamber of Commerce, joining the industrial trade group in calling for voluntary code reductions, agreed that Roosevelt was planning a general reduction in hours before the election to forestall 30-hour legislation.[62] Harvey Firestone of Firestone Tire and Rubber Company remarked gloomily that these developments surely meant that "shorter hours are here to stay: they will never go back to where they were."[63]

Adding fuel to these speculations, the AFL conducted a noisy convention in San Francisco in early October, stridently demanding the passage of the Black–Connery bill and threatening "universal," nationwide strikes if 30-hour legislation was held up any longer. Calling 30 hours the AFL's "paramount purpose," and noting the "disillusionment of labor with the workings of section 7a," William Green warned that "all congressional candidates were being asked to give their views on the Black–Connery bill and that these replies would be broadcast to the voters." The convention committed labor to "use all means at its disposal to gain the thirty hour week; economic and political." If the election did not return a Congress willing to grant this demand, then national strikes, what Green called "class war practically," would be the likely result.[64]

But just as the AFL convention was ending, the Chamber of Commerce issued a statement expressing its confidence that Roosevelt would oppose the unions. In marked contrast to their fevered efforts to compromise with labor on a 36-hour week in August, the chamber noted calmly that "renewed demands for a statutory thirty hour week will be made in the next Congress. Fortunately there is no evidence that the administration, which in the last session opposed [it], has changed its position. [The administration] feels with business that adjustments of hours of work should be made through the NRA." The chamber expressed its "high confidence" that Hugh Johnson's successors at the NRA, especially S. Clay Williams, the new NRA chairman, could be trusted to exercise the restraint on this measure that the administration had shown throughout 1934.[65]

The chamber had detected or been informed rightly that the so-called change in administration policy to general endorsement of industrywide share the work, so widely regarded in September as signaled by the 10 percent reduction in hours in cotton garments, was an illusion. Instead, Roosevelt held fast to the course set by the administration early in the summer—to the standard of 40 hours. Moreover, with the departure of Hugh Johnson from the NRA on September 27, a new leadership emerged that was much less interested in reductions in hours, wages, and production controls. Men such as Williams and Leon Henderson, legal adviser for the NRA, felt that "most of the NRA's energy should be concentrated on positive stimulants to greater productivity" and the "increasing volume of goods and services," which alone could end unemployment. Both Henderson and Thomas Blaisdell, head of the consumer division, questioned whether the codes had value any longer, since they were so widely ignored, and advised that the politically vital parts of the NRA, such as labor's right to organize and bargain collectively and the prohibition of yellow-dog contracts, should be written as specific laws.[66]

At this time, a set of proposals emerged from the Department of Agriculture; these proposals were alternatives to the NRA's existing policy of "co-coordinated scarcity." Led by the institutional economist Mordecai Ezekiel, the agricultural group offered a systematic federal program for "industrial expansion," which Henry Wallace presented to the Executive Council in October. In essence it was, as Ezekiel said, "AAA (Agricultural Adjustment Administration) in reverse." But instead of a program to limit farm production, this was a system to encourage industrial production with the federal government "balancing" the market forces of supply and demand, using AAA-like programs such as support prices and quotas. For example, Ezekiel proposed an "ever-normal warehouse" where industrial products would be held and released as the marketplace warranted. Such measures would allow and encourage industries to expand in an orderly, concerted fashion. This proposal in the form of an "Industrial Expansion Act," appealed to Wallace and others in the administration and found support in Congress.[67]

Ezekiel thought that share-the-work efforts were counterproductive. Questioning whether a 30-hour bill would "make jobs for all," he reasoned that the result of such forced work sharing coupled with minimum wages might "cause an immediate increase in business." But over the long term, "that increase would disappear as other costs followed prices up." Toeing the administration line, Ezekiel admitted that "undoubtedly there is need to prevent unduly long hours . . . in sweatshop industries to prevent competition there from becoming competition to see how far down wages and working conditions can be pushed." But he rejected the idea that "shorter hours of themselves will inevitably produce more employment and more income." Instead, temporary gains made through work sharing would evaporate as inflation increased, and the result would be more unemployment.[68]

Ezekiel argued:

> As compared to the 30-hour bill, Industrial Expansion is less spectacular but more substantial. The benefits of a 30-hour bill would seem large at the start but then would gradually disappear. The gains from Industrial Expansion would only seem moderate at the start, but would steadily grow more and more. Industrial Expansion provides for a sustained and continuing increase in production and business activity.[69]

Ezekiel equated shorter hours with less production and with inflation. As such, he saw little good in the measure. He was willing to concede that hours might possibly be reduced as "improvement in technology justifies." But he was careful to point out that, in any event, shorter hours meant less production, less spending, and less economic growth. But it was exactly these things—expanded production and consumption—that provided more total work and were at the heart of economic progress. It was improved productivity that was, in the last analysis, able to provide real wage increases and a guard against inflation.[70]

Thus, by the 1934 election, the administration had arrived at a firm stand against a general reduction of working hours in the codes and a firm opposition to labor's demands for legislated work sharing. This was a risky stand. The political consequences were liable to be fearsome given labor's militancy and increasing political prominence. The 30-hour issue again confronted Roosevelt directly in the 1934 elections.

Like other observers, the political reporter Turner Catledge felt that Roosevelt, "if [he] determines to stand by those members of his administration who contend that American industry cannot be standardized with a uniform work week," would be in trouble during and after the elections. Yet Roosevelt had apparently listened to advisers who were telling him that "his recovery program as a whole would be thrown out of balance were a general thirty hour week adopted."

According to Catledge, Roosevelt's "closest advisers" had agreed that such a measure "would so increase the per unit cost of production as to nullify a great portion of the purchasing power that has been restored" during the New Deal. But having accepted this point of view as his own, Roosevelt was facing the prospect of looking foolish and paying a high political price. Nearly everyone in Washington realized that "nothing short of a miracle can stave off a showdown on the question of [shorter hours]." The forces behind 30 hours were so strong that "if the administration emerges from the next congress without a statutory work week tied around its neck, it will be by . . . the cleverest pieces of political magic yet evoked by President Roosevelt."[71]

But Catledge recalled that "the last time agitation for a . . . limitation on work hours reached anything like present proportions, Mr. Roosevelt reached into his hat and pulled out NRA. As it is almost too much to hope now that even the unpredictable Roosevelt has anything up his sleeve that would outdo that." Catledge concluded that if Roosevelt had any chance of escaping the 30-hour threat, it would be in an unprecedented "show of great leadership." If he were able to put together "a permanent industrial policy, coupled with a social security program of unemployment insurance and old-age pensions," he might be able to satisfy labor and "make the thirty-hour agitation look small in comparison."[72]

Other pundits, such as Arthur Krock, agreed with Catledge that labor might be willing to "horse trade" over 30 hours. Although few believed that this reform was not labor's ultimate goal, reporters were convinced that in the short term, labor might be willing to hold off in return for concessions.[73]

The 1934 elections have often been seen by historians as posing a threat to Roosevelt from the left, from demagogues and disgruntled reformers, from a new coalition of dissatisfied farmers, labor, the lower middle classes, and the unemployed. The "thunder from the left" has been seen as causing Roosevelt to shift his policies in the winter of 1934–1935. This new departure was designed to provide security and larger incomes for the masses through such measures as increased deficit spending, larger government payrolls, taxation policies, social welfare legislation, and industrial regulations.

But of all the "thunder from the left," none was as persistent and as widely heard, none represented as realistic a political threat in Congress, as the Black–Connery measure. Yet Roosevelt consistently opposed it and never accepted the 30-hour principle—the legislated share-the-work plan that labor endorsed. On this issue, Roosevelt found himself on the side of business and even the leading conservative organization, the American Liberty League. In the face of labor's constant pressure and the forces in Congress that made him pay a high political price, Roosevelt held out, offering the second New Deal's social and industrial accomplishments to labor, not as compromises, but as a series of alternatives and compensations.[74]

Roosevelt responded in masterful fashion, engaging the Black–Connery threat on two main fronts. First, he took the initiative during the elections and committed his administration to the creation of new work opportunities as the way to reemployment—a direct alternative to work sharing. He presented new programs, such as the Works Progress Administration (WPA), that created jobs for the unemployed and stimulated business activity, adding his Social Security plan to protect those who could not be reemployed (see next chapter). In addition, as he had done in 1933 and 1934, he took a reactive stand to the 30-hour bills throughout 1935, offering bits and pieces of the NIRA to labor as discrete pieces of industrial regulation legislation as pressure built in Congress for passage of Black–Connery.

After the congressional elections, the administration reaffirmed its position. As director of the National Emergency Council, Donald Richberg addressed the Associated Grocery Manufacturers in New York City and warned against 30 hours. He pointed out that the flexible provisions in the NRA that allowed working hours and conditions to be set by labor and management working together were still better than legislation that would put industry and workers in a straitjacket.[75]

In addition, the NRA, under the influence of Henderson, began to lift the curbs on production that Johnson had instituted. In so doing, the agency continued its evolution from policies based on the acceptance of economic maturity and toward policies of full economic growth—policies that had no ideological place for reductions in working hours. Consistent with this development, supervisors of some four hundred basic and supplemental manufacturing codes agreed to recommend a uniform 40-hour week late in November, a move widely seen as a outright rejection of labor's demands. After Perkins called a Conference on Labor Standards in mid-December, which endorsed the 40-hour standard, there could be no mistaking the administration's position.[76]

On December 14, Green went to the White House and presented Roosevelt with a list of labor's legislative demands. Afterward, he told reporters that the AFL would "carry direct to Capitol Hill a fight for a thirty-hour week." But Green stopped short of attacking Roosevelt for his administration's obvious opposition. In discussions with the President, Green had been reassured that Roosevelt would "horse trade" over the 30-hour issue. Green was told that the administration would support renewal of the NRA, due in June, and would consider other concessions, among them that the collective bargaining sections of 7a would be made a separate and permanent law, a move that Roosevelt had opposed in 1934. Hence Roosevelt managed to distance himself from the actual legislative battle.[77]

As the new year began, Black and Connery reintroduced their original bills (Connery had discarded his attempt to legislate 30-hour industry code maximums). Harold Moulton and Maurice Leven of the Brookings Institution attacked the bill on the day it was introduced, January 3. Even though Moulton, as director of the institution, was hardly an official spokesman for the administration, his views about Black–Connery were widely regarded as reflecting Roosevelt's own. The Brookings Institution chose this time to release what became its very influential report *America's Capacity to Consume*. Written in part by Moulton, it presented the economists' case against 30 hours.[78] Moulton and Leven admitted that the 30-hour week had become "the primary national issue" because of the election and labor's powerful showing and called the bill "more revolutionary in its economic and social implications" than any bill ever considered by Congress.[79]

The *New York Times* reported in early February that "the thirty-hour bill is the piece of legislation most feared by industry in the current session." This assessment was based on a meeting of prominent industrial trade association executives in New York City that had concluded that the measure was even more dangerous than the Wagner bill and the huge expenditures being made by the federal government. Even though many businessmen agreed with the Chamber of Commerce that Roosevelt would oppose Black–Connery and that, without his endorsement, it could not get through Congress, the fear remained in most conservative and anti-New Deal circles that such strong sentiment for the bill was developing in Congress that the administration would be forced to give in, down the line, to the rest of labor's legislative agenda.[80]

The bill disappeared from view temporarily in House and Senate committees, where hearings produced the same sorts of debates as in three previous hearings; in most cases, arguments were made by the same people. But in late March, the bill was reported out of the Senate committee just at the time that Congress was dragging its heels on renewal of the NIRA. Senator Black admitted that his bill "was closely connected with NRA" and that if congressional leaders were not ready to renew the agency and support tougher industrial codes, then the sterner measure of 30-hour legislation would be the result. Connery, on the House side, shared Black's confidence, commenting that "sentiment for the thirty hour week is predominant in both the House and the Senate . . . if we could get it on the floor it would pass the House in a minute."[81]

Business fears that 30 hours would be used to force passage of other prolabor legislation seemed to be coming true. Even though opinion was divided among businessmen over the wisdom of renewing the NRA, many opponents were brought around to support it by this development. For example, the National Council of Shoe Retailers thought small business faced a Hobson's choice, but urged its members to write their congressmen in support of the NRA's renewal in hopes that the Black–Connery measure would be shelved.[82]

When the Senate voted against consideration of the Black bill on April 8, postponing debates until "the NRA matter" was settled, labor stepped up its pressure. Strikes were held in Philadelphia on April 15, and the next day Green delivered some of his strongest language. To the mass meeting of "thousands" of workers in that city, Green, punctuating his remarks by pounding on the speaker's table hard enough to knock over lamps, water pitchers, and glasses, warned that the form of government was liable to be changed if Congress continued to hesitate on 30 hours and play politics with the bill. Sharing the speaker's platform, the socialist Norman Thomas added that 30 hours was "absolutely vital" but was only the first step.[83]

Green's rhetoric and emphatic delivery notwithstanding, the AFL was certainly playing its own political game. Louis Stark wrote that although labor was dead serious about the Black–Connery bill and would be happy to have the legislation pass, the reporting of the bill out of Senate committee and its simultaneous appearance on the House floor were signs that labor, together with several congressmen, had a larger strategy. In addition to pushing 30 hours as a way to increase support for the NRA's renewal in Congress, labor was using 30 hours as a stalking horse to force the administration to support the Wagner bill, in the form that labor endorsed, and the Guffey–Snyder Bituminous Coal stabilization bill. Labor's strategy became more apparent when pressure mounted in the Senate to tack 30 hours onto the NRA renewal act in order to block the Clark resolution that would have limited the NRA's life to ten months instead of the two-year extension labor supported.[84]

Labor's strategy was successful. The NIRA was renewed in early May for two years. Even though Roosevelt continued to oppose the Wagner bill, saying that he preferred the protections of Section 7a, Frances Perkins threw her support behind the stronger version of the Wagner bill, which kept the National Labor Relations Board in the Department of Labor. And with such tacit approval by the administration, the bill passed the Senate on May 16. But the whole legislative picture was thrown into confusion with a series of Supreme Court decisions on May 27, "Black Monday."

Among these decisions, the *Schechter* poultry case had the greatest impact on the New Deal's industrial and labor legislation. The NRA was ruled invalid because, as the Court saw it, Congress had delegated its legislative power "to persons wholly disconnected with the legislative functions of government." Moreover, Congress had misused its constitutional authority over interstate commerce to regulate intrastate manufacturers and businesses. Observers such as Robert LaFollette concluded that both the Wagner and Guffey bills were brought into question by the Court's rulings.

According to the AFL and its congressional allies, the Black–Connery bills were immune. Even though such Democratic leaders as Senator Robinson thought that it would be impossible to enact maximum-hour and minimum-wage laws that would pass constitutional muster, Black disagreed. He argued that since his bill did not delegate legislative authority, it was constitutional. Moreover, he argued, maximum hours had been ruled constitutional several times in the past, although most of these rulings applied to state laws. Even so, such federal legislation as the Adamson Act had stood the constitutional test. Black concluded: "There is not one word in the decision that stands as an obstacle to the bill that I have introduced. This bill invokes the constitutional powers of Congress [to regulate interstate commerce] that are well recognized and have been for years." Urging passage of his bill, Black warned against relying on business "to legislate for itself," a clear reference to remarks that Donald Richberg had made calling for industry to continue voluntary compliance with the outlawed NRA codes—the so-called codeless NRA.[85]

Other legal experts, such as Charles Wyzanski, solicitor for the Department of Labor, shared Black's views that 30-hour legislation, if carefully limited to interstate commerce, could very well be accepted as constitutional.[86]

For several liberal congressmen, the Black–Connery bill seemed the way out of the constitutional tangle, and support to replace the failed NRA with 30-hour legislation began to gather steam. Most of the initial efforts made in Congress to salvage the NRA revolved around the existing Black–Connery bill, since it already contained minimum-wage, maximum-hour, and collective bargaining provisions—the very things that the Court had outlawed in the NRA. Moreover, the bill had a strong constituency that had persevered for over two and a half years.[87]

William Green felt that the Black–Connery bill's chances had been much improved and that "the Supreme Court [made] the passage of the measure more necessary than ever." The AFL announced that it would intensify its efforts because of what the Court had done. Expressing dissatisfaction with Roosevelt's apparent willingness to go along with business efforts to keep the NRA alive through voluntary compliance with the old codes, the AFL spelled out what it saw as a necessary response to the Court's decisions. In addition to 30-hour legislation, labor demanded passage of the Wagner bill, the Guffey coal bill, and the "omnibus" Social Security bill.[88]

Harper Sibley, the new president of the National Chamber of Commerce, spoke for business when he congratulated Roosevelt on his opposition to the 30-hour "nonsense." He also embraced what he understood to be Roosevelt's new tack: the "codeless NRA." Sibley explained that it was "exactly what business wanted"—the ideal opportunity for self-regulation and control.[89] But the chamber's confidence was misplaced and its membership in for a shock when Roosevelt reversed himself and warned that he could no longer sanction voluntary agreements that violated antitrust laws, despite the supposed delegation of such emergency authority to the President under the NIRA. Although Sibley was right about Roosevelt's continued opposition to Black–Connery, he had misjudged the President's willingness to continue his lax approach to the antitrust issue. He also had failed to detect the more profound shift within the administration on the whole question of the enforcement of antitrust laws to more of a "new freedoms" approach.

Instead of continuing to support the "codeless NRA" or trying to revise the NIRA to make it constitutional, Roosevelt attempted to save components of the act. Casting aside his deeply felt suspicions in order to placate labor, he abruptly threw his full support behind the Wagner bill, which rapidly became law on July 5. In addition, he approved the Connally Act, which regulated the oil industry along the lines of the NRA codes, but more effectively, prohibiting the shipment of oil in interstate commerce not produced in accordance with interstate compacts. The administration also supported passage of the Guffey–Snyder Coal Conservation Act in August and was able to get Social Security through Congress and signed the same month.

Thus labor saw its legislative program enacted less than two months after the *Schechter* decision, with the exception of hours regulation. The explosion of activity by the administration in July and August eclipsed the congressional move to renew the NRA in the form of the Black–Connery bill. The administration, while it continued its firm opposition to 30 hours, did not have to confront the congressional support for wage-and-hour legislation directly until it sponsored the Walsh government contracts bill.[90]

Consistent with his attempts to have the important parts of the NRA written as separate laws, Roosevelt, having dealt legislatively with the other outlawed 7a sections, endorsed the Walsh bill in an attempt to satisfy labor and the congressional forces that were clamoring for some kind of wage-and-hour legislation throughout the summer. But this bill simply imposed NRA standard hours (40) and wages on government contractors; as such, it fell way short of the controls that labor demanded. Even its supporters spoke of it as a "skeleton NRA." While Roosevelt was said to be willing to compromise and support legislation for industrywide 40 hours at this time, he and his advisers pointed out that such a measure was probably unconstitutional and that the half-loaf of the Walsh measure was better than nothing.

But on August 9, 1935, as the Senate was ready to vote on the Walsh bill, Senator Clark, in a surprise move, offered the Black bill as a substitute. Labor and several 30-hour supporters in Congress had agreed that the Walsh bill was an attempt by the administration to drain off pressure for legislation on hours. Since they did not share Roosevelt's supposed fears about the constitutionality of the Black bill, they believed that now was the time to revive the issue in unmistakable terms. At the least, they claimed, their measure would regulate interstate businesses and thus be a much more effective law than the mere regulation of government contractors. But this was a move born of desperation, and the revolt was short-lived. Finding scant support for their substitution, labor and the Black forces were able to do little more than postpone the passage of the government contracts bill.[91]

Hence Roosevelt countered the forces behind 30 hours, offering a series of measures once contained in the NRA as alternatives. But the New Deal went beyond this reactive position. At the same time he was opposing 30 hours and across-the-board work reductions, Roosevelt took the initiative, offering a set of positive steps aimed at creating more work, stimulating the economy, and providing security. Paralleling his efforts aimed at industrial stabilization were new initiatives: the WPA, Social Security, and monetary policies designed to deal with unemployment by guaranteeing more work to more people.

CHAPTER 7

Idleness Reemployed: Public Works and Deficit Spending

THE NEW DEAL'S commitment to guarantee the "right to work" took definite form in 1934 and 1935. Policies were put in place that Roosevelt used to oppose 30 hours in the political arena and offer his positive alternative in the battle against unemployment: work creation.

From the start, the NIRA included provisions for public works, funded at $3.3 billion. Hugh Johnson viewed the Public Works Administration (PWA) as a vital part of the NRA, and would have used the PWA to promote hirings and stimulate business activity immediately, spending as rapidly as possible to speed recovery. Johnson, more than any other member of the administration, played both sides in the work-creation, work-sharing debate in 1934, because he saw no necessary contradiction. But the administration's conservatism during Roosevelt's first two years was nowhere more evident than in the handling of public works. In spite of Johnson's threats to quit the NRA, Roosevelt turned over administration of Title I to Secretary of the Interior Harold L. Ickes, who moved at a snail's pace as far as Johnson was concerned.[1]

Ickes, mindful of the scandals that had racked Washington ten years earlier, was extremely careful to avoid any hint of favoritism or corruption. Moreover, he was concerned that every PWA project be "useful" and pay for itself in a reasonable amount of time by the obvious benefits it provided communities and the nation. The result was an outstanding list of accomplishments: hospitals, schools, highways, waterworks. But insofar as working as a recovery measure to stimulate business activity and promote new hirings on a large scale, the WPA under Ickes was a failure.[2]

With the coming of winter 1933–1934, relief became an even more pressing issue. Harry Hopkins maintained that it was infinitely better for people to be at work on public jobs than to be idle and on the relief rolls. Without work, job skills would be lost, and workers would sink into despondency and despair. The nation's mental health was at stake. By so arguing, he was able to convince Roosevelt to divert $400 million from the PWA to a large-scale work-relief program under Hopkins's control. The result was the short-lived Civil Works Administration (CWA). Designed to put people on relief to work at whatever public job could be found or created, the CWA, within weeks of its November 1 beginning, discovered work for 4 million unemployed. Hopkins was able to sustain the CWA through the winter of 1933–1934, but with the coming of spring, he saw CWA projects canceled and the relief effort focused again in the Federal Emergency Relief Administration (FERA).[3]

Historians have argued whether CWA was the start of the New Deal's attempts to provide workers with jobs directly when the private sector failed to do so. There is no doubt that Hopkins supported this approach and felt that "work relief" simply meant the use of public funds to create as much work as possible. But during the winter of 1933–1934, Hopkins's views were still in the minority. Competing approaches to both public works and unemployment relief held sway.

The dominant views about public works within the administration at the time were divided between people such as Hugh Johnson, who were more interested in using the measure to stimulate business activity and help heavy industry than to provide direct unemployment relief, and people like Harold Ickes, who were concerned more with the cost effectiveness of federal projects than with promoting local economic "boomlets."[4]

As unemployment–relief remedies, Hopkins's ideas and the CWA faced equally stiff competition. Trade unions and other supporters of Black–Connery were a much more potent political presence than the unorganized unemployed, and labor's attempts to revise the major industrial codes on hours downward were more of an immediate legislative concern to the administration than was continued funding for the CWA. Moreover, the CWA was bedeviled from the start by direct opposition from union leaders. For the most part, organized labor stood by its traditional opposition to "makework" projects (even though Hopkins had dug up an obscure article in the *American Federationist* by Samuel Gompers that envisioned a work-relief program somewhat similar to what he had in mind). Most union officials shared Johnson's general views about public works; such projects should be used to provide employment for existing labor pools, thereby expanding those pools, not for "busywork" or "makework" for the unemployed. According to

Matthew Woll, most workers had had enough of digging holes and then filling them up when they were in the army. But by maintaining this position, the AFL faced critics who pointed out that such views were self-serving and that unions opposed offering work relief only to those on the relief roles because they wanted the jobs for their members.[5]

Labor countered that workers were more interested in getting to the root of the depression's distress: unemployment. Immediate relief was necessary; the FERA needed more funds. As for providing relief by providing work, labor was clearly more committed to the share-the-work approach and Ickes's brand of public works. With mandated shorter hours, the invention of outlandish kinds of new work would not be needed. Existing labor pools would be more equally distributed; traditional jobs would reappear as workers became more secure and confident. According to Green, work relief was the purpose behind the 30-hour measure. Such legislation would provide jobs for the unemployed quickly, obviating the need for expensive and degrading "makework." While Green and Hugo Black (in 1934) were pragmatic enough to accept the relief offered by CWA projects, they nevertheless put their main effort into 30 hours.[6]

Hopkins had to struggle to have his case heard within the administration. Just when he was trying to get support to extend the CWA into the spring, Johnson and Perkins were joining together to support labor's frantic calls for reductions in hours in the NRA codes. Thus Hopkins's programs for work creation vied with work regulation in the tangle of Washington politics and were lost for a time in the shuffle.[7]

But the demise of CWA was only a temporary failure in Hopkins's attempts to establish government as the employer of last resort. In contrast to Roosevelt's opposition to labor programs of widespread work sharing, which became firm at the time of the CWA's demise, his opposition to Hopkins's brand of work relief lasted only until the 1934 elections. After discarding the share-the-work solution to unemployment, Roosevelt turned increasingly to Hopkins's work-creation remedy.[8]

The congressional elections did return a more liberal House and Senate, but the results were far from clear in terms of specific policies. Some observers, citing the political rise of the unemployed and unskilled workers, interpreted the results as a mandate for new federal relief efforts; others recognized organized labor's strength and saw the opportunity for labor to enact its legislative agenda. But for Hopkins, it was clear that whatever else the election had shown, the day had come for work relief.[9]

In his annual message to Congress on January 4, 1935, the President confirmed Hopkins's view, vowing to replace the dole, the cash handouts, and degrading "marketbaskets" with constructive work programs. Slums needed to be cleared, parks and recreation facilities built, rural areas provided with electricity and adequate housing, and forests reseeded. So many things needed doing; so many were unemployed, looking for a job. The obvious solution was for government to bring the two together, the worker and the work. The burden of care for the chronically unemployed, those incapable of work to support themselves, would fall again on local agencies. But able-bodied persons on relief would be given what they needed most: work. Roosevelt also pledged to support the omnibus Social Security plan, which included unemployment insurance and retirement programs. Together, work relief and Social Security constituted the new unemployment policy and replaced most of what had been tried the previous two years under industrial stabilization.[10]

The only reference Roosevelt made to shorter hours was a vague and indirect assurance "that the ambitions of the individual to obtain for him and his a proper security, a reasonable leisure and a decent living throughout life is an ambition to be preferred to the appetite for great wealth and great power."[11] Reductions of work and the hours of work had given way to work's creation and elaboration.

On April 8, Congress authorized $5 billion through the Emergency Relief Appropriations Act for the work-relief effort. On May 6, 1935, Roosevelt launched the Works Progress Administration (WPA), appointing Ickes as head of the planning division and Hopkins as WPA administrator and the man with the real power.

These events occurred just when the Black–Connery bill emerged from House and Senate committee hearings. The timing was not accidental. By launching his relief program at this time, Roosevelt increased his control over the legislative and political situations, both of which were in considerable need of repair because of the "logjam of legislation" in Congress (caused partly by the 30-hour legislation) and the likes of Huey Long, Charles Coughlin, and F. E. Townsend roaming the country practicing their incendiary political arts.[12]

By creating the WPA, Roosevelt appealed to an emerging labor constituency, skilled and unskilled workers in the great mass production industries who, led by John L. Lewis, were in the process of breaking away from the AFL. By so doing, he was able to bypass the congressional logjam, making an end run around Black–Connery and the AFL forces that were holding up other legislation. Even though John L. Lewis pressed almost as hard as William Green for 30 hours, the unemployed and unskilled workers that labor was now seeking to represent were much more interested in work-relief programs than were the craft unions and were more willing to accept work relief as compensation for Roosevelt's opposition to Black–Connery. Unskilled workers and the unemployed were also considerably more interested in minimum wages and a weekly cap on hours than mandatory reductions in hours. Hence Roosevelt, with the WPA, was able to divide the share-the-work forces politically at the same time that he supported what he felt was the more viable unemployment remedy: work creation.[13]

Following Hopkins's lead, Roosevelt, after the Hyde Park conference in late 1934, began to support WPA projects that provided the maximum work creation for the minimum amount of federal spending. "Light projects" that were as labor intensive as possible were supported over the longer term, heavy construction projects favored by Ickes and the PWA. The majority of the large construction projects were postponed in favor of projects that "tapped unemployment pools . . . could move promptly . . . could be completed in a relatively short period of time . . . and could utilize more man-power rather than materials."[14]

On these lighter projects, much of the work was unskilled, and more funds flowed as wages to workers who were more likely to spend them immediately for consumer items; less went to managers and administrators, less was tied up in capital expenditures—or so Hopkins argued. The WPA programs, then, were designed to provide a direct stimulus to consumer spending and give a boost to retail business. Thus Hopkins shared Johnson's concern with increasing retail consumption. But instead of the Blue Eagle's consumer campaigns, Hopkins used the more direct approach of putting a work-relief paycheck into the hands of men and women who were in considerable need and would spend without delay.[15]

In ordinary private employment, skilled and management personnel are usually required for the effective employment of unskilled workers. Their numbers vary with the state of technology and the use of machines, but an efficient ratio of unskilled to skilled to management often exists in occupations, below or above which productivity declines on the margin. Since Hopkins had determined that work, not efficiency or product, was the WPA's primary aim, much of the newfound WPA work involved unskilled work but often did not require machines and efficient techniques—the shovel and pickax became almost synonymous with the WPA. Such deliberate labor intensification troubled Green and the AFL, who saw this as a trend toward reenslaving the worker to ways of work long outgrown by industrial advances. Green feared that such manufacturing of work, if continued on a large scale, would result in less efficiency and less production and would impair not only the prospect of higher wages but future reductions in labor's work burden. Such work would become a barrier to shorter hours. Conservative observers joined in the criticism with the observation that without proper supervision and management, WPA work was wasteful. Businessmen complained loudly about haphazard "makework," kibbitzing that not only was the work not worth doing but it was being done by lazy oafs who, unsupervised, were not working hard enough at it. With the symbol of the shovel came the image of the Civilian Conservation Corps (CCC) man leaning on it, waiting patiently for the unlikely appearance of his foreman.[16]

Nevertheless, government figures showed that the monthly cost to the government of employing a worker on WPA projects under Hopkins was $82, compared to $330 under PWA and Ickes. Such assessments convinced Roosevelt that the future lay with Hopkins's brand of public works, labor efficient or not.[17]

Ickes and Hopkins disagreed about the mechanics of job creation, and their running battle about how to spend public works money, a battle that erupted periodically in the press and amused FDR a good deal, reflected a deeper division.[18] For Ickes, public work had to be "useful." Since the free marketplace could no longer be counted on to find meaningful employment for everyone, government had to take a hand and create work projects that benefited the nation substantially.

Ickes believed that enough work for everyone was "a precious heritage," a "priceless ingredient" of American optimism and self-reliance. He took issue with the work sharers, observing that

> no one can reasonably contend that the standard of living in this country is so high that we can afford to . . . require the employed portion (of the population) permanently to divide their work with the unemployed. Such a course is economically and morally untenable. It would compel a lower standard of life for everybody. . . . Our task is to find useful work and employment for all of our people by increasing the interchange of goods and services among them. Only thus can we permanently utilize the progressive advances in technology and not have the machine become our undoing.[19]

But until this happened, until the private sector provided the essential expansion of "the interchange of goods and services," public works, intelligently administered, had to take up the slack. Such projects were critically important national tasks: to "conserve and develop our natural resources, to prevent soil erosion and recurring periods of droughts and floods." Public work was not busywork.[20]

Ickes was willing to admit that many projects "were, or will be, undertaken with the primary object of giving work, directly and indirectly, to the unemployed." But he insisted that public works "involve more than this." He consistently argued that "an improvised public works program that merely 'makes work' must always be inadequate. . . . We must go far beyond any such limited conception. . . . We need public works to preserve the human . . . resources of the nation."[21] Public works that are useful give something of enduring value to the community.[22]

If "makework" and the restoration of spending power were the only justifications for government projects, these objectives "could be attained more speedily by loading our public-works money into coal cars and shoveling out a million dollars every mile or so in the course of a swing around the country."[23]

Ickes believed firmly that if work relief were to succeed and be more than shoveling out money every mile or so, it had to be worthwhile. Pointless work, even work on useful projects, that was inefficient and a "throwback to primitive days" of hand labor, degraded the worker almost as much as the dole. He saw no reason to go "back to the hand loom or the foot-propelled spinning wheel, back to man-blown glass or hand-built carriages." Instead, he envisioned a "social order . . . which would have the advantage of scientific technical advances preserved in a democratic system."[24]

Public works needed a larger purpose. It had to be more than work for work's sake. It required a vision, a national objective and clear social purpose that called forth the worker's best effort and deserved the use of the best machines and techniques. Such PWA projects as the conservation and recreation operations in the Great Smoky Mountains provided such larger purposes, transcending private gain or individual advantage. The nation offered "infinite possibilities" for such transcendent goals. Limitless opportunities to "make our country more productive, more convenient, and more beautiful" existed. Hence Ickes asserted that "public works [was] a continuing . . . task" with the responsibility of providing "Americans with meaningful work for years to come."[25]

Moreover, such useful projects were economical both in terms of manpower and in terms of long-term investments. As Ickes put it: "Public works . . . are not an enforced extravagance arising out of dire necessity. They are—always provided that they are well conceived and well carried out—an economy. They use labor and tools that would otherwise be idle."[26] The unemployed represented billions of dollars of wasted, idle time—a "social surplus" that could be turned to the public good. Until such time as private industry could employ those idle hours, the government had the responsibility of making good public use of them as proof against the time when the country's posterity would demand an accounting:

> Public works are as profitable an investment as can be made, whether or not they are in any literal sense self-liquidating. They should not be thought of as an enlargement of the public debt, reluctantly assented to in the hope of tiding over a depression. They are, in effect, a transfer of some of the social surplus which private enterprise cannot at the moment profitably use, to perfectly sound public investment . . . which would benefit ages to come. [Public works added] billions of dollars of real wealth to the nation in the form of new school buildings, sewer and water systems, power plants, river and harbor improvements, vast areas of irrigated and reclaimed desert land and many other types of socially and economically desirable capital assets.[27]

Ickes called the public works projects under the New Deal the largest national endeavor in history. They far surpassed the great national feats of the past; the Pyramids and the Great Wall of China seemed "petty" in comparison. But more important, the New Deal's projects embodied the unique American spirit. The Pyramids were the work of overweening individual pride; the Great Wall the result of a nation's paranoia. By contrast, PWA, CCC, CWA, and the Tennessee Valley Authority (TVA) were the fruits of a nation's noble purpose and indomitable will, springing from care for the public's welfare and concern for the security of the people. This larger purpose and meaning were transmitted through the New Deal's projects to the individual at his particular public work job, which became, in turn, uplifting, "useful," and "meaningful."[28]

But by 1935, Harry Hopkins and the WPA chairman of the Division of Applications and Information, Frank C. Walker, had lost what few qualms they had shared with Ickes about national goals or transcendent purposes. In May, Walker observed that the WPA had advanced beyond old-fashioned notions about "utility, engineering, and soundness" and had introduced "a new conception of public works." From then on, WPA projects would be undertaken "on the simple basis that they will provide employment. . . . A new yardstick must be applied to all works projects and the emphasis on all engineering and economic soundness must be subordinated . . . to the acute unemployment problem." The primary object was simply to get people off the relief rolls and back to work.[29]

Hopkins pointed out that the "great public works" under Ickes had "little or nothing to do with unemployment relief." Work provided by these projects was taken by people in only a few occupations, mostly in construction, heavy industries such as steel, and transportation. The unemployed in other fields, "waitresses, chauffeurs, the professions and the whole unhappy white collar army," needed work the PWA could never provide. This was the WPA's first responsibility.[30]

For Hopkins, work needed no transcendent purpose. It was worthwhile on its own, aside from product or result. It was the end for which other parts of the economy and government were the means. Without work, people suffered much more than the simple absence of income. They suffered extreme emotional, social, mental, and "spiritual" distress. The whole of the personality deteriorated. Work skill was the first to go, followed by community esteem, family respect, "pride, courage, self-respect, ambition, and energy."[31] For the individual, work was life's center, a point of reference and stability without which existence was confusion. Men and women had found "no substitute for work to keep themselves sound in body and mind." For the state, work was one of its principal reasons for being and a primary way to maintain national identity, order, and cohesion. Work "conserves [human beings] as a national asset, the lack of work lets them sink into a national liability." In Hopkins's mind, maintaining "the right to work" was the state's first responsibility to its citizens and absolutely essential for the survival of democracy.[32]

Like Roosevelt, Hopkins was at first somewhat sympathetic to labor's shorter-hour campaign. Testifying before the House Labor Committee in 1934 on the Connery bill, he repeated the administration's position that NRA codes for maximum hours were a good idea in general; they would put a limit on the chiselers, provide a few jobs, and thus serve as a temporary expedient. Pressed to deal with 30 hours, he was coy and vague, a model of evasiveness. He was clearly uncomfortable and kept wandering off the topic into other areas that interested him more, principally work relief. He had little interest in the question of increased leisure or with Representative Connery's idea that as industrial productivity improved, workers could and should be freed increasingly from their jobs. Hopkins's overriding passion was for more work, not less.[33]

Hopkins never endorsed 30 hours or the principle of industrywide reductions in hours. On the contrary, he laid out the economists' indictment of shorter hours several times. He quoted Moulton and the Brookings group, and made reference to Walter S. Gifford, director of the Employment Stabilization Research Center of the University of Minnesota, all of whom agreed that share the work put all the burden of unemployment relief on the shoulders of the American worker,

instead of dividing it with industry and government. He also tended
to identify the "spread the work" idea with the "outmoded" policies
of the Hoover administration. Tracing the lineage of public works, he
described how the Committee on Public Works of Hoover's President's
Organization for Unemployment Relief had rejected the "spread the
work idea" presented then by several groups. Instead, the Committee on Public Works presented a long report in favor of a five-part
public works proposal. For Hopkins, it was clear that, since then, public works had demonstrated its superiority over shorter hours as an
unemployment measure—even Hoover's administration had begun to
see this.[34]

In any event, Hopkins devoted as little of his attention to shorter
hours as politically possible. For Hopkins, increased productivity did
not offer the opportunity of increased leisure; instead, it presented
the massive problem of generating more work. He delved into the
question of productivity and concluded that "due to the growth and
improvements of machines the average worker can produce 39 per
cent more [in 1936] as he could in 1920 . . . 10 per cent more than
in 1929." For Hopkins, it followed logically that "to reduce unemployment to the 1929 level we would have to produce 10 per cent more
goods than we did in 1929." But only if population had remained
constant. Under the real conditions of a growing population, "total
production would have to be 20 per cent above the 1929 level."[35]

This was the challenge for government and industry alike: to put
to use the "surplus labor" left in the path of industrial efficiency by re-
gaining and surpassing previous production levels. Hopkins compared
this challenge to the challenge of the original American frontier:

> The passing of the frontier left a gap which we have not filled;
> as long as we had a frontier, aggressive and resourceful indi-
> viduals could repair the ravages to their families caused by the
> ups and downs of the business cycle. The new frontier is idle
> men, money, and machines . . . [which required] tremendous
> organization of productive forces, such as only government can
> supply.[36]

Like Ickes, Hopkins counted the cost of the "work famine" in billions of dollars:

> Our failure to conquer this new frontier of idle overhead has
> cost us at least $200,000,000,000 in lost income we might
> have produced but didn't since 1929. That $200,000,000,000
> is about equal to the 1932 value of the entire wealth of this
> nation. We have been losing since 1929 almost two-thirds of the
> entire national debt.[37]

Time freed by machine efficiency had cost a frightening national price.

Reporting on what it called the "Frontiersman Hopkins," *Time* magazine quoted him as estimating that 15 percent of "U.S. Citizens will forever remain dependent on Government for daily bread." The choice for Hopkins, then, was between the permanent dole and permanent government works programs. Consequently, Hopkins envisioned the government as the employer of last resort, conducting an ongoing work program to provide for the "standing army of able-bodied workers who have no jobs," employing whatever varying fraction of people was not used by private industry, creating what *Time* called "a socialistic appendix" to the capitalist system.[38]

But work provision was a challenge to industry as well. The "new frontier of idle men, machines and money," could be conquered "only if government works with business and business works with government toward a common end." Permanent federal jobs' programs had to combine with increased production and consumption in the private sector. By providing direct employment, the federal government could do its part and get things started; it could stimulate consumer spending, "provide a broad base of purchasing power and increase the stability of the economic system." But American free enterprise had to do its share. Hopkins trusted that it could and would: "I do believe that the needs of the United States require the services of all . . . in the production of goods and services. Any other view is a defeatist one to which I cannot subscribe."[39]

The first problem was "to get the national income up [so that] the underprivileged one-third of the American people can become consumers, and thus participate in our economy." "What caused the present decline in business? It is very apparent that consumer incomes did not increase fast enough to take goods off the market."[40]

Having given his reasons for the federal provision of work so often, Hopkins was able eventually to condense his argument to a tight, logical chain. He reasoned closely thus: To put people back to work, production had to increase by more than 20 percent; to support this increased production, consumption had to increase; since industry was not supplying the necessary purchasing power and capital was sitting around, unused, the federal government had to spend enough to make up the difference—balancing consumption with production by whatever monetary and physical policies required. Hopkins's ideas about the centrality of work were obvious. Government had to increase consumption to support more production to create more work.

Roosevelt shared Hopkins's ideas about idleness reemployed. Speaking at the dedication of Boulder Dam on September 30, 1935,

Roosevelt observed that public projects stimulated the "financial and industrial mechanism of America" to ever greater heights:

> Labor makes wealth. The use of materials makes wealth. To employ workers and materials when private employment has failed is to translate into great national possessions the energy which would be otherwise wasted.... It is a simple fact that government spending is already beginning to show definite signs of its effect on consumer spending; that the putting of people to work by the government has put other people to work through private employment.[41]

Most public works supporters—economists, mayors, bureaucrats, statisticians, and politicians—used this kind of reasoning more than any other justification. The Bureau of Labor Statistics kept running tabs in the *Monthly Labor Review* on "employment created by public works funds."[42] Economists such as J. M. Clark and William Foster published numerous articles defending public works in these terms.[43] Idleness reemployed became the hallmark of public works, its chief reason for being and best case for spending large amounts of money and running up large public debts. As with Social Security, proponents of public works looked to Germany's example, noting that Germany was the model of a progressive state that provided work for its people when the marketplace failed to do so.[44] To many supporters, it seemed logical for the state to employ workers' time in national efforts, filling the time vacuum left in the wake of the machine and mass production.

But the public works and work-relief initiatives of 1935 were far from the most important development that year. For all of Hopkins's and Ickes's posturing and grabbing of the headlines, their act was a prelude to the main events. Historians have tended to see the WPA as an "emphemeral phase" of the second New Deal. Much longer in their effects on the nation's future development were labor legislation (discussed above) devised to replace the NRA, Social Security, and new monetary policies. Like labor legislation and the WPA, both Social Security and the administration's monetary policies had a good deal to do with share the work. Each was used in a political sense to placate the AFL and the emerging CIO for Roosevelt's opposition to Black–Connery in mid-1935; each presented an explicit ideological alternative to 30 hours.[45]

Harry Hopkins's views about public works and the deficit, as well as his management of the WPA, dovetailed with what Marriner S. Eccles, new governor of the Federal Reserve Board, thought and did about monetary policy. In 1935 Eccles was influential in drafting the administration's banking bill to include a restructuring of the Federal

Reserve System. This restructuring centralized control of the system in the public board in Washington and removed a good deal of the autonomy of individual Federal Reserve banks, taking away in the process what *de facto* central control existed and had been exercised by the New York Reserve Bank.

As Eccles saw it, the Federal Reserve Board needed three key powers in order to manage the nation's banking. First was the power to set rediscount rates for the Federal Reserve System—changing rates for all reserve banks for the good of the total economy. Second was the authority to determine the proportion of dollar reserves as against deposits of member banks. Third was authority over "open-market operations"—the buying and selling of government securities.[46]

Hearings on the banking bill dragged on during the early part of 1935. Carter Glass, considering the Federal Reserve System to be his private creation, inviolate of change by anyone but himself, tried to have Title II removed. The senator from Virginia objected to Eccles's proposals, which were contained in this section, but was willing to go along with the rest of the bill—the Federal Deposit Insurance Corporation (FDIC) and the provisions for reform of bank examinations.

Roosevelt's patience wore thin in May. Faced with a legislative logjam in Congress and threatened from the left by labor and its forces and from the right by an increasingly hostile business community, Roosevelt put pressure on Congress to take care of the Federal Reserve reform before leaving town. Because of Carter Glass's opposition, Roosevelt was not able to get Eccles's restructuring proposal through Congress unchanged. But Walter Lippmann assessed the banking bill that did pass as a victory for Eccles "dressed up as defeat."[47] Glass's Senate bill differed little from Eccles's House draft, but a few concessions to the banking community gave Glass the sense of control he needed.

After the banking bill cleared Congress and was signed by the President on August 24, 1935, Eccles was able to exert effective control over monetary policy and for the first time use the Federal Reserve Board as a tool for the implementation of an administration's economic policy in the management of the economy.[48]

As Eccles's put it, that policy could be summed up as one of "easy money": "government spending" and credit expansion.[49] Although Roosevelt was much too pragmatic and eclectic in his approach to monetary matters to be called a Keynesian, Eccles and some of the men around him, such as Lauchlin Currie, were certainly influenced by the British economist and pursued what many observers, among them James Warburg, saw as a "frankly inflationary" course. By lowering the rediscount rate, reducing reserve requirements, and expanding the eligible paper on which member banks could issue loans, Eccles increased the total volume of the nation's money supply.

But Eccles, departing from economic orthodoxy, argued that these policies would not cause inflation. Although he may have followed Keynes's theories in this matter, he was not overly preoccupied with scholarly respectability, nor did he mention Keynes in the hearings on his appointment as governor of the board. Instead, he acknowledged his intellectual debt to William Foster. Moreover, in a practical, political sense, Eccles depended more directly on the niche, the rhetorical foothold, that Ickes and Hopkins had carved out of the legislative tangle when they defended the WPA and PWA—and the deficit spending these programs required. Like these two men, Eccles built his case on the fact that so much idleness existed in the economy.[50]

Following his colleagues' lead, Eccles argued that since so much potential wealth was being lost because of "idle time" and "surplus labor," the Federal Reserve Board should make money more readily available to underwrite increased production. Like Hopkins, Eccles equated increased production with the creation of new work:

> I have been and still am an advocate of an easy money policy, and expect to continue to be an advocate as long as there are large numbers of people who are unable to find employment in private industry, which means that full productive capacity of the nation is not being utilized. Under such conditions, to restrict the available supply of capital and thus make it difficult, if not impossible, to employ these people would not only be anti-social but uneconomic.[51]

The way to control inflation was not to tighten rediscount rates, reserve requirements, or definitions of eligible paper to be used for loans. These measures would slow the economy and spill more time out of the marketplace as idleness—time that should be employed to increase the nation's wealth. The way to control inflation was to increase total production by means of a liberal monetary policy. The large amount of idle time that existed in the economy would act as a buffer, absorbing the new "liquidity." Idle men and women would be put to work with the newly available funds, producing new goods and services—real wealth that would give substance to the banks' paper promises. Consumption would also expand, and new production would be encouraged as the multiplier effect did its work. Thus a consumption–production spiral would be set up to lift the economy to "full employment" and "full production." If and when "full employment" was reached, such policies, if continued, would surely be inflationary. New measures would then have to be put in place, such as paying off the national debt. But until all the unused time was taken back into productive use, "easy money," like deficit spending, was the wise course.[52]

To advocates of share the work, Eccles pointed out that both "unjustified" wage increases and hourly reductions "limit and actually reduce production." As such, they were "not in the interests of the public or in the real interests of the workers themselves." He argued that shorter hours "retard and restrict production" and thus were a prime cause of inflation—of too many dollars chasing too few goods (given his monetary policies). "Surplus labor" should be employed to create new wealth, not drawn down and wasted by shorter hours.[53]

> The remedy for price inflation when the country has unused manpower, natural resources and capital, is through more not less production, through an orderly, balanced use of these three fundamental factors, and not by creating a needless, artificial shortage of any one of them. . . .
>
> Reductions of hours for purposes of sharing the existing volume of work, however, raise many intricate problems relative to costs, increased shortages in individual lines, of loss of total output and, therefore, in national income. There is a danger that it may mean sharing poverty rather than sharing wealth.[54]

In the face of labor's political threats, Eccles was diplomatic enough to admit that once full employment existed, hours might be shortened. Workers would be entitled to more leisure in good times, but only to the extent that they had won it, only to the degree that they and industry became more productive. This was equally true for wages. But he was not willing to admit that existing labor, machine, and capital surpluses could be alleviated by share the work. The "free time" of the depression was "unemployment" to Eccles. As such, it was idleness and waste. It needed to be reemployed by economic growth. Otherwise, this free time would continue to cost billions in lost wealth to the nation, and Eccles's monetary policies would turn out to be as inflationary as his critics feared.

Turning to tax matters, Eccles continued his "idleness, reemployed" theme. Although the "banking system could influence the volume of money," Eccles argued that tax policies could and "must influence the velocity of money."

Immediately after the *Schecter* decision, pressure mounted on Roosevelt to come up with some kind of tax reform. In order to finance the New Deal, Roosevelt turned to a plan that the Treasury Department had presented in 1934. This tax program promised a sweeping tax reform: the inclusion of inheritance and gift taxes, a corporate dividend and a corporate graduated income tax, and a tax on undistributed corporate profits. Designed to penalize large businesses and industrial conglomerates, this tax plan was vigorously opposed in Congress and was so altered that it proved to be largely ineffective as a revenue source. But the administration's interest in the measure is revealing. In addition to demonstrating that Roosevelt had changed directions and was following a "neo-Brandeisian," antimonopoly course, the Revenue Act of 1935 showed that the administration was attempting to use tax policies for social ends.[55]

Eccles agreed with Robert H. Jackson, general council of the Bureau of Internal Revenue, that taxes on consumption, which had come to constitute nearly 60 percent of federal tax revenues, should be reduced and replaced by heavier taxes on incomes, gifts, corporate profits, and estates. The problem of the growing concentration of capital and industrial control could be dealt with in part by the Treasury's tax scheme; but equally important, the tax burden would fall more heavily on those better able to pay. Moreover, the "oversaving" and the vast reserves of unused capital would be put to use—if businesses were slow to spend their profits, government could show them some real spending. In short, a tax plan that took more money from the well-to-do who would "oversave" it and left more to those who were in immediate need and hence would spend it speedily on the necessities of life, would increase what Eccles called the "velocity" of money. As more money (resulting from his liberal monetary policies) was spent more rapidly, more production would be stimulated, work created, and the upward spiral speeded on its way. In answer to business critics who complained that such a tax policy would discourage individual effort, Eccles explained that without some redistribution of wealth to the government and to those who would turn the money over quickly, spending power would remain insufficient, and the motive force pulling economic growth ahead would be lost permanently.

But, according to Eccles, a balanced budget was more likely to be achieved by his monetary policies than by substantial tax hikes for the mass of workers and consumers. He thought it was madness to increase taxes in 1935 for the small wage earner. Given tax breaks, these were the very people who would spend money and spend it fast. If anything, taxes should be reduced, not increased.

More money left in circulation by a restrained tax policy would have the same effect as liberal monetary policies. Both would encourage increased consumption and act as a stimulus to more production and hence more work; additional jobs would be created to take up the "surplus labor." As previously idle workers were put back to work, they would then pay more taxes as a matter of course. No tax rate increase would be needed. As the tax base grew, the federal deficit would be reduced; emergency outlays such as those used for public works and unemployment insurance would be less needed. Hence the "idle hours" of American workers were a potential source of tax revenue, a source that would, if productively employed, become an asset rather than a liability and go a long way to help pay off the deficit.

> I am as anxious as anyone to see the federal budget balanced. In my judgment this cannot be accomplished until the national income is higher than it will be this year. I do not believe that it can be done at this time either by reducing government expenditures or by increasing Federal taxes, particularly those that bear most heavily upon consumption. I believe that the only way the budget can be brought into balance is through increased Federal revenue from an increased national income. . . . The only way that we can impoverish ourselves is by failing to utilize our idle man power, resources, productive facilities and money in the production of real wealth.[56]

Eccles did not see his tax measures enacted in the Revenue Act of 1935, but he was able to convince Roosevelt that taxation, like monetary policies, could be used to stimulate production and consumption. Subsequently, Eccles's views were to prevail. In his State of the Union message to Congress in 1937, Roosevelt echoed Eccles's point of view, suggesting that the budget could indeed be balanced without additional tax increases. Thus, in both the tax policy and monetary measures Eccles espoused, the importance of reemploying the nation's surplus labor was of central importance.[57]

Finally, Eccles's views about the federal deficit mirrored those of Ickes and Hopkins; countercyclical spending was near to becoming the administration's accepted position by 1935:

> I *do not* believe in government spending at any time for spending's sake. I *do* believe in government deficit-spending in depression periods as a supplement and stimulant to private spending, using only the manpower, materials and money that otherwise would be idle . . . the object always being a maximum of private employment.[58]

In all three areas that concerned him as governor of the Federal Reserve Board—monetary reform, tax policy, and the deficit—Eccles centered his attention on the "idle hours" and "wasted time" of unemployed Americans. In each area he supported specific policies that were, in his judgment, likely to "reemploy" this idleness, pointing out the potential benefits to the nation and the federal government when this waste was stopped. In each area he offered his policy solutions as alternatives to share the work in terms of the wisdom of putting idleness to the service of economic growth and the folly of wasting it on expensive shorter hours. In each area he went out on a limb insofar as the conventional wisdom of the time was concerned, supporting policies that built on the potential that the nation's idle time could, if "reemployed," pay back the deficit, make good the banks' paper extensions, and make the tax structure the engine for economic growth rather than a great barrier to individual effort. These views came to be more and more important in setting the "second New Deal's" political and legislative course after mid-1935. Eccles was to change some of his ideas about the Revenue Act by 1937, but his "idleness, reemployed" theme remained constant.

CHAPTER 8

Social Security and the Fair Labor Standards Act

IN SEVERAL important respects, the development of the "omnibus" Social Security bill, passed in August 1935, influenced and was influenced by the share-the-work movement and the Black–Connery bills. Many early supporters of government retirement and unemployment compensation measures agreed with 30-hour advocates that technological overproduction was chronic and that the resulting unemployment could be remedied through reducing the supply of work, both by shortening the worklife and shortening the workweek. But this commonality was two-edged. In the first years of the Roosevelt administration, a partial coalition was formed by the two groups. But the partnership was replaced by rivalry when Roosevelt played the groups off against each other in Congress, rejecting 30-hour legislation at the same time he endorsed the Railroad Pension Act of 1934. But then Roosevelt's administration abandoned, for the most part, the effort to use pensions to stabilize industry and create jobs for younger workers on a large scale, turning instead to social insurance primarily for unemployment relief and old-age security. As a consequence, the two work-sharing factions joined in alliance and fought together for a while in 1935 to amend the Social Security Act to include stronger provisions for industrial stabilization. Roosevelt was able to counter that insurgency by making small concessions to retirement as work sharing in Social Security and using labor's rhetoric about the need to make reductions in work supply—while doing little that was substantial. By the time Social Security became law, Roosevelt had abandoned the course of work reduction and fully committed himself and his administration to the creation of more work as the primary method to deal with the depression.

As the movement for state-run and state-supported old-age pensions and social insurance programs grew independent of European influence in the 1920s, supporters, looking for additional ways to justify their reforms, turned increasingly to the idea of work sharing. Certainly the notion that pensions were good things because they took older people out of the job market, and thus out of competition with younger workers, was part of the movement for decades. But this "work sharing" over the life span became more popular in the late 1920s and early 1930s—a welcome, "hard-headed" economic approach that toughened social welfare rhetoric. At first, some supporters of share the work and the leaders of government-supported old-age assistance programs recognized one another as natural allies; both used the rhetoric of the shorter-hour solution to unemployment; both used some of the same arguments concerning the value of increased leisure; both agreed on the importance of reducing the workforce to maintain wage levels; both thought of themselves as inheritors of the tradition of Progressive reform.

Similarly, unemployment insurance, as it developed in the early 1930s, had some of the same goals as the shorter-hour movement. Part of the public support for unemployment insurance had to do with its potential to help stabilize industry and thus industrial jobs. The influential Wisconsin law that John R. Commons helped draft, for instance, penalized establishments that experienced chronic seasonal or cyclical unemployment. The penalty would, in theory, encourage industrial managers to distribute work and production over the year and take more care to avert wide swings in production and employment levels. By the same token, supporters of the Black–Connery measures believed that shorter weekly hours would act to spread the work not only among more people but from periods of surplus work to times of work famine. Thus, before 1934, advocates of unemployment insurance, state old-age pensions, and share-the-work programs held similar views about the cause of unemployment and the need to control and reduce the supply of labor.

To be sure, there were dissenters; they saw their reforms as better than, or exclusive of, any others. For instance, some supporters of old-age pensions thought that it was more reasonable to apportion "leisure" to the older or "superannuated" worker than it was to shorten the hours of work across the board. H. S. Peterson, director of the Taylor Society, argued that retirement should be given a higher priority than shorter weekly or yearly hours because younger workers were more capable of harder work and longer hours. He reasoned that young workers ought to keep their noses to the grindstone while they could, putting aside savings or building an insurance program for security in old age. Retirement was the time for "leisure"; in youth, it was a pitiful waste. "[I]nstead of converting increased social income immediately into a shorter work-week or shorter work day, which emphasize *immediate* leisure and spending, a substantial portion of increased social income should be converted into ultimate leisure, comfort and enjoyment; enhanced in value by the element of security."[1]

Peterson denied that he was opposed to increased leisure in principle. He agreed that given the threat of overproduction, some plan for steady work reductions was called for. But he viewed shorter hours, distributed indiscriminately, as unwise. The scientific manager, put in charge of things, would be able to devise a plan that would divide work rationally as leisure increased, a division that would allow for the gradual reduction of hours to be geared to the worker's age and/or capacity to work. By such divisions, total industrial efficiency would be increased by a workforce pruned, in humane fashion, of the less able and less productive workers. But this pruning had to be controlled scientifically to make sure that hours were reduced proportionate to increased industrial productivity; otherwise, runaway inflation would threaten the economy.[2]

Douglas Brown, director of industrial relations at Princeton, agreed with this view. Together with others in his new profession, Brown felt:

> Whether or not we accept the proposition that underconsumption is the cause of the present maladjustment of production, pensions as a means of providing workers with purchasing power as well as leisure after sixty-five will be a better remedy than leisure on Saturday and no purchasing power after sixty-five, if both are not possible.[3]

In contrast, some social workers supported pensions and unemployment compensation primarily because they saw them as essential parts of social welfare; they looked askance at those who would use these things for industrial stabilization. Fearing that the focus on relief and security would be lost in attempts to restructure the workplace, they tended to tolerate the work sharers more than they actively sought them out. There was also some concern among social workers that the industrial manager and welfare capitalist were encroaching on reforms that social workers had championed for so long, taking away the prestige rightfully theirs and diluting the movement's moral purpose with a crass, self-serving economic logic.

But even with the factionalism of the industrial relations experts, scientific managers, and social workers, a significant degree of political agreement and mutual support was to be found among the groups before 1934. For example, politicians prominent in support of shorter hours were also prominent in leadership for old-age pensions and unemployment insurance. One of the main congressional leaders of the 1934 and 1935 railroad retirement bills, Representative Robert Crosser of Ohio, was also the chief sponsor of the railroad brotherhood's 6-hour day for 8-hours' pay bill.

In addition, William Connery of Massachusetts, who introduced 30-hour legislation in the House, made his reputation in Washington by becoming involved with the fight for veterans' bonuses and pensions. His interest in retirement grew, and Connery emerged in the forefront of old-age assistance in 1932–1934. He was joint sponsor of the Dill–Connery bill, which provided for retirement at age sixty-five in state pension plans as a condition for the state's receiving federal old-age assistance up to one-third of total benefit payments, with authorization of $10,000,000 per year. This bill would have also created an Old Age Security Bureau in the Department of Labor to administer the act and continue work on enlarged assistance for the aged and further development of retirement programs.[4]

First introduced in the Senate, hearings on Dill–Connery were held by the Subcommittee of the Committee on Pensions as early as February 1931 and were conducted by the chairman of the subcommittee, Thomas Schall. Senator Clarence Dill of Washington presented the bill and did much of the questioning. These early hearings focused on old-age distress and the difficulty workers had after age forty in getting a new job (superannuation of workers) because of technological advances and the premium employers put on youth and new skills. Consequently, the people who testified before the subcommittee stressed the need for old-age relief without mentioning industrial stabilization. Nevertheless, led by Connery in the House, supporters of Dill–Connery began to focus on the work-sharing possibilities of federally supported state pensions.

The House Labor Committee held hearings on Connery's bill in 1933 and 1934, and such notables as Abraham Epstein of the American Association for Old Age Security testified in support. There were numerous similarities between the hearings on these bills and the hearings the House Labor Committee was conducting simultaneously on Black–Connery. In both hearings, the same arguments about overproduction, technological unemployment, and the necessity to reduce the supply of labor to balance consumption with production were rehearsed. Some of the same people, such as Monsignor Ryan, offered their support in testimony and in publications.[5]

Hugo Black entered the arena and introduced his own, stronger version of Dill–Connery to the Senate. Senator Norton joined Black, and together they presented legislation to set the age limit at sixty for federal matching assistance payments, rather than the Dill–Connery age of sixty-five to seventy; they claimed that a younger eligibility age would encourage more marginally employed older workers to withdraw from the workplace. Hence, both House and Senate versions of Dill–Connery developed from specific relief measures for distress in old age into a recovery bill, augmented in design to encourage the use of old-age relief and assistance funds by the states to promote work sharing over the life span.[6]

Notwithstanding the solidarity of the leadership in Congress, supporters of 30-hour legislation began to quarrel with those whose primary aim was federal retirements. At first, the quarrels had to do with priorities, that is, which work-sharing measure should be presented first in Congress and which was more vital if a trade had to be made. The AFL had made its decision to support 30 hours first and foremost. Social workers and the two senior railroad brotherhoods struggled to have retirement placed first on the legislative agenda. With divisions about priorities came other wranglings, other points of controversy having to do with who benefited most from shorter hours or shorter work lives. And the more labor and other work sharers split on the issues, the better Roosevelt was able to blunt the political pressure for 30 hours by throwing his support behind pensions in 1934 and 1935, ostensibly because retirement was more reasonable than work sharing.[7]

The division within labor was most apparent in the development of the Railroad Retirement Acts of 1934 and 1935. The railroad brotherhoods were the first unions to begin agitation for a 6-hour-day, five-day-week schedule. Six months after the Crash on Wall Street, when other unions were just beginning to talk about the need for a 40-hour week, each of the seven major brotherhoods called for 30 hours in railroads. Recognizing their common aims and the need for concerted effort, the Brotherhood of Locomotive Firemen and Engineers (BLFE), the Order of Railroad Conductors (ORC), the Brotherhood of Locomotive Engineers (BLE), the Brotherhood of Railroad Trainmen (BRT), and three lesser organizations met in October 1930 for a conference. Seven hundred local union chairmen gathered in Chicago to review the unemployment that had decimated railroads and assess its causes. Technological displacement had hit workers in railroading especially hard—according to speakers at the convention, harder than any other group. New, larger locomotives that pulled enormous trains reaching a length of 120 cars, the increased capacity of each railcar, faster trains, and the capacity of better roadbeds to sustain more speed—

all meant that fewer crews were needed. The crews required were in danger of being reduced—firemen's jobs were threatened, as was the requirement for two brakemen on each train.[8]

Led by Alexander Whitney, president of the BRT, the conference began by calling for a "six hour day with eight hours' pay," claiming that this was the only way to provide long-term relief for their 350,000 unemployed brothers. Speakers demanded a concerted drive, based on the example set by train service employees in 1916, which had resulted in the passage of the Adamson Act, reducing working hours in railroading from 10 to 8 a day. Conventioneers recommended this plan over several others because, judging by what the Court had determined about the Adamson Act, it was founded on Congress's constitutional authority to regulate interstate commerce.

The BRT and BLFE introduced a new twist to the proceedings by calling for an immediate, voluntary reduction of monthly road time to twenty-six days, pointing out that some of the "old heads" were often accumulating the equivalent of more than thirty-five days a month of "excess mileage." (The seniority system on railroads was based on advancement of firemen to engineers and trainmen to conductors. When work was scarce, engineers and conductors with the least seniority signed up for runs as firemen and trainmen, bumping the regular firemen and trainmen below them in seniority. Hence the brotherhoods were organized roughly according to seniority.) The BRT and BLFE urged that this measure was essential for the "immediate relief" of workers who were not getting any jobs. These workers were in the greatest distress and would benefit immediately from the twenty-six-day monthly limit. Moreover, they urged the convention to begin a drive for 6-hour legislation at once, following in the footsteps of the Adamson Act.[9]

This initiative elicited two responses. First, the conductors and engineers bolted the convention and prepared their own minority report. Whitney's arguments about the need to make a choice between increased leisure and increased unemployment impressed the conductors and engineers not at all. They pointed out that the twenty-six-day limit would cut heavily into their paychecks and would thrust all the burden of railroad relief on them. They continued to support the 6-hour-day, 8-hour-pay option. But they became hesitant and unsure even on this issue, opposing for the time being an immediate campaign for federal action. They proposed instead the circuitous route of forming a special subcommittee from the conference, calling a meeting with Hoover to be followed by the protracted collective bargaining process.[10]

The second result of the twenty-six-day proposal was to bring railroad officials into the picture. Lawrence A. Downs, president of Illinois Central, W. B. Story, president of Atchison, Topeka, and the Santa Fe, and Milton W. Harrison, president of the National Association of Owners of Railroads and Public Securities, seized on the voluntary twenty-six-day limit as a way to hold the line against the 6-hour day for 8 hours' pay, which they vigorously opposed. Harrison cabled the conference to support the shortening of work hours and suggested that the voluntary 6-hour day (with a pay cut) and the voluntary twenty-six-day maximum would solve the railroads' unemployment problems "without disturbing total payroll or imposing an undue hardship on the men now employed."[11]

The trainmen and firemen were dissatisfied with conference decisions to hold off on an immediate 6-hour-day legislative campaign in favor of protracted negotiations, and were displeased with the engineers' and conductors' veto of the monthly limit. Hence, beginning the next month in Spokane, Washington, they joined together to start a voluntary share-the-mileage program of their own, in hopes that the movement would spread to the more senior men. Late in December 1930, the BRT and the BLFE, led again by Whitney, called for their unions to begin a national, voluntary share-the-mileage effort based on the twenty-six-day maximum, and as a threat, they opened negotiations with the AFL for affiliate status. They also kept up pressure on the other unions to begin a drive for 6-hour legislation.[12]

In the meantime, a good number of conductors and engineers, separate from their national unions, had been conducting their own grass-roots movement—but for retirement legislation. Organized by the Railroad Employees National Pension Association (RENPA), they had abandoned the brotherhoods' orthodox shorter-hour solution to unemployment and embraced federally supported retirement programs.

From the beginning of the depression, W. W. Royster had championed the retirement cause and fought against negotiated or legislated shorter hours. In Minnesota, as state legislative chairman of the BLE, Royster had convinced his union to end its endorsement of the state's share-the-work program and begin a campaign for the pension plan he had drawn up. His plan's influence spread to Washington State's railroad employees, who drew up their own version, the "Washington plan," which grew in turn to national prominence with the establishment of RENPA at roughly the same time that the 6-hour movement was taking shape in the brotherhoods.[13]

Royster and RENPA accepted the arguments that the brotherhoods made about technological displacement and unemployment. But they came to very different conclusions about what ought to be done.

They agreed with the brotherhoods' position that the amount of work required in railroading had declined, and would continue to decline as prosperity and productivity increased, creating a permanent unemployment problem. But the way to ensure a proper balance of production, consumption, and employment was through flexible pension programs—in the case of railroads, programs that awarded the paid leisure of retirement to workers as the reward for long service. RENPA was successful with the rank and file (RENPA claimed that 95 percent of railroad workers supported its pension plan) because it appealed to men of all seniority ranks; the older worker had the promise of a secure pension, and the younger worker had the prospect of seniority advance as senior men retired.[14]

The brotherhoods vigorously opposed RENPA initially, not allowing the organization use of union publications or giving its leaders a chance to speak at conventions. The overriding reason for this antagonism was Royster's and RENPA's own stated opposition to 6 hours. Whitney felt that RENPA was guilty of creating a "dual outlaw movement," a rival organization based on a rival purpose. Moreover, Whitney pointed out that RENPA had given employers a lever with which to divide labor. This factionalism was also bound to dilute the unions' ability to be effective in Congress. D. B. Robertson of the BLFE agreed that RENPA had divided railworkers and had diverted attention from the most important issue: shorter hours for higher wages.[15]

The BRE and the Conductors' union were never as adamant, even though they sided with the firemen and trainmen on the primary need for 6 hours. In fact, since the strength of RENPA drew most heavily from engineers and conductors, these unions tended to be sympathetic to the independent pension movement.

With the unions split, railroad officials were in a position to delay action. D. B. Robertson, as chairman of the special subcommittee formed by the 1930 conference, reported that the brotherhoods' efforts to "thrash out the wage issue" with management and reach some sort of compromise between 6 hours with the same pay and 6 hours with a proportionate pay cut had failed. Railroad executives had simply "refused to deliberate over the problem." Hence, the brotherhoods met again in June 1932 in Cleveland to discuss the impasse. By this time, the sentiment in the BLE and ORC for 6 hours had strengthened because of the trainmen's and firemen's voluntary campaign for twenty-six days, management's intransigence, and a new call for wage reductions. Consequently, a compromise was achieved: The junior men agreed to the inclusion of the retirement insurance issue in the collective bargaining process, a concession that attracted some of the engineers and conductors in RENPA. The brotherhoods were then able to agree to seek congressional action on the 6-hour day, returning to their original position that this measure was the "only" workable solution to unemployment. The threat of a replay of the Adamson Act moved railroad officials to speed collective bargaining, and at a Chicago meeting in January 1932, they began work on a settlement with labor.[16]

This conference was remarkable for what it presaged for the New Deal and Social Security politics. The brotherhoods' representatives presented management with an enlarged agenda, explaining in public that this would increase the freedom of both sides to maneuver, compromise, and reach an agreement. In addition to the 6-hour-day for 8 hours' pay proposal, the Railroad Labor Executive Association (RLEA) included three other measures to stabilize employment: a railroad-run national placement bureau, a joint call for federal provisions for accident compensation, and, most important, a plan for a government-run retirement insurance plan. Even though Robertson denied reporters' assertions that the unions were still divided by 6-hour versus retirement issues, it was clear from conference events that the union representatives had different priorities and that the railroad presidents were making trades.[17]

The railroad presidents had their own priority—a 10 percent wage cut. And because of the weakness of the industry, they were in a position to get what they wanted. As negotiations wore on through January, the main question became how much unions could get in terms of employment stabilization in return for agreeing to wage reductions. Dismissing new, "radical" proposals from labor for things such as a year's guarantee for existing jobs, the railroad presidents accepted the unions' requests to set up a railroad employment bureau and explore with the unions the possibility of legislation for a federal workmen's compensation plan and retirement insurance. But the RLEA leadership presented a common front for a while, holding out for its central negotiating point—the 6-hour-day for 8 hours' pay—deadlocking the negotiations until the end of the month. The railroad presidents would not even consider a compromise to join with the unions to ask Congress to establish an investigative committee on the measure. Donald R. Richberg, council for the labor association, was then instrumental in persuading James Couzens of Michigan to introduce a resolution in the Senate calling on the Interstate Commerce Commission (ICC) to conduct hearings on labor's 6-hour demand—a resolution passed by the Senate in late January and passed by the House (introduced by Crosser of Ohio) shortly afterward. This development broke the deadlock, and the RLEA agreed to pay cuts with only two weak employment stabilization concessions from management—a committee appointed to study workmen's compensation and retirement insurance, and some assurances of support for these measures.[18]

After labor's poor showing in the January settlement, pressure mounted from the rank and file and RENPA for immediate pension legislation. Under pressure, RLEA prepared its own version of railroad retirement insurance. But RLEA had moved too slowly for Royster and RENPA; its pension legislation was tainted by cooperation with railroad officials. Moreover, RLEA's provisions for an employee-supported system were too conservative for their tastes, and its actuarial plans would not have eliminated enough workers through retirement to have an appreciable effect on railroad unemployment. Notwithstanding RLEA's repeated efforts to block them, RENPA and Royster had their own version introduced in Congress by Senator Henry Hatfield from West Virginia and Congressman Kent Keller from Illinois. Subsequently, a new, extraunion workers' organization was formed in Chicago with L. A. Filbert as chairman to lobby for the Keller bill, promising that it would "immediately create jobs for 112,000 furloughed workers." Filbert stressed that this bill was much better than the brotherhoods' plan in terms of retirement work sharing. In the meantime, RLEA acted, and with the help of Richburg, had its own retirement bill introduced by Senator Wagner and Representative Crosser in March 1932. Hence, even before the ICC began its hearing on 6 hours, the brotherhoods were forced by their own internecine struggles to support the secondary unemployment strategy of retirement, deploying their forces on two major fronts and thus slowing progress toward their primary share-the-mileage objective. With the simultaneous introduction of the railroad retirement bills and the beginnings of the ICC hearings, the brotherhoods' internal divisions were given expression as separate political agendas in Washington.[19]

But trainmen and firemen, supported by this time by the AFL, kept up the pressure for their primary goals at ICC hearings. Whitney's testimony in May 1932 is revealing because of what it shows about the development of the brotherhoods' and indeed the labor movement's shorter-hour position. Whitney reviewed the various depression measures that politicians were proposing in the election year and found many of them wanting. For example, plans being formulated for abolition of antitrust laws by those who would substitute "self-government of industry through trade-associations" departed so far from the American tradition of individualism that they were "revolutionary." He asked,

> Why indulge in doubtful speculations and revolutionary plans designed to tear down our present system when we have one

course open to us which is as old as labor itself, tried and found workable in our present system, and especially fitted to the modern needs of the machine age and mass production?

Shorter hours for all workers were the "most effective course open to the country":

Potentially prosperous markets for all industries lie dormant beside idle factories because modern efficiency has short-sightedly sacrificed men on the altar of machine economy. The adoption of shorter work hours will compensate workers for their increased efficiency; it will give our part-time employed and unemployed workers an opportunity to work, which is their right, and it will re-establish purchasing power with all that it means to every industry of the country.[20]

Whitney's was one of the earliest and most direct statements of what became labor's standard position throughout the depression.

But hearings on the railroad retirement bills, held at the same time as the ICC investigations, produced some of the same arguments. The BLE spokesmen claimed that they had found a way to get rid of all un-employment in the railroad industry. They maintained that pension plans that "adjusted the retirement age," depending on unemploy-ment levels, would work well enough to eliminate the need for un-employment insurance. Being considered as two separate sets of bills in Congress while 6 hours was still before the ICC, pensions gained visibility, strength, and support daily. By mid-1932, work sharing as retirement on the railroads had gained a clear early advantage.[21]

The ICC then made its report in late 1932, finding that the 6-hour day for 8 hours' pay plan was feasible. Even though it would cost the railroads a considerable amount in new labor costs, it would act, as the unions claimed, to reemploy rail workers and increase their spending power. Encouraged by the ICC report, Whitney and the brotherhoods renewed their efforts and found backing from the National Committee on Economic Recovery early in 1933. They also found an able and will-ing ally in Senator Hugo Black, who introduced their bill in early April, just at the time of the near-passage of the Black–Connery–Perkins bill. But shorter hours for the railroads suffered the dual disadvantage of being ignored by Roosevelt's administration from the start and being introduced long (over a year) after the railroad pension bills.[22]

Nevertheless, RLEA conducted a vigorous campaign. Whitney vowed to "repeat the successes [the rail unions] had with the Adamson Act" and make their Black bill become for Roosevelt's Presidency what

Adamson was for Wilson's: the shining achievement of progressive reform. Whitney and the RLEA made common cause with the Black–Connery, national 30-hour bill, proudly claiming leadership of the movement and repeating organized labor's old call for the "progressive shortening of the hours of labor" to match industrial efficiency. The brotherhoods were able to put on a show of solidarity as well, with the active support of conductors and train dispatchers who testified in congressional hearings in favor of the measure.[23]

But union hopes dimmed as their bill languished through 1933 and into 1934. The administration's attempts to block Black–Connery's general 30-hour bill were transmitted as passive opposition to the railroad measures, which were kept bottled up in committee until early 1934. But this was true for nearly all of labor's legislative agenda. As the 73rd Congress neared its end, William Connery observed that virtually nothing had been accomplished for labor; none of its major bills had been passed. The Black–Connery bill for a nationwide 30 hours, the Black–Crosser bill for 6 hours on the railroads, the Dill–Connery bill for industrial pensions, the Hatfield–Keller and Wagner–Crosser bills for railroad pensions, Wagner's bill for fair labor practices, and the Dill–Crosser bill for fair labor practices on the railroads had all been held up in committees. Connery observed that, notwithstanding his and labor's congressional supporters' best efforts to persuade the President and his administration to "do something for labor," time was running out.[24]

Consequently, labor's congressional supporters, faced by the prospect of adjournment with nothing to show their constituents in the 1934 election, began on their own to force the issues, maneuvering as best they could to break the legislative logjam of May and June 1934. They began with the Black–Connery and Black–Crosser measures, since these were labor's first priorities. Connery introduced resolutions to discharge his 30-hour bill (H. R. 295) from committee for consideration on the House floor. Similarly, Representative Crosser began a campaign to bring his 6-hour railroad bill to a vote, confident that it had a good chance of passing. Labor supporters in the House circulated a petition for a motion to discharge this bill, collecting 145 signatures in short order. Momentum for the railroad measure grew faster than any of the other initiatives, and observers predicted that amendment riders would soon be affixed by supporters of other 30-hour measures. Since Roosevelt opposed Connery's 30-hour NRA codes bill, work sharers intended to use Crosser's bill as a vehicle to keep 30 hours in the NRA alive. At this point, Crosser and Connery also offered resolutions for the discharge and consideration of the railroad retirement and the labor relations measures.[25]

Adding to the congressional pressure on Roosevelt, the Dill–Connery bill for federal funding of state pensions programs, which had emerged from the House Labor Committee on March 17, 1934, with a favorable report, passed the House of Representatives and came near passage in the Senate in May. Roosevelt took no open stand on the bill, but he called supporters to the White House and persuaded them to delay passage until the administration prepared its own, "more comprehensive version."[26]

Roosevelt then announced, on June 8, 1934, that he planned to appoint the President's Committee on Economic Security (CES) to investigate the feasibility of a federally run old-age assistance program. In a statement widely regarded by the press and in Congress as signaling that no action would be taken on Dill–Connery in the current session, Roosevelt promised that his administration was committed to introducing and supporting new, inclusive Social Security legislation in the 74th Congress. According to Edwin Witte, executive director of the CES, the Dill–Connery bill provided the push needed to set the Roosevelt administration in motion. Wilbur Cohen, Witte's research assistant in 1934, agreed that Dill–Connery's favorable report out of committee and the hearing conducted in the House Ways and Means Committee on unemployment insurance "were the immediate stimuli for President Roosevelt to establish the Committee on Economic Security in order to make a comprehensive and coordinated study of all aspects of economic security."[27]

Pressure also mounted on the administration from outside Congress. Steelworkers were threatening to call a national strike that promised to be violent if something was not done about labor organization in, and relief of, that industry—over and above the NRA codes.

Forced to "do something for labor" in the 73rd Congress, Roosevelt turned first to the Dill–Crosser measure as a stopgap solution to the steelworkers' threat. Since Roosevelt still opposed Wagner's bill, the more conservative Dill–Crosser bill, which was originally designed as the Emergency Railroad Transportation Act to settle labor–management disputes in the railroads, was pressed into service as an administration, omnibus labor organization measure. This act, as amended, called for the President to establish a federal labor board to settle labor disputes in organized industries and oversee election of workers' representatives in unorganized industries such as steel. In return for temporarily accepting this watered-down version of the Wagner bill, the administration promised labor's congressional allies that it would support the railroad pension bill in the 73rd Congress.[28]

Roosevelt then turned to railroad pensions. He had been interested in the measure for some time, having been convinced by Secretary

Perkins and Senator Wagner that it would help to relieve unemployment in railroads. His interest was strengthened by a Committee on Railroad Employment report that a pension plan would produce a healthier kind of work sharing than 6 hours because it would improve efficiency by creating a younger, more highly skilled workforce. Prominent among the members of this committee was J. Douglas Brown, who was to become influential in the drafting of the Social Security Act. But in spite of his advisory committee's recommendation and Perkins's endorsement, Roosevelt was never more than lukewarm to the bill, finding nearly as many drawbacks as benefits in it.[29]

Before adjournment, the Senate and House passed a compromise (between the RENPA and RLEA versions) railroad pension bill, the Railroad Retirement Act of 1934, and on June 31, Roosevelt, using the same work-sharing rhetoric that RENPA had employed, signed the bill, observing that the mandatory retirement age of sixty-five would provide 50,000 new jobs as "superannuated workers" on the railroads were "replaced by younger workers" who were unemployed or working part-time.[30]

But while supporting railroad pensions, the administration continued to oppose Connery's 30-hour measure for the NRA codes and withhold support from Black–Crosser's 6-hour-day railroad bill. Notwithstanding AFL pressure on Roosevelt and Green's threat of a national strike, Connery's bill was defeated on June 20. Moreover, administration loyalists in the House took direct action to counter Crosser's attempts to have his bill brought to the floor. Before the House could vote on the petition to discharge, the House Committee on Interstate and Foreign Commerce, led by Sam Rayburn, reported the bill out of committee without recommendation. As such, it was referred to the Committee of the Whole House and then to the House Rules Committee, where it was again stalled. Crosser filed a minority report, pointing out that the "obvious purpose" of Rayburn's move was to prevent a vote on the motion to discharge, a vote that, if successful, would have allowed any supporter of the discharge motion to call for an immediate House vote. Crosser pointed out that the 145 names attached to the motion to discharge should have been sufficient under House rules to require a vote on the motion and, if passed, on the bill itself. But Rayburn's maneuver was successful, and the 6-hour railroad bill was not brought to a vote in the 73rd Congress, or indeed ever afterward.[31]

For the time being, Roosevelt and his supporters had found in the railroad pension bills and the Dill–Crosser labor relations act ways to circumvent the support building in the House for a vote on the 6-hour railroad bill—a vote that would almost surely have meant consideration of amendments for 30 hours in most other major industries under NRA codes. Without having to oppose the brotherhoods' 6-hour day directly, Roosevelt was able to claim a victory for labor, even though, for labor, it was a victory for measures of secondary importance. He was also able to claim to support share the work, notwithstanding the fact that he had killed Connery's bill and that railroad pensions were far short of what the AFL or the brotherhoods had in mind. But such claims, made often enough and couched in labor's own rhetoric, proved to be credible and appealed to many railroad workers who had been supporting RENPA.[32]

Moreover, with the appointment of the Committee on Economic Security, Roosevelt gained enough time to consider carefully the role of retirement and unemployment compensation in his administration's industrial recovery program. While retirement as work sharing figured prominently in the Dill–Connery and Black versions of federal old-age relief and pensions, and in many of the twenty or so pension plans before Congress at the time, Roosevelt was not sure that this was the best road to reemployment. His blocking of Dill–Connery and the reservations he voiced when he signed the railroad bill are indications that Roosevelt and the administration, while not committed to any positive alternative, were not ready to endorse such a retirement work-sharing policy on a national scale.[33]

Roosevelt's delaying strategies worked only for a while—until the end of 1934. Beginning in October, federal courts began to question the constitutionality of the Railroad Pensions Act, and with alarming frequency began to rule against it. (The Supreme Court finally found it unconstitutional in May 1935.) As the courts were chipping away at pensions, the brotherhoods renewed their 6-hour drive, pointing out that, based on the precedent of Adamson, the Black–Crosser measure would doubtless succeed where the Railroad Pension Act was failing. Disregarding warnings given them by Federal Railroad Coordinator Joseph E. Eastman, the RLEA told Roosevelt directly that the 6-hour day was still the brotherhoods' number-one priority in early 1935, adding that if government ownership of the rails was necessary for the measure to be taken, then "so be it." Railroad officials had reduced hourly pay again on the first day of 1935, so the measure had increased importance as a wage issue for the unions.[34]

The administration then threw its support behind a redrafting of railroad pensions. The courts were finding that the 1934 pension act was flawed because it was designed to create employment opportunities, not because it imposed a tax to provide security in old age—a purpose covered by the welfare clause of the Constitution. Redrafted in 1935 as the Wagner–Crosser pension plan, the work-sharing features of the 1934 bill were practically eliminated; the final bill, signed by Roosevelt, emphasized old-age security and protection. For the second time, Roosevelt was given an object lesson in the use of retirement programs to placate labor and blunt the shorter-hour insurgency. With passage of the 1935 Railroad Act, the brotherhoods' 6-hour-day for 8 hours' pay campaign, with two minor flareups in 1936 and 1937, was repulsed for good.[35]

The political events surrounding railroad pensions were mirrored in several ways by the history of Social Security from May 1934 until passage in August 1935. Like the railroad pension bill, Social Security evolved. In 1934, both concepts were designed with unemployment and industrial recovery in mind; by August 1935, both had become largely relief measures. Like the railroad pension planners, the CES moved away from the reemployment issue and toward the issue of security in their reports and recommendations. Roosevelt supported both the railroad pension bill of 1935 and the Social Security Act mainly by using arguments that social workers made about the need to provide for the welfare of the old and unemployed. In both cases, he abandoned the substantial measures necessary for retirement work sharing, measures still very much alive and controversial well into 1935.[36]

William Graebner, a revisionist historian, makes a convincing case that the Social Security Act was originally conceived as an industrial stabilization measure. He cites the work of the Advisory Committee on Railroad Employment and the memoirs of the principal architects of the CES report to show that, at least in early 1934, unemployment and labor unrest were among the administration's and the CES's paramount concerns. A principal response to these concerns was retirement as work sharing.[37] Graebner quotes Wilbur Cohen, a member of the CES staff and Witte's research assistant in 1934, who remembered that "the roots of the social insurance movement came out of the work and consideration of people in the field of labor legislation. Social insurance was to them a form of remedial legislation to deal with the problem of labor unrest and industrial society which grew out of labor–management problem[s]."[38] Graebner quotes other influential members of the CES, such as J. Douglas Brown, an economist from the Industrial Relations Section at Princeton, who recalled that unemployment was the committee's chief concern and that one of the administration's appeals to labor was based on the CES's "plan to take men out of the labor market when they were superannuated."[39] According to Barbara Armstrong, CES member and former professor of law at the University of California at Berkeley, work sharing was "in the minds of [Murray] Latimer, [J. Douglas] Brown, Armstrong, and [Otto] Richter, and it was in the mind, I think, of everyone who ever worked on social insurance." Even Roosevelt, Armstrong remembered, thought that he faced a choice between employment of the young or the old. She said, "The interest of Mr. Roosevelt was with the younger man . . . there were two reasons why Roosevelt had acted at all. One was great concern for the unemployment problem, and the young people [who] were without hope and without a chance."[40] Graebner also cites the testimony of Armstrong and Latimer in the congressional hearings on Social Security during the 74th Congress as evidence of the continued interest, at least among CES members, in Social Security as a reemployment measure.

Indeed, such ideas about work-sharing reemployment were current in the administration in the spring and early summer of 1934 when the CES began its work. Roosevelt's trial balloon in February for the voluntary 35-hour week, Perkins's endorsement of Connery's efforts to lower hours in the NRA codes, Hugh Johnson's call for reductions in hours, and Roosevelt's hesitant approval of the Railroad Retirement Act are all further indications that some support remained in the administration. But administration opposition to nationwide 30-hour legislation and the 6-hour day on the railroads had remained, and it had grown. Hence, support for work sharing within the administration tended to collect around pensions and modest reductions in hours in the NRA codes. Moreover, apart from industrial stabilization, the administration had other political uses for Social Security (i.e., pacifying labor and preventing Black–Connery and Black–Crosser from being brought to a vote in Congress). Finally, evidence for the strong link between the work-sharing Dill–Connery bill and the initial work of the CES is additional proof that Social Security was deeply rooted in the administration's early efforts to achieve industrial stabilization and settle its accounts with labor in 1934.[41]

But however deep the roots of the CES were in Dill–Connery, the Railroad Pension Act, and support for retirement work sharing within the administration in early 1934, the fruit of the Committee on Economic Security was a very different variety. After early summer of 1934, Roosevelt's position on work sharing, both as a shorter workweek and a shorter worklife, hardened. The administration turned to public works and fiscal policies for industrial stabilization, and to social insurance for job and old-age security. By January 1935, the administration, having established at last a definite set of legislative alternatives, no longer felt the need to propose a substantial program of retirement work sharing as a compromise with labor on Black–Connery.[42]

Developments inside the CES reflected these policy changes. As early as August 13, 1934, a "Formal Statement of Purpose" was adopted by the committee's technical board and approved by the CES. The committee conceded that economic security was "a much broader concept than social insurance, embracing all measures to promote recovery and to develop a more stable economic system, as well as assistance to the victims of insecurity and mal-adjustment." Other agencies, "the NRA, the AAA and the National Resources Board," had been given the jobs of industrial recovery and industrial stabilization. The committee recognized that "these subjects . . . lie outside" its presidential commission and understood that "the field of study to which the committee should devote its major attention is that of the protection of the individual against dependency and distress." Hence, by August, the CES had formally acknowledged that security, not industrial stabilization or reemployment, was its domain and was the primary reason for the retirement legislation and the unemployment insurance programs it was investigating.[43]

Nevertheless, under the influence of Harry Hopkins, the CES did commission studies on reemployment, but not the work-sharing kind. Instead, the CES turned its attention to public employment at the suggestions of the Federal Emergency Relief Administration (FERA) officials and the direction of the technical board. Emerson Ross headed these studies and was given a staff of workers paid by the FERA. In addition, members of the technical board with connections with the Department of Labor had studies made on employment opportunities in the private sector. Directed by Meredith Givens of the Social Science Research Council, these studies were never used by the CES, but they are evidence that the committee was changing direction, heading away from work sharing.[44]

Hopkins also led a move in the administration to combine Social Security with his work-relief program (WPA) in one piece of legislation. He was even able to persuade Roosevelt for a time, but was prevented from carrying through with such legislation by D. W. Bell, acting director of the budget, who objected to this procedure. These events are all indications that the administration's move in the second half of 1934 toward a reemployment policy based on expanded work opportunities and increased employment influenced the CES in its work, leading it farther away from its original acceptance of retirement work sharing.[45]

Labor leaders such as William Green, congressmen such as Connery, and even some administration officials, such as Albert Deane, resisted this process and tried to keep up pressure for a work-sharing Social Security bill. In term of old-age assistance, the primary work-sharing issues were age of retirement, amount of annuity, mandatory retirement, and a "retirement test." Work sharers supported lower

age limits and higher annuities to attract more older workers from
their jobs and favored mandatory retirement and the "retirement test"
for the same reasons. Each of these issues had been debated in the
73rd Congress in committee, and the twenty or so Social Security bills
considered then presented a range of alternatives from frankly work-
sharing measures such as Monaghan's, which set retirement age as low
as fifty and annuities as high as the average industrial wage, to conservative bills with age limits well above sixty-five and annuities well below
the poverty line. During CES public meetings and some of its private
sessions and communication, more liberal members of the committee
and public representatives of some of the major public organizations
presented their cases for early retirement, high annuities, and compulsory retirement. William Green, for example, was displeased by what
he saw as a rigid attitude in the CES about these things, and all through
1934 and 1935 he tried to have the age limit reduced to sixty.[46]

The CES accepted the Dill–Connery age limit of sixty-five and held
fast. This age limit was a compromise reached in the 73rd Congress—
individual state's pensions averaged sixty-eight to seventy, and most
Social Security measures had limits below sixty-five. According to
Wilbur Cohen, the committee never gave any consideration to other
age limits:

> At no time did the committee give consideration to recom-
> mending any alternative to 65 as a retirement age. . . . The
> simple fact is that at no time in 1934 did the staff or mem-
> bers of the CES deem feasible any other age than 65. . . . Not
> a single actuarial study of costs or financing was made on any
> other assumption. The committee made no detailed studies of
> alternative ages or of any proposals for voluntary retirement
> at earlier ages or of compulsory retirement or of any flexible
> retirement programs.[47]

Yet, one reason Cohen gave for opposing a lower retirement age
was costs. Certainly, during the debates on the Social Security Act
in 1935, actuarial studies were made and presented to prove that
reductions below age sixty-five increased costs geometrically but that
increases above age sixty-five reduced them much less in comparison.
From Cohen's own account, however, it is far from clear that cost was
the major factor in the committee's decisions about age sixty-five.

Much more convincing and consistent is Cohen's description of
"public pressure." He remembered that

> a higher retirement age was never considered because of the
> belief that public and congressional opposition would develop

against such a provision in view of the widespread unemployment that existed. . . . Undoubtedly the large number of unemployed at the time and the desire of many people in the country for the retirement of older persons as a way of alleviating unemployment conditions were factors in achieving the enactment of the legislation and its acceptance by the Supreme Court.[48]

But the CES was also aware that the pensions they were proposing and the qualifications they were setting up would have little or no impact on the existing workforce. Few employed older persons were likely to be lured from work by the annuities they were recommending. No unemployed older worker under age sixty-five would be eligible for retirement, and so would still be on state relief or looking for work. Notwithstanding the fact that

> there was strong sentiment in the early 'thirties for the establishment of an old age security program as a method of retiring older workers and thereby alleviating the unemployment condition, this was never a significant factor in the minds of the staff or members of the committee in designing the specifications of the old age security plan.[49]

The committee, then, knew that labor and the work-sharers' support was vital "in assuring congressional and public acceptance of the plan." Yet the committee had lost whatever interest it may have had in any substantial work-sharing measure. Consequently, the CES presented a work-sharing facade. For appearance' sake, the committee endorsed the "retirement test," that is, the provision that a worker not be employed in order to be eligible for pensions, making a great show of its support of retirement work sharing. But this requirement was the least important of the four principal work-sharing issues. Moreover, the " 'major' reason for the retirement test was to prevent the labor market from being depressed by subsidizing wages." Thus the committee claimed this as a work-sharing measure virtually as an afterthought. And even while endorsing the "retirement test," the CES rejected, out of hand, the much more important work-sharing measure of mandatory retirement.[50]

The CES's final report confirms that the committee, rejecting the major measures required, had put aside retirement work sharing. The report also demonstrates the extent to which the committee had come to concentrate on public works and private employment for recovery and to understand social insurance primarily as security. The focus of attention had shifted 180 degrees from May—from reductions in the workforce to work creation:

Since most people must live by work, the first objective in a program of economic security must be maximum employment. As the major contribution of the Federal Government in providing a safeguard against unemployment we suggest employment assurance—the stimulation of private employment and the provision of public employment for those able-bodied workers whom industry cannot employ at a given time. . . . We regard work as preferable to other forms of relief where possible. While we favor unemployment compensation in cash, we believe that it should be provided for limited periods of time. . . . Public funds should be devoted to providing work rather than to introduce a relief element into what should be strictly an insurance system. . . .

In our economic system the great majority of workers must find work in private industry if they are to have permanent work. The stimulation and maintenance of a high level of private employment should be the major objective of the Government. All measures designed to relieve unemployment should be calculated to promote private employment and also to get the unemployed back into the main channel of production.[51]

With the administration, the CES settled on a set of specific recovery measures designed to create more jobs by creating more work, not by reducing the number of workers or the hours, day, months, or years on the job. Unemployment compensation and old-age pensions were only "complementary" parts of a larger unemployment strategy. Private employment was the first line of defense and accordingly, "the stimulation and maintenance of a high level of private employment should be a major objective of the Government." The second line of defense was public employment, which should be expanded "when private employment slackens." The committee used the same justifications for public works that Hopkins was using: the need of the unemployed for work as well as money, the social value of public projects, and the "stabilizing effect" increased purchasing power would have on private industry. Concluding its report, the CES characterized its efforts and distinguished its recommendations from European social insurance policies precisely in terms of "[our] primary emphasis on employment."[52]

In the catalogue of security programs proposed to ward off the "hazards of industrial life," amid suggestions for employment services and unemployment bureaus, the CES included the topic of education. As a means to economic security, education, training, and vocational guidance had proven their worth. The main idea behind the employment services the CES proposed was to "readjust" displaced people and retrain the "superannuated" worker. Even as the CES was recommending more training, however, it had become "tragically evident" that education and training were no longer any "guarantee against dependency and destitution." Graduates with worthless degrees were everywhere in evidence. But instead of abandoning or "losing faith in our democratic system of education," the committee proposed a reformation along the lines that Rexford Tugwell and Leon Keyserling were advancing. They suggested that "education, to fulfill its purpose, must be related much more than it has been to the economic needs of individuals." The depression had made it abundantly clear that there was a difference between "schooling and education." The need was for less "schooling" (i.e., general education) and more "education" geared directly to work. In the "attack against economic security [*sic*]," the committee recommended that the federal government accept responsibility for such education and together with the states and local governments create curriculums and adult retraining programs centered on "economic rehabilitation." Of particular importance was workers' leisure:

> In the years ahead . . . there is a peculiar need for educational and training programs which will help the worst victims of the depression to regain self-respect and self-support. While men have so much leisure time, those who can profit from further education and training should be afforded an opportunity to make such use of their leisure. Particularly for the young worker and those who have little hope of returning to their old occupations, the need for educational training and vocational courses and retraining programs is clearly indicated.[53]

Here the committee turned the work-sharers' argument on its head, urging that leisure was important as a means to learning work rather than as the purpose or logical result of work's advance and perfection.

More generally, the committee distinguished "employment assurance" from Social Security. The first was the touchstone of economic recovery and industrial progress; it was founded on governmental programs for increased private and public employment, education, and training programs. The second had to do with unavoidable circumstances and was a form of relief. Of course, when "employment assurance" led to recovery, many of the unemployed would be off the relief rolls—so in a sense reemployment was permanent relief. But even with the best government attempts to increase work and provide jobs for those able to work, many Americans would still be faced with financial distress. This was a fact of industrial life. Even in "normal times," the relief problem was greater than private and state resources.[54]

After the initial section on "employment assurance," the committee focused its report on the need for security for the old, sick, handicapped, dependent children, and mothers in need, and of course workers who were unemployed. But the focus on relief for unemployed workers was not on using pensions or unemployment compensation to resolve the larger problem of unemployment. The emphasis was on the government's providing relief for workers between jobs, helping to shoulder the burden of technological displacement and providing some security against the hazards of being a worker in the twentieth century. It was true that Social Security would have a positive influence on the economy. But that influence was indirect, coming as a result of improved worker morale and confidence. With unemployment insurance, workers would take economic risks, such as spending more of their money, that they otherwise would avoid, and such risks would reinvigorate the economy. Similarly, old-age insurance was primarily a form of security and relief. The CES gave no hints about the benefits retirement might have as work sharing and no indication of the importance such a consideration had in the committee's origin.[55]

Subsequently, Thomas Elliot, council of the committee, prepared a draft of the Social Security bill along the lines of the report and delivered the draft to the President on January 15. Elliot, on his own, had placed the old-age assistance title first because he considered it to be the most popular by far and the most easily understood.[56]

The political maneuvering began immediately. Friction developed over which congressman would introduce the bill, with Lewis, Ellenbogen, Connery, and Kelley vying for the honor. Connery and Lewis both made strong bids, claiming that since they had been involved with this measure for so long and had sponsored the major legislation in the 73rd Congress (the Wagner–Lewis and Dill–Connery bills), their names should appear on the 74th Congress's bill. Instead, Robert L. Doughton, powerful chairman of the House Ways and Means Committee, prevailed on the President and insisted on introducing the measure. Even though Roosevelt felt that the House members who had offered Social Security to the 73rd Congress had a legitimate claim, Doughton and Lewis together ended as joint sponsors. A more important and revealing fight along similar lines developed over which committee would consider the measure. In the Senate there was no question; the Finance Committee received the bill. In the House, however, Connery fought to have Social Security sent to the House Labor Committee, arguing that since Dill–Connery and most of the original

Social Security measures had been in the Labor Committee, of right the bill was theirs. After a long and bitter debate, however, Connery's motion to this effect was defeated, and the Speaker of the House referred the bill to Doughton's House Ways and Means Committee.[57]

Since the House Labor Committee was a hotbed of liberals and work sharers, with members such as Connery, Lundeen, and Monaghan of Montana, it is hardly surprising that administration supporters in Congress were unwilling to turn Social Security over to them, preferring the more tractable Ways and Means Committee. Moreover, these three representatives were on record as favoring much more liberal provisions for pensions and unemployment compensation. Lundeen and Monaghan immediately turned to the Lundeen proposal. Connery testified that had Social Security been given to his committee, he would have insisted on a complete overhaul of the bill, substituting the Deane plan for the CES's recommendations for unemployment compensation.[58]

The Deane plan was one of the few major alternatives to Social Security. Together with the Townsend plan, social credit proposals, and the Lundeen amendment, it commanded national attention and support. The CES had staff studies (mostly done by Cohen) made of these proposals, only to reject them. The Deane plan was the least publicly known, but had commanded the most respect within the administration. In July 1933, Albert L. Deane, president of the General Motors Holding Company, and Henry K. Norton presented "a method for automatically sustaining consumption, production and employment" to the Institute of Public Affairs at the University of Virginia. One of the first of the countercyclical spending proposals set before the administration, this plan was turned over to Secretary of Commerce Daniel C. Roper, who gave it in turn to his assistant secretary, Dickinson, who then consulted with General Johnson. Interest grew, and Frances Perkins called a conference at the University of Virginia to consider the proposal, bringing together some of the most influential members of the administration.[59]

The House Ways and Means Committee considered the Deane plan during the 73rd Congress (H.R. 1620), and the "whole matter was brought before" the President in January 1934. At the time, the administration was considering various work-sharing proposals, and Roosevelt, prepared by Perkins, was interested enough to spend over two hours with Deane. Throughout the spring, Deane continued to promote his plan to administration officials and then was appointed deputy director of the Federal Housing Administration (FHA) in midsummer, continuing in his official position to lobby the CES. In September, at the closing session of the Human Needs Conference in Washington, he struck out on his own and began a more public campaign aimed at congressmen, offering his plan as an alternative to the CES proposals. In October, he again presented his plan publicly, this time before the National Conference of Catholic Charities in Cincinnati. At the beginning of the 74th Congress, Perkins forwarded a copy of the plan to Connery and the House Labor Committee, who invited Deane to Capitol Hill to explain his proposal. The committee then had a bill drafted containing its major features. But, as Connery remembered the story, since the Social Security bill was sent to the House Ways and Means Committee, "nothing came of it [the bill's draft]." But Connery also opined that since Deane's plan received such a favorable response in the Labor Committee, if Social Security had been given them, "we would have reported favorably on the Deane plan as part of security legislation." Hence, throughout 1934, the Deane plan had a quasi-official standing in the administration and, as such, found some support in Congress as a compromise between the CES recommendation on unemployment compensation and more liberal proposals.[60]

The Deane plan was a complicated and thus little understood unemployment compensation proposal that, like the Wisconsin law, contained strong industrial stabilization provisions. Deane called his measure "the American Plan" and envisioned the establishment of a revolving fund for unemployment compensation supported by a tax on employers. This tax would be geared to industry's "excess producing capacity" by means of a surcharge on worker "overtime." The overtime would be calculated on the basis of the average weekly hours of all workers, employed and unemployed, in the country over the preceding ten years. This would represent the "highest average employment we have been able to attain," and as such would constitute the basic national workweek—would define "full employment." The second step would be for the designated Labor Department board to ascertain total work hours in individual industries by a monthly survey, dividing that total by the number of workers in the industry, employed and unemployed, to find the monthly average workweek. If the monthly average fell below the ten-year industry average, this would indicate a slump in economic activity, and the countercyclical spending feature of the plan would be put into operation. Workers falling below the ten-year average would receive a wage supplement at the rate of one-half their normal hourly pay for the weekly shortfall. But whenever a worker was employed more hours in any week than the monthly or ten-year average (whichever was lower), the employer would be required to pay double for the overtime. The worker would receive time-and-a-half pay, and the remaining half-time wages would be paid as a tax into a "National Employment Fund," which would

be used as a cushion for recession. All unemployed workers would
be paid half their normal salary from this fund, but workers with a
weekly hour deficit would benefit only during an "hours recession."[61]

This revolving fund would in theory have had two results. Its provision for countercyclic spending was designed to keep consumption
levels within a tolerable range. Deane reasoned that "inasmuch as
workers in this country constitute the primary market they must be
provided with sufficient purchasing power" on a permanent basis.[62]
The measure would also have acted to redistribute work by discouraging employers from working their employees more than the ten-
year industry average. Employers would have the choice of paying the
overtime premium to workers and an excise tax on "surplus hours" or
hiring new workers. Because of this requirement, the tax would work
to limit "excess production," that is, production in excess of demand,
by providing a mechanism to balance consumption with demand and
with wages and employment. Similar in purpose to the Wisconsin
unemployment compensation system in the countercyclical measures,
the Deane plan added a sophisticated work-sharing scheme to unemployment compensation and found support among both work sharers
and supporters of a more liberal unemployment insurance plan in
Congress.[63]

Moreover, Deane included provisions for the use of a revolving
fund to finance public works. From 1933, Deane had offered this
funding source for federal projects. Much earlier than Hopkins, he
rejected the long-term dole in favor of government-sponsored work
programs. Thus his plan found supporters within the administration
who were looking around for just this sort of financing alternative to
debt and taxes. Deane concluded that under his plan, "unemployment
would be entirely eliminated." A person would "either find employment in the private sector or . . . would be guaranteed a job on Public
Works, his wages paid out of the National Reserve Fund." Moreover,
Deane openly opposed Social Security's unemployment insurance as a
"palliative based on class progress and not germane to the American
scene."[64]

Connery, of course, was most interested in the plan's work-sharing
potential. The bill that Connery and the Labor Committee had drawn
up as a substitute for Social Security's unemployment insurance, while
based on Deane's plan, looked very like the 30-hour measures. In
the "declaration of policy" section, the bill's drafters located the cause
of unemployment in the "indiscriminate, arbitrary, and unequitable
distribution of the total work-hour requirements of the nation." In this
situation it was Congress's responsibility "to relieve unemployment
and so regulate [its] custodianship that there will be available to all

the people some portion of the total work-hour requirements of the nation."[65]

Moreover, in contrast to the administration's use of countercyclical spending, drafters of the Deane bill intended to counter only short-term, "weekly-hours recessions." Similarly, they used the overtime provisions to discourage short-term, "over-expansions," making no attempt to try to influence long-term (ten-year average) developments by such countercyclical measures. Supporters such as Connery, and Deane himself on occasion, concluded that the "total-work hour requirements of the nation" were declining.[66] Connery and the Labor Committee considered long-term trends to be out of the realm of possible legislation and federal action, and left them to the free market.

Roosevelt continued into 1935 to exhibit some interest in unemployment compensation proposals such as Deane's. For example, Witte recorded that the first draft of the President's January 17 message, prepared by Arthur Altmeyer, contained nothing at all about the stabilization of employment. Coming "as a complete surprise to the [CES] committee," Roosevelt discussed the role that unemployment compensation would play in industrial recovery. He suggested that unemployment compensation be geared to public works and rejected the CES restrictions on state laws, inviting the states to use measures along the lines of the Wisconsin statute to "induce industries" to stabilize employment through tax and other incentives. Even though the President was not critical of CES, the committee and some members of Congress understood the January 17 message to be an indication "that the President was not entirely satisfied with the committee's recommendations in this respect."[67] Witte remembered that "the language [in the message] was added by Professor Moley" and that throughout 1935, Roosevelt remained interested in the potential that unemployment insurance measures had to counter extreme fluctuations in the labor market.[68] Other than the Wisconsin law, the Deane plan was the only politically viable unemployment compensation scheme to include plans for industrial stabilization. Roosevelt's unexpected endorsement of this function of unemployment compensation on January 17 may indicate that the administration was still interested in aspects of the Deane plan. If true, this would support the revisionist historians' contention that the labor relations experts continued to wield their influence in the administration at the expense of the social worker.

But Roosevelt was certainly not interested enough to back such amendments to Social Security in Congress. Connery and Monaghan appear to have tried to compromise with the administration through such measures as the Deane plan, but Roosevelt offered few concessions to the work sharers on his political left in 1935, at least in terms of specific changes in Social Security. He understood that even though the measure had been stripped of practically all its work-sharing and industrial stabilization features, his appeals to Social Security and welfare would carry the left. His main concessions in that direction were rhetorical; the main opposition in Washington to Social Security was coming from the right. Consequently, those less interested than Connery in compromising with Roosevelt and more interested in forcing the issues took the lead in the House Labor Committee and on the floor.[69]

Lundeen's proposal surfaced in the House Labor Committee immediately after the administration's bill was given to the House Ways and Means Committee and Connery's efforts to find support for the Deane plan failed. One of the most radical of all the retirement and unemployment measures, the Lundeen bill eliminated any retirement age restriction by the simple expedient of defining retirement as unemployment. Unemployment due to any cause—old age, sickness, pregnancy, disability, or injury—was unemployment and was to be compensated under Lundeen's proposal. Moreover, there was no question about benefits being attractive enough to lure the marginally employed; rates of unemployment compensation were to be the same as average weekly paychecks, except if the average wage was less than $10 a week plus $3 for each dependent, which was to be the minimum compensation. In contrast to other unemployment compensation schemes, which depended on special funds and reserves built up by a tax on payrolls, Lundeen looked to general tax revenues and proposed additional taxes on individual and cooperate income over $5000 and a new tax on gifts and inheritances to support such payments. Lundeen would have covered all workers under his bill and would have had the program run by representatives elected by "the workers."[70]

Before the House Ways and Means Committee could complete hearings on the administration's bill, the Labor Committee hurriedly conducted its own hearings on the Lundeen bill and reported it out of committee favorably on March 15. But the administration blocked this move, and the Lundeen bill was not placed on the House calendar. Connery introduced a resolution for a special rule for consideration of Lundeen, and a petition was circulated for discharge from the Rules Committee, but only a few signatures were collected. Not until the Lundeen bill was offered as a substitute to the Social Security Act did the House vote on the measure, defeating it soundly.[71]

It is hard to understand why the Lundeen bill, as radical as it was, should have had such ready support in the House Labor Committee. Apart from Lundeen himself, who had strong communist ties, others in the committee, such as Connery, Crosser, John S. McGroarty, Vito Marcantonio, Maury Maverick, and Joseph P. Monaghan were not wide-eyed iconoclasts and were surely aware that such a radical version, almost a caricature, of the most extreme position on every Social Security issue had no chance of becoming law. The Lundeen bill did make a point of showing how far the administration measure was from making any important impact on unemployment—how far it was from being an industrial stabilization and reemployment measure, and the extent to which it had become a security and welfare measure. As such, Lundeen served to clarify the work-sharing issues once again. In defending his measure, Lundeen and his supporters played heavily on the inevitable acceleration of technological unemployment and the need to support the growing army of the unemployed, as well as to find some method to distribute the remaining work equitably. A good case may be made that the House Labor Committee used the Lundeen measure as a work-sharing stalking horse mainly to draw their colleagues out on issues such as retirement age and pensions large enough to make an impact on reemployment, issues that the administration was sweeping under the rug.

Even more radical than the Lundeen proposal, the Townsend plan, although it generated a good deal of publicity, had less of an impact on the legislative development of Social Security. Nevertheless, it demonstrated the widespread, continuing interest in the country in retirement work sharing. The movement's official slogan, "Youth for Work—Age for Leisure," and its insistence that the aged give their work to the young were as influential in winning public support as its more extreme wealth-sharing proposals—the sending of $200 a month to everyone over age sixty, providing that they spend it in sixty days. The Townsend bills, H.R. 3977 and H.R. 7154, introduced in early 1935, were given to a hostile House Ways and Means Committee and were not taken seriously. Nevertheless, like the Lundeen measure, Townsend and his supporters raised the question of work sharing in unmistakable terms and exhibited the extent to which Roosevelt had abandoned the cause. Like Lundeen, Townsend raised again the critical retirement work-sharing issues: age of retirement, amount of annuity, and mandatory retirement.[72]

Following the Townsend and Lundeen proposals, a short-lived insurgency of moderates did develop around the retirement-age issue. More successful than more radical proposals, the move to reduce the age for retirement benefits from sixty-five to sixty ultimately received 160 votes on a House motion to recommit Social Security for this and other measures. The origin of this insurgency was complex, combining the interests of several groups. Some of the 160 votes for recommittal were conservatives trying to sabotage Social Security. Serious supporters included representatives such as Gerald Boileau of Wisconsin, who were attracted to the Townsend plan but could not support some of its more radical features and so fixed on its age sixty limit as a form of modified support. Others followed Harold Knutson of Minnesota, who, as a member of the House Ways and Means Committee, opposed the committee's recommendations on Social Security and issued his own minority report, which included the age sixty provision. Still others, such as Monaghan (and other former sponsors of Social Security legislation), had supported earlier retirement ages since the 73rd Congress. Finally, liberal representatives such as Charles Trax of Ohio, a member of the House Labor Committee, who had supported the Lundeen measure, joined the age sixty movement as a fallback position after having lost their main objective to Roosevelt's forces.[73]

Most of those in the insurgency were united about why age sixty was preferable. They used the same work-sharing language as supporters of shorter work hours. Several representatives saw the similarities. For example, Dunn of Pennsylvania commented on his experiences at the House Labor Committee hearings on the 30-hour legislation and related that testimony directly to the age sixty debates. Others, such as Knutson, felt that "shortening the hours of toil" alone would not be enough and concluded that retirement at age sixty was a necessary part of a total work-sharing system.[74]

One of the more perceptive observations was offered by John Marshall Robsion of Kentucky. He was in favor of age sixty, but he was not as doctrinaire as other work sharers. He agreed that efficiency had increased and production had expanded so fast that they had somehow managed to outrun consumption. Unemployment and the depression had resulted. Even after the most pressing needs of the depression were met by expanded spending and increased economic activity, the nation would face long-term work scarcity. Robsion saw two possible remedies: "There are but two things. We must work out a plan to create more work and provide more jobs, or divide the work and jobs that now exist."[75] In these two sentences, spoken on the House floor on April 15, Robsion identified the crux of the debate and the whole point of efforts to compromise on such things as age sixty or sixty-five. Cutting through the complex political events, in these few words he epitomized Roosevelt's new, vigorous industrial policy and summed up the opposition: the old, and fading, work-sharers' solutions.

Hence, Roosevelt withstood at least four important attacks on his version of Social Security: The Deane plan promoted by Connery and the House Labor Committee, the Lundeen and Townsend plans, and the attempts in Congress to amend Social Security to include age sixty for retirement. Each attack was designed to put work sharing back into federal retirement and unemployment legislation. From its origin and through its passage, Social Security and work sharing were linked. Roosevelt had his hands full politically when he and his administration abandoned its original interest in retirement work sharing and turned to security and welfare as the major functions of retirement legislation. From the CES report, it is clear why Roosevelt made this move. By 1935, he and his advisers had come up with a positive alternative, work creation, and were using measures like the WPA and monetary policies to achieve industrial stabilization and growth.

With the passage of Social Security, labor saw its 1935 legislative program enacted less than two months after the *Schechter* decision, with the exception of wage-and-hour regulation. But, beginning in August, labor renewed pressure to enact such legislation to complete the restoration of the NRA. John Frey, president of the AFL's Metal Trades Department, joined Green in repeating the call for 30 hours, explaining that "at present our nation is endeavoring to cope with this rapid elimination of workmen by paying out billions for dollars in relief and billions more for the purpose of stimulating the nation's industry and commerce. But the process of increasing the workman's per capita production has not stopped, instead it is being stimulated in every industry." Frank Morrison, veteran secretary of the AFL, observed that the administration's expectation that workers forced out of old industries would be reemployed in new ones was flawed, explaining that "the new industrial revolution operates in new industries as well as in established industries."[76] Morrison argued that "low paying jobs, such as employment at gas-filling stations and mass production industries, are no solution to unemployment" among skilled workers, concluding that "labor demands the five-day week, six-hour day and a wage that will enable his family to live in reasonable comfort."[77] Green vowed to continue the fight for 30 hours, calling the problem of "reemployment of the vast army of idle workers the most pressing problem" facing the nation and "the increased replacement of men by machines" the greatest threat.[78] Green, Frey, and Morrison, in a series of Labor Day speeches, agreed that 30-hour legislation was the only solution to unemployment and urged Congress to pass Black–Connery. At the October 1935 convention, the AFL renewed its demand for Black–Connery, calling it "the paramount objective" in 1936. Green observed that "we are going to fight for this as we have never fought before."[79]

Moreover, in September, Hugh Johnson, in a letter to Roosevelt announcing his resignation as WPA director for New York City, attacked the demise of the NRA and noted that there had been a 20 percent increase in the hours of labor, an increase he blamed directly on the ending of the codes. Johnson continued: "A lot of new unemployment has been created here [in New York City] in the last few weeks because of a marked extension of the hours of labor." In October, Johnson, speaking to a conference of trade association representatives, said that sixty days after the President's reemployment agreement, reducing the workweek to 35 hours, nearly 3 million new jobs had been created, and he called again for the renewal of regulations on hours.[80]

Reporting on business response to labor's pressure, the *New York Times* concluded that businessmen in New York were in favor of a modified recovery act in preference to 30-hour legislation. Trade association representatives, meeting in the city, "were sufficiently impressed" by the AFL's drive to be more receptive to a revival of wage-and-hour regulations in the NRA. At least one industrialist continued to favor 30 hours by voluntary agreement. W. K. Kellogg had maintained this work schedule for five years in his operations and felt that the plan was a permanent solution to the depression.[81]

Green kept up the pressure in January 1936. Meeting in Miami, the AFL Executive Council announced that 30 hours would top labor's legislative agenda, calling it labor's "standing remedy" for the depression. Green and the Executive Council also suggested that a constitutional amendment might be necessary if Black–Connery failed to pass that year.[82]

With the election coming up, Roosevelt again tried to placate labor in a concerted drive to show administration support of regulation of hours. Early in the year, he promised to present a minimum-wage, maximum-hour plan in 1936. Speculating that legislation could be written that would be declared constitutional, Roosevelt remained vague about the actual wage-and-hour levels, and the administration of such a plan. He promised only that regulation of hours would be included in the plan.[83]

In addition, Perkins and administration officials tried to show how successful the New Deal had been in reemployment in terms of the hours-of-labor question labor was still asking. Perkins observed that "more than 70,000,000 man-hours of employment have been created since August 1933, in producing and transporting the cement used in the public works projects." And 450 million man-hours had been created in mining, fabricating, and transportation of iron and steel products.[84]

Roosevelt also reaffirmed his faith in business recovery. He observed early in 1936 that "the ultimate answer to unemployment is with private industry. . . . Only if industry fails to reduce substantially the number of those now out of work will another appropriation and further plans and policies be necessary." While he said that antitrust laws must be "fully and vigorously" enforced, he saw nothing in them or any other laws that would "prohibit managers and business from working together to increase production and employment." Nevertheless, labor persisted. Having heard this rhetoric before, the AFL made support of the 30-hour bill an allegiance test for political candidates in the elections.[85]

Kicking off his campaign with a speech in Baltimore, Roosevelt tried another tactic. He suggested that work sharing was still a good idea, but not if it was achieved through 30 hours. Instead, he offered a plan through Social Security to limit work to persons between the ages of eighteen and sixty-five, adding that wage-and-hour standards were important not so much for reemployment but as a way to prevent "overly long hours" in "cutthroat" competition.[86]

Roosevelt also tried to make peace with labor by urging business and industry to make "reasonable reductions" in work hours voluntarily.[87] Secretary Roper asked the Chamber of Commerce to develop a program for "proper hours" along the lines of the old Teagle campaign.[88] In spite of Roosevelt's hardening position concerning antitrust enforcement, by October he was concerned enough with the shorter-hour issue in the campaign to say that shorter hours were "good for business" and that businesses should act together, voluntarily, to cut hours.[89]

Roosevelt also said that he sided with Green concerning the issue of the increasing average workweek. Green had brought this up in April, noting that while industry was increasing the hours of those with jobs, chronic unemployment remained and, according to Green, was growing. This, he noted, was share the work in reverse. Along with General Johnson, the AFL cited the longer work periods as a prime cause for continuing unemployment. Consequently, the administration tried to check this increase in work hours primarily through its efforts to promote voluntary reductions.[90]

Reflecting the administration's efforts, the Democratic convention and platform called for legislated wage-and-hour standards. And both contained a promise to seek a constitutional amendment for these purposes if legislation was blocked by the courts.

Still, little progress was made that year in Congress. Most developments were rhetorical, having to do with the campaign. Roosevelt's and the administration's support of shorter hours in 1936 was for show, used to blunt the adverse effect on the election of their opposition in 1935 to work sharing.[91]

Relentlessly, Green and the AFL continued to press for share the work after the election. Green, referring to Roosevelt's Baltimore speech in April and his proposal to reserve work for people between the ages of eighteen and sixty-five, called for amendments to Social Security for higher benefits and a lower age limit to alleviate unemployment. The AFL Tampa convention in November proclaimed, in what was sounding more and more like a Greek chorus: "Thirty hours [is] the only means of mastering unemployment." Moreover, labor had made an even more impressive showing in the election of 1936 than they had in 1934. Again, 30 hours topped their list of tests for candidates' allegiance to labor.[92]

Early in January 1937, Roosevelt again seemed to side with labor, complaining that hours were getting longer. "An average of 33.3 hours per week in manufacturing industries in September, 1934" had grown to "more than 40 per week in October, 1936." Every such action by employers "tends toward stepping up production without an equivalent stepping up of employment."[93]

On January 11, the AFL laid out its position to the President. Green remarked that the AFL "would not agitate for a constitutional amendment" if minimum-wage and maximum-hour legislation were passed. On January 16 and 21, FDR met with Black and Connery, both of whom, leaving their meetings, indicated that they would reintroduce their bills, for the fifth time, during the current congressional session.[94]

But FDR again stopped short of endorsing work sharing. Instead, he continued to oppose industrywide reductions in hours and tried to find a way to work around the congressional work sharers and labor to head off the perennial pressure for Black–Connery. At first he was inclined toward a proposal presented by the Industrial Council's coordinator, George Berry, to eliminate "sweatshop" hours and unfair practices by giving the Federal Trade Commission (FTC) mandatory authority to set hours and wages.[95]

Furthermore, in a series of meetings in late January with Lewis, Hillman, and C. P. Howard, Frances Perkins tried to reach an accord. After these meetings, reports circulated that the administration was considering a "new NRA" to spread work and spur reemployment. In order to spike demands for a constitutional amendment, a bill would be written to answer the Court's objections. The proposed bill would be modeled after the PRA and the blanket codes, and would impose a 40-hour limit on clerical workers and a 35-hour limit on factory and industrial workers, a compromise with the work sharers.[96]

On January 30, Hugh Johnson presented Roosevelt with a tax plan that would levy an excise tax on overlong hours, explaining that such a measure was a constitutional way to raise revenues, not to regulate commerce, and so would avoid the unconstitutional issues raised by imposing direct industry standards.

But the Business Advisory Council then met with Secretary Roper. The council opposed these measures and insisted that industrial growth and *increases* in working hours were desirable courses of action, pointing out that Roosevelt had been following these measures with success. In addition, in early February, Richberg warned Roosevelt once more against work sharing.[97]

At a February 3 press conference, FDR observed that wage-and-hour legislation was his primary concern and that he would go ahead regardless of the growing pressure in Congress (which Senator Borah was leading) for a constitutional amendment. These assurances were widely regarded as a ploy to "spike" the move for a constitutional amendment.[98]

As the administration was formulating its own wage-and-hour measure, opposition increased to the proposed legislation as a work-sharing measure. The Brookings Institution kept up a running battle with work sharing and in its *The Recovery Problem in the United States* concluded that "to keep on reducing hours to offset every gain in productive efficiency . . . would be to freeze the volume of national production." Other administration leaders joined in the condemnation. For example, Eccles opposed any wage-and-hour plan, stating that "money must be used as the servant to increase production and employment . . . and not to restrict employment and production."[99]

Throughout February, FDR moved closer to a bill designed to limit "excessively low wages and long hours" rather than work sharing. The *New York Times* reported that the Roosevelt administration "scraps the Black–Connery bill and will offer its own plan." Moreover, in the spring, with a series of cases, the Supreme Court began to reverse its position on industrial regulation in *West Coast Hotel* v. *Parish* and five Labor Board cases, holding that the Labor Relations Act was a constitutional use of the federal government's power to regulate interstate commerce.[100]

With this change in the Court's position, on May 22 the administration unveiled its proposal for a 40-cent-per-hour minimum wage and a 40-hour-per-week maximum on hours. Included in the proposal was a three-man commission with authority to alter maximum and minimums, to average work out in seasonal industries to the 40–40 standards. Labor was wary of these proposals; it was disappointed in the 40-hour maximum and suspicious of the minimum wage. Green met with Roosevelt and expressed fears that such a minimum wage might well lower minimums currently in place, established by collective bargaining. He also told Roosevelt and the press that the 40-hour provision would create few new jobs and would apply only to a limited number of firms; again he pressed Roosevelt at least to compromise and lower the maximum hours from 40 and toward labor's baseline of 30.[101]

Finally, on May 4, FDR unveiled his wage-and-hour law, calling on Congress "to extend the frontiers of social progress." But Congress and the President were far apart on the measure. After a last-minute conference with the President, Connery and Black, who had been chosen as the logical members to submit the administration's bill to Congress, changed the administration's draft before they introduced it, deleting the 40-hour-maximum and 40-cent-minimum-wage provisions and announcing that they would press for provisions for a five-member board empowered to set hours between 40 and 30 a week. Joseph Taylor Robinson, the Senate majority leader, joined with Black and Connery to convince the President to demur and let Congress set specific wage-and-hour levels.[102]

The bill, as introduced, simply left these sections blank. Thus the fight continued in Congress, with work sharers versus those opposed to share the work and favoring regulation of overlong hours.

At first, Green and the AFL threatened to fight the bill, believing that minimum wage could easily become a maximum wage. In Cincinnati, Green suggested that the old Black–Connery bill should be passed instead, and the AFL Executive Council officially endorsed this call on May 28.[103]

But because of opposition from businessmen and from southern congressmen, Roosevelt was able to sway labor and gain tentative support. Green finally endorsed the bill in principle, hoping that Congress would set limits that would actually reduce work hours. Hillman and Frey, questioned by reporters whether the 40-hour-week provision would not destroy their hopes for a substantial reduction in hours, responded, "We feel that a quick limitation of hours and the establishment of minimum wages . . . will bring us closer to a 30 hour week than a 40 hour week." Labor, at this point, remained hopeful that the administration bill, managed by Black and Connery, would emerge as a work-sharing rather than a "sweatshop" bill and would thus achieve some compromise with 30 hours.[104]

Hearings on the bill, which the press still called "Black–Connery," began June 2 before the combined Senate and House Committees on Labor. Green, in his testimony before the committees, supported the 40-hour "minimum maximum," with the provision that the board be empowered to set hours as low as 30. In addition, the AFL endorsed fixing the minimum wage at 40 cents an hour, but objected to allowing the board to fix wage rates at a later date, insisting that collective bargaining have this role and that the board accept, as industry standards, hour-and-wage levels achieved by labor in specific occupations. John L. Lewis concurred with Green in this position.[105]

But the administration and its congressional allies began to link wages and hours together and talk more in terms of an "annual wage" than an hourly wage rate. They were successful in shifting the issue from work sharing to total wages paid, stressing the fact, in Hugh Johnson's words, that hours per week was the "multiplier" and hourly wages the "multiplicand." Hence, demands to shorten hours were countered by the argument that total annual wages would be reduced. For example, in the clothing trades, Hillman accepted these terms and stressed the need for an $800 annual wage (40 cents an hour × 40 hours per week × 50 weeks a year). In this way, the administration forced labor to make a choice between wages and hours legislatively that economists close to Roosevelt had always thought existed in the labor marketplace, a theory that labor had always rejected.[106]

Still, during the June hearings in the House, William Connery continued to try to fashion a compromise that would keep work sharing in the administration bill and bring it more in line with his 30-hour proposal.[107] But much of Connery's old enthusiasm had dimmed. He and John Ryan reminisced together about the 30-hour legislation they had been advocating for more than four years. Ryan observed that "no legislative proposal has given me as much satisfaction as the Black–Connery bill." Connery responded, recalling how they had continued to fight for share the work throughout the New Deal. He suggested that all of the labor and industrial stabilization legislation that Congress had enacted had at one time or another been part of his and Black's bill and that the administration had simply enacted Black–Connery piecemeal, shying away from its central feature, 30 hours.[108] He had made these observations several times earlier, noting that

> the committee feels that by the Black–Connery bill . . . into which we wrote the abolition of child labor, the abolition of the yellow-dog contract, the right to collective bargaining, the right of labor to organize, and the thirty hour week, we were not only the father but also the mother of the National Recovery Act.[109]

But now the administration was trying to pass hour-and-wage standards that would have little real impact on reemployment, thus completing the process of picking 30 hours apart as a depression measure.

Shortly after this exchange, Connery became suddenly ill. Rushed to a hospital, he died overnight of food poisoning on June 15, 1937. He was replaced as chairman of the House Labor Committee by Mary Norton, Democrat of New Jersey, who was much more sympathetic to the administration. With Connery's death, the most influential congressional supporter of work sharing was lost, and with Norton's rise to the chairmanship, Roosevelt's support in the House was assured. Since Black had already abandoned 30 hours, Roosevelt had much smoother sailing in Congress.[110]

Subsequently, the major opposition to Roosevelt's bill came from businessmen and from southern congressmen who were able to delay passage by bottling up the bill in the Ways and Means Committee until the session ended. Roosevelt then issued a call for a special session of Congress, to begin November 15, to pass the wage-and-hour bill.

Southern opposition continued into 1938. But apart from a few calls for 30 hours by the United Mine Workers, labor joined forces with Roosevelt. Still, a Democratic congressman, John O'Connor of New York, chairman of the House Ways and Means Committee, opposed Roosevelt's bill and kept it locked up in committee.

In his annual message to Congress in January 1938, Roosevelt reiterated his reasons for supporting the labor standards bill. He called for wage-and-hour limits to protect "the under-paid and the overworked," not to cure unemployment. His aim was to eliminate "starvation wages and intolerable hours." In addition, he underscored his concern with the "annual wage." Following the Brookings Institution's and Richberg's suggestions, he linked hours to wages as an either–or choice in a roundabout fashion: "Regularizing the work of individual workers . . . thinking more in terms of the worker's total pay for a period over the whole year than just . . . hourly wages" was the administration's basis for labor standards.[111]

Following his message, Roosevelt began negotiations with the southern forces, offering at a conference of southern governors that the southern freight-rate structure would be reexamined and a regional differential would be included in the new law. These were moves that the AFL opposed.[112]

Finally, after a public appeal by the President on April 30, the House approved the bill May 23. Signed by FDR on June 25, it became effective October 24. The bill, now called The Fair Labor Standards Act (FLSA), established a wage-and-hour division in the Department of Labor to enforce its provisions. Covering workers in interstate commerce, the measure set minimum wages at 25 cents per hour in 1938 and 30 cents in 1939. Maximum hours were set at 44 in 1938, 42 in 1939, and 40 for 1940 and following.[113] The issue of a minimum weekly wage increase was resolved by this formula:

Weekly Wages	Weekly Rate
First year	$11.00 (44 × $.25)
Second year	$12.60 (42 × $.30)
Third year	$14.00 (40 × $.35)
Fourth year and after	$16.00 (40 × $.40)

Administration supporters argued that millions of workers would be covered by the measure. But opponents, among them labor, were hard put to find anyone to whom the bill applied, especially in the provision on hours. Certainly some southern textile mills were covered. But since the average workweek was at 40 hours in industry, the bill was recognized for what Roosevelt had meant it to be: a cap to "overlong hours" and not a method to reduce unemployment.[114]

The administration, having rejected work sharing in the Fair Labor Standards Act, turned again to its alternative programs. Because the recession, which began in the autumn of 1937, had worsened through 1938, Roosevelt sent a special message to Congress in April, announcing that he planned to follow Eccles's suggestions, loosening credit restrictions and increasing deficit spending on public works. Congress responded by authorizing $3 billion for the WPA and increasing expenditures for the TVA and CCC. By this time, there was no doubt that Roosevelt and the administration had made its choice about how to deal with the depression: expanded employment and economic growth. Share the work had been branded a regressive measure, destined to share the poverty. Additional decreases in work hours, below 40, were shown by FLSA tables to be a drain on weekly and yearly earnings, and would henceforth be included as a leading negative economic indicator, predicting or showing a measure of economic downturn. The forces behind share the work and the continuation of the progressive shortening of the hours of labor had been routed.[115]

Lawrence Connery, appointed to serve out his brother William's unexpired term, expressed bitterness at these developments. Before the administration's bill passed the House, he insisted that the bill not carry his brother's name. Since it had been so changed by the administration and by amendments, the bill had little resemblance to what the elder Connery had devoted his life's work to in Congress; it was "no longer in accord with Billy Connery's aims."[116]

Thus Roosevelt, as several reporters predicted he must, had pulled another political trick out of his hat. He put together just the sort of "permanent industrial policy, coupled with a social security program of unemployment insurance and old-age pensions," that reporters predicted would be necessary to make "the thirty-hour agitation look small in comparison." And in so doing, Roosevelt completed the "second New Deal."[117]

Roosevelt displayed his well-known political agility throughout these events. But he was more than a political opportunist when it came to opposition to the shorter-hour cure for unemployment. Although he was not doctrinaire in this matter, and was willing to accept parts of the share-the-work strategy in retirement provisions of Social Security as pragmatic measures as late as 1934, in 1935 he and his advisers had developed ideological and policy alternatives to share the work that they consistently put forth as the better unemployment remedies, even at a considerable political price.

Whereas the Black–Connery forces would have divided a stable "lump of labor," Roosevelt was consistently more interested in increasing total work effort and creating new jobs. Supporters of shorter hours dreamed of increased leisure as a basis for individual freedom and progress, but the administration envisioned government acting to assure everyone the "right to work" a "full time job"—looking to secure work, not freedom from work, as the social desideratum.

The political contest that raged over Black–Connery reflected an ideological division of the first importance, a division between views of progress and views about the fate of work in the depression. With the ascendancy of Roosevelt's views about the importance of economic recovery and vitality, visions of increased leisure as the basis of culture and a healthy social order waned. With the coming of the "right to work," made sure by government support, the politics of shorter hours faded. With the emergence of the second New Deal, the shorter-hour process in America ran up against its first successful adversary, and the salvaging of work from the steady erosion of shorter hours began.

In a letter to Arthur Schlesinger dated April 9, 1958, Leon Keyserling stressed that Roosevelt came to Washington without a "systematic economic program." The "highly experimental, improvised and inconsistent" programs of the first New Deal defy categorization. They were the products of "schools of reformers" that had been promoting diverse programs that Roosevelt, higgledy-piggledy, picked up. According to Keyserling, the PWA, CWA, NIRA, and the rest were not parts of any systematic plan or overall purpose. The only coherence given these events came from outside the administration. It was the "desire to get rid of the Black bill" that prompted the administration to draw up such things as the NRA, "to put in something to satisfy labor." This same point was made by other notables in Roosevelt's administration, among them Raymond Moley.[118]

Throughout the depression, 30-hour legislation goaded Roosevelt to action. The Black–Connery bill, introduced in each depression Congress until passed in highly modified form as the Fair Labor Standards Act in 1938, with all the work-sharing teeth pulled, continued to function as a sort of reverse polestar, enabling Roosevelt to chart his course by the simple expedient of sailing in the opposite direction. Roosevelt's instinctive reaction against 30 hours matured to positive approaches to industrial stabilization and reemployment. They were built on work creation, not work spreading, founded on industrial growth and increased spending as the wellsprings of progress. In the process, he and his administration discarded the century-old notion that work reduction had the potential for social and individual advancement.

From the point of view of someone like Representative William Connery, who pushed for 30 hours from 1932 to 1937, the New Deal had a coherence, a reason for happening when and as it did, that was lost on others not so positioned. From Connery's perspective, the New Deal was what it was because of its opposition to 30 hours.

CHAPTER 9

Intellectuals and Reformers Abandon Shorter Hours

JUST AS the 30-hour bill seemed about to be passed by Congress in 1933, Rexford Tugwell published *The Industrial Discipline and the Governmental Arts*. This work, more than any other single document, presented what was to become the administration's position on work creation vis-à-vis work reduction. As such, it stands as representative of a view of government's role in progress and reform shared increasingly by intellectuals and reformers as the depression wore on.

Tugwell devoted his book to challenging the idea that reductions of work were necessary or desirable in the depression and detailing specific policy alternatives that were to be embodied in the New Deal. Tugwell later described the last chapter of this book as "a preview of the NRA."[1] More important, in his opposition to work reductions, Tugwell outlined an alternative philosophy of progress that gradually emerged as one of the New Deal's few political and social dogmas. Although Tugwell had developed these themes before, and would reiterate them later in the depression, *The Industrial Discipline* remains the most complete and succinct presentation of his ideas.

Tugwell began with the issue that was troubling many of his contemporaries. He reviewed the progress of inventions, mechanization, and industrialization, and found that the end of labor was in sight— "within a stone's throw."[2] While it was possible to criticize the machine for taking away work, and it was tempting to look back longingly to preindustrial days when such problems did not exist, such talk was idle, such dreams useless. The machine would go on taking away work. It would continue to make traditional occupations routine, if not obsolete, and while it removed much of work's drudgery, it also removed its creative and human dimensions. Not only were machines "devital-izing" work but advances in industrial organization, the "serialization" of machines and regimentation of workers, represented more pro-found dimensions in mechanization—machines were being made that made other machines. With such quantum advances in inventions and industrial organization, work was being lost to the machine exponen-tially.[3]

But Tugwell could not bring himself to accept the possibility that the goal of industrial progress was the elimination of work. This sort of "climax" could hardly be said to have been intended through the centuries of effort and improvement. The caveman who first used a stick as a lever to pry at a stone, if he had anything in mind, did not in-tend this. Inventors down through the centuries had specific purposes for their machines, specific jobs that had to do with immediate need and not with some distant elimination of effort.[4] This "crisis of inven-tion" was an ironic accident. For while humans had been using their ingenuity in such a way as to ensure the end of labor, they had at the same time made a virtue of hard work, praising most "he who works longest and hardest." Perhaps, Tugwell wrote, this final "climax" was part of some obscure, subterranean human motive, a sort of uncon-scious desire that was opposite conscious intention and had somehow been able to assert itself in the collective actions of toolmakers and inventors.[5]

How this unintended or unconscious "climax" came to be "within a stone's throw" was not as important as what to do about the prospect, for Tugwell "knew of no question which interest[ed] him more than this one."[6] He wrote: "Is it too much to ask that we should seize on the prospect of the final release from labor and put it for a time at the center of our thinking; that we should not be ashamed to desire it and scheme to bring it about?" He ventured to guess that 1933 was the time when people were finally ready to entertain such a "grand hypothesis," and accordingly he devoted his book "largely [to] the statement of it."[7]

Putting the "release from labor at the center" of his thinking, Tugwell saw two alternative ways this release could come about. One "path" would be to accept the machine and its routine work, finding freedom in the "reduction of hours of work and days of work to the lowest minimum, finding relief . . . in higher wages, more leisure, bet-ter recreation, and in like ways." Or, release and freedom could take the form of new and better kinds of work, free from drudgery and routine and transformed by government and industry into something new. Looking around him at the time, he found that "tendencies in both these directions can be discerned," both in the political arena and in the world of the intellectual. But he felt he had to take a stand and show how one form of "release" was infinitely better than the other.[8]

The "release" into freedom as leisure, while a form of "immediate relief" and a kind of repose from the centuries of work effort and tension, was a dead-end. Tugwell was willing to admit that "there is a certain playful restlessness in men that ought not to be stopped from expression in a variety of amateur activities."[9] But leisure and amateurism, the antipodes of work, as the sole content of the new freedom and the direction for new progress, were anathema. They could never create "a new worker's world."[10] Supporters of share the work who talked nonsense about the promise of leisure were nihilists. They had "elaborated a despairing notion" that there was only a limited amount of work to be done and that what was left by the machine "must be shared out carefully." This notion was "thoroughly inconsistent with what any person of sense knows."[11] It was not useless leisure that men needed and longed for, it was worthwhile jobs. True progress lay on the frontiers of new work, not in the backwaters of mass idleness.

Government and industry had to take the lead and, transforming work, offer authentic progress as an alternative to the nihilism of leisure. The release from "old labor" must be the release into "human work." It was true that "work, in its physical sense, [was] no part of man's destiny, but the sphere of machines." This fact had confused people, especially those in the labor movement who resisted innovation and understood progress only as higher wages and shorter hours. Rightly understood, "the obvious lesson of the industrial revolution" was that an opportunity had arisen to "remake human occupations" and choose a "different orientation of industrial effort."[12] Work had to be recast; it had to be freed of drudgery and compulsion and transformed into creative, fulfilling, and freely chosen careers and "occupations." Industrial effort had to be turned from traditional concerns with producing more and meeting "basic needs" to the service of "worthwhile effort." Furthermore, industrial progress was no longer to be measured by increases in output and reductions of effort. On the contrary, industry and government now had another, nobler goal: the creation and sure provision of good jobs.[13]

Having given his thoughts about what progress ought and ought not become, Tugwell proceeded to outline what the transformed work would look like and practical ways to provide more of it. In a general sense, transformed work would be marked by cooperation and joint effort and not, as work had been for so long, marred by competition and self-seeking. The primary goals of cooperative work would be social, not individual; fairness, for example, would replace the ethic of dog-eat-dog. Common purposes such as the "public interest," the encouragement of cooperation and assistance of technological advances, would emerge and guide work; older, selfish work motives would be replaced by concern for the welfare of the whole social and economic order.[14]

Transformed work would also "multiply thinking tasks." As the machine took over repetitive operations, as it should, men and women would be given useful employment that was uniquely human—jobs that challenged and developed the mind rather than taxed the body. Increasingly, workers would enter the "managerial range" and begin to work controlling "complex operations," building up "an executive operation with . . . expanded personnel and with the elaborat[ion] of duties."[15] The major contribution of innovations such as paperwork, for example, was "to enlarge the grasp of the human mind so that it can take in wider areas and more complicated problems than it could do unaided."[16]

In addition to overseeing the introduction of new machinery and making sure that boring and unrewarding jobs were given to the machine, some new workers, the cream of the crop, would have the awesome responsibility of finding new worthwhile work; they would have to work on work. These new workers, in the upper echelons of universities, businesses, and government, would be at "the heart of the process by which we are redefining and readapting modern work." They would have to "distinguish in men their special abilities" and go on to the "fitting of tasks to [these abilities] and defining work in human terms." By taking a "scientific approach to a definition of man's role in the working life," they would produce intrinsically satisfying jobs, not old-fashioned goods and services.[17]

Some workers on work, probably those in universities, would "continue to set new problems for solution." As the day approached when "a standardized machine series [could] turn out goods indefinitely," then "we [would] ask for new inventions which make new problems. For specially gifted individuals with the requisite training, we set up wonderfully equipped institutions for research and experiment, perhaps in direct connection with an industry, perhaps in a university . . . the results we get are equally disturbing—and equally valuable." New frontiers with new challenges to overcome, new problems to work through, would come along if American institutions responded to the challenge and did their duty to "multiply the thinking tasks."[18]

Other workers on work, in both government and industry, would, as they had already begun to do, bring more kinds of human relationships and dealings into the marketplace and convert more "worthless" activities and pastimes into useful work. Tugwell used the general term "functionalization" for this process and saw such efforts as a part of a larger development whereby "effort was thought of in terms of what it is intended to accomplish rather than what it is." The key to progress was understanding what effort was for, not what it was in and of itself. Human effort and human beings had meaning only as they were "instruments of a social purpose, rather than as object of social solicitude."[19]

> We work, consume, live, together; we are social. Programs and purposes must be group programs and purposes. The individual, to get anywhere himself, must subordinate himself. . . . He must consent to function as part of a greater whole and have his role defined for him by the exigencies of his group. We need . . . a direction for individual and group functions which shall subject each to a larger purpose and give each a sense of unity in a wider functioning. . . . For definition nothing short of a national view will be effective.[20]

Work was the expression of meaning and function within the social group. Leisure was a void for the solipsistic, meaningless gesture of the isolated individual.

New methods had to be developed to provide this new work. The old-fashioned free marketplace and laissez-faire capitalism were not equipped for the task. They had led to overproduction and mass idleness and the threat of leisure. A complete overhauling of industry by government was called for. The economic situation had to be stabilized immediately by "extensions of present government controls which would in a sense direct production and even consumption." These controls would mean concessions from "the present owner–employer group" and labor's withdrawal "from dependence on bargaining for higher and higher wages and shorter and shorter hours as the sole means of making progress." These controls would also involve "recasting our notions of property rights . . . deeply embedded in our legal system." Both labor and management would have to turn to cooperation and hence, more and more, to government supervision.[21] But these adaptations were essential in order to avoid chronic unemployment or, equally bad, the "leisure" of an enduring work famine. In a virtual blueprint for the NRA, Tugwell prescribed government controls and direction of industry for the short-term goal of industrial stabilization and the enduring purpose of job creation.[22]

Tugwell concluded that the main fear people had about the depression was the loss of work—the prospect that with so much production and with the advance of technique and efficiency, "we shall discover no way of using people's time."[23] This fear had paralyzed government and society, creating a reluctance to accommodate institutions to the advance of industry. But once government took the lead and accepted the primary moral imperative—"we ought to be working long hours and many days"—then the needed adaptations would follow.[24] Models for this adaptation were available in things like federal farm-relief programs. All that was needed was the political will and skill to get the job done.

In support of his vision of recasting progress in terms of new work, thereby transcending "mere higher wages and shorter hours," Tugwell reemployed the rhetoric used during "the economy of scarcity." It was clear enough to him that not only were work sharing and the "new leisure" inadequate as a philosophy of progress, they were ridiculous responses to the national economic emergency. Even as the machine was revolutionizing production, "there are still people insufficiently supplied with goods, the city and the countryside alike cry out for physical reconstruction. . . . Everyone knows there is work to be done, plenty of it." The position of the work sharers was "thoroughly inconsistent with our conspicuous need for goods."[25] Although it was true that when one looked at the economy in terms of decades, the industrial problem of overproduction and the need to make new work were paramount. But in the short term, for the sake of economic recovery, more production, not less, was required. Tugwell saw no inconsistency in these positions. More work, not less, was essential for recovery. More work, not less, was the ultimate goal and enduring product of a mature industrial society.

Tugwell returned often to these themes: the ending of "old labor" because of productivity, the waste of idleness and threat of increased "leisure," the need for more work and production for recovery, and the necessity of applying American institutions to the creation of new forms of "worthwhile work" over the long term. Tugwell centered his political philosophy in these simple precepts. The policies he promoted in the New Deal and his subsequent writings were guided by them. Moreover, he was able to put them into common-sense terms, arguing, with what he believed was considerable impact on Roosevelt, that the solution to the depression was to create "a situation in which everybody could employ everybody else and everybody work for everybody else"—what critics were to brand the "take-in-each-other's-washing" argument. Tugwell remembered that this bit of reasoning "appealed to Roosevelt," and for the first time "offered him a way out [of the depression]."[26]

In line with his ability to express his basic precepts simply and effectively, Tugwell was able to use them to shape administration policies. His ideas were at the heart of the NRA, in things such as the setting of hours by the codes at 40 a week, and the efforts to encourage consumer spending. Even when he supported temporary production controls, he cautioned that if short-term policies, which idled men and machines, were made permanent, "this would not be progress . . . it would be an admission that we have created a Frankenstein which we are unable to master."[27]

The public works section of the NIRA also dovetailed with Tugwell's basic principles. As Tugwell remembered events, he and Wagner were principal supporters of the inclusion of public works in the NIRA, and were able to prevail amid the "pretty bad mix-up" of events and conflicting pressures that swirled around the drafting of the legislation.[28] By 1935, Tugwell was speaking about the "third economy" when he reviewed the progress of public works. Recounting the advances the administration had made in the control of soil erosion, new land-utilization policies, rural housing and city sanitation projects, development of community recreational, educational, artistic and cultural programs, the CCC, the PWA and WPA, Tugwell saw clear indications that a completely new category of jobs, a "third economy," had been created. From a profit-and-loss standpoint, these jobs were "unprofitable." Nevertheless, they were "necessary." These efforts were designed to "preserve both the individual and the State, without immediate advantage to either." They focused on long-term, collective goals: the conservation and preservation of "the national patrimony" and the construction of an infrastructure on which to build new jobs for common purposes. Newly built community recreation facilities, for instance, would continue well into the future to provide useful occupations for recreation professionals, who would work for the public good to make leisure worthwhile and socially beneficial; the nation could even work on its play. To his satisfaction, Tugwell saw much of what he prescribed in 1933 coming to pass by 1935. The nation was well on its way to developing new work in the service of new social and national purposes.[29]

Tugwell shuddered to think what would have happened if the Puritan ways of life had held in the modern world, if "people were content with a subsistence level of life" and the "old ascetic ideal that man is richest whose needs are least" had been followed. It was not the elimination of desires that was needed; it was the creation of new "means to satisfy them." In defense of public works, Tugwell argued that idleness was waste on a giant scale. For him, it was "part of national self-preservation" to make good use of unemployment, instead of retrenching into a parsimonious existence.[30]

Not only had technology made imperative an ever-higher standard of living, it had also created a "huge national resource in the form of human energy" released from basic work tasks, a "margin of skilled and useful workers no longer required by the kinds of production which furnishes our ordinary goods." But until Roosevelt came along, the nation had not recognized that unemployment represented "the greatest of our national resources" gone to seed. If all the idle hours that had been wasted during the depression had been put to use, "we could have given every family in America a brand new $5,000 house." For Tugwell, this idleness was an "appalling waste." But public works was only one answer.[31]

Tugwell recalled that he and the administration took an "experimental attitude," believing that "we shall learn by experience how to utilize for the common good the human energy which is being released from the task of production by our steady increase in technical skill and industrial efficiency." Tugwell's and the New Deal's well-known willingness to experiment did not take place in a vacuum. For Tugwell, at least, the experiments had a firm purpose.[32]

As the depression wore on, Tugwell was even willing to turn to the private sector for the generation of jobs. As far as he was concerned, the administration's efforts to stimulate private industry and business were designed for the same purposes as public works. For instance, he defended the administration's deficit-spending policies in much the same way as he defended public works. Asking "How shall we pay for all of this?" he observed that the money borrowed and spent on things like public works would generate new spending and new jobs in numerous industries and businesses. Since taxes came out of the national income, increased private activity would increase the amount of taxes collected. As idleness was reemployed, revenues would increase enough to pay off the debt without an increase in the tax rate. If "the present efforts [to stimulate the private sector by government spending] succeed and industry under private management provides work, the increase in national income will give the government a big reservoir of wealth upon which to draw for paying the bill." Tugwell was one of the first people in the administration to sound this "idleness reemployed" theme and one of the first to use it to justify the New Deal's spending and monetary policies. But Tugwell was careful to add that "if present measures fail and industry does not provide work, then public authority may be expected to step in more decisively to insure the providing of work and of goods. . . . We have capacities we are not using. These are not lost. All we need is the courage and the intelligence to put them to work."[33]

As he had done in *The Industrial Discipline*, Tugwell continued to attack the work sharers as the New Deal unfolded, contrasting the New Deal's reasonable policy of work creation with their absurd work reductions. For instance, in 1935 he pointed with pride to the administration's "intelligent solution of the main problem of production through coordination and through the cultivation of the 'Third Economy.'" A "flood of activity" had been released; new work, new goods and services, and new energy were replacing the lassitude and virtual paralysis of the early depression. These things had been accomplished in spite of continued support for "shared work or shared leisure which still [in mid-1935] *dominate* [emphasis added] our sentimental wishful thinking." But the New Deal's policies, which "realiz[ed] that there is work here for at least five million men as far ahead as we can see," had given the lie to the work sharers.[34]

In addition to enlisting private industry and business in his cause, Tugwell appealed to public institutions other than government to get the job done. His main pitch was to education. In fact, Tugwell's earliest appeals were to the schools. Even before publishing *The Industrial Discipline*, Tugwell had wrestled with the problem of technological displacement, which he renamed "occupational obsolescence," and called for a "revolution in teaching" to meet the problem. He recommended that schools establish "a vocational heart to the educative process," and commit fully to "the necessity of preparing children for an industrial career."[35]

He observed that "it ought not to be impossible . . . to reeducate men to continually new tasks." Except for one "important obstacle," the way was clear. As usual, Tugwell cast the work sharers as the villains in his story. The "important obstacle" was nothing more than "our prevalent council of despair . . . the feeling at large that we have too many goods and too many workers." As he did so many times, he saw "everywhere . . . talk of surplus, of the need of reducing stocks of goods, of withholding efforts to produce. Never . . . in history has economic nonsense got itself into so many heads." Even educators had been misled.[36]

Sounding the same themes that guided him as a presidential adviser, he explained to teachers that it was true that technology was taking jobs away and superannuating old occupations. But instead of giving up on education for jobs and retreating to a fantastic "education for its own sake" or education for leisure, Tugwell recommended the acceptance of "the obsolescence of occupations as . . . desirable." Then "unemployment becomes another sort of problem." Workers "will not have to become useless; but the nature of their work will have changed." It was man's destiny to find new kinds of employment and the schools' responsibility to recast occupations in new and creative forms.[37]

Speaking about his "third economy" before the Rochester Teacher's

Association in April 1935, Tugwell voiced some of his most desperate fears about "the threat of idleness." He had found that "Satan still finds some ill for idle hands to do." The manpower released by the machine "demands to be used, and would be used" for ill or for good. If that "surplus energy" was not channeled to "constructive" social purposes, it would lead to despair and then be exploited for "military or imperialistic purposes. This is the lesson of history." Unless the nation was able to divert "our idle man-power into tasks contemplated by our 'Third Economy,'" war was inevitable; human suffering and chaos on a gigantic scale were just around the corner.[38]

> It is only by utilizing the surplus man-power which has been set free by the machine to develop our national heritage and to reconstruct our ways of living that we can avoid the temptation of war and the risks of revolution. In other words, unless we reshape our society so as to use the great human resources now sardonically represented by unemployment, these resources will demand expression and that expression will be catastrophic.[39]

Tugwell called for a "new spirit" in education and a "revolution in teaching," an "entirely new kind of school" to meet this threat. Schools had to turn to "adult retraining" so that "we can substitute technological replacement . . . for technological unemployment." Teachers had the responsibility to lead the way in creating new, rewarding work for the social welfare and, indeed, the well-being of the world.[40]

Schools also had a vested interest in seeing to it that Roosevelt's policies, such as the WPA, were funded. With the administration, schools had to advance to "brainwork" and persevere in training students for those "enlarged mental tasks" that were the future of work. One of the greatest tragedies of the depression was that "trained brains" were sitting at home with degrees and nothing to do. Harry Hopkins and the administration had taken the lead and set these "trained brains" doing tasks "which heretofore [were supported by] university or foundation funds." The alternative was to give such people unskilled jobs, and "this is a waste for which our generation should not be responsible." Working together, government and school could center education on work, with government providing the jobs and the schools the appropriate training, and so begin to deal with the threat of idleness that gave every indication of becoming a twentieth-century plague.[41]

A second reformer, Walter Lippmann, was late coming to the topic of leisure and was interested in it but a short while. Years after Stephen Leacock, John Ryan, and Stuart Chase had written seriously about leisure, Lippmann published his extraordinary contributions. But when he did write, in the early 1930s, he added a special historical perspective coupled with unique insights. The most important of his writings on the subject was an article in the *Woman's Home Companion* titled "Free Time and Extra Money."[42]

He admitted that mass leisure was a new issue for him. "Who would have thought it?" he asked. Only the utopian writers of his youth had dared to imagine such a thing. But it was apparent to Lippmann that the day had arrived, albeit unexpectedly, when poverty was "almost abolished." With this abolition, a new trouble had sprung up to plague the sons and daughters of Adam, "the problem of leisure." Reformers of Lippmann's generation, those who "stood at Armageddon with Theodore Roosevelt," never had foreseen this turn of events or worried themselves with such remote possibilities. Those who, like Lippmann, had fought alongside labor for shorter hours had done so when the need was clear; the pain of overwork and fatigue cried out to be healed, the necessity for rest and some family life was manifest. But that free time itself would become a "problem"! The old Progressives assumed that with the cessation of drudgery, workers would do good and even noble things automatically, "would spend their energies writing poetry, painting pictures, exploring the stellar spaces, dancing with Isadora Duncan . . . and producing Ibsen in little theaters." All the reformer had to do was "rearrange the environment," reducing the hours of overwork, for instance. Freeing people from the chains of convention and industry would free them for expression of their own sound judgment and the exercise of their innate goodwill.[43]

But now, in the 1930s, these optimistic and Progressive knights who had stood at Armageddon were "wrinkling their brows" at the freedom for which they had longed and struggled, the spectacle of mass leisure. Many had lost faith, coming face to face with "the automobile, the moving pictures, the radio, parties, bridge, the tabloid, and the stock market." Those who had in their innocence yearned for the "Freedom of Man" now indicted the "freedom of ordinary men and women." This indictment was "perhaps the chief theme" of a whole school of social critics—from H. L. Mencken to Leon Keyserling to *Main Street*, with "*Babbitt* standing as the masterpiece" of the genre and the *American Mercury* producing "an almost pedantic record of the phenomena." Even the "experts," the professionals, were drawn into the discussion. Charles Beard and Stuart Chase had written about "the problem." But here, at least, one found some objectivity and much less the passion of condemnation that disillusionment had excited among so many.[44]

In *Whither Mankind*, Beard and Chase had laid out the indictment, traced "the problem's" origin, and offered some typical and perhaps even helpful remedies. Lippmann reviewed the "points of the indictment": Mass production was beginning to meet basic needs and create surpluses of "leisure, power, and luxuries." With the dual temptations, leisure and luxury, the moral fabric was rotting. One aspect of the decline and "sterility which appears in an overripe civilization" was the "mass production of pleasure." A "dreary thing," mass leisure was commercial, appealing to the lowest threshold of amusement, just below which boredom beckoned. "Second-handed" things—spectator sports, movies, and radio—destroyed the individual's sense of control and even the exercise of will. Pleasure had become an "antidote to boredom" more than the "accompaniment of a spontaneous harmony in man's life." As such, the dosage had to grow ever larger, and the time would come when it would fail to beguile; it would cease to amuse and finally become the disease (boredom) itself.[45]

Beard and Chase presented what Lippmann viewed as a typical response, the case for social reform and improvement. Given something better than mass leisure—for example, hobbies, education for the worthy use of leisure, more individual control of free time, availability of better public recreation facilities, and trained people to direct the leisure of the community—the "leisure problem" would be addressed as the problem of child labor had been addressed, by social and political action.

But on this issue Lippmann parted company with his reformer friends. Here, he said, was a limit to social welfare and liberal reform. Here was a problem that could not be solved by the statesman. Unlike farm relief or public health, which could be addressed by "laws and policies and organized effort," leisure was on a "wholly different plane where each person must find for himself what it is that engages and satisfies him."[46]

Lippmann maintained that widespread leisure presented Americans with some hard questions that they had been able to avoid for so long because they were concerned, perhaps rightly, with the practical business of making a living. But now leisure, together with economic abundance, forced consideration of and decisions about matters heretofore dismissed as too academic and philosophic: hard questions about freedom.

Lippmann called leisure "the substance of liberty, the material of free will." In leisure was the "stuff to surpass our compulsions," requirements and necessities, and the opportunity to step into another dimension of existence, the realm of freedom and "disinterestedness" —a chance to do the thing-for-itself.

Ideally, all human activity should be so free—work and leisure.

But for most people, "a life of creativity was not possible, and to them the expenditure of their free time and energy is a matter of great moment." Because it was the essence of freedom, leisure had the potential to become the "best part of life," the time in which one was "directed by things within." In those free times of self-movement, "man attains his full stature."[47]

The sad part about commercial and mass amusements, then, was that they were proof that the ordinary person had no stomach for such freedom, that "men and women accept and submit to organized pleasures because they would find their own leisure intolerably nerve-racking if they had to dispose of it themselves." This fear of freedom, this escape back to the chains of mass leisure the very instant that liberation from alienating work was offered, was indicative of a disease of the soul. Lippmann located the obvious causes of this fear in the fact that the "problem of leisure" was so new and industrialization had weakened ancient social structures such as the family, the community, the codes of manners and culture of the people—things that could have given direction to leisure and a place for individual expression. Above all, the weakening of the old systems of belief contained in the Judeo–Christian tradition, and the exposure of modern men and women to a vacuum of meaning, had caused leisure to be a frightening thing.[48]

There was no real remedy in the indictment of the movies or radio, or even in the control or abolition of them. Mass leisure was a symptom of a disease, and fear of freedom was the disease. What, then, could be done? Lippmann turned to the regeneration of men and women one at a time—to individual, not social, reform.

Lippmann, a good journalist with a good story to tell, began by hinting at what he had in mind as a prescription for the new disease. "It consists of finding how to absorb this free energy so that it intensifies rather than fights against the order of our being." A person could recognize it in "the capacity to find exhilaration in solitude . . . the sense of . . . being replenished."

He continued with descriptions of what the regeneration was *not*. It was not a naive desire for pleasure. Most pleasures could be distinguished from this regeneration because they were found outside the individual. Such ordinary desire either became satiated or grew "upon what it feeds upon and therefore remains unsatisfied, bringing tension, anxiety, and frustration in its train." The outside search for pleasure and satisfaction could go on to absurd lengths, to the point where the searcher "possesses whole provinces for his estates, armies for his retinue, museums for his toys, and establishments for his lusts." Such pursuit never ended. The chase brought only the plagues of disappointment, boredom, confusion, despair; and "in the chaos of desire the human imagination picks out portents and monstrous things." Terror was the last, worst symptom of boredom.[49]

The remedy for the problem of leisure was not the "effort to satisfy desire, but in desires which are themselves satisfying. . . . It was customary once to state this in another language and to say that a man could not be happy until he had been born again." Unless in the "intimate places of the heart" there was reform and peace and unity, the whole world would not do to solve leisure. No amount of rearranging and reforming the external world would replace "that radical rearrangement of the inward activity which in its many manifestations men have called religion."

The problem of leisure, then, forced the asking of religious questions:

> It is from this experience that most of us shrink for it is profoundly disturbing. It does not comport well with the ordinary tenor of modern life, where it has become established convention not to reach too high or to look too deeply into the hidden regions. . . . But [man] does not domesticate perfectly. There is a strain of wildness and excess in him which cannot be caged . . . which may drive him to the savage or the sublime, he cannot satisfy with mediocre distractions.[50]

Instead of an exact religious prescription, Lippmann concluded more with a challenge and a warning. Freedom, in its modern epiphany, leisure, could lead either to despair and the savage or to the sublime. The religious questions that had occupied the Western mind for millennia were not put aside by the machine and technology; they were simply being asked in another form. The modern man and woman were not as immune to religious concerns as they had imagined; the "problem of leisure" was proof enough that this was true.

After Lippmann finished this splendid essay, he spent very little of his time on the subject. Like many who "stood at Armageddon," he went on to support Roosevelt's New Deal in varied degrees and from time to time. With many others, Lippmann became a convert to Keynesian economics and for the most part adopted the New Deal's solution to the depression: the creation and multiplication of work, the expansion of the "realm of necessity" to which he contrasted leisure so well in 1930. He opposed the share-the-work campaign, especially in the form of the retirement programs that Townsend had championed. By 1935, in opposition to Townsend's and labor's shorter-hour scheme, he observed that "idleness does not produce wealth, and those that think it does are trying to make gold out of sea water and invent a machine for perpetual motion."[51]

Lippmann's brief and luminous interest in leisure exemplifies the thinking of many of his fellow reformers from the days of the New Freedom and New Nationalism. Like Lippmann, many old reformers had only a brief encounter with the promise of leisure, having ignored it when they fought for shorter hours and then having forgotten about it after their conversion to Roosevelt's gospel of work. But for that brief time—that false spring of the late 1920s and early depression— some of the best of the old reformers' hopes were pinned on leisure, some of the best of their heretofore hopelessly ideal dreams were given practical dimensions.

Reformers' defections from shorter hours to the right to work were legion. Educators, for example, abandoned "education for the worthy use of leisure" after the winter of 1933–1934 when the movement reached a high point as educators began gearing their schools to the progressive shortening of hours of labor. Afterward, educators accepted the role that Tugwell outlined for them: the responsibility for creating new occupations and training and retraining children and adults for work, not leisure.[52] But one of the best examples of these critical defections was by American scientists.

CHAPTER 10

A Case in Point:
Scientists

O F THE MANY GROUPS affected by the depression, American engineers and scientists (in traditional areas such as the natural and
physical sciences and the mechanical arts) were particularly hard hit.
Unemployment was as much a threat to them as to everyone else.
What was unusual was the challenge that technological unemployment
presented to their role in society and their contribution to progress.
For generations, scientists and inventors understood technology as the
application of science to human life in order to relieve human bur-
dens: easing work and meeting material needs. For decades, they had
justified their place in society by pointing out how their discoveries and
machines had increased efficiency, helping to improve the standard of
living while reducing work hours. Few trends marked the Progressive
era in the United States more than this interest in efficiency among
scientists and politicians. The promise of increased productivity was
the hallmark of the "scientific managers" for the first three decades of
this century. As a group, they sought to create a world of neat, orderly
work, with "maximum production" at its center. The proportion of
work product to work time had been vitally important for science and
technology for years, and few questioned science's mandate to improve
that proportion by increasing it.[1]

With this solid ideological foundation, scientists had been able to
find increasing governmental support in agricultural and mechanical
experimentation in the 1910s. For example, the National Research
Council was instrumental in convincing the federal government to
support such legislation as the Newlands, Smith-Howard, and Gronna
bills, which provided support for scientific research. With efficiency

as their slogan, scientists found an increasing role in industry after World War I when "the movement of scientists into industry became a virtual tide."[2] The Nobel Prize winning physicist R. A. Millikan, for example, found widespread agreement in government and industry that "the scientist is, in a broad sense, a creator of wealth as truly as is the man whose attention is focused on the application of science."[3] As secretary of commerce, Herbert Hoover stressed the importance of scientific research in agencies such as the Bureau of Standards, which provided information and advice for the "coordination" and "effectiveness" of business efforts, including for the first time in the report of the secretary of commerce in 1926 an entire section on scientific research.[4]

Of course, critical voices were heard from time to time. Henry Adams and Mark Twain questioned the tendency of "pure science" to amass knowledge with no thought given to its application or hope for progress toward certainty and a final resolution of scientific truth. This kind of disenchantment increased with the appearance of Freudian psychology, Einstein's relativity, and Werner Heisenberg's uncertainty principle. Toward the close of the 1920s, other critical voices were heard; people such as Christian Gauss, dean of Princeton University, pointed to the "Threat of Science" represented by the misuse of scientific inventions for war and human exploitation. Still, notwithstanding the intellectuals' questionings, the importance of science in the economic life of the nation and the course of progress was generally secure until the Great Depression and was founded on technology's continuing successes in increasing productivity.[5]

With the coming of the depression, technological unemployment emerged as a potent threat to this extremely successful ideology. Paradoxically, efficiency and productivity, once answers to social ills, became the problems. Science and technology were made to appear in the press as having succeeded too well, as having put scientists as well as everyone else out of their jobs. Moreover, government support for research was cut severely. The sharp rise in industrial research that had taken place from 1927 to 1931 was replaced by a steep drop through 1933. Leading scientists felt attacked and beleaguered. They believed they had been singled out as scapegoats for the depression. As a consequence, the future of research and scientific advance in America was seen to be threatened as never before.[6]

Technological unemployment's threat to the ideology of efficiency caused scientists to reassess their role in society. A dialogue emerged among scientists about possible avenues for future development that echoed the more general social debates and political developments of the time. One group, formed by such people as the notorious technocrats and more respectable engineers such as Arthur O. Dahlberg, continued to support the doctrine of increased efficiency and to embrace its paradoxical results—continued work reduction and the growth of free time—as continued indications of scientific progress. The dominant response, however, was represented by scientists who turned away from a reliance on efficiency. Leading scientists and engineers began to see technology in a new light, as science in service of the creation of new work instead of mere work reduction. They began to do what Rexford Tugwell, one of the scientific community's most important champions in Roosevelt's administration, was suggesting: "to work on work." They set out to open new and "endless frontiers" of knowledge, invention, and work, and in the process found new, important, and serious jobs for themselves, securing again their status as "pioneers of progress."[7]

Supporting many of the New Deal's reemployment efforts, leading scientists and engineers turned to work creation and redirection with the same zeal that had characterized the centuries they had devoted to work's relief. Instead of finding some kind of fantastic respite from seriousness in leisure, this majority group set about finding new worlds to explore and conquer and new challenges to meet that would require the services of "an army of workers." This was an extremely important development in the history of science and technology; it marked a turning point from simple justification through efficiency.

Moreover, this dialogue among scientists had important political implications: The first group supported and directly influenced the politics of the shorter-hour solution to unemployment, and the second became deeply involved with the New Deal and its efforts to generate jobs. Although the dialogue was a microcosm of the larger social and political debates, it did not occur in a vacuum. Scientists were active politically and publicly, finding concrete public issues to support or attack that corresponded exactly with their internecine struggles.

The group of scientists that continued to serve the ideal of efficiency had an advantage in the sense that they spoke first to the issue of technological unemployment. Notwithstanding the fact that theirs was a minority voice, they were able to choose the ground for the debate, forcing their opponents to respond to their solutions and proposals.

Although written by an engineer and addressed specifically to "technicians and managers," Dahlberg's book *Jobs, Machines, and Capitalism*, published in 1932, influenced businessmen, politicians, and academicians. Arthur Schlesinger, Jr., wrote that Dahlberg presented the "most effective statement" for the limitation of work hours. According to the historian, the book received support in influential business circles; more important, it directly influenced Hugo Black, who used Dahlberg's arguments about technological unemployment and the need to spread work when he introduced and defended 30-hour legislation.[8] In addition, notables such as Edward Alsworth Ross, who wrote a foreword for the book, Kimball Young, and E. A. Filene lent their support. Louis Rich traced Dahlberg's ideas directly to Thorstein Veblen and to the work of engineers who had followed Veblen in the 1920s.[9] Dahlberg, however, maintained that two books—David Friday's *Profit, Wages, and Prices* and Stephen Leacock's *The Unsolved Riddle of Social Justice*—had the most impact on him and "started [him] upon a train of thought which eventuated in this book."[10]

Dahlberg's major premise was that the dramatic improvements in industrial efficiency that science and technology had made possible had ushered in "an Age of Leisure." But the central issue remained "whether we take that leisure in the form of shorter hours . . . or in the form of unemployment and lose it."[11] This question had profound implications for the American economic system. Pointing to the threat posed by competing economic arrangements, communism and government socialism, Dahlberg argued that unless the question "Unemployment or leisure?" was answered in the right way, "capitalism would fail" and would be replaced. Maintaining that he was not "an apologist for capitalism," Dahlberg nevertheless distinguished himself from other critics by pointing out that he was interested in giving the system "a fair trial." Since its beginning, capitalism had never been "permitted to function under a chronic 'scarcity of labor.' It has always been forced to operate under a scarcity of job . . . opportunity." He proposed that under a "chronic and genuine scarcity" of labor, created and maintained by shortening work hours, capitalism would be given its "fair trial" and would be "potentially almost an ideal system of economy," one that provided for economic abundance and security at the same time it promoted liberty. The "Age of Leisure" under the capitalist system could develop a new kind of freedom from work and material concerns and new opportunities for autonomy of the individual, and thus avoid plunging the nation into the authoritarian planning and tyrannical state controls being tried in Europe.[12]

The key failure in the capitalist system was resistance to shorter work hours. Keeping workers at work for longer than was necessary had several unfortunate results. Workers did not receive enough wages to buy necessities. The richer classes, given the opportunity to buy the new goods, were slow to do so. A great amount of time and energy was expended trying to move these new, "sluggish" goods; advertisers, window dressers, stylists, and salesmen were devoting their lives to "unproductive" pursuits.[13] Great amounts of savings were channeled into these new industries and into building up existing capital goods, many of which were already idle a good deal of the time because of weak demand. The whole direction of industrial advance was diverted into a dead-end. Dahlberg reasoned:

> Our failure to shorten the length of the working day . . . is the major cause not only for our unequal distribution of wealth but also of our inefficiency of production and waste in consumption; . . . the cause of low wages . . . the primary cause of our wasteful production, our excess industrial plant, our economic imperialism, and our commercial and pecuniary standards.[14]

Instead of accepting shorter hours, business and industry had made the mistake of trying to create new markets, new jobs, and new goods and services in the age of abundance. Dahlberg, like many others of his day, took issue with Hoover's Committee on Recent Economic Changes and its contention that consumption and human needs and desires could be expanded indefinitely. He argued that the newer classes of goods (e.g., automobiles, chemicals, electrical appliances, radios) were different from the old (e.g., agriculture, mining, textiles, rails) in the sense that they were not "spontaneously" wanted. The shift in the economy toward production of such goods and services created inefficient consumption, a problem "big enough to upset the whole capitalistic process."[15] "Men displaced by machinery today can be reemployed only if and when the appetite for a new good has been created. This results in a continuous lag in the demand for labor."[16]

Dahlberg attempted to show that the venerable economic law that "'production creates its own demand' embraces several errors." It was founded on a wrong premise: "the maxim that human wants are insatiable."

> If human nature were such that people with purchasing power demanded their "higher" wants as spontaneously and imperatively as they demanded their basic necessities; if they demanded their yachts and aeroplanes and new styles as spontaneously as they demanded their milk and meat, the historic view that "demand must always equal supply" could be accepted without modification.[17]

But this view had been disproved by the depression. The obstacle to the resumption of business was rooted in "social psychology," in the fact that people were not behaving according to Say's law. This was more than a breakdown in the system of finance.

Like John Ryan and the labor leaders, Dahlberg reasoned that if hours were shortened, wealth would flow from the richer classes to the productive ones. Workers with more urgent needs, given more wages, would buy necessities immediately and spontaneously; this would stimulate economic recovery and guide the formation of capital goods away from the production of luxuries and back to food, clothing, and shelter. The elaboration of work in silly, unproductive forms would cease as hoards of salesmen, "stylists," entertainers, advertisers, "intellectuals," and social critics gave up their pretense of "working," their "make-believe" jobs, and returned to production.[18] Dahlberg felt that neither the multiplication of work nor the discovery of new markets would promote recovery. These were forms of waste and inefficiency that needed to be controlled. Everyone working shorter hours in traditional and necessary occupations—carpenters and plumbers, farmers and food processors, spinners and cutters—would produce more than enough for all. Individuals who desired to entertain or amuse, write or paint, or do research in science or history would have more than enough time to do these things when they got off from "real" work. They would not then be lumbered with pretensions about truth, significance, and relevance, most of which such people had given up intellectually, if not occupationally, years ago.

Necessities produced before luxuries, productive work superseding the elaboration of unnecessary tasks; these were Dahlberg's guiding principles. Louis Rich's point about Dahlberg's debt to Veblen was well made.[19] There are strong hints in *Jobs, Machines and Capitalism* of Veblen's influence regarding such things as waste, unproductive work, and the need to shift economic control and power back to the producing classes. Veblen's influence is suggested by such a passage as

> economists have inferred that, if under capitalism, the working day were cut from, say, 8 hours to 4 hours a day, the output would roughly be cut in half. But I contend that . . . a drastic shortening of working hours would merely forcibly exchange the inefficiencies of capitalism for leisure, increase real output, and—because of the change in bargaining power—increase the share of this output going to workers and managers.[20]

Dahlberg also argued that government spending and pump priming were inappropriate responses to the depression. It was true that government spending during World War I had a stimulating effect on the economy. Industry ran full-time, and efficiency improved so much that more was produced when a substantial part of the population was in Europe fighting than was produced before and just after that time. But such spending had a purpose: winning the war. In the depression, indulging in a "wasting spree" of spending to stimulate the economy might lead to more employment and thus be "economically

. . . the same as shortening the length of the working day." In social and human terms, this was a bad choice.[21]

Such policies would work toward the creation of antidemocratic institutions when those with political influence were able to control state funds and thus be able to determine what kind of work was done and what was produced, outside the control of the marketplace. Workers would be subject to the whims of bureaucrats and "professionals," and made to work at "freakish" government and institutional jobs, the need for which was clear to no one, since the whole point of this "makework" was to assure the status and control of the new, nonproducing classes. This would be a new slavery for productive workers.[22]

Moreover, state support for capitalism's new markets perpetuated the worst trends in capitalism rather than accentuated its strengths. Support for the retention of long working hours, measures that propped up new, "inefficient" consumption would continue to inject "materialistic social standards" into American life. Workers would have to continue to make goods that reflected the cultural wants of those with purchasing power rather than their own necessities. The course of progress under capitalism would be diverted from its just and proper conclusion: sufficient necessities for everyone and freedom from work and material concerns. A retrogression would occur.[23]

State-supported capitalism would begin to curtail freedom. A cultural outlook with an accentuated militaristic bias would evolve. Capitalism was

> likely to produce socially desirable goods when it attempts to satisfy our bodily needs, but not so when it attempts to satisfy our psychic needs. The first needs are prescribed by nature, they remain the same regardless of the motive . . . but the latter needs are man-made, they are subject to creation, and when selfishness becomes the spur to this creation . . . then these wants are as apt to be socially undesirable as to be socially desirable. When selfish producers have satisfied the demand for necessities they can find work for themselves, with which to fill the long working day, only by appealing to materialistic standards. . . . Thus . . . by not shortening the working day when all the wood is in—we force the selfishness of the profit motive to become both the creator and the satisfier of spiritual needs. *Here lies the root cause of our materialistic civilization.* The selfish producer becomes the most powerful director of all human effort and aspiration. Our long day, then, forces our producers to lead us

into a commercial religion and materialistic philosophy. Energetic salesmen, impelled by selfishness, determine the course of our spiritual expression and become the priests of our religion. They impel us to worship wants and ends and methods. . . . When selfishness can turn nowhere else, it wraps our soap in pretty boxes and tries to convince us that that is solace to our souls. When hunger is satisfied, it appeals to snobbery.[24]

The "Calvinistic worship of toil" had created a new brand of false religion in which production was "an end and a world of itself," where "we automatically anoint our business men as the high priests of our religion" or "the swirl of economic forces tosses them into the pulpit."[25] Coincidentally, "the manufacturer thus becomes the modern shepherd" who seeks "some human frailty which he can cultivate into a new demand." He is continually trying to convert the buyer to the true faith "that consuming more physical goods is spiritual expression. Advertising campaigns are his sermons. 'Consume More' is his text."[26]

Leaving its proper place, the satisfaction of necessities, and embarking into nebulous realms of "psychic need," social "meaning," and human relationships, capitalism was causing the nation to be "spiritually poverty stricken; [in which condition] we labor and die. For poverty is more than a matter of bread. But as things stand now, our energies are so completely devoted to economic ends and concerns which have no [authentic] spiritual meaning for us—we have no energy remaining."[27]

Dahlberg concluded that these trends could be stopped and capitalism saved by *"federal statutory enactment"* of shorter hours. The fact that the state would have to intervene in this way was unfortunate. But at least this state control would "not make our Capitalism into 'Socialism,'" as would other kinds of government interventions to "stimulate the market." Instead, it would free capitalism and the market to do what it did best: produce necessities.[28]

Leadership in such an effort would have to come from those most closely connected with industry, those "technicians and managers" to whom Dahlberg addressed himself specifically. He argued that it was in their own best interests to lead the way to the establishment of "economic arrangements that favor the mass of consumers [rather than] support [measures] . . . which favored the owners of industry." Technicians and managers would have to be "the prime movers," leading the way to social and industrial support of the "chronic scarcity" of labor. Without this leadership, "capitalism can never be put under better operating conditions . . . and life under capitalism is destined to become increasingly severe."[29]

Shortening the working day would undoubtedly accentuate the "problem of leisure." But, according to Dahlberg, "we have that problem now in a worse form—in unemployment." He had no sympathy for "those who oppose shorter hours because of their fears for the '[im]moral behavior' of workingmen during their leisure hours. After all, what is so 'moral' about endless and meaningless drudgery?" He suggested that what "Americans need most urgently is a new attitude toward work and the working day. We must sometimes regard work as a preliminary to living—as a chore to be done as quickly as possible in order that the individual in us may be free."[30] Moreover, adjusting working hours "to secure economic freedom . . . would undoubtedly decrease the cultural subserviency of the . . . workingman. The spunk which has oozed out of him in recent decades might return," and the nation would experience "a cultural revival the like of which the world has never seen. It would be a revival untrammeled and free,"[31] constrained by neither a cultural or intellectual aristocracy nor industrial bosses.

> For by the mere act of shortening its hours of labor and constantly maintaining a genuine scarcity of labor, Capitalism can eliminate unemployment and the fear of unemployment; it can eliminate industrial wastes and inanities of consumption; it can eliminate exploitation of personality and the corruption of values; it can eliminate insecurity and get at the kernel of all economic evil by giving economic power to the mass of the people; it can remove the brakes from its marvelous machine, give engineers a free reign to spin the wheels of industry, and rekindle the American beliefs that the material world can be molded to our will.[32]

Early in 1933, Dahlberg was called to testify before the Senate Subcommittee on the Judiciary on Black's 30-hour bill. Dahlberg gave the senators a synopsis of his book and reviewed the arguments of other supporters of shorter hours, especially Leacock. Dahlberg's influence on Black was evident during the hearings; Black's praise and obsequiousness verged on being embarrassing. But after this, Dahlberg lost interest in 30-hour legislation. As the depression wore on, he came to feel that 30 hours alone was not going to solve the nation's problems and embarked on more popular courses. But during the interregnum, Dahlberg's influence on shorter hours was significant.[33]

Orthodox economists such as Frank Knight attacked *Jobs, Machines and Capitalism* for not being scholarly. Knight doubted that Dahlberg had ever read a modern textbook on economics.[34] But others, such as Louis Rich, praised the work as "one of the most thought provoking . . . within recent times."[35] Dahlberg's themes were picked up by John H. Finley, associate editor of the *New York Times*, who argued in March that the new era of scientific achievement would lead to "spiritual accomplishments" and "the wisdom that comes with leisure" when machines produced more than the world "actually needs of the absolutely pivotal necessities of life."[36] Ralph Flanders of the Jones and Lamson Machine Tool Company and later a senator from Vermont joined in a sort of partnership with Dahlberg, trying to create interests in the scientific community in Dahlberg's solutions.[37]

Other scientists and engineers began to respond to the problem of technological unemployment soon after Dahlberg's book appeared. Some took a defeatist attitude about technology and efficiency; they advised scientists to retreat from attempts to find applications for their knowledge and to retrench in the universities, devoting themselves to "pure research and science." At the opening of the Merck Laboratories in April 1933, Henry H. Dale counseled such a course. Edward Elliot, president of Purdue University, quoted Sir William Bragg and observed that "it is when the results of ["pure"] science are incorporated into business and trade that trouble begins."[38]

But Dexter S. Kimball, dean of the College of Engineering at Cornell University, was more representative of mainstream scientists and engineers, who were still making up their minds. Kimball offered his own reassessment of science's role in society and observed that "for the first time technological unemployment . . . appears as a vital issue and as a possible factor, in a large way, in the general problem of unemployment." The "greatest and most immediate menace to the worker" seemed to have become "industrial progress" and technological efficiency. This, he concluded, had come about unexpectedly. "Until quite recently, our industrial progress was viewed with considerable satisfaction. . . . It appeared to many of us that we had really entered a new era and that we had in some measure solved the problem of living through higher wages" and increased productivity. Over the previous thirty years, there had been "an unprecedented improvement in the science and art of production." The "entire philosophy of industrial management had been rebuilt" and founded on the principle of scientific efficiency. But technological unemployment threatened this principle. "For the first time a new and sharp question is raised concerning our manufacturing methods and equipment, and the fear is expressed that our industrial equipment is so efficient that permanent overproduction. . . . has occurred and that consequently technological unemployment has become a permanent factor."[39]

Even though most academic economists were assuring the public that permanent technological unemployment was unlikely, Kimball had his doubts. The facile assumption that displaced workers would naturally find work someplace may have been true "when industry was simpler." But in the modern age, "this is not so easy to do." He argued that "we cannot continue the present uncertain methods [of laissez-faire capitalism] faced with even moderate technological progress." He suggested that the domestic markets "must be developed" and foreign trade expanded with government help. Kimball pinned his hopes on "new inventions," which, unlike previous technological improvements, would be designed to "absorb the surplus labor" instead of "displacing workers." Inventions such as the radio and the automobile were in this new category, employing more people than they replaced. Even though "no such inventions are on the present horizon," forward-looking industrialists and scientists had embarked on the search for machines whose "economic and social value" rested, not in how much labor was saved, but in how many workers found employment. But this was not the automatic process which economists imagined. Moreover, the individual entrepreneur could no longer be counted on to solve a problem grown to national proportions. Reemployment required large-scale, organized thought, effort, and invention; time, work, and government support were needed in order for it to succeed.[40]

Kimball did make concessions to a continuation of the old sorts of efficiency. Like Dahlberg, he thought that the shorter working week was "inevitable" and that the "deeper significance" of technological advance was that it had added "economic freedom" to traditional political and religious liberties. This new freedom was the release "from physical drudgery and an opportunity for all men to live like men and not like the beasts of the field." "Delight in both work and in leisure" were overdue and had become necessities.[41] Kimball, then, had it both ways. While offering the creation of new employment as the key to scientific advance, he nevertheless agreed with Dahlberg to some degree, hanging on to the traditional notion that freedom from work was a desirable result of technology. But such moderate and conciliatory arguments were soon shoved aside with the appearance of the technocrats, who effectively polarized scientific opinion.

Historians have had a tendency to dismiss the technocrats as an anomaly, a cipher in the unfolding of American history, rightly discredited by scandals and Nazilike trappings and quickly discarded in the dustbin of the past before World War II. In reality, the technocrats represented more than a national craze engendered by depression trauma. They brought to fruition an important, long-term intellectual development reaching back to the utopian writers of the nineteenth century and to scientists such as Thorstein Veblen and Charles Proteus Steinmetz. More than any one person or group, the technocrats publicized the fact that technological unemployment threatened the ideology of scientific efficiency; in so doing, they sparked consideration among other scientists about science and technology's future. But because of their fame, they also spoke powerfully, however briefly, to central social and economic issues of the early depression years. The importance of the technocrats, then, was not limited to the dialogue among scientists. Their significance included their contribution to the larger public issues and political debates of the time.

Few primarily intellectual movements have had such a dramatic impact. Over the winter of 1932–1933, technocracy dominated the national news. The editors of the *Nation* proclaimed that the technocrats' work, more than any other economic research in recent American history, had captured the attention of the country.[42] Charles A. Beard called one book on technocracy "the most important . . . of the twentieth century that has come within my kin . . . [marking] an epoch in economic thought."[43] Even the comedian W. C. Fields got into the act, being grilled in one of his movies by a pesky child prodigy, "Daddy, what is technocracy?"[44]

The technocrats became one of the nation's top news stories simultaneously with the introduction of the Black–Connery bills. These two events were directly related. In the congressional hearings, witnesses discussed the technocrats and their 660-hour year, presenting the case for 30 hours based on what the technocrats called the "inevitability of declining employment." In turn, the technocrats discussed attempts to share the work being made by private industry and by Congress, only to reject such measures as being too little, too late. While agreeing that work sharing was the right idea, they judged it, like all such efforts to find a remedy for the depression in the existing economic and governmental frameworks, impractical and doomed by the waste and inefficiency of tradition-bound institutions.[45] For the technocrats, free time was bound to occur. Under the then-current economic system, it was bound to take the form of unemployment. Only under a completely different political and economic system could it be transformed into leisure.[46]

The major contribution the technocrats made to the ongoing intellectual and political debates was their *Energy Survey of North America*. Funded by the New York Architects Emergency Relief Committee, Howard Scott and his cohorts in the Committee on Technocracy concluded from their survey of employment in some three thousand major industries that, quite simply, to the extent industry was becoming more efficient, employment had been decreasing—an inverse proportional relation existed between productivity and employment.

In this situation, work was bound to be ever more taken over by the machine. Even in 1933, "it is necessary for the adult population ages 25 to 45 to work but 660 hours per year per individual to produce a standard of living for the entire population . . . above the average income of 1929."[47]

But this "dialectic of technology," which should have been an occasion for rejoicing, had become a gigantic problem. Americans had the "capacity . . . to produce [enough] physical wealth . . . that we are assured of a sufficiency to keep us going for a thousand years."[48] But living in the "new era" of abundance, Americans were nevertheless experiencing their greatest economic depression. The reason for this patently illogical situation was the obviously illogical "price system." And the reason that the price system did not work was basically because the work time needed to produce the material needs of human beings was being reduced.[49]

Like Kimball and Dahlberg, the technocrats questioned the orthodox economic view that chronic unemployment was impossible and that people would eventually find new jobs as new markets opened up. According to Scott and his followers, this fine theory had been disproved by events. Their survey demonstrated that basic needs and material requirements were at long last capable of being met. The technocrats used phrases such as "economic sufficiency" to describe what they believed was a characteristic of the recent past. Certainly they had as little patience as the next empiricist with nineteenth-century abstract notions about "human nature" and some kind of predetermined, absolute limit on what people needed and would be willing to work for. By contrast, their conclusion that a "stationary" economic state had arrived was based on what they considered a legitimate, longitudinal analysis: a time-series study of what was actually occurring. That human needs could be divided into "absolute" and "contingent" categories, as John Maynard Keynes was suggesting at the time, had been established empirically. The evidence was simply that employment was decreasing as productivity increased. New goods and services, and the desire for them, were not emerging quickly enough; new work was not being created in great enough quantities to offset industry's increasing productive capacity. This was adequate indication that "sufficiency," "abundance," or "enough" were appropriate "descriptors." This concrete fact of the inverse proportion between productivity and employment signaled the inevitable decline of work as surely as if God Himself had written the list of human industrial needs in the immutable laws of Nature.[50]

Because needs were being met and work was declining, the existing economic arrangement, the "price system," was no longer viable. It had become unstable, causing the Great Depression, and would go on creating chaos until it was replaced by reason and a scientific system. At one time, the price system made sense. When men and women had to struggle for survival without the benefit of technology, then work time was an adequate measure of "value." The process of buying and selling was based on the exchange of workers' time for the goods and services they produced. But as technology replaced work time with machines, this exchange lost its logic. Scott summed up his complex argument by pointing out that the existing economic order "demands man-hours [for the exchange of goods] if it is to succeed, and manpower for production steadily becomes more and more [*sic*] a thing of the past."[51]

Moreover, the existing profit system put a premium on productivity; businesses that replaced more man-hours with more machinery won out in economic struggle. The profit system had combined with the ability of science and technology to meet the most pressing of human material needs. The result was less work time, which meant less purchasing power and more economic dislocation.[52] In this situation, the "distribution of human labor becomes impossible . . . [working] against the increase of wages."[53] In the simplest terms, and in the way that most people understood what the technocrats were saying, expanded free time was undermining the profit system and would eventually topple capitalism.[54]

Over the recent past, attempts had been made to mitigate this inevitable process of "time dislocation." Debt had been tried as a substitute for the coin of work time. Bankers had attempted to sustain increased production by creating webs of debt, spinning larger and increasingly unstable nets of paper currency, encouraging installment buying and foreign trade. Even governments had spun webs of public debt to keep the economy aloft and consumption up to the level of production. But before long, these webs, requiring increasingly large debt levels, would also collapse. Paper promises could never be the representative of value in the way that work time once had been. Only the few were able to buy more because of the extensions of credit; and being well-off, more often than not they were investing in more machines, which took more work time out of circulation. The majority still had to depend on the exchange of work time for their right to consume.[55]

Attempts to reemploy men in new industries and create new markets in foreign trade and by advertising had also been made. These were good ideas, in theory. In a fantasy world, new industries, new goods and services, and new work could go on being created forever. But in the real world, they would not keep on saving the overbuild economy. Infinite industrial growth and the infinite creation of new work were pipe dreams. A point was bound to come when industrial growth ran up against the finite limits of what humans needed to live and what nature was able to provide. In fact, the "energy survey" demonstrated that this limit had already been reached.[56]

Like Dahlberg, some technocrats went on to argue that advertising and the creation of new work and new needs were retrograde developments. Most of the new "mass of commodities" being produced were contradictions of wealth and abundance. They were "useless" products, and as such, a form of created and willful inefficiency. As a response to the problems of modern industry, they were as bad as the deliberate misuse or insane destruction of machine power and potential. Stuart Chase called these new consumer goods "illith," a term that Graham Laing approved of and elaborated upon:[57]

> Practically the whole of the patent medicine industry was included [as a form of "illith"]. A large number of the tremendous cosmetic business would also come under that head. An enormous number of gadgets and trivialities are totally unnecessary and serve little real purpose. . . . And in [the persuasion to buy] a great deal of wasted effort exists in the advertising industry.[58]

Harold Loeb observed that the majority of advertising and new goods being created were based on "appeals to [the] . . . lowest instincts—vanity, envy, ostentation, and fear." Above all the rest was fear, "fear of missing something, fear of being laughed at, . . . of being surpassed, fear, even—and the misery this must cause, the hours of sniffing and smelling—fear of odors.[59]

At this point, Scott and his followers wandered off into their own never-never land of "energy credits" to replace the "price system" and government by a technocrat elite to replace wornout democracy. Their fantastic technocratic dream world, so removed from political realities and the mainstream of public discourse, is indeed of marginal and only passing interest, matching in no way the important role they played in the public and intellectual debates about technological unemployment. Leaving their castles in the air and their internecine organizational squabbles aside, and turning to their conclusions about what leisure time could become in a more orderly world, one finds them speaking again to the mainstream political and intellectual issues. In many ways, their fantastic technocratic creation was designed to accomplish free time's reformation and leisure's transformation of culture; as such, they were well within the rhetorical mainstream, struggling with the same issues of work and freedom from work that were occupying the attention of the nation.

The technocrats centered much of their writings on leisure; even technological unemployment was given secondary status, since it was seen as transitory. They reasoned that this free time, although it could take the form of unemployment for a while and cause profound misery, must eventually be changed into leisure because people had enough common sense not to live forever in a depression. Like many around them, the technocrats spoke of the choice before Americans, either to accept passively the time freed by the machine as unemployment or to take action and reform that time into leisure. Much of what they had to say about technocracy and government by a scientific elite came back to this choice.

Scott, for example, found that "man, in his age-long struggle for leisure and the elimination of toil, is at last confronted not only by the possibility but by the probability of its arrival." The result would be a "new era."[60] Wayne Parrish, technocracy's journalist, called this "the most potent and significant statement made in the 200,000 or so years of man's habitation on this small planet."[61] Harold Loeb described his discussion of the use of leisure as "the crux of the problem." If technocracy succeeded "only in ameliorating material condition," it would be only "of little value."[62] Its true significance lay in diverting "the race's surplus energy . . . from the obsolete money competition to a search for vital values." For Parrish, although hidden by "the riffraff of a thousand and one sideshows," this was technocracy's central point: Leisure was coming, it would overthrow the existing economic order and would usher in a "new era" of freedom for the really important human drama.[63]

The technocrats tended to divide the world into the realms of freedom and necessity. Given the fact of abundance, of technology's capacity to meet rational material needs, the realm of necessity was not as important as it had once been; it was not as pressing and as deserving of attention, energy, and effort. In fact, necessity could be safely turned over to the engineer–servant, who, as he had done with sewers, could manage according to the rules of nature and assure that operations such as the distribution of goods and services functioned smoothly. In the realm of work and necessity, scientific law could best rule; rule by man and his whims would mean waste and confusion. But far from curtailing freedom, rational acceptance of law and a logical system would make real freedom possible for the first time in history. For the technocrats, perfect freedom was the result of submitting to the laws of the universe instead of kicking at the traces of necessity and reason.

The realm of necessity—of function, product, and control—would naturally contract as the rational need for work diminished. As workers were freed from work and assured by rational systems that their material needs would be taken care of, they would have leisure to do whatever they really wanted—free from the controls of government, industry and the rich. This would be a revolution, a "new era" of freedom, not an age of new restrictions. Graham Laing, a leading technocrat and professor of economics at the California Institute of Technology, observed: "After all, there is no need for human beings to be obsessed with economics."[64] Loeb added that "the definite and final disposing of the whole problem of material wants should release most men from the terrific preoccupation which now obtains with this relatively boring and unfruitful aspect of life."[65] Frank Arkright concluded that since the machine would "require two eight hour days a week from each worker . . . why should we do more, when, as [Bertrand] Russell says, 'the morality of work is the morality of slaves.'"[66]

But tradition held back a rational response to abundance. Outdated institutions, such as the price system and the marketplace, obstructed things. Equally important as a barrier were confused notions about work. Lang pointed out that "our preoccupation with work has led us to the confirmed habit of thinking that there is nothing else worth doing." This "fallacy" has resulted in a virtual "obsession" with work, with "necessity," and with the seriousness of existence, which has "almost killed the understanding of the purpose of life. We cannot live until we have controlled work" and put it in its proper, "subservient place."[67] Scott repeated again and again that "the importance of man as a worker has dwindled and is dwindling even more rapidly now."[68]

Mixing up the realm of free activity with the realm of work and necessity produced profound confusions, where "two purposes are jumbled."[69] Work could not be transformed into a place for freedom and for activities and values that were "intrinsic" (i.e., worthwhile in themselves). Work was, by definition, for a product; it was complete not in itself but in the act of consumption. Making music and art and even "pure" science into jobs was a mistake. It made for activity that was neither necessary by any rational understanding of need nor free in the sense that it was done simply for itself. The future was not in the elaboration of work and the extensions of necessity into areas of life that had, first and foremost, to be free; but in continuing the rational divisions between work and leisure, between necessity and freedom, and going about reducing the former and augmenting the latter.[70]

Harold Loeb presented the most systematic and detailed of the technocrats' descriptions of what leisure could become in a technocracy and what this free time would mean for traditional American institutions and values. In his descriptions of "life in a technocracy," Loeb did much more than engage in utopian speculation. He offered a critique of American institutions founded on the "morality of work" and presented the case for reforming these institutions for the service of leisure.[71]

In the service of leisure, religion would be transformed, not eliminated. The churches would be freed from the "mysticism of money," their current "fundamental faith," and strengthened in their true calling: the "inculcation of joy" and ethics based in "spiritual values." Freedom from work could be the occasion for a renewed appreciation of the spiritual and reverential aspects of life. Given free time, men and women could be expected to direct their energies, instead of their money, in these directions—that is, if churches were important mainly for the life of the spirit and not just as a way to "inculcate resignation" to work and the "immortal dollar."[72]

Education would undergo a similar transformation. "Industrial schools," which taught practical work skills, needed to be separated from schools that "sought culture [and knowledge] for its own sake." This was necessary because learning was naturally, and had been historically, divided between "knowledge for the sake of use and knowledge for the sake of the student's satisfaction."[73] Education for "culture, the cultivation of the aesthetic and intellectual appreciations and the extensions of human knowledge," was, rightly understood, leisure education, not work education. "Knowledge for its own sake" should bring together, in freedom, those who loved to teach with those who loved to learn. "Such loosely bound aggregations of teachers and students [would] resemble the Universities of the Middle Ages instead of our contemporary school." This would be a vast improvement over modern education, which "jumbled" the utilitarian servile arts with the classic liberal studies, trying to make the former "classy" and the latter "useful" or relevant to work. Since the advent of leisure, all people could have the benefit of both kinds of education. Those areas of training previously reserved for the elite could become the domain of the many, while everyone could be expected to pull his own weight in the realm of the practical. The spectacle of the poet–bricklayer lost its poignancy when that worker could count on devoting his main energy to the muse instead of the timeclock. Similarly, the "Artist" and "Scientist" as elite leaders of culture and progress had been outmoded.[74]

In leisure, social organization would change. Although it was logical to seek ever greater collectivism in work and to accept the regimenting of worker and machines according to the dictates of scientific principles, in leisure individualism would flourish. Work required great collectives; leisure needed small, intimate communities. Leisure activities of "study, play, art, and worship," freely chosen and not controlled or centralized by the state or by the commercial marketplace, would generate small play groups that allowed for a much wider range of individual choice and variety.[75] The commercialization of leisure had produced standardized, inactive, and boring amusements. Freeing leisure from the constraints of advertising and the marketplace would increase the possibilities for more and better kinds of human relationships in small-scale community activities.[76]

Art, for example, would flourish in leisure. Although it was true that the "mysticism of money" had produced wonderful works of architecture and art, these were hothouse growths.[77] The "Artist" had been enshrined as a special genius by capitalism, but in the process, human creativity was captured as another form of work and subordinated to the business of buying and selling. With increased leisure, this part of life could open up again to everyone, as men and women, "humble in the knowledge that the good life is not to be attained by satisfying [unreasonable] material needs, would gradually, inevitably, and with cumulative intensity, turn to art."[78]

But, like "leisure education" and "leisure communities," "leisure art" would be transformed art and so hardly recognizable as its poor imitation, "serious" work art. According to Loeb, it would be "quite unmixed with any utilitarian purpose."[79] It would be more like the cavorting of swallows "before the setting sun," the "exult[ation] in . . . rhythmic motion" resembling not at all "serious art" and its "studios with 'crossed legs' . . . filled with experiments in combining oddly colored shapes and empty highball glasses." Instead, it would be the recovery of the primitive capacity for the "sense of imminent wonder and beauty—no words exactly describe it—which all living things are heir to."[80]

But this free, leisured "art" would be more than an immediate animal response because it was to be done consciously:

> The artist is infinitely more [than unconscious response]. [While] he has regained the natural gift of all living free things . . . he is more than an animal. In his moments of conscious vision he is akin to those supernatural deities evoked by the human imagination. He sees and he knows he sees . . . man's so-called progress is a retrogression unless he regains his animal birthright and at the same time keeps the self-consciousness acquired during the millenniums of self-imposed discipline.[81]

In comparison with this "art," even the magnificence of ordinary science paled. The science of the merely useful "can discover only how things work." But "art" included the higher regions of science in the greater, more sublime attempt of humans to "discover, freely, the why of things." This "art–science" transcended the merely useful and engaged the "ecstatic." Here was evident the human search for the "meaning of life." Here the "sorrow, the tragedy, even the ostensible evil which is woven of necessity into the texture of our temporal days" was given proportion and "reduced to their proper importance." The great teachers of both "ethics and aesthetics glimpsed this consummation," this goal of human struggling and working. But the renunciation and rigors of the "various religions," even the modern religion of science, were no longer called for in order to gain this beatitude. Instead, "man may enjoy all earthly goods and still have time to delve into these mysterious and satisfying aspects of existence."[82]

While such a vision was shared by the other technocrats, few of Loeb's contemporaries were able to express it as well as he. But he owed his insights to others. Charles Proteus Steinmetz, for example, had made similar observations in the 1920s, in equally eloquent terms, some of which Loeb lifted directly.[83] B. F. Skinner, in turn, was to devote his utopia, *Walden II*, to Loeb's topics in the 1940s, concluding in one central passage that, "leisure's our levitation," thus using the possibilities of leisure that Loeb had explored to defend his behaviorism against attacks that it was tyranny and arguing that freedom was the product, not the price, of scientific control.[84] The trace of these ideas about leisure and its significance to science and technology, then, extend forward and backward from technocracy's advent. But they never before or since had such popularity and relevancy to the times, to actual public issues being debated and to viable legislative proposals in the U.S. Congress.

Technocracy and the 30-hour legislation constituted the most visible responses to the depression by those who continued to advocate the shorter-hour solution to unemployment; and in the public debate on increased leisure, both figured prominently, one the "scientific," the other the political expression. Although most supporters of the shorter-hour solution had turned their attention to the 30-hour campaign during the 1930s, politicizing their cause as never before, the technocrats remained aloof from the rough-and-tumble politics of the New Deal, preferring to offer their observations and prescriptions objectively and present a sweeping, radical, and, for the most part, impolitic program to achieve their goals.

Nevertheless, there is no doubt that technocracy was a high-water mark in the American consideration of the "new leisure." As intellectual movements go, it was exceptionally effective in spelling out issues in terms that appealed to a mass audience, explaining simply the advantages of increased free time for the saving of many traditional American institutions and values, but at the same time detailing in unmistakable terms the threat that free time represented to the existing economic order. In doing so, the technocrats served to clarify the alternative political solutions to the depression being offered and improved the debates that raged over work's reduction.

Thus the importance of what the technocrats had to say was matched and even surpassed by the effect they had on public debates and on scientists, engineers, and businessmen. Although the majority of these people rejected the technocrats' ideas, they nevertheless were prodded by the popularity of the movement to explain their positions on technological unemployment and the decreasing need to work. One story is illustrative of the way the technocrats, despite their radicalism, did have a powerful effect in clarifying issues and forcing those around them to take a stand. Albert Einstein, the nation's adopted guru of mystic science, was visiting California at the time the technocrats were gaining celebrity status. The press approached the great man, hoping to tie two headline stories together in some way. But those who expected all scientists to speak with one voice about economic matters were disappointed; newspapermen were not able to proclaim Einstein a technocrat. Instead, his few words about technocracy were given relatively small play in the newspapers. What he did answer to reporters' questions spoke volumes and set the tone for how other scientists would respond. Einstein simply replied that "power as applied to production must not be halted, but at the same time, men must have work." These few words sum up the characteristic response of engineers, scientific managers, and orthodox economists. The ideas they expressed were reiterated time and again by technocracy's critics; but while elaborated in more complex detail, they were never expressed with such eloquent simplicity.[85]

Technocracy's historian, William E. Akin, also summed up the dominant response to technocracy, concluding that "[a]ccelerated economic growth, expanded consumption, enlargement of service industries, and government stimulation provided a convincing way out of the technological dialectic."[86] Certainly businessmen, faced with the technocrats' radicalism, tended to reassert their faith that the economy would right itself and that demand would increase enough so that technological unemployment would be eliminated, repeating the "gospel of consumption" formula that human needs for industrial products and services were infinite. Similarly, the Council of Engineers and the editors of *Scientific American* dismissed the technocrats in a few words as radical and unscientific. Nevertheless, taking the larger issue of technological unemployment seriously, they argued that the creation of new work was necessary and would be accomplished when scientists and engineers accepted the challenge and developed new inventions "to take up the slack." They assured the public that technology, far from continuing to reduce work and necessity, could easily create new challenges and new generations of problems to worry over and take seriously—"demanding an army of workers."[87]

But the problems of the scientist and engineer were only beginning. As the popularity of the technocrats faded, scientists and engineers continued long after to struggle with technological unemployment. The debate about technocracy, despite its brief intensity, was simply one installment in the larger dialogue among scientists about the decline of work and the challenge posed to the ideology of scientific efficiency. The theoretical threat to science presented by the technocrats was quickly overshadowed by the very real threat offered by what the Roosevelt administration was saying and doing, by the more general public outcry against the scientist as villain in the depression tragedy, and the very real loss of research funds and industrial jobs. All underlined what the technocrats had maintained: Science, in the singleminded pursuit of efficiency, had come to a turning point.

Some of the most disturbing threats to scientific research came from within Roosevelt's administration. Research funds had been slashed, and some scientific agencies, such as the Bureau of Standards and the Biological Survey, had experienced budget cuts of more than 50 percent of their 1931–1932 appropriations.[88] Roosevelt had shown some interest in the plight of scientists in July 1933 when, at the suggestion of Secretary of Agriculture Henry Wallace, he had appointed a Science Advisory Board (SAB) and named Karl Compton, president of MIT, as its chairman. The board promptly presented Roosevelt with a plan for a public works programs for unemployed scientists, a $16 million scientific renewal project that Compton called "The Recovery Program of Scientific Progress." Under the control of the National Research Council, the program was designed to give employment to scientifically and technically trained young men just out of college who could not find satisfactory positions. The proposal also emphasized scientific research to help with the implementation of other public works programs and the basis for the creation of new jobs in new industries, suggesting development in employment in such areas as meteorology, soil mechanics, sewage disposal, cryogenic research, heavy hydrogen, mineral resources, and social problems of mechanization. Nevertheless, Roosevelt had turned a deaf ear to Compton and the board's suggestions.[89]

Moreover, during the winter of 1933–1934, when Roosevelt and his advisers were softening their position on shorter hours and Roosevelt floated his trial balloon for 36-hour NRA codes, Secretary of Agriculture Wallace, the most prominent administration advocate of federal support for scientific research, appealed to scientists to consider a "wider and better controlled use of engineering and science to the end that man may have a higher percentage of his energy left over to enjoy the things which are non-material and non-economic." To the list of leisure pursuits, "music, painting, literature and sport for sport's sake," Wallace added "particularly" the "idle curiosity of the scientist himself." He then suggested that "even the most enthusiastic engineers and scientists should be heartily desirous of bending their talents to serve these higher human ends [leisure pursuits]. If [scientists] do not recognize these ends, there is grave danger that Spengler may be proved right after all." Even Wallace, their champion, endorsed the idea that science and technology were important because they provided and served leisure. And equally upsetting, Wallace seemed to understand pure science as nothing more than "idle curiosity," just another leisure activity. Traditional research was being placed in a subservient role and the magnificent temple of science approached with no more respect than one would approach a playground. In his concern with the social impact of increased free time, Wallace added insult to injury, suggesting that scientists "have turned loose upon the world new productive power without regard to social implications" and that they would have to shift their attention to "social life" and the needs for economic planning.[90] He had elevated social scientists to the level of natural scientists and given the social scientists the more significant tasks of evaluating and solving the problems of unemployment and increased free time.[91]

In addition, during this cold winter for scientists, the NRA issued regulations in some of the industrial codes controlling the introduction of labor-saving machinery, and there was talk in the administration and in public about a national "moratorium on inventions."

Natural scientists and engineers detected in such developments a national phobia. They perceived that they were being made the scapegoats of the depression and that a new, "anti-intellectual" tide was running against them. Robert A. Millikan termed the "reaction against science the worst in 300 years," characterized by "retreat into superstition and irrationally where sentimentalists reign."[92] It seemed that the nation had risen up against scientists, attacking them for being responsible for the very labor-saving machines that had once been so widely praised.[93]

The scientists launched a counterattack in the form of a public campaign of information, concerted attempts to lobby for federal relief of unemployed scientists, and restoration of government funding for research. In late February 1934, the American Institute of Physics and the New York Electrical Society sponsored a national symposium on

"Science Makes Jobs" in New York City. Among those who attended were Millikan, Karl T. Compton, Nobel Laureate Orestes H. Caldwell, president of the Electrical Society, Frank B. Jewett, vice-president of AT&T, and Henry Barton, director of the Institute of Physics. Considerable effort went into publicizing the event; radio addresses were made, and newsreel interviews were granted. A special exhibition at the Museum of Science and Industry was created on the symposium topic. On prominent display were statistics about the increases in employment brought about by discoveries and inventions such as rayon manufacture, incandescent lighting, aircraft, telephone, radio, motion pictures, and electrical appliances. Inventions that had led to the automobile, for example, were shown to have resulted in the employment of 2.5 million workers. Finally, speeches were made and letters from Roosevelt and other leading politicians were read to those assembled.[94]

Special attention was given in newspaper accounts to letters from Roosevelt and Owen D. Young, former president of General Electric (who had helped create the Dawes plan in the 1920s and had gained prominence as a leading conservative Democrat by his managing of German reparation payments). Roosevelt's letter exonerated scientists from the widespread charge that they were "responsible for the current economic ills" and supported the continuation of scientific "thought and development" for the purposes of reviving industry and creating "markets for raw materials."[95]

It was Owen, however, scheduled to speak at the symposium but unable to attend, who set the tone for the meeting. In his letter, read to the symposium, he observed that "the notion that science and technical development have resulted in unemployment and financial panic is a characteristic of the Depression." Such farfetched "attacks against science" had hidden the truth that science was not the "Devil that caused the depression but the most promising Angel to lead us out of it." He railed at the idea, "which many today advocate," that scientists should "focus all our ingenuity and energy on reducing the cost of [production]." That would only "reduce the labor content [of manufacturing], and so the work to be divided among the people would surely grow less and less." He observed that "there is no hope in that direction." Shorter hours and declining opportunities to work were dead-ends for science.[96]

Instead, coining a phrase picked up by the media and widely circulated for a month or so after February, Owen observed, "Science is the mother of obsolescence." He argued that it was "not wear-out" but the new products made possible by science that had "kept our people at work and has produced more and better things." Hence, to the "extent that we paralyze [invention and research], we will limit employment."[97]

Millikan followed the reading of Owen's letter, and in a speech complicated by his own struggle as a scientist redefining the role of science, observed that "every labor-saving device creates in general as many, oftentimes more, jobs than it destroys." He continued: "The progress of human civilization consists primarily in the multiplication of human wants. If you want a stagnant civilization you have only to destroy the influences that cause these wants to multiply." Among these influences, Millikan counted scientific inventions first on the list. He went on to dismiss the whole issue of technological unemployment; there was "no such thing," he concluded. He attacked the public pressure and the political "wisdom" that was pushing for a halt in scientific research and development. Those who were suggesting that it would be "wise to let development in the natural science wait until the social sciences have caught up" were engaging in the worst kind of "muddy thinking." To stop the development of the natural sciences would be to lose the "chief stimulant to the progress of civilization."[98]

The next day, the *New York Times* reported that Millikan "slaughters those pressing for a 'research holiday'" and "puts to rest the superstition" that "science is at the root of the current economic distress."[99]

Compton explained to the press that the symposium's purpose was to "combat the prevailing idea that science is responsible for the present difficulties of the world." He agreed with Millikan that

> the idea that science takes away jobs, or in general is at the root of our economic and social ills, is contrary to fact, is based on ignorance or misconception, is vicious in its possible social consequences, and yet has taken an invidious hold on the minds of many people. It has become evident that the spread of this idea is threatening to reduce public support of scientific work and in particular, through certain codes in the NRA, to stifle further development in our manufacturing processes.[100]

Like Millikan, he attacked NRA codes that contained clauses that forbade the introduction of labor-saving machinery and added, bitterly, his own thoughts about Roosevelt's refusal to fund the Science Advisory Board's "Recovery Program for Scientific Progress." He also attacked social scientists who were suggesting that natural science should slow down so that "lagging" knowledge in other areas could catch up.

After the symposium, these leading scientists and engineers continued pressure on the administration to restore research money for existing federal agencies and fund Compton's $16 million project. Using the slogan "Science Makes Jobs," they widened the campaign to convince the public they were not to blame for technological unemployment but were in the vanguard of work creation. Prominent figures such as Charles F. Kettering, research vice-president of General Motors Corporation, and W. W. Campbell, president of the National Academy of Sciences, joined the cause, repeating the arguments that Compton, Owen, and Millikan had outlined.[101]

In May 1934, Alfred P. Sloan, president of General Motors, organized a round-table symposium at the opening of the Century of Progress Exposition in Chicago on the topic "Previews of Industrial Progress in the Next Century." In preparation for his symposium, Sloan sent telegrams to prominent scientists throughout the United States, asking, "What is to be the progress of science and industry during the next decades?" and, "Is there any logical reason to assume that progress is to be halted at this particular point in our development?" He received some three hundred responses, which he characterized as "tremendously encouraging." The prevailing opinion was that "science is ready to show the way to greater industrial progress" and that higher standards of living and "greater opportunities" for research and employment were on the horizon.[102]

For example, Arthur A. Noyes, director of the Gates Chemical Laboratories at the California Institute of Technology, maintained that "if science and industrial research are stimulated and not handicapped there will result in the future . . . a stimulation of the wants of men and a much greater employment of labor than the unemployment resulting from the displacement of old industries. Recent chemical research affords striking illustrations, such as light metals . . . , cellulose industries, and biochemical investigations."[103]

Charles Kettering attended the Chicago meeting and in his presentation gave a brief history of the changes in scientific opinion. He said the public still thought that "science and industry are only interested in the development of labor-saving devices." This was understandable because for over fifty years labor saving had been science and technology's "most important" concern. But in the last five years, scientists had come to be "very much more interested in the production of labor-producing projects . . . than labor saving." Kettering thought the purpose of the symposium was "to present . . . this point of view," correcting public misconceptions and finding additional support in the scientific community.[104]

But the campaign continued to run up against new threats. In late March 1934, at a meeting of the British Association for the Advancement of Science, the economist Josiah Stamp led a discussion about the need for a "scientific holiday" to deal with technological unemployment. In addition, Stamp published *Must Science Ruin Progress*, a book that was widely discussed in the press and among scientists. The suggestions by an English bishop, Edward Arthur Burroughs, that a ten-year moratorium be imposed on scientific investigations were dug up from seven years' obscurity, refurbished, and widely circulated in the American popular press. These events added urgency to the "Science Makes Jobs" campaign, but little progress was made that year.[105]

In December 1934, Compton, in a feature article in the *New York Times*, complained that whereas science had once "created vast employment," it was "not being called on to create new employment when this is desperately needed." As before, he traced this lack of research support to "depression hysteria," which put the blame for unemployment on scientists, and he decried the clamor for a "scientific holiday." He noted with approval that Roosevelt was trying to provide for employment in public works, but questioned the wisdom of the administration's failure to include scientific research in such efforts. He also praised Roosevelt's attempts to "stimulate the development of new industries," agreeing that, "like babies," new industries needed "shelter and nourishment which take the form of patent protection, and financing." But, "before all," he maintained, "they need to be born, and their parents are science and invention." In addition, the needs for military preparedness were being ignored. Trained scientists were being forced to take unskilled jobs in industry, and a whole generation of new scientists was being wasted. Their skills, vital to the nation's defense and to maintaining a competitive edge in international trade, were being lost, atrophying through lack of proper employment.[106]

Compton reiterated the need for opening new directions for scientific and technological progress. Most people were "chiefly impressed with the fact that efficiency experts have found, in the products of science, ways of lowering labor costs of production." This narrow view about efficiency had led people to view "science as a menace." But "economic pressure [would] continue to force the development of labor saving devices." Therefore, significant scientific discoveries in the future would "most likely be in other fields than mechanics, as in chemistry, electricity, biology or medicine." Moreover, traditional research would doubtless change. For example, agricultural research in the past had led to greater yields. But "what we need now is to find new uses for old products which will create new social value or replace the consumption of our exhaustible natural resources (such as grain alcohol mixed with motor fuel)." He believed that "experience justifies reasonable hope that a large fund of wisely expended research along these lines will contribute toward a positive and permanent solution to the problem of agricultural overproduction . . . a far better solution than the present emergency expedient of huge year by year expenditures to pay farmers to reduce their production." Other "frontiers begged to be opened," such as "complete electrification of the country," new housing, and better refuse and sewage systems.[107]

In December, Compton proposed a new, expanded version of his $16 million public works project, suggesting that .5 percent of the public works emergency appropriations be diverted to scientific research. He also called for the permanent establishment of government scientific bureaus for research and information and for a $5 million annual appropriation for research outside government. The totals for his new project were $15 million per year and $75 million over its five-year life. In the same month, Compton was elected president of the American Association for the Advancement of Science, and during the Pittsburgh convention appeared to have the backing of a major part of the scientific community for his proposals. Again, at Pittsburgh, he justified such a measure with the "Science Makes Jobs" rationale.[108]

Nevertheless, F. A. Delano and the National Resources Board rejected Compton's plans as too expensive. After a meeting with Compton in January 1935, Delano prepared a letter to Roosevelt for Ickes's signature. The NRB's proposal, in effect, absorbed the Science Advisory Board into the National Resources Board, creating an omnibus science committee in the NRB that included natural science along with social science and education. In place of Compton's massive program, the NRB recommended that Roosevelt increase funding for existing federal research agencies and fund specific research projects that the NRB would propose in the future. Roosevelt approved the NRB's suggestions, and in a memorandum to Ickes, called for the board to develop a national plan for research and for employment of scientists "remembering always that 90 percent of the amount expended must go to direct labor paid to persons taken from the relief rolls."

Very little was left for Compton and the Science Advisory Board to do but pack up and go home. The NRB had effectively established itself as the clearinghouse for federal support of the sciences and the arbiter of federally supported research projects. As a result, the "Science Makes Jobs" campaign lost some momentum, and federally supported research took other directions.

In 1936, in a letter to Compton (back at his old job as president of MIT) and the heads of other major schools of technology and engineering, Roosevelt lectured the educators on "the responsibility of engineering." Roosevelt wrote that "in respect of the impact of science and engineering upon human life—social and economic dislocations as well as advance in productive power—the facts are revealed with distressing clearness in public records of unemployment, bankruptcies and relief. . . . The design and construction of specific civil engineering works or of instruments of production represent only one part of the responsibility of engineering. It must also consider social processes and problems, and the modes of more perfect adjustment to the environment, and must cooperate in designing accommodating mechanisms to absorb the shock of the impact of science." Roosevelt called for the engineering schools to redesign their curriculums by including courses that taught social responsibility for scientific achievements. Compton responded with "Science Makes Jobs," and came close to accusing the President of being one of the uninformed masses "chiefly impressed by the fact that science . . . has displaced human labor." Nevertheless, Roosevelt's letter was indicative of the climate of opinion in the NRB.[109]

The National Resources Board, renamed in 1935 the National Resources Committee, appointed its own science committee in that year, contacting the National Academy of Sciences, the Social Science Research Council, and the American Council on Education for nominations. In this new committee, social scientists outnumbered natural scientists, and as a result, emphasis shifted from exclusive concern with the natural sciences. Responding to Roosevelt's directive, the National Resources Committee conducted extensive investigations on the impact of inventions, publishing a series of reports from 1937 to 1941.[110]

The first major report, *Technological Trends and National Policy*, submitted by the science committee under the direction of William F. Ogburn, focused on the *social* consequences of technological unemployment. Compton and the natural scientists' influence was evident in committee findings that "although technological unemployment is one of the most tragic effects of the sudden adoption of many new inventions (which may be likened to an immigration of iron men), inventions create jobs as well as take them away."[111] But, unlike Compton's plan to focus scientific research on new inventions for new jobs, the science committee, with its preponderance of social scientists, recommended that economic and social studies be first undertaken to gauge the impact of existing inventions such as the mechanical cotton picker, air conditioning, plastics, and artificial fibers had on employment. They also recommended that the National Planning Committee form a special joint committee to "keep abreast with [future] technological developments . . . ascertaining and noting the occupations and industries which are likely to be affected by imminent technological changes and the extent to which these inventions are likely to result in unemployment."[112]

David Weintraub, director of the WPA's National Research Project on Reemployment Opportunities and Recent Changes in Industrial Techniques, prepared his own report, *Unemployment and Increasing Productivity*, for inclusion with the science committee's publication. Like the social scientists on the committee, Weintraub concluded that "full study" of the impact of new "machinery on the volume of unemployment" was needed before effective governmental action could be taken.[113] Weintraub emphasized the complexity of such a study and the fact that sufficient data were not available to make any conclusions about whether new machinery created or destroyed work. Nevertheless, he presented "the current thinking of many economists" about the matter, quoting J. M. Clark's recently published *Economics of Planning Public Works* in detail. Clark had concluded that there were *prima facie* grounds for believing that increased productivity in the age of "material progress" had "created dislocations in our economic system because we cannot make the necessary adjustments fast enough. . . . Mere technological progress seems capable of bringing on a state of chronic inability to use all our labor power." Technological improvements made since 1929, and other advances waiting in the wings for economic recovery, made it likely that "unless there is some shortening of the hours in industry . . . there may be a considerable amount of unemployment even after the current [1936] revival has gone as far as it can." Weintraub agreed, and in his conclusions about the outlook ahead, noted that since "our economic system has not yet evinced an ability to make necessary adjustments fast enough, it may be expected that the dislocations occasioned by technological progress will continue to present serious problem of industrial, economic, and social readjustments."[114]

In addition, Charles E. Merriam, a member of the National Planning Board, was bold enough to give a speech in Minneapolis to a meeting of the American Association for the Advancement of Science stressing the importance of scientific research for increased free time. Merriam observed that science, after helping to relieve the "burden of hunger, disease and fear," could open the "book of leisure . . . and the treasures of human appreciation and enjoyment be made available to the mass of mankind."[115]

The struggle between natural scientists and social scientists in the NRC's science committee continued until the coming of the war, with social scientists questioning easy acceptance of the "Science Makes Jobs" formula and channeling research funds into studies on the economic impact of new machinery. In many cases, they subordinated "basic" research and new inventions to their economic impact studies. The social scientists' point that more social studies had to be funded to catch up with mechanical and physical advances carried the day.

Moreover, ideas about scientific progress for leisure continued, with highly placed people such as Merriam perpetuating the arguments.

Nevertheless, the basis for future research had been laid. The NRC concluded that research was a national resource and made firm the connection between national planning and scientific research. Moreover, in practical terms, even though Roosevelt rejected Compton and the American Association for the Advancement of Science's (AAAS) massive research and reemployment program, he restored funding for existing federal research agencies: weather, soils, standards, mines, etc. By 1937, budgets were returned to pre-depression levels and continued to grow afterward.[116]

It is hard to judge how much impact scientists such as Compton, Millikan, and the AAAS had with their "Science Makes Jobs" campaign, since their influence in the NRC was diluted by social scientists and it was clear that Roosevelt was far from convinced. But as the depression wore on and the NRC's influence grew, attacks against science as the cause of the depression lessened, and scientists were able to recover most of their losses.

In any event, with the coming of World War II, called by some "the physicists' war," natural scientists reasserted their influence as funding for military research skyrocketed. Roosevelt created the Office of Scientific Research and Development (OSRD) just before the war to mobilize science, providing funds through this agency that met and surpassed the wildest dreams of Compton and the Science Advisory Board. And as the war was ending, Roosevelt asked the OSRD director, Vannevar Bush, a former vice-president of MIT and president of the Carnegie Institution, to submit a report on ways that wartime mobilization of scientists could continue and their efforts be turned to peacetime uses. The result was *Science: The Endless Frontier*. Published in July 1945, this report, according to Robert Kargon, "has become a classic . . . statement," justifying subsequent increases in governmentally supported research programs and laying a foundation on which has been built modern, massive research structures.[117]

In this report and in subsequent grants for research through the National Science Foundation (created in 1950), "Science Makes Jobs" finally came into its own. In his letter to Bush, Roosevelt predetermined OSRD's principal conclusions. Roosevelt suggested that research be turned "in the days ahead to the improvement of our national health, the creation of new enterprises bringing new jobs and the betterment of the national standard of living. . . . The diffusion of such knowledge should help us stimulate new enterprises, provide jobs for our returning servicemen and other workers, and make great strides for the improvement of the national well-being."[118]

Bush displayed as the frontispiece of *Endless Frontier* Roosevelt's conclusion that "new frontiers of the mind are before us, and if they are pioneered with the same vision, boldness, and drive with which we have waged this war we can create a fuller and more fruitful employment and a fuller and more fruitful life."

Responding to this letter, Bush reasserted the importance of research in the natural sciences, noting that Roosevelt had made it clear that "in speaking of science he had in mind the natural sciences, including biology and medicine. . . . Progress in other fields, such as the social sciences and the humanities, is likewise important; [but] the program of science presented in my report warrants immediate attention." Bush reiterated Roosevelt's other points: "The pioneer spirit is still vigorous within the nation. Science offers a largely unexplored hinterland for the pioneer who has the tools for the task. . . . Scientific progress is one essential key to our security as a nation, to more jobs, to a higher standard of living and to cultural progress."[119]

Continuing to follow Roosevelt, Bush outlined the three reasons scientific research was necessary in the future—"for the war against disease . . . for our national security . . . and for the public welfare"— a tripod that has been the basis of most subsequent governmentally supported research. Bush noted in the section on public welfare that "one of our hopes is that after the war there will be full employment." To reach that goal and "create new jobs . . . we must make new and better and cheaper products. . . . But new products and processes are not born full grown. They are founded on new principles and new conceptions which in turn result from basic scientific research. Basic scientific research is scientific capital . . . essential to our goal of full employment." He added that expansion of existing research and development and dissemination of information were also essential to avoid unemployment. Bush noted that millions of people were employed in industries that did not even exist before World War I, citing "radio, air conditioning, rayon, and plastics" as examples. But these were only the beginning "if we make full use of our scientific resources."[120]

In addition, federal support for scientific research would provide government jobs for scientists directly, and in so doing would conserve one of the nation's most valuable resources at the same time that it prevented unemployment. Military research could employ thousands in the defense of the nation. Government-supported industrial and medical research would open job opportunities and new occupations for an army of nonscientists. But these were not makework public jobs. Although funded by the government, they were essential tasks thrust on the nation by the threats of hostile nations, diseases, and unemployment.

Trying to list all possible benefits of increased "scientific capital," Bush included "more leisure for recreation, study, for learning how to live without the deadening drudgery that has been the burden of the common man." But this was an afterthought and in no way rivaled his paean to science as the great creator of new work and the dynamo of employment.[121]

By the end of World War II, most scientists had resolved the issue of technological unemployment. With Bush and the OSRD, they had found their place at last in Roosevelt's administration. Social scientists who had questioned the importance of "pure" research (what had by then been renamed "basic" research) had been banished—not "warranting of immediate attention." Economists' suggestions that employment impact studies be made before new machines were introduced were ignored, and the true faith, "Science Makes Jobs," was affirmed in its simplicity. People such as the technocrats, Dahlberg, and Wallace, who had tried to hold on to the old belief in simple efficiency were forgotten. The idea that science's importance was limited to the efficient creation of necessities and service of human freedom in leisure were transcended in the "endless frontier" of new, important work. The heresy that science was for itself, apart from "application," and a form of "mere amusement," was abolished. Free time, a potent threat to science and research during the depression, was tamed, and leisure was added as a comfortable afterthought to the long list of science's pioneer achievements.

CHAPTER 11

The Age of Work

O NE FOREIGN OBSERVER of the American scene during the depression was H. G. Wells. Announcing that he would make a movie depicting life in the year 2054, Wells arrived in the United States in mid-1934 at the height of the shorter-hour agitation, when Roosevelt was making overtures to labor and the technocrats were still popular. Wells dined at the White House, observed the political scene, and set to work on two movies that were completed in 1936 and 1937.[1]

Things to Come and *The Man Who Could Work Miracles* were released to lukewarm reception in the United States but have remained two of Wells's more popular films; they still may be seen on late-night television. Both seem woefully out of date, with stilted dialogue and hackneyed plots. But when they were released, they spoke directly to the unique political and cultural situation that existed in the United States and, to some degree, in Britain. Both films are "period pieces" in the best sense of that phrase.

Things to Come begins with the "opening effect . . . of walking and hurrying crowds. Across this scene appears and fades the legend 'Whither Mankind?'" This was Wells's original title for his film and was a direct reference to Charles Beard's book of that name. Beard had begun his book this way: "In America, where Europeans have renewed their youth, conquered a wilderness, and won wealth and leisure by the sweat of their brows, the cry ascends on all sides: 'Where do we go from here? *Vivere deinde philosophari*—the stomach being full, what shall we do next?'" This question occupied Wells's attention throughout his film.[2]

Wells portrays a catastrophic war that he calls "World War II," for which the film is best remembered as a prophecy. The war is followed by an extended portrayal of the "period of barbarism," a late-twentieth-century Dark Ages with pestilence, starvation, and continuing warfare on a smaller scale. But at the heart of the film is Wells's portrayal of a new golden age, beginning in the mid-twenty-first century with the reconstruction of machinery, technology, and order.

This "brave new world" of 2054 is not yet perfect. It still contains two competing groups. But unlike previous social divisions, between those with power and those without, or between the "haves" and the "have-nots," this world is divided between "doers" and "do-nots."

The "do-nots" are led by Theotocopulos, a rebel artist, and the "doers" are led by a group of scientists, headed by Oswald Cabal, who are busy building a giant gun to shoot astronauts to the moon, a project that symbolizes the larger issues that divide the two groups.

Theotocopulos is introduced saying, "I do not like this machinery. All these wheels going round. Everything so fast and slick. *No.* . . . I will *go* for this Brave New World of theirs—tooth and claw."[3]

The scene shifts to a discussion between Cabal and Passworthy, a character who takes a moderate position between Theotocopulos and the scientists.

> PASSWORTHY: I grant you the reality of the progress the world has made. . . . It has been a century of marvels. But cannot we have too much progress? Here I agree is a lovely world in which we are living. A little artificial—but admirable at last. The triumph of human invention and human will. Comfort, beauty, security. Our light is brighter than the sunshine. . . . We have got the better of nature. Why should we drive on so urgently?

> CABAL: Because it is in the nature of life to drive on. The most unnatural thing in life is contentment. . . . Science asks for the best.

> PASSWORTHY: I'm out of sorts with this modern world and all this progress. . . . Why can't we rest at this. Why must we go on and go on more strenuously than ever?

> CABAL: Would you stop all the thinking and working for ever more?

> PASSWORTHY: Oh, not exactly *that*.

> CABAL: Then what do you mean? A little thinking, but not much? A little work but nothing serious? . . . No. Nature drives. . . . Beneath this surface of plenty and security she is still contriving mischief. Now she wants to turn our very success against us, tempt us to be indolent, fantastic, idlers and pleasure-lovers —betraying ourselves in another fashion. . . . Life couldn't be

better. Let the new generation *play*—waste the life that is in them. . . . A planet-load of holiday makers, spinning to destruction. Just a crowning festival before the dark.[4]

The scene shifts again. The lovers Rowena and Cabal are separated by their differences:

ROWENA: Reproach me! All the same I care. Who left me love-hungry? Cabal, have you no pity? Have you no imagination? . . . Hard you are and terrible. What are you doing with life, Cabal? You turn it to steel.

CABAL: You fritter it away. I hated your going. But you made life too distracted and vexing for me. I loved you—but loving you was an all-time task. I had work to do.

ROWENA: *What* work?

CABAL: The everlasting work of fighting danger and death and decay for mankind.

ROWENA: Fanatic! Where are danger and death today?

CABAL: In ambush everywhere.

ROWENA: You go out to meet them . . . if you are hunting danger and death all the time, what is there left of life?

CABAL: Courage, adventure, work—and an increasing power and greatness . . . let me live after my nature. You may want love, but I want the stars.

ROWENA: But love too. You wanted human love once, Cabal.

CABAL: I wanted work more. . . . Do you think that everything else in human life is going to alter, scale and power and speed, and men and women remain as they have always been? This is a New World we are living in. It drives to new and greater destinies. And that desperate old love story which has been acted and told so often, as though it was the very core of life, is almost finished with. [The new man and woman] live for the endless adventure. . . . And that is the increase of human knowledge and power—for ever.[5]

The scene shifts again. Theotocopulos appears on a "mirror screen," a 2054 television set.

THEOTOCOPULOS: What is all this progress? What good of this progress? Onward and upward. We demand a halt, we demand a rest. The object of life is happy living.

CABAL (*talking to the screen*): One would think the object to life is everlasting repetition.

THEO: We will not have life sacrificed to experiment. Progress is not living, it should only be the preparation for living. . . . Let us be just to these people who rule over us. Let us not be ungrateful. They have tidied up the world. . . . Order and magnificence is achieved, knowledge increases. Oh God, how it increases! [*Laughter*]

CABAL (*to the screen*): So they laugh at that.

THEO: Still the hard drive goes on. They find work for all of us. We thought this was to be the Age of Leisure. But is it? We must measure and compute, we must collect and sort and count. We must sacrifice ourselves. We must live for—for what?—the species. We must sacrifice ourselves all day and every day to this incessant spreading of knowledge and order. We gain the whole world—and at what a price! Greater sacrifices and still greater.[6]

The scene changes to the "world audience" in the form of a many-voiced dialogue about Theotocopulos's speech.

THEO (*continues in a "discourse of Theotocopulos" in voiceover*): *Thou shalt and thou shalt not,* oppressing the free hearts of men. You have learnt about these tyrannies of the spirit in your histories. But have they really left us—or have they merely adopted new names and fresh marks? I tell you this science and exploration of theirs is no more and no less than the spirit of self-immolation returning to the earth in a new guise . . . the old dark seriousness—the stern unnecessary devotions.[7]

Then comes the world audience. A nursery, old men drinking, a scientific laboratory where groups discuss the merits of work, adventure, exploration, seriousness versus the end of progress as leisure and living.[8]

Then mobs collect to fight against the space gun. Wells describes this as "not a traditional social conflict we are witnessing. It is not the Haves attacked by the Have Nots; it is the Doers attacked by the Do-nots."

As the social unrest intensifies, Cabal begins the countdown for the moon launch and closes with these opinions:

CABAL: Rest enough for the individual man. Too much of it and much too soon, and we call it death. But for MAN no rest and no ending. He must go on—conquest beyond conquest.

This little planet and its wiles and ways and all the laws of the mind and matter that restrain him. Then the planets about him, and at last out across immensity to the stars. And when he has conquered all the deeps of space and all the mysteries of time—still he will be beginning.[9]

These were themes that Wells had explored earlier. In *The Time Machine*, he had populated the future with two kinds of human creatures: those who worked with and were slaves to machines, and those freed by machines and the exploited workers for a life of leisure. Both groups, the workers and the leisured, were miserable. Those with leisure had degenerated without the challenge of work to subhuman stupidity; those with work were doomed to an eternal underground in a hell-like existence of heat and whirling machinery. But the workers had turned the tables and were preying on the leisured above ground. Because the leisured ones were so stupid and devoid of will, they were easily converted to food.[10]

In *Things to Come*, Wells is not so harsh about the future's possibilities. Work and leisure seem to him to be worth considering, and he gives both a chance to be represented by articulate spokespersons. The antagonism between the two remains in the form of a social and cultural contest, not in the older, cannibalistic form.

In *The Man Who Could Work Miracles*, one of Wells's best-known films, he again treats the problem of industrial growth and the possibility of leisure. Here he is at his most optimistic, but he still has reservations about whether humans can ever stand too much freedom, too much power and control. In this film, he addresses the possibility of increased leisure directly.

The story is a model of simplicity. The gods, or "great elementals," named "the Observer," "the Indifference," and "the Player or the Giver of Power," decide for amusement to give humans power over nature. Since they judge it a bad idea to give all mankind power, they decide on one individual, George McWhirter Fotheringay. A meek and mild-mannered clerk, Fotheringay is given the ability to work miracles. Much of the film is spent depicting Fotheringay working small-scale miracles to the astonishment of those around him, accomplished by some very innovative special effects.[11]

Wells's social comments are given in dialogues toward the end of the film. Fotheringay's friends tell him that he ought to make greater use of his powers. Those at his boardinghouse suggest that he make himself rich, and make them rich in the process, by going into business. Selling some good or service miraculously would be heaven-sent indeed. Fotheringay responds that he could, with a gesture, give everybody in the world enough to satisfy them. Bampfylde, a banker, is horrified:

BAMPFYLDE: What would they DO? What incentive would there be for anybody—to do anything?

FOTHERINGAY: Couldn't they have some fun—like?

BAMPFYLDE: I can assure you, Mr. Fotheringay. . . . I have studied these questions—very profound questions—before you were born. Human society, I repeat, is based on want. Life is based on want. Wild-eyed visionaries . . . may dream of a world without need. Cloud-Cuckoo-Land. It can't be done.

FOTHERINGAY: It 'asn't been tried, 'as it?

MAJOR GRIGSBY: You take my word . . . You can't go *heaping* things on people without a *quid pro quo,* it would ruin everything. Universal bankruptcy. Lassitude. Degeneration.[12]

Fotheringay, discouraged by such advice, and tempted to use his power to become much more successful with the women around him, turns to Mr. Maydig, the Baptist minister. The opening scene with Maydig finds the reverend gentleman reading from Bertrand Russell's *Freedom and Organization,* commenting at length on its wisdom:

MAYDIG: Ah-ah! Wonderful, wonderful. "To take this sorry scheme of things entire and mold it better to the heart's desire." Yes, my dear beloved friends, this poor disordered world, this rich and marvelous world. Do you ever . . . No! Do we ever— No, no, no. When do we ever lift our eyes from the things—the sordid urgent little things about us—think—dream. . . . If we only had the power—if we only had the faith to do that.[13]

Fotheringay breaks in on this scene and engages Maydig with questions about the wise use of his miraculous powers. Visions of peace and plenty fill Maydig's imagination, and he describes a golden age to Fotheringay.

But Fotheringay has had his confidence shaken by Bampfylde and company; he fears that "there may be a catch in it somewhere." He quotes the banker to Maydig—that people are "held together by money, really, and by wanting things, and that if they didn't want they wouldn't have anything to do."

Maydig finds this "absolutely intolerable," a complete lack of trust in human beings. Hovering over Fotheringay, he exclaims, "Is there no art? Is there no beauty? Are there not boundless seas of knowledge yet unplumbed?"

Fotheringay repeats the banker's observation that people are not "likely to go in for that sort of thing all at once."

Maydig scoffs. "Because the man has no imagination. Because he has no soul. Because he has forgotten the clouds of glory he trailed from heaven in his infancy. The business man! The banker! Save me from them! Man bankrupt—in a world of plenty. . . . Oh Heaven! . . . Are we to remain needy to please bankers and business men?"

Maydig sways Fotheringay for a while, and together they plan to institute the "Golden Age" sometime in the mid-afternoon of the following day.[14]

But before this comes about, Fotheringay meets Colonel Winstanley, who repeats the banker's admonitions, but with more passion. Fotheringay pleads his and Maydig's case, that "the Want System" would have to give way to "the Plenty System. There's no need for people to be hard up now." The colonel answers that with the end of competition, work will be unnecessary, raising a problem: "What are people going to DO, sir? What are they going to *do?*" Fotheringay is still puzzled by this question, but quotes Maydig that "we ought to just go about loving one another."

This sets the colonel off on a tirade. Jumping up, he shouts, "Are you mad, sir? Are you human? Have you no sense of decency? The most private—the most sacred feelings!"

Fotheringay tries suggesting "arts and science and making things," adding that Maydig "had seen the possibilities in such a different way."

The colonel, gasping apoplectically, replies, "Fretwork and—fretwork and foolery!"

After Fotheringay departs, Colonel Winstanley plots to kill him. Conferring with bankers Bampfylde and Grigsby, he points out that Fotheringay is on the verge of destroying business, credit, and "the cash nexus" by which "the human world is held together . . . if it goes—everything goes." The colonel decides to take matters into his own hands when his partners shy from murder and leaves to get his service rifle.[15]

In the meantime, Fotheringay has met with Maydig, and they sit together, Maydig savoring the moment just before the "millennium," Fotheringay troubled by doubts. He asks the minister Colonel Bampfylde's question: "What are people going to do" without work, want, and necessity to drive them?

Maydig responds: "As to the question of leisure, it's been raised already by science and invention and rationalisation and all that. It's not a *New* question. . . . Scientific progress has warned us already. The answer is the intelligent pursuit of happiness, artistic work, creative energy."

Fotheringay objects, using the colonel's reasoning that "people—as a general rule—would not want to do those things." Maydig responds that "we must *make* them want."

Fotheringay objects again: "Won't a lot of new—desires get loose?" confessing that "powerful desires" are already growing within him. But Maydig counsels self-restraint and tells him to seek "guidance" from his church and its representative, Maydig.[16]

Just then, the colonel takes a shot at Fotheringay, who, shaken by the experience, makes himself invulnerable and then loses all control.

Rejecting any and all advice, he sets himself up as ruler of the world, adorning himself in splendor, creating a lavish palace and surrounding himself with a harem. Maddened by power and ego, he brings all the most powerful people in the world to his presence and demands that they give him a perfect world before the sun goes down. But since the sun is already setting, Fotheringay decides to stop the world's spinning to provide more time—a bad decision, since this destroys the world. But in the last moments of consciousness, Fotheringay works another miracle, demanding that everything be "as it was—a minute before" he received his powers. Then, standing outside the pub where the film began, Fotheringay makes his last wish, that his powers end.[17]

The "great spirits"—Player, Observer, and Indifference—comment on these events. Indifference says that he had thought all along that humans could never handle power, that they were ruled by "egotism and elementary lust." But Player observes that they were "apes only yesterday" and that in time, "if I give them power . . . bit by bit. If I stir thought and wisdom into the mess to keep pace with the growth of power. Broaden slowly. Age by Age. Give the grains of gold time to get together," and humans had the potential to discover something to do other than want and need, fight and lust. *The Man Who Could Work Miracles* ends with Fotheringay his normal self once again, except with a new appreciation of the paradox in the power to work miracles.[18]

In these two films, Wells represented the political and cultural debates going on at the time. He made specific references to current events on occasion; for example, in *The Man Who Could Work Miracles*, one character describes his own, "Bill Stoker's, New Deal."[19] Like other observers, Wells saw a contest between views of progress occurring in the United States and Britain, a competition over Charles Beard's question, "The stomach being full, what shall we do next?" But unlike the cultural partisans in the 1920s and the political activists of the 1930s, Wells was a neutral observer for the most part, presenting each point of view evenhandedly. The real political contests were represented fantastically—as a social conflict in a future world or as a series of dialogues about miraculous powers. But Wells's message is unmistakable: The issues of work and freedom from work, the questions "Why create more work in plenty?" and "What would people *Do* if they were not working and governed by 'necessity?'" were far from settled and would occupy the Western mind for years to come. Wells did not try to resolve these issues. In *Things to Come*, the social unrest is left hanging in the air; in *The Man Who Could Work Miracles*, Fotheringay goes back to being a clerk.

Although Wells envisioned the debate continuing into the twenty-first century, national policies begun during the depression that continue to develop today have proved him largely wrong. Where Wells left the outcome of the contest between the "doers" and the "do-nots" in question, history has shown a clear winner: work creation.

With the failure of the Black–Connery bills and the advent of governmentally managed capitalism, the shorter-hour movement lost its short-lived political momentum. More important, the New Deal committed the federal government to assuring workers a 40-hour week, and in so doing institutionalized a bias against free time in any form, leisure or unemployment. The two were virtually defined in terms of each other. Since the depression, few Americans have thought of work reduction as a natural, continuous, and positive result of economic growth and increased productivity. Instead, additional leisure has been seen as a drain on the economy, a liability on wages, and the abandonment of economic progress. No Theotocopulos has arrived on the scene to lead a mass countermovement.

Certainly, the end of shorter hours has many dimensions and causes that must be explored. But the narrative presented in this book suggests two important causes, one social and the other political. Among the reasons for the ending of the shorter-hour movement was the change in American attitudes toward free time.

For over a century, American workers and their supporters had valued work reductions. They did so for a variety of reasons, some economic, some nonpecuniary. Only higher wages competed with this issue for workers' attention. During the 1920s and 1930s, labor and other groups saw in the "progressive shortening of the hours of labor" a practical foundation for old Romantic dreams, as well as a necessary remedy for the economy's ills. But during the depression, free time took the form of massive unemployment. Instead of accepting the 30-hour remedy, Roosevelt and the majority of Americans saw this free time as a tragedy that had to be eliminated by increasing economic activity and governmental provision of work. The idea that free time could be leisure—a natural part of economic advance and a foil to materialistic values—was abandoned. The reform continuum was broken during the New Deal by subsequent adherence to economic growth as the only road to progress.

The changes in attitudes found concrete forms in federal law and policy established during the depression that have been perpetuated to the present day. Hence, the end of shorter hours is to be explained partly in political terms.

Since the depression, public policy has been designed to maintain "adequate demand" and "full employment." Government deficit spending, liberal Treasury policies, increased government payrolls, expanded public works projects, and increased military spending have usually been employed when the economy has become "sluggish." Beginning with Roosevelt's administration, and continuing through such things as the Full Employment Act of 1946, the Commission on Money and Credit in 1961, the Humphrey–Hawkins employment bill in the 1970, and Reagan's massive deficits for military buildup, the government's policy has been constant. In the words of the Employment Act of 1946, it is "the continuing policy of the Federal government . . . to promote maximum employment, production, and purchasing power," by means of "federal investment and expenditure as will be sufficient to bring the aggregate volume . . . up to the level required to assure a full employment volume of production." In practical terms, the government has acted as a permanent stabilizing force in the economy, spending whatever is necessary to stimulate "full employment" and "full production."[20]

The shorter-hour cure for unemployment has been forgotten for more than forty years, partly because of the public policy described above. Share the work and increased leisure have simply not had a political constituency since the depression. Leisure has not been a critical issue politically or socially. The decisions made during the depression about the waste of increased free time and the importance of economic growth and work as "full employment" have become articles of conventional wisdom, conservative as well as liberal. This dogma is demonstrated by public policy. But it is manifest in the fact that the shorter-hour movement has been dormant for nearly half a century.

The lasting political and social changes that occurred during the depression added to events in the 1920s that may have slowed down the drive for shorter hours: the weakening of the traditional, practical arguments for shorter hours (fatigue, health, and safety); business doubts about the link between increased productivity and shorter hours; the gospel of consumption; and the waning influence of worker subcultures.

For example, limitations on immigration and the lessening of internal migration from the farm, coupled with the adjustment of native workers to the needs and ways of the industrial state, may also have been important, if E. P. Thompson's musings are correct. From his perspective, and that of a number of historians, as workers became more used to the industrial setting and their work in it, and as fewer new workers showed up to create management problems, the pressure for shorter hours may have decreased. And if "the transition to a mature industrial society entailed a severe restructuring of working habits—new disciplines, new incentives, and a new human nature upon which these incentives could bite effectively," then workers could well have come to prefer work and wages to shorter hours.[21]

Business opinion may also have been a factor. It has been shown that employer attitudes toward increased leisure became more negative in the 1920s. Businessmen and advertisers recognized the marketing potential of existing free hours and exerted considerable effort in commercializing them. The role of these attitudes in employers' decisions about how to set working schedules is revealing, contrasting as it does with earlier business ideas about fatigue's bad effects on productivity.

In addition, labor's position, so adamant during the New Deal, softened after the compromise with the Fair Labor Standards Act. On occasion, as during John Kennedy's administration, labor has raised the issue on the national level, only to be swayed from it by the federal government's promises to stimulate the economy.

Work sharing made an appearance in the U.S. Congress as recently as 1979 in the form of H.R. 1784, a bill that would have modified the Fair Labor Standards Act of 1938 by setting the standard workweek at 35 hours. The following quote is from a letter circulated in Congress by Representative John Conyers of Michigan, the bill's sponsor. Conyers made points about work sharing that have been made for over a century in America:

> One of the chief methods of keeping unemployment in check during the Depression was the adoption of the 40 hour work week. During the past 30 years, however, the work week has remained substantially unchanged, despite the frequency of massive unemployment, large-scale technological displacement of human labor, and considerable gains in productivity. We ought to look at reducing the working week and spreading employment among a greater number of workers, once again, as a means to reducing joblessness without sacrificing productivity.[22]

Conyers was not successful in his effort. He found little support from labor; and this, the first serious effort to amend the Fair Labor Stan-

dards Act, disappeared with little notice in the press or the political
arena.

That labor has not continued to press vigorously for shorter hours
may have to do with the issue of weekly or annual wages and the
political linking of hours and wages together as an either–or choice.
Just as labor accepted, temporarily, the productivity theory of wages
after 1925, organized workers since the depression have tended to
agree that if concessions are made to shorter hours, then the *quid pro
quo* is naturally a reduction in total wages. The theory that, in the
long run, reductions in hours would improve wages for all of labor
has given way to practical considerations of the short-run need to
exchange hours for wages in actual negotiations.

World War II also had an impact. During mobilization, critics complained loudly that 40 hours a week was not enough work to win the
war. Labor's pressure for shorter hours was branded at this time, not
as sharing the poverty, but as shrugging off responsibility for world
citizenship. Since then, military spokesmen in the cold war have continued to equate diligence and hard work with peace and preparedness. What Felix Cohen called this "new industry, war," has employed
hundreds of thousands of workers.[23] Military spending is also justified
by its advocates as a way to create jobs. So, since World War II, advocates of strong national defense have often followed, not led, public
and political opinion in these areas. It has been more a case of jobs
justifying military spending then of national defense calling for continuation of the work ethic.

Changes in American leisure behavior could have also played a
role. From simple inspection of the wage-and-hour record, and from
total recreational spending statistics, it is evident that Americans have
used more and more leisure goods in the time they had free from
work. S. B. Linder has described this development as a trend from
"time intensive" to "goods intensive" leisure. Ironically, leisure itself,
becoming more expensive, could well have encouraged an increased
preference for work and wages. Or, as de Grazia and others point
out, this commercial leisure may be ever less satisfying, and hence
less desirable, as it becomes ever less active, creative, personal, and
connected to others.[24]

Advertising and what John Kenneth Galbraith called the "impera-
tives of consumer demand" may have been related to this phenomenon. Galbraith supposed that insofar as capital growth depended more
on production and consumption than on leisure taking, capitalists have
had a vested interest in convincing people to continue to work to buy
new things, rather than abandon the marketplace for leisure. In more
extreme fashion, Marxists have argued that a capitalist conspiracy has

been afoot, plotting to convince workers to buy things they do not need (thereby alienating workers not only from their work but from their leisure), rather than take their free time to accomplish what Herbert Marcuse called their "liberation, instinctual as well as intellectual." [25]

Lippmann's observations, made in 1930, also offer a possible clue. With Lippmann, others such as William James and Erich Fromm have commented on the fear of freedom characteristic of modern men and women. The weakening of the Judeo-Christian tradition and the community- and family-centered folk cultures have made time away from work too free. Without traditional forms of community and older patterns of conviviality and ritual, modern leisure runs the risk of boredom, and, as Lippmann said, "In the chaos of desire the human imagination picks out portents and monstrous things." [26]

Finally, John Ryan detected great questions about progress and about views-of-the-world at stake in the division of time between work and leisure. In 1931 he wrote:

> It all depends on what we mean by progress. Just why a people should spend its time in turning out and consuming a hundred kinds of luxuries which minister only to material wants, instead of obtaining leisure for the enjoyment of the higher goods of life, is not easily perceptible. After all, neither production nor consumption is an end in itself. The former is only a means to the latter and the latter is beneficial only in so far as it is exercised upon goods which promote genuine human welfare. . . .
>
> One of the most baneful assumptions of our materialistic industrial society is that all men should spend at least one-third of the twenty-four-hour day in some productive occupation. [27]

Ryan was aware of a change in the work ethic: Catholic, Jewish, and Protestant. In its traditional forms, the work ethic was bound to a larger, religious vision; it was part of a theological superstructure that placed all work in context as a means to an end. In the older formulations, work had definite and obtainable purposes: satisfaction of "necessaries" and the road to higher things. But by the 1920s and 1930s, work had become its own justification. It was no longer a means to an end, but had been transformed into an end in itself, for which other parts of the economy, government, and culture were the means. As the "thing-for-itself," work emerged as a sort of fetish—a part of an older tradition broken off and worshipped for itself. Meaning, justification, purpose, and even salvation were now sought in work, without a necessary reference to any traditional philosophic or theological structure. Men and women were answering the old religious questions in new ways, and the answers were more and more in terms of work, career, occupation, and professions. The new, secular versions of the "work ethic" differed dramatically from the religious one. Work for itself was much stronger with such a faith, and work indeed could be without end, an eternal quest with no recognized goal and a necessity in its own right.

The older visions of progress and subordinated work have been rare since Ryan's day. In the light of the new orthodoxy—self-justifying work—the idea that progress involves material advance through higher wages and some kind of nonmaterial, "higher life" progress through shorter hours, seems curious today. But the ebbing of such a vision, shared by many of Ryan's contemporaries, such as Steven Leacock and Abba Silver, may be counted among the reasons for the turnaround from the era of increasing leisure to the Age of Work.

But even in the midst of the modern religion of work, a few countercurrents continue to flow, echoes of the past debate that moderates somewhat this book's generally pessimistic conclusion about the future of increased leisure. Although amounting to a modern heresy, arguments for freedom from unnecessary work and a transcendence to higher things may still be found. The leftist European Green movement, the counterculture of the 1960s and 1970s, and some modern philosophers have continued to struggle with questions about the need to work in economic abundance and the possibilities inherent in the freedom from work. These are questions that H. G. Wells imagined would be critical and important. The debate between the "doers" and the "do-nots" is still viable, although much less evident in the political and cultural mainstream. Monsignor Ryan thought of his position as conservative, more traditional than that promoted by the "new economic gospel of consumption." By no measure was Ryan a radical. But his arguments, expressed today, have become radical.

Those who have written about the possibilities of play and leisure in this Age of Work have recognized this radicalism. Staffan Linder points out that the consumer society is so structured in its values that a change to shorter hours and increased leisure, rather than increased luxuries, would mean a change in Western culture, a change of historic proportions.[28] The radical writer Hebert Marcuse bases his radicalism, not so much in a change of government forms, but in his attacks on the religion of work. After all, communism has as high a regard for industrial work as the rest of the world. Recent statements testify to this. For example, when Pope John Paul II visited Poland in June 1987, the Polish leader General Jaruzelski proposed that East and West find common ground, not in the communist bloc's movement toward capitalist practices, but in the recognition that each major political system has, as its supreme goal, what he called "the Theology of Work."[29] Hence, Marcuse's radical view, as he points out in the Preface to *Eros and Civilization*, is based in the fact that

> automation threatens to render possible the reversal of the re-
> lation between free time and working time: the possibility of
> working time becoming marginal and free time becoming full
> time. The result would be a radical transvaluation of values,
> and a mode of existence incompatible with the traditional cul-
> ture. Advanced industrial society is in permanent mobilization
> against this possibility.[30]

NOTES

Introduction

1. M. C. Cahill, *Shorter Hours: A Study of the Movement Since the Civil War* (New York, 1922), pp. 14–19, 43–46, 156–159, 211; J. D. Owen, *The Price of Leisure* (Montreal, 1970), pp. 62–67; J. S. Zeisel, "The Work Week in American Industry," *Monthly Labor Review* 81 (January 1958): 23–29; U.S. Department of Commerce, Bureau of the Census, *Historical Statistics of the United States: Colonial Times to 1970* (Washington, D.C., 1975); J. Kreps, *Lifetime Allocation of Work and Income* (Durham, N.C., 1971), pp. 17–24; E. B. Jones, "New Estimates of Hours of Work per Week and Hourly Earnings, 1900–1957," *Review of Economics and Statistics* 45 (November 1963): 374–385; U.S. House of Representatives, *Hours of Work, Hearings Before the Select Subcommittee on Labor of the Committee on Education and Labor*, 88th Cong., 1963, pp. 1 and 2, pp. 73–104.

Portions of the Introduction and Chapter 2 appeared in B. K. Hunnicutt, "The End of Shorter Hours," *Labor History* 25 (Summer 1984): 373–404. The author acknowledges with thanks permission given by *Labor History* to include them here.

2. J. R. Commons et al., *History of Labor in the United States*, 4 vols. (New York, 1918–1935), 1:170–172, 384–386, 479, 546; 3:97–113; H. A. Millis and R. E. Montgomery, *The Economics of Labor*, 3 vols. (New York, 1938–1945), 1:481–483; 3:423; I. Bernstein, *The Lean Years: A History of the American Worker, 1920–1933* (Boston, 1960), pp. 476–484; F. R. Dulles, *Labor in America* (New York, 1966), pp. 106, 107; Cahill, *Shorter Hours*, pp. 14–19, 43–46, 156–159, 211; S. Perlman, *A History of Trade Unionism in the United States* (New York, 1950): originally published (1921), pp. 4, 45, 46; S. Fine, "The Eight-Hour Day Movement in the United States, 1888–1891," *Journal of American History* 40 (1953): 441–461.

3. Owen, *Price of Leisure*, pp. 62–67; Millis and Montgomery, *Economics of Labor*, I:iii–v, 468–473; Cahill, *Shorter Hours*, pp. 11–58, 250–256; R. Hofstadter, *The Age of Reform* (New York, 1955), p. 242; A. Link, *Woodrow Wilson and the Progressive Era* (New York, 1954), pp. 226–239; A. M. Schlesinger, *The Crisis of the Old Order* (Boston, 1957), pp. 111–116; Bernstein, *Lean Years*, pp. 70–82; L. Wolman, *Hours of Work in American Industry* (New York: National Bureau of Economic Research, 1938), p. 20; R. McClosky, *The American Supreme Court* (Chicago, 1960), pp. 153–156; N. Pollack, *The Populist Response to Industrial America* (Cambridge, 1962), pp. 28–31; *New York Times*, July 5, 1892, and August 8, 1912.

4. See, for example, J. D. Owen, "Workweeks and Leisure: An Analysis of Trends, 1948–75," *Monthly Labor Review* 99 (August 1976): 3–8, for the claim that there has been no increase in leisure for American workers since World War II. See also Y. Barzel and R. McDonald, "Assets, Subsistence and the Supply Curve of Labor," *American Economic Review* 63 (September 1973): 621–633; D. H. Dalton, "The Age of the Constant Workweek: Hours of Work in the United States Since World War II" (Ph.D. dissertation, University of California, Berkeley, 1975); E. B. Jones, *An Investigation of the Stability of Hours of Work per week in Manufacturing, 1947–1970* (Athens, Ga., 1970), passim; E. Jones, "Hours of Work in the United States: 1900–1957" (Ph.D. dissertation, University of Chicago, 1961), pp. 8–9; Jones, "New Estimates of Hours of Work per week," pp. 375–383; T. A. Finegan, "Hours of Work in the United States: A Cross Sectional Analysis," *Journal of Political Economy* 70 (October 1962): 452–470; T. J. Kniesner, "The Full-Time Workweek in the United States, 1900–1970," *Industrial and Labor Relations Review* 30 (October 1976): 3–15; S. Linder, *The Harried Leisure Class* (New York, 1970), p. 135; H. Northrup, "The Reduction of Hours," in *Hours of Work*, ed. C. Dankert et al. (New York, 1965), passim; J. D. Owen, *Working Hours: An Economic Analysis* (Lexington, Mass., 1979), chap. 3; A. Rees and D. Hamermesh, *The Economics of Work and Pay*, 3d ed. (New York, 1984), chap. 2.

5. In 1900, the life expectancy of American males was 48.2 years; by 1940, it had increased to 61.2 years; by 1960, to 66.6 years; and by 1970, to 67.1 years. As a result, more people have lived to retirement age. In 1900, 39.2 percent of males lived to age 65; by 1974, 67 percent reached that age, a 27 percent increase. In addition, as more males lived to age 65, they could expect more years of life. The life expectancy after age 65 in 1900 was 11.5 years. In 1974, it was 13.4 years, a 1.9-year increase. Fred Best has noted that free time during old age has increased nearly 5 years from 1900 to 1970. But nearly 2 years of that increase has come about by longer life expectancy at age 65 (39 percent of the total), and at least another 27.8 percent was caused by more people reaching retirement age; see F. Best, "The Time of Our Lives: The Parameters of Lifetime Distribution of Education, Work and Leisure," *Loisir et Société* 1 (1978). Hence, over 67 percent of the increase in free time during old age is the result of the longer life span. The advent of general retirements is necessary to explain increases in this kind of free time, to be sure. But it is not sufficient. One must conclude that the longer life span is also a principal reason for longer retirements, a primary source of increased free time (as well as increased working time). The longer life span also explains why the average male worker today works more than 8 years longer in his lifetime than his counterpart in 1900. Of this century's average 18.9-year extended life span, about 8 years, or 42 percent, has been devoted to work; 5 years, or 25 percent, to retirement; and 6 years, or 32 percent, to longer periods of education in youth and later entrance into the work force. See U.S. Department of Health, Education and Welfare, *Vital Statistics of the United States, 1971*, (Washington, D.C., 1975), vol. 2, pt. A.

Juanita Kreps has pointed out that the increases in nonworking hours per year have been distributed as follows from 1890 to 1974:

Reduction in workweek	1,100 hours
Reduction in worklife (average 9 years added by retirement and longer education)	435 hours
Vacations	48 hours
Holidays	32 hours
Sick leave	40 hours
Total averaged annual increase in nonworking time	1,655 hours

Sources: Kreps, *Lifetime Allocation of Work and Income*; Jones, "New Estimates of Hours of Work per Week."

From these figures it is clear that about two-thirds of the total increase in free time in this century came about before the stabilization of the workweek during the 1930s, and only one-quarter of the total has resulted from retirement and later entrance into the work force.

6. U.S. Department of Commerce, *Historical Statistics of the United States*, p. 127; Jones, *Stability of Hours of Work per week in Manufacturing*. See also M. Killingsworth, *Labor Supply* (Cambridge, 1983), pp. 437–440; B. Hunnicutt, "The Economic Constraints of Leisure," in *Constraints on Leisure*, ed. M. G. Wade (Springfield, Ill., 1985), pp. 257–265.

7. The historical alteration of occupational structures has been viewed as related to this change insofar as jobs, shifting from the primary and secondary sectors of the economy to the tertiary sectors, were viewed by workers as being more "desirable" or "attractive," or at least less burdensome. In marginalist terms, if work became less of a disutility, then the "stick" driving people toward free time became less important. Related to the changes in job structure, the "fatigue factor" has been suggested as important in determining the attractiveness of leisure. For example, when the workday was more than 8 hours, the fatigue factor encouraged leisure taking; in the age of the 40-hour workweek, this factor has been less important. Owen suggested that "the great proliferation of educational opportunities . . . has tended to discourage the demand for leisure time"; see Owen, *Working Hours*, p. 78. He also cited the increase in commuting time as another factor discouraging leisure.

Unemployment may also be understood as a factor in the age of the constant workweek. Unemployment has been seen to increase leisure taking when labor demand has declined in periods of recession. Alternately, work hours have seemed to increase during times of reducing unemployment and increasing labor demand. Dalton, in "Age of the Constant Workweek," opined that the rise in consumer debt, allowing many middle-class people access to things like single-family housing and consumer durables, has discouraged workers from seeking gains in their leisure. He also talked about a "psychological propensity to work," a concept amorphous at best, a simple renaming of the hours' reduction stabilization phenomenon.

8. H. Gutman, *Work, Culture and Society in Industrializing America* (New York, 1976), p. vii.

9. F. H. Knight, *Risk, Uncertainty, and Profit* (New York, 1921; 1964) pp.
116–117. Knight's speculation has led economists to make what Robert Lane
called "the Claim" (see R. Lane, "Markets and the Satisfaction of Human
Wants," *Journal of Economic Issues* 12 [December 1978] 803–812). Some economists have contended that the free market automatically assigns "value" to
most if not all human motivations and satisfactions. See, for example, Alfred
Marshall's *Principles of Economics*, 5th ed. (London, 1907), p. 17; J. Barbash, *Job
Satisfaction and Attitude Studies* (Paris, 1976), p. 19; and J. Heckman, "Shadow
Prices, Market Wages and Labor Supply," *Econometrica* 42 (July 1974): 679–
694. "The Claim" is founded on the economics of time use. It rests on the
assumption that any extraeconomic activity a person chooses, that any nonpecuniary source of gratification he or she pursues, has a certain "opportunity
cost." Going to church, visiting friends, or spending time with the children
involves giving up the chance to work. Because of this, a rational person
allocates his or her limited time carefully, and maximizing the utilities of
money—work and leisure, imputes a value to these activities. Using this idea,
economists have indexed a "price" for such extraeconomic activities as visiting one's mistress or paramour. See R. C. Fair, "A Theory of Extramarital
Affairs," *Journal of Political Economy* 86 (February 1978): 45–61. W. Nordhaus
and J. Tobin, in "Is Growth Obsolete?" in *The Measurement of Economic and
Social Performance*, ed. M. Moss (New York, 1975), developed a new "measure
of economic welfare" by adding the value of leisure to the traditional GNP mea-
surements, concluding that leisure represents over one-half of total consumer
income.

Chapter 1

1. E. P. Thompson, "Time, Work-Discipline and Industrial Capitalism,"
Past and Present 38 (December 1967): 56–97. See also E. J. Hobsbawm, *Labour-
ing Men: Studies in the History of Labor* (New York, 1964), esp. chap. 17; K.
Thomas, "Work and Leisure in Pre-Industrial Societies," *Past and Present* 29
(1962): 50–62; S. Pollard, "Factory Discipline in the Industrial Revolution,"
Economic History Review 16 (1968): 254–271; G. S. Jones, "Working Class Culture: Working Class Politics in London, 1870–1900," *Journal of Social History*
9 (1974): 460–508; S. Pollard, *Work and Play: Ideas and Experiences of Work and
Leisure* (New York, 1976); H. Gutman, *Work, Culture and Society in Industrializing America* (New York, 1976), pp. 3–78; D. R. Roediger, "The Movement for
the Shorter Working Day in the United States Before 1866" (Ph.D. dissertation, Northwestern University, 1980), pp. 4–12.

Portions of this chapter appeared in B. K. Hunnicutt, "Historical Attitudes toward Free Time," *Loisir et Société* 3, no. 1 (November 1980): 195–218.
The author acknowledges, with thanks, permissions granted by Presses de
l'Université du Québec to include them here.

2. J. R. Commons et al., *History of Labor in the United States*, 4 vols. (New
York, 1918–1935), 1:170–172, 384–385. Compare with 1:479, 546, and

2:89–90, 102–110, 475–479. See also Roediger, "Movement for the Shorter Working Day," p. 43.

3. Commons et al. *History of Labor*, 1:169, 171.

4. Ibid., 3:97, 98.

5. H. Sumner, "Causes of the Awakening," in ibid., 1:169–192.

6. H. A. Millis and R. E. Montgomery, *The Economics of Labor*, 3 vols. (New York, 1938–1945), 1:491–493, quote on p. 491; see also 3:423.

7. I. Bernstein, *The Lean Years: A History of the American Worker, 1920–1933* (Boston, 1960), pp. 476–484, quote on p. 476. See also F. R. Dulles, *Labor in America* (New York, 1966), pp. 106, 107; M. C. Cahill, *Shorter Hours: A Study of the Movement Since the Civil War* (New York, 1922), pp. 14–19; S. Perlman, *A History of Trade Unionism in the United States* (New York, 1950; originally published 1921), pp. 4, 45, 46; S. Fine, "The Eight-Hour Day Movement in the United States, 1888–1891," *Journal of American History* 40 (December 1953): 441–461.

8. D. Brody, "The Old Labor History and the New: In Search of an American Working Class," *Labor History* 20 (1979): 111–125.

9. D. Montgomery, "Gutman's Nineteenth Century America," *Labor History* 19 (1978): 416–429, quote on p. 419.

10. S. J. Ross, "Workers on the Edge: Work, Leisure, and Politics in Industrializing Cincinnati: 1830–1890" (Ph.D. dissertation Princeton University, 1980), pp. iii–v, 317–404.

11. J. T. Cumbler, *Working-Class Community in Industrial America: Work, Leisure, and Struggle in Two Industrial Cities, 1880–1930* (Westport, Conn., 1979), pp. 7–12, 28–38, 114–128. See also R. Rosenzweig, *Eight Hours for What We Will: Workers and Leisure in an Industrial City, 1870–1920* (Cambridge, 1983), pp. 222–228; D. Montgomery, *Beyond Equality: Labor and the Radical Republicans, 1862–1872* (New York, 1967), pp. 234–238; D. Brody, *Steel Workers in America: The Nonunion Era* (New York, 1960), pp. 171–173.

12. V. Y. McLaughlin, "Patterns of Work and Family Organization: Buffalo's Italians," *Journal of Interdisciplinary History* 2 (Autumn 1971): 299–314; E. Peck, "Family Time and Industrial Time," *Journal of Urban History* 1 (August 1975): 365–389; A. Keosler-Harris, "Organizing the Unorganized: Three Jewish Women and Their Incomes," *Labor History* 17 (Winter 1976): 5–15; B. K. Hunnicutt, "The Jewish Sabbath Movement in the Early Twentieth Century," *American Jewish History* 69 (December 1979): 196–225.

13. Rosenzweig, *Eight Hours for What We Will*, pp. 222–228, quotes on p. 223.

14. Roediger, "Movement for the Shorter Working Day," pp. 264–267.

15. Roediger observed that the demand for increased leisure, although bound tightly to practical concerns having to do with fatigue and wages, nevertheless "evoked broader, even visionary, hopes for a radically reshaped society" among the middle-class reformers who became the dominant spokespersons for the 10-hour movement. For example, Richard Trevellick, a nineteenth-century organizer for the National Labor Union, wrote: "Add another two hours to the liberty term, and we shall increase the ratio of progress three-

fold . . . laboring men and women educated to a standard of physical, mental, moral and social excellence that will be its own security against idleness, vice, degradation and misery." Quoted in ibid., p. 5.

Roediger also argued that the 10-hour movement had ideological roots in the revolutionary period and that workers used the iconoclastic rhetoric of the time to press for shorter hours during the Jacksonian era. For example, he cites the Boston carpenters who in 1825 assailed the "despotic servitude" enforced on them by the dawn-to-dusk schedule in the summer (ibid., p. 46). Philadelphia journeymen carpenters, striking for 10 hours in 1827, resolved that "all men have a just right, derived from their Creator, to have sufficient time each day for the cultivation of their mind and for self-improvement" (ibid., p. 5). Such an argument, founded on revolutionary notions of natural rights, were echoed by the famous Boston "Ten-hours Circular" of 1835, which attacked long hours as an offense against God and natural right in these words: "The God of the Universe has given us time, health, and strength. We utterly deny the right of any man to dictate to us how much of it we shall sell" (ibid.). See also J. R. Commons and associates, *A Documentary History of American Industrial Society*, 10 vols. (Cleveland, 1910), 6:94–99.

The influence of the waves of religious revivalism before 1866 was also evident in the 10-hour movement; it was an influence that worked both for and against work reduction. On the one hand, the Protestantism of the revival movements strengthened the work ethic and sanctioned the capitalistic order in other ways, especially with a defense of sobriety, prudence, and gain. But certain other principles strengthened the workers' position. Long hours in pursuit of materialistic aims and destructive to morals, religious observances, and spiritual advance were condemned by spokespersons such as Charles Douglas, Seth Luther, and Frederick Robinson, who held up increased leisure as a legitimate avenue for human improvement—a realm of free action especially suited to spiritual advance.

16. See J. D. Owen, *The Price of Leisure* (Montreal, 1970), pp. 61, 62; E. Jones, "Hours of Work in the United States: 1900–1957" (Ph.D. dissertation University of Chicago, 1961), pp. 8–9; E. Jones, "New Estimates of Hours of Work per Week and Hourly Earnings, 1900–1957," *Review of Economics and Statistics* 43 (March 1963): 375–383.

17. U.S. Department of Labor, *Wages and Hours of Labor, Nineteenth Annual Report of the Commissioner of Labor* (Washington, D.C., 1904), table 4. See also U.S. Bureau of the Census, Special Reports, *Occupations at the Twelfth Census* (Washington, D.C., 1905); U.S. Department of Labor, Bureau of Statistics, *Unemployment in the United States*, Bulletin 195 (Washington, D.C., 1916), and *Wages in the United States to 1928*, Bulletin 604 (Washington, D.C., 1934); U.S. Department of Commerce, Bureau of the Census, *Historical Statistics of the United States: Colonial Times to 1970* (Washington, D.C., 1975), pp. 126, 168. For the longitudinal analysis, see also Jones, "New Estimates of Hours of Work per Week," pp. 375–383.

18. Ibid.

19. Ibid.

20. A. Rees, *Real Wages in Manufacturing: 1890–1914* (Princeton, 1961), pp. 3–17, quotes on pp. 3, 5. For a review of the three principal studies that found no improvements in wages from 1900 to 1914, see ibid., pp. 8–12.

21. P. H. Douglas, *Real Wages in the United States, 1890–1926* (Boston, 1930), pp. 105–132, 204–222. Compare with C. D. Long, *Wages and Earnings in the United States: 1860–1890* (Princeton, 1960), pp. 109–118; S. Ratner, J. Soltow, and R. Sylla, *The Evolution of the American Economy: Growth, Welfare, and Decision Making* (New York, 1979), p. 309.

22. Cahill, *Shorter Hours*, pp. 164, 165, quote on p. 164.

23. Ibid., pp. 52–57, 86, 87, 165–167, 180.

24. Jones, "Hours of Work in the United States," pp. 51–67, quote on p. 67.

25. Ibid., p. 63.

26. Cahill, *Shorter Hours*, pp. 177–183.

27. A. S. Link, *American Epoch* (New York, 1963), p. 57.

28. Cahill, *Shorter Hours*, pp. 261–282.

29. Link, *American Epoch*, pp. 56–60; Cahill, *Shorter Hours*, pp. 57, 87–89, 165.

30. Cahill, *Shorter Hours*, pp. 23, 97, 98, 118–133.

31. Ibid.; see also F. Frankfurter and J. Goldmark, *Brief for the Defendant in Error: The Case for the Shorter Work Day*, U.S. Supreme Court, October term, 1915; *Franklin O. Bunting, Plaintiff in Error vs. The State of Oregon, Defendant in Error*, reprinted by the National Consumers' League (New York, 1915), passim.

32. W. Lippmann, "Free Time and Extra Money," *Woman's Home Companion* 57 (April 1930): 31–32.

33. Link, *American Epoch*, pp. 210–212.

34. Ibid.

35. Cahill, *Shorter Hours*, pp. 232–241; U.S. Industrial Commission, "Relations between Capital and Labor," *Report*, 19 vols. (Washington, D.C., 1900–1902), 14:659; J. Goldmark, "Standard Working Hours," *Human Engineering* 1 (1911): 150; I. Fisher, "Industrial Hygiene as a Factor in Human Efficiency," *Human Engineering* 1 (1911): 254. See also J. Goldmark, "Study of Fatigue," *Survey* 22 (July 10, 1909): 534–536; L. H. Gulick, "Time to Quit Work," *World's Work* 14 (August 1907): 9196–9198; J. Goldmark, "Fatigue and Efficiency," *Survey* 28 (May 4, 1912): 206–210; F. S. Lee, "The Nature of Fatigue," *Popular Science* 76 (February 1910): 182–195; "Occupational Fatigue," *Scientific American* 75 (June 28, 1913): 410–411; C. B. Lord, "Cause of Industrial Fatigue," *Industrial Management* 55 (April 1918): 310–311; H. Bentinck, "Industrial Fatigue—and the Relation between Hours of Work and Output," *Contemporary Review* 113 (February 1918): 113–144.

36. Owen, *Price of Leisure*, pp. 80–93, quote on p. 84. See also J. F. Kasson, *Amusing the Millions: Coney Island at the Turn of the Century* (New York, 1978), pp. 3–9, 87–112; Rosenzweig, *Eight Hours for What We Will*, pp. 226–228.

37. Rosenzweig, *Eight Hours for What We Will*, pp. 222–228.

38. W. I. King, *The Wealth and Income of the People of the United States* (New

York, 1917), pp. 175–177; U.S. Immigration Commission, *Report of the Immigration Commission: 1907–1910*, 42 vols. (Washington, D.C., 1911), 1:38–39; I. A. Hourwich, *Immigration and Labor: Economic Aspects of European Immigration to the United States* (New York, 1922), chap. 13. Hourwich reviews the charges that immigrants had lowered the standard of living, giving detailed references to what he took as a general point of view; see ibid., Chaps. 1 and 2.

39. Rees, *Real Wages in Manufacturing*, p. 3.

40. R. Higgs, "Race, Skill, and Earnings: American Immigrants in 1909," *Journal of Economic History* 31 (June 1971): 420–428; F. McGouldrick and M. B. Tannen, "Did American Manufacturers Discriminate against Immigrants Before 1914?" *Journal of Economic History* 37 (September 1977): 723–746; W. B. Harrison and J. H. Yoo, "Labor Immigration in 1890–1914: Wage Retardation vs. Growth Conducive Hypothesis," *Social Science Journal* 18 (April 1981): 1–12.

41. Hourwich, *Immigration and Labor*, pp. 311–316, quotes on pp. 314, 316.

42. Rees, *Real Wages in Manufacturing*, p. 13.

43. For example, see B. K. Atrostic, "The Demand for Leisure and Nonpecuniary Job Characteristics," *American Economic Review* 72 (June 1982): 428–440; W. A. Barnett, "The Joint Allocation of Leisure and Goods Expenditure," *Econometrica* 47 (May 1979): 439–463; J. Clarke and C. Zech, "An Empirical Estimation of the Labor Supply in Response to Primary and Secondary Wages," *American Economist* 22 (Spring 1978): 46–50; M. S. Feldstein, "Estimating the Supply Curve of Working Hours," *Oxford Economic Papers* 20 (March 1968): 74–80; T. A. Finegan, "Hours of Work in the United States: A Cross Sectional Analysis," *Journal of Political Economy* 70 (October 1962): 452–470; R. Gronau, "Leisure, Home Production, and Work—The Theory of the Allocation of Time Revisited," *Journal of Political Economy* 85 (March 1977): 1099–1123; A. O. Quester and J. Olson, "Sex, Schooling, and Hours of Work," *Social Science Quarterly* 58 (March 1978): 566–582; R. Ray, "Estimating Leisure Goods Models on Time Series of Cross Sections," *Empirical Economics* 7 (1982): 175–189; L. Robbins, "On the Elasticity of Income in Terms of Effort," *Economica* 10 (June 1930): 123–129; S. Smith, "Estimating Annual Hours of Labor Force Activity," *Monthly Labor Review* 106 (February 1983): 13–22; T. J. Wales and A. D. Woodland, "Estimation of Household Utility Function and Labor Supply Response," *International Economic Review* 17 (June 1976): 397–409; T. J. Wales and A. D. Woodland, "Estimation of the Allocation of Time for Work, Leisure and Housework," *Econometrica* 45 (January 1977): 115–132.

44. See Carroll Wright's reports in U.S. Department of Labor, *Wages and Hours of Labor*, table 4. See also U.S. Bureau of the Census, *Occupations at the Twelfth Census*, table 43; L. E. Gallaway, R. Vedder, and V. Shuka, "The Distribution of the Immigrant Population in the United States," *Explorations in Economic History* 11 (Spring 1974): 213–226.

45. P. F. Brissenden and E. Frankel, *Labor Turnover in Industry: A Statistical Analysis* (New York, 1922), pp. 78–102, quote on p. 87. See also D. T. Rodgers *The Work Ethic in Industrial America: 1850–1920* (Chicago, 1978), pp. 155, 163–

170; U.S. Department of Commerce, *Historical Statistics of the United States*, pp. 126, 182.

46. J. B. Gilbert, *Work without Salvation: America's Intellectuals and Industrial Alienation, 1880–1910* (Baltimore, 1977), pp. vii–xv, 31–66, quote on p. vii.

47. Ibid., p. xiv.

48. Rodgers, *Work Ethic in Industrial America*, pp. 28, 29, 65–124, quotes on p. 28.

49. Ibid., pp. 90, 107.

50. Ibid., p. 160.

51. G. Cross, "The Political Economy of Leisure in Retrospect: Britain, France and the Origins of the Eight Hour Day" (Pennsylvania State University, Department of History, 1985).

52. W. S. Jevons, *Theory of Political Economy* (New York, 1957; originally published 1870), pp. 11–19.

53. J. K. Galbraith, *The Affluent Society* (New York, 1958), p. 121. Portions of this economic discussion appeared in B. K. Hunnicutt, "The Economic Constraints of Leisure," in *The Constraints of Leisure*, ed. M. Wade (Springfield, Ill., 1985), pp. 242–286, and are used here courtesy of Charles C Thomas, Publisher, Springfield, Illinois.

54. R. B. Ekelund and R. F. Hebert, *A History of Economic Theory and Method* (New York, 1975), p. 111.

55. A. Marshall, *Principles of Economics*, 5th ed. (London, 1907), pp. 527–529, 681, 719, quote on p. 529. See also Robbins, "Elasticity of Income in Terms of Effort," pp. 123–129; G. S. Becker, "A Theory of the Allocation of Time," *Economic Journal* 75 (September 1975). For a basic college text treatment, see R. L. Heilbroner, *The Economic Problem*, 7th ed. (Englewood Cliffs, N.J., 1984), p. 453. For a good history of this theory, see Ekelund and Herbert, *History of Economic Theory and Method*, pp. 35–47.

56. F. H. Knight, *Risk, Uncertainty and Profits* (New York, 1964; originally published 1921), p. 117.

57. Galbraith, *The Affluent Society*, p. 121.

58. J. S. Mill, *Principles of Political Economy* (London, 1923), pp. 748, 749.

59. Ibid., p. 750.

60. Ibid., p. 751. Italics added.

61. S. Patten, "The Economic Causes of Moral Progress," *Annals* 3 (1893): 129–147; S. Patten, *The Consumption of Wealth* (Philadelphia, 1889), pp. 30–60. See also D. Fox, ed., *The Discovery of Abundance* (Ithaca, N.Y., 1967), passim.

62. S. Patten, "The New Basis of Civilization," in Fox, *Discovery of Abundance*. See also S. Patten, "The Effects of the Consumption of Wealth on the Economic Welfare of Society," in *Scientific Economic Discussions*, ed. R. T. Ely (New York, 1886).

63. W. Weyl, *Tired Radicals* (New York, 1921), p. 73.

64. W. Weyl, *The New Democracy* (New York, 1912), p. 333.

65. A. O. Dahlberg, *Jobs, Machines, and Capitalism* (New York, 1932), Foreword.

Chapter 2

1. Garrett, "Business" in *Civilization in the United States*, ed. H. Stearns (New York, 1922), p. 414; J. A. Hobson, *Economics of Unemployment* (New York, 1923), p. 23; J. A. Hobson, *Incentives in the New Industrial Order* (New York, 1923), p. 50; J. A. Hobson, "The Limited Market," *Nation* 120 (April 11, 1925): 350–352; F. J. Boland, *Wage-Rates and Industrial Depressions: A Study of the Business Cycle* (New York, 1924), pp. 4–7, 75. See also W. M. Persons, "Crisis of 1920 in the United States," *American Economic Review* 12, Suppl. no. 1 (March 1922): 5.

2. *New York Times*, January 1, 1923, January 1, 1925, January 1, 1926, October 26, 1926, January 1, 1927, October 10, 17, 1927. See also *New York Herald Tribune*, January 2, 1926. For other pessimistic views about saturated demand, see J. L. Wright, "Need We Be Afraid of a Job Famine?" *Nation's Business* 15 (January 1927): 22–24; and "Volume, Production, and 'Stabilized Prosperity,'" *Nation's Business* 15 (August 1927): 88, 89; P. M. Mazur, "Mass Production, Has It Committed Suicide?" *Review of Reviews*, October 1927, pp. 74–76; H. E. Krooss, *Executive Opinion* (New York, 1961), pp. 92–94.

3. K. Yung, "Some Aspects of the Business Depression of 1921" (master's thesis, University of Iowa, 1926), pp. 79, 80. See also the following issues: *New York Times*, December 5, 1920, p. 20; December 28, 1920, p. 18; September 21, 1921, p. 16; January 8, 1921, p. 18; January 10, 1921, p. 28; February 16, 1921, p. 4; September 29, 1921, p. 1.

4. *New York Times*, April 29, 1931, p. 17.

5. *New York Times*, April 27, 1921, p. 12.

6. *New York Times*, January 10, 1921, p. 28.

7. *New York Times*, January 8, 1921, p. 18.

8. *New York Times*, January 18, 1926, p. 23. See also Krooss, *Executive Opinion*, pp. 92–94. For other pessimistic views, see *New York Herald Tribune*, January 2, 1926; *New York Times*, October 26, 1926, May 20, 1927, October 10, 17, 1927.

9. *New York Times*, January 31, 1926, sec. 10, p. 1.

10. V. M. Cutter, "Our Greatest Economic Problem," *Current History* 27 (October 1927): 74–76.

11. See, for example, the following issues: *New York Times*, December 5, 1920, p. 20; December 28, 1920, p. 18; September 21, 1921, p. 16; January 8, 1921, p. 18; January 10, 1921, p. 28; February 16, 1921, p. 4; September 29, 1921, p. 1.

12. M. Leven, H. Moulton, and C. Warburton, *America's Capacity to Consume* (Washington, D.C., 1934), pp. 115–117; W. Foster and W. Catchings, "Business under the Curse of Sisyphus," *World's Work* 52 (September 1926): 503–511; C. Southworth, "Can There Be General Overproduction? No!" *Journal of Political Economy* 32 (December 1924): 722–723.

13. "Attitude of Certain Employers to the Five-Day Week," *Monthly Labor Review* 23 (December 1926): 1168–1170; W. B. Craig, "Business Views in Review," *Nation's Business* 14 (December 1926): 72–75; "Mass Production of

Time," *Nation's Business* 14 (May 1926): 33. See also "Business Attitudes toward the Five Day Workweek," *Nation's Business* 15 (April 1927): 32; "Manufacturers Discuss Ford's Five-Day Week" *Iron Age* 118 (October 28, 1926): 592; A. H. Young, "Some Considerations in Reducing Working Time," *Iron Age* 119 (June 2, 1927): 1599; J. Edgerton, "Annual Address of the President," *Proceedings of the National Association of Manufacturers* (New York, 1929), p. 23; J. Edgerton, "Annual Address of the President," *Proceeding of the National Association of Manufacturers* (New York, 1930), p. 17.

14. National Industrial Conference Board, *The Five Day Week in Manufacturing Industries* (New York, 1929), pp. 52–54.

15. See *Pocket Bulletin* 27 (October 3, 1926): 2–12; the entire issue is devoted to criticism of the 40-hour week.

16. Ibid., p. 6.

17. Ibid., p. 9.

18. Ibid., p. 3.

19. Ibid., p. 10.

20. J. E. Edgerton, "Industry Has Advanced Further Than Religion," *Pocket Bulletin* 27 (April 1927): 4; Edgerton, "Annual Address" (1929), p. 23.

21. W. H. Grimes, "The Curse of Leisure," *Atlantic Monthly* 142 (April 1928): 355–360, quotes on pp. 355, 358.

22. E. Cowdrick, "The New Economic Gospel of Consumption," *Industrial Management* 74 (October 1927): 208; "Prosperity and Production," Report of the 15th Annual Meeting of the Chamber of Commerce, *Nation's Business* 15 (May 20, 1927): 40, 41; W. Foster and W. Catchings, "What Is Business Without a Buyer?" *Nation's Business* 14 (June 1926): 27; W. Craig, "Digest of the Business Press," *Nation's Business* 14 (June 1926): 14; G. Buck, "This American Ascendancy," *Nation's Business* 15 (March 1927): 15; "Business Views in Review," *Nation's Business*, July 1927, p. 117, and August 1927, p. 95; "Other Times, Other Occupations," *Nation's Business* 13 (July 1925): 35; L. Pierson, "Looking Ahead for Business," *Nation's Business* 16 (June 1928): 13; J. Hammond, "Look Back—and Ahead," *Nation's Business* 16 (December 1928): 35; A. W. Shaw, "Is This Why the Overproduction Bogy-Man Is a Bogy-Man?" *Magazine of Business* 54 (September 1928): 263–265; P. U. Kellogg, "When Mass Production Stalls," *Survey* 59 (March 1, 1928): 683–686; H. S. Dennison, "Would the Five-Day Week Decrease Unemployment?" *Magazine of Business* 54 (November 1928): 508 (for relevant quotes from *Dow Jones Financial Bulletin*); G. E. MacIllwain, "Mortgaging Tomorrow Puts Pep into Today: Installment Buying Is Giving the Worker Something to Work For," *Forbes* 18 (March 1, 1926): 12–13.

23. I. S. Paull, "When Is Industry's Job Complete?" *Nation's Business* 15 (December 1927): 28, 29; J. L. Wright, "Is the Machine Replacing Man?" *Nation's Business* 15 (September 1927): 78–80 (for views about increased consumption by James Maloney and Secretary of Labor Davis, who agreed that "the luxuries of yesterday become the necessities of today"); M. Thorpe, "The Amazing Decade," *Nation's Business* 16 (September 1928): 9; Cowdrick, "The New Economic Gospel of Consumption," p. 210; J. H. Collins, "Pro-

ducer Goes Exploring for the Consumer," *Saturday Evening Post* 195 (April 7, 1923): 8; T. C. Sheehan, "Must We Limit Production?" *Magazine of Business* 53 (February 1928): 150–152; E. S. Martin, "Advertising as a World Power," *Harpers* 147 (March 1924): 553–554; E. J. Kulas, "Whip of Prosperity: Curtailment of Production—A Mistake," *Saturday Evening Post* 201 (June 29, 1929): 5; "We Have Because We Spend," *Collier's* 80 (September 2, 1927): 146; I. F. Marcossen, "Production and Prosperity," *Saturday Evening Post* 189 (August 14, 1926): 12.

24. C. Kettering, "Keep the Consumer Dissatisfied," *Nation's Business* 16 (January 1929): 31.

25. J. Dorfman, *The Economic Mind in American Civilization*, 5 vols. (New York, 1949), 4:57, 58, 84, 343.

26. Committee on Recent Economic Changes, *Recent Economic Changes* (New York, 1929), pp. xvii, 15, 52, 59, 80, 81, 578; quote on p. xv. See also T. N. Carver, *The Present Economic Revolution in the United States* (Boston, 1925), pp. 59–65; Edgerton, "Industry Has Advanced Further Than Religion," p. 4; J. E. Edgerton, "Annual Address of The President," *Proceedings of the National Association of Manufacturers.* (New York, 1925), p. 12; L. Wolman, "Consumption and the Standard of Living," in *Recent Economic Changes*, pp. 13–20; R. S. Lynd, "The People as Consumers," in President's Research Committee on Social Trends, *Recent Social Trends* (Washington, D.C., 1933) p. 857.

27. *Recent Economic Changes*, p. xv.

28. W. W. Rostow, *The Stages of Economic Growth* (London, 1960), pp. 9–11; see also *Recent Economic Changes*, pp. 12, 81, 82, 321, 531–544.

29. Dorfman, *Economic Mind*, 5:593–594.

30. T. C. Cochran, *Two Hundred Years of American Business* (New York, 1977), p. 192; T. C. Cochran and W. Miller, *The Age of Enterprise: A Social History of Industrial America* (New York, 1961), pp. 310–324.

31. Krooss, *Executive Opinion*, pp. 90, 91; *Recent Economic Changes*, p. 531.

32. C. H. Hession and H. Sardy, *Ascent to Affluence: A History of Economic Development* (Boston, 1969), p. 666.

33. F. L. Allen, *Only Yesterday: An Informal History of the Nineteen-Twenties* (New York, 1964), p. 140.

34. D. N. Potter, *People of Plenty* (Chicago, 1954), pp. 173–175; see also *Recent Economic Changes*, pp. 402, 424.

35. D. Riesman, *The Lonely Crowd* (New Haven, 1950), pp. 74, 75, 96–98, 116–123, 150, 189–191, 227, 290.

36. W. Leuchtenburg, *Perils of Prosperity, 1914–32* (Chicago, 1958), p. 278.

37. Dennison, "Would the Five-Day Week Decrease Unemployment?" p. 508. See also *Recent Economic Changes*, pp. xv, xvii, 52, 59, 80, 81, 574–578; "National Distribution Conference Meeting, 1925," *Outlook* 141 (December 30, 1925): 656–657.

38. H. Ford and S. Crowther, "The Fear of Overproduction," *Saturday Evening Post* 203 (July 12, 1930): 3.

39. Cowdrick, "The New Economic Gospel of Consumption," p. 209.

40. *Recent Economic Changes*, p. xvi.

41. H. Ford, "Why I Favor Five Days' Work with Six Days' Pay," Interview, *World's Work* 52 (October 1926): 613. See also "The Five-Day Week in the Ford Plants," *Monthly Labor Review* 23 (December 1926): 1163. For Ford's views during the depression, see H. Ford and S. Crowther, "Unemployment or Leisure," *Saturday Evening Post* 203 (August 1930): 19.

42. T. M. Kappen, "Can We Work Less and Earn More?" *Magazine of Wall Street* 39 (February 26, 1927): 788–791; Craig, "Business Views in Review," pp. 72–75; D. A. Laird, "This Bunkum about Hard Work," *Printer's Ink* 147 (April 18, 1929): 33–34; T. H. Price, "Employing the Labor Saved by Machinery," *Commerce and Finance* 17 (June 20, 1928): 134–137; J. L. Wright, "Need We Be Afraid of a Job Famine?" *Nation's Business* 15 (January 1927): 22–24.

43. Edgerton, "Annual Address of the President" (1929), p. 23.

44. Ford, "Why I Favor Five Days' Work," p. 614.

45. Southworth, "Can There Be General Overproduction?" p. 722.

46. Dennison, "Would the Five-Day Week Decrease Unemployment?" pp. 508–510.

47. "Shorter-Hours Cure for Overproduction," *Literary Digest* 90 (September 18, 1926): 16; Dennison, "Would the Five-Day Week Decrease Unemployment?" pp. 508–509; L. Ardzrooni, "Philosophy of the Restriction of Output," *Annals of the American Academy of Political and Social Science* 91 (September 1920): 70–75; Sheehan, "Must We Limit Production?" pp. 150–152; Kulas, "Whip of Prosperity," p. 5.

48. Such phrases may be found in T. Read, "The American Secret," *Industrial Management* 73 (June 1927): 321–323; C. Stelzle, "Religious Ideal Dignifies the Work of Man," *Forbes* 21 (January 15, 1928): 26–28; F. M. Trumbull, "Work," *Industrial Arts Magazine* 16 (August 1927): 281–282; J. Klein, "Can Industry Provide New Jobs as Machines Take Away Old Ones?" *Magazine of Wall Street* 44 (October 19, 1929): 1078–1081.

49. B. Barton, *The Man Nobody Knows* (Indianapolis, 1924), pp. 23, 162, 179. This work was a nonfiction bestseller in both 1925 and 1926.

50. Ford and Crowther, "Fear of Overproduction," p. 3. See also A. C. Laut, "Taking the Curse Off Labor," *Nation's Business* 14 (April 1926): 15–17; E. B. Clark, "Abolish 'Common' Labor," *Nation's Business* 14 (October 1926): 16.

51. W. T. Pitkins, *The Twilight of the American Mind* (New York, 1927), pp. 2–20.

52. H. S. Dennison, "Management," *Recent Economic Changes*, p. 517.

53. W. Feather, "A Fourth of July Speech—New Style," *Nation's Business* 14 (July 1926): 14.

54. A. C. Bedford, "What Is a Captain of Industry?" *Nation's Business*, November 1925.

55. D. Nelson, "Scientific Management and Labor," *Business History Review* 48 (May 1974): 479–481; O. Tead, "Trends in Industrial Psychology," *Annals of the American Academy of Political and Social Science* 149 (May 1930): 110–119; M. L. Putnam, "Improving Employee Relations," *Personnel Journal* 6 (February 1930): 25–32; W. F. Ogburn, "Psychological Basis for Increasing Production,"

Annals of the American Academy of Political and Social Sciences 90 (July 1920): 83–87; Dorfman, *Economic Mind* 4:60; "Teaching Joy in Work," *Journal of the National Education Association* 13 (February 1924): 60.

56. J. Prothro, *Dollar Decade: Business Ideas in the 1920's* (Baton Rouge, 1954), pp. 5–15, 67.

57. Ford, "Unemployment or Leisure," p. 19.

58. *Recent Economic Changes,* p. xv.

59. R. T. Bye, "Some Recent Developments of Economic Theory" in *The Trend in Economics,* ed. R. C. Tugwell (New York, 1924), pp. 275–277. See also O. F. Boucke, "A Unique Situation in Economic Theory," *American Economic Review* 12 (December 1922): 603–608. That marginalism continued to "dominate" the field of economics but in highly modified forms before World War I, see Dorfman, *Economic Mind,* 4:354–360; see also Paul T. Homan, "Consumption," in *The Encyclopedia of Social Sciences* vol. 15 (1934), pp. 293, 294; Lionel Robbins, "On the Elasticity of Income in Terms of Effort," *Economia* 10 (June 1930): 123–129. Robbins designed this article as an attack on the inevitability of the "income effect," but in so doing he presented the argument in its finest form, citing the numerous authorities that had argued the case, such as Dalton, Robertson, and Wickstead, as well as Knight and Pigou.

60. J. K. Galbraith; *The Affluent Society* (Boston, 1976), pp. 120, 121.

61. See Chap. 1, pp. 31–32.

62. F. H. Knight, *Risk, Uncertainty, and Profit* (Boston, 1921), pp. 116–120, quote on p. 117.

63. A. C. Pigou, *A Study of Public Finance* (London, 1928), pp. 83, 84 (quotes), 116–120; A. C. Pigou, *The Economics of Welfare* (London, 1920), pp. 87, 463, 593.

64. P. Douglas, *The Theory of Wages* (New York, 1934), pp. 310–314.

65. T. N. Carver, "Shorter Working Time and Unemployment," *American Economic Review* 20 (March 1932): 8. See also Carver, *Economic Revolution in the United States,* pp. 59–65; here Carver summed up: "The question in the broadest aspect is simply this: do we prefer to take our increasing prosperity in the form of more goods or more leisure?" (p. 162).

66. J. M. Clark, "Recent Developments in Economics," in *Recent Developments in the Social Sciences,* ed. E. C. Hayes (Philadelphia, 1927), p. 303.

67. P. T. Homan, "Consumption" in *The Encyclopedia of Social Sciences,* vol. 15 (1934), p. 294; F. H. Knight, "Value and Price," in ibid., p. 219.

68. Dorfman, *Economic Mind,* 5:590.

69. H. Kyrk, *A Theory of Consumption* (Boston, 1923), p. 172; T. S. McMahon, *Social and Economic Standards of Living* (Boston, 1935), pp. 401–407.

70. Robbins, "The Elasticity of Income," pp. 123–129, quote on pp. 128–129. See also J. O. Owen, *The Price of Leisure* (Montreal, 1970), pp. 62–67; Southworth, "Can There Be General Overproduction?" p. 722.

71. Kyrk, *Theory of Consumption,* p. 69; Southworth, "Can There Be General Overproduction?" p. 722.

72. Dorfman, *Economic Mind,* 5:570, 575, 594.

73. Kyrk, *Theory of Consumption,* p. 172. See also Z. C. Dickinson, "Kyrk's

Theory of Consumption," *Quarterly Journal of Economics*, February 1924, p. 343; McMahon, *Social and Economic Standards of Living*, pp. 401–407. Other economists concerned with the "dynamic theory of consumption" include J. W. Angel, "Consumer Demand," *Quarterly Journal of Economics* 39 (May 1925): 584–611; C. P. White, "Shall We Control Demand or Follow It?" *Annals of the American Academy of Political and Social Sciences* 89 (September 1928): 126–135; C. Frederick, "New Wealth, New Standards of Living and Changed Family Budgets," *Annals of the American Academy of Political and Social Science* 115 (September 1924): 74–82.

74. Kyrk, *Theory of Consumption*, p. 278.

75. Ibid., pp. 263, 292–293.

76. McMahon, *Social and Economic Standards of Living*, pp. 401–407, quote on p. 405.

77. W. Thomas, "The Economic Significance of Increased Efficiency of America," *American Economic Review* 18 (March 1928): 128.

78. W. Mitchell, "A Review," in *Recent Economic Changes*, pp. 841–910, quote on p. 874.

79. W. T. Foster and W. Catchings, "Dilemma of Thrift," *Atlantic* 127 (April 1926): 544; L. H. Haney, "Hen of Production, Egg of Consumption," *North American Review* 225 (May 1928): 530.

80. Dorfman, *Economic Mind*, 4:57; W. Foster and W. Catchings, *Money* (Boston, 1923), pp. 305–331; see also W. Foster and W. Catchings, *Profits* (Boston, 1925), pp. 398–406. Foster and Catchings, "Business under the Curse of Sisphyus," pp. 503–511, is a restatement of their original overproduction thesis found in *Money*. This is the article for which the publishers of *World's Work* called for responses.

81. For a typical negative response, see H. B. Fitt, "Ancient Virtue: Reply to Dilemma of Thrift," *Atlantic* 127 (July 1926): 138.

82. Southworth, "Can There Be General Overproduction?" p. 722.

83. W. Foster and W. Catchings, *Business Without a Buyer* (Boston, 1928), pp. ix–xi, 11, 118–120; W. Foster and W. Catchings, *The Road to Plenty* (Boston, 1928), pp. iii–iv.

84. Foster and Catchings, *Business Without a Buyer*, pp. x, 11, 115–125.

85. See chap. 2, pp. 00–00.

86. Mitchell, "A Review," pp. 841–910, quote on p. 877.

87. Clark, "Recent Developments in Economics," pp. 304, 305.

88. Galbraith, *Affluent Society*, pp. 67–99.

89. Clark, "Recent Developments in Economics," pp. 304–305.

90. Homan, "Consumption," pp. 293, 294.

91. Ibid., p. 295; Foster and Catchings, "Business under the Curse of Sisyphus," pp. 503–511, quote on p. 507.

92. J. M. Keynes, *The Economic Consequences of the Peace* (New York, 1920), p. 21.

93. J. M. Keynes, *Essays in Persuasion* (New York, 1931), pp. 365–373, quote on p. 366. Compare Keynes's view of leisure in this book and his *Economic Consequences* with his views developed later in the depression and found

in his *General Theory of Employment* (New York, 1935). On page 326 of *General Theory* he wrote: "Another school of thought finds the solution of the trade cycle, not in increasing either consumption or investment, but in diminishing the supply of labor seeking employment; i.e. by redistributing the existing volume of employment without increasing employment or output. This seems to me to be a premature policy—much more clearly so than the plan of increasing consumption. A point comes where every individual weighs the advantages of increased leisure against increased income. But the present evidence is, I think, strong that the great majority of individuals would prefer increased income to increased leisure." What "evidence" Keynes had in mind is not clear, especially since Paul Douglas's study, published the year before as *Theory of Wages*, was the only investigation that had been made, and Douglas found conclusive evidence that leisure preferences had been quite strong for three decades—a third of the gains made in wages had been expressed as shorter hours. The only conclusion possible is that Keynes had made a political decision and taken a normative position in keeping with Mitchell and his fellow economists, that is, that work had to be saved by increasing consumption and investment, and by government intervention if necessary.

94. Keynes, *Essays in Persuasion*, p. 367. Keynes was impressed with the implications of abundance. Patten had an indirect influence on this economist through J. R. Commons at the University of Wisconsin. Commons, although not a supporter of Patten's themes, still was impressed with his suggestions about the economic transition from scarcity to abundance. Commons in turn influenced Keynes to a great extent in this matter. See D. M. Fox, *Discovery of Abundance* (Ithaca, N.Y., 1967), pp. 167–169.

95. McMahon, *Social and Economic Standards of Living*, pp. 401–407.

96. S. Gwinn, "Days of Drudgery Will Soon Be Over: Interview with Walter S. Gifford," *American Magazine* 56 (November 1928): 25.

97. M. Heald, "Management's Responsibility to Society: The Growth of an Idea," *Business History Review* 31 (Winter 1957): 375–379; M. Heald, "Business Thought in the Twenties: Social Responsibility," *American Quarterly* 13 (Summer 1961): 126–139; G. Kolko, *The Triumph of Conservatism*, (Glencoe, Ill., 1963), p. 2; Krooss, *Executive Opinion*, pp. 39, 40; *Recent Economic Changes*, pp. 81, 82; R. Wiebe, *Businessmen and Reform* (Chicago, 1962), pp. 192, 193, 205; R. Wiebe, *The Search for Order* (New York, 1967), pp. 175, 176; S. P. Hayes, *The Response to Industrialism* (Chicago, 1957), pp. 4–13.

Chapter 3

1. For example, see "Shorter-Hours Cure for Overproduction," *Literary Digest* 90 (September 18, 1926): 16; "Would the Five-Day Week Decrease Unemployment?" *Magazine of Business* 54 (November 1928): 508–509. One way of understanding the position of the advocates of limited production is by reviewing their opponents' attacks. For the businessmen's and economists' views of the limited production idea, see L. Ardzrooni, "Philosophy of the Restric-

tion of Output," *Annals of the American Academy of Political and Social Science* 16 (September 1920): 70–75; E. J. Kulas, "Whip of Prosperity: Curtailment of Production—A Mistake," *Saturday Evening Post* 201 (June 29, 1929): 5.

2. H. A. Millis and R. E. Montgomery, *The Economics of Labor* (New York, 1938–1945), p. 469.

3. The Commission of Inquiry, the Interchurch World Movement, *Public Opinion and the Steel Strike* (New York, 1921), pp. 25, 82, quote on p. 82.

4. Ithaca, New York, School of Industrial and Labor Relations Collections, The Consumers' League of New York Papers, Box 5-B, File Folder 19, and Box 6A. See especially *Report of the Executive Secretary Meeting of the Board of Directors, February 8, 1927*; quotes are from this report. See also pamphlet held by Wisconsin Historical Society, Madison, Wisconsin: The Consumer League of New York, *The Forty Eight Hour Law: Do Working Women Want It?* (New York, 1926–1927); and "Amalgamated Clothing Workers," *Advance* 12 (March 11, 1927): 10.

5. U.S. Department of Labor, *Bulletin of the Women's Bureau*, Bulletin 58 (Washington, D.C., 1927); "Women's Bureau Report," *American Federationist* 35 (June 1928): 709. See also U.S. Department of Labor, *Women in Delaware Industries*, Bulletin 58 (Washington, D.C., 1928).

6. Opinion that the 8-hour day, 48-hour week was becoming standard was expressed in such articles as "Doom of the Twelve-Hour Day," *Outlook* 121 (June 7, 1922): 245–246; "Triumph for the Eight-Hour Day," *Outlook* 134 (August 15, 1923): 572–574; "Death Struggles of the Twelve-Hour Day," *Literary Digest* 70 (June 9, 1923): 7–9; M. B. Bruere, "48 Hours Shalt Thou Labor and Do All Thy Work," *Survey* 58 (April 15, 1924): 80–81; A. B. Buse, "Digging in for the Eight-Hour Day," *Survey* 52 (April 1, 1924): 12; J. C. Bowen, "48-Hour Week in Industry," *Monthly Labor Review*, December 1923, pp. 1305–1326. The idea that the five-day week was a new direction taken by labor and was a trend that, like the 8-hour day, was becoming a national force may be found in "Labor Now Out for a Five-Day Week," *Literary Digest* 41 (October 16, 1926): 9–11; "Prevalence of the Five-Day Week in American Industry," *Monthly Labor Review* 23 (December 1926): 1153–1169; "How the Five-Day Work Week Works," *Literary Digest* 34 (March 31, 1928): 12–13; "New Era, Five Days a Week," *Business Week*, September 7, 1929, pp. 5–6; "Five Days Shalt Thou Labor," *Literary Digest* 101 (May 18, 1929): 8; "Extension of Five-Day Week Movement in New York State," *Monthly Labor Review* 23 (October 1925): 747–748; "Is the Five-Day Week Practical? Pros and Cons," *System* 51 (January 1927): 6–9; "Five-Day Week," *World's Week*, July 1930, pp. 59–60; F. T. De Vyver, "The Five-Day Week," *Current History* 33 (November 1930): 223–227; "Extent of the Five Day Week in Manufacturing Industries," *Monthly Labor Review* 30 (February 1930): 368–371.

7. For labor's position in general, see "Labor Now Out for a Five-Day Week," pp. 9–11; *New York Times*, October 17, 1926; "Prevalence of the Five-Day Week in American Industry," pp. 1153–1169; "How the Five-Day Work Week Works," pp. 10–11; "Coming: A Five-Day Working Week," *Literary Digest* 36 (March 31, 1928): 12–13; "New Era, Five Days a Week," pp. 5–6; "Five

Days Shalt Thou Labor," p. 8; "Extension of Five-Day Week Movement in New York State," pp. 747–748; "Is the 5-Day Week Practical?" pp. 6–9; "Five-Day Week," pp. 59–60; De Vyver, "Five-Day Week," pp. 223–227; "Extent of the Five Day Week in Manufacturing Industries," pp. 368–371.

8. National Industrial Conference Board (NICB), *The Five Day Week in Manufacturing Industries* (New York, 1929), pp. 15–24; "History of Movement for Shorter Hours in Industry and the Five-Day Week," *New York Times*, June 2, 1929; "Prevalence of the Five-Day Week in American Industry," pp. 1153–1169; J. P. Frey, "Labor's Movement for a Five-Day Week," *Current History*, December 1926, pp. 25, 369–372.

9. A. Link, *American Epoch* (New York, 1955), p. 238.

10. "Prevalence of the Five-Day Week in American Industry," pp. 1153–1169. See also "Boston Fur Workers Win 40-Hour or Five-Day Week After Five Weeks Strike," *Labor*, November 20, 1926, p. 2; Brotherhood of Painters, Decorators and Paperhangers of America, *Reports of the General Officers to the 12th General Assembly, Dallas, Texas* (Lafayette, Ind., 1921), p. 76; "Five Day Work Week Already in Effect at Many Plants," *Trade Union News*, November 4, 1925, p. 5; G. F. Hedrick, "The Five-Day Week," *Painter and Decorator, Department of Labor Industrial Bulletin* 4 (August 1925): 284; "Conference on Paper Box-Board Manufacturers on Shorter Working Hours, Washington, D.C., May 2, 1924," *Monthly Labor Review* 21 (June 1924): 1187–1196; NICB, *Five Day Week in Manufacturing*, pp. 15–24. See also "History of Movement for Shorter Hours in Industry"; "Prevalence of the Five-Day Week in American Industry," pp. 1153–1169; Frey, "Labor's Movement for a Five-Day Week," pp. 369–372; *New York Times*, December 10, 1926, p. 27, and January 4, 1927, p. 27.

I. I. Hourwich observed that immigrant workers tended to show a higher than average preference for shorter hours of labor from 1900 to 1909, contrary to "preconceived notions." See his *Immigration and Labor: The Economic Aspects of European Immigration to the United States* (New York, 1922), pp. 316–317. But D. Brody noted that immigrant steelworkers in the period wanted more work for more money, believing that "a fat pay envelope overshadowed heavy labor and long hours"; see his *Steelworkers* (New York, 1969), pp. 94, 100. But he also noted some willingness to forego wages (especially among workers' wives) for shorter hours around 1919 when the Pueblo steelworkers wanted the 8-hour day "despite the cost" (pp. 235–236).

11. M. Josephson, *Sidney Hillman: Statesman of American Labor* (New York, 1952), pp. 177–180. See also the following issues: *Monthly Labor Review* 16 (August 1923): 503; 18 (June 1924): 1366–1368; 23 (December 1926): 1153; 20 (June 1925): 1390–1391. And see U.S. Bureau of Labor Statistics *Bulletin 439*, June 1924, pp. 373, 374, 573–575, and *Bulletin 435*, pp. 20–21.

12. See the following issues: *Advance* 2 (May 31, 1918): 4; 2 (October 25, 1918): 4; 3 (January 24, 1919): 4; 3 (February 28, 1919): 4; 15 (May 10, 1929): 2; 16 (February 7, 1930): 4; 20 (January 12, 1934): 3. See also *Advance*, January 17, 1919, p. 1, and January 24, 1919, p. 24. See also the following issues of ILGWA *Journal* 2 (August 27, 1920): 4–5; 10 (February 3, 1928): 4; 12 (January 2, 1930): 1; 12 (March 14, 1930): 4; 12 (November 7, 1930): 5.

13. NICB, *Five Day Week in Manufacturing*, p. 28. See also De Vyver, "Five Day Week," pp. 223–227.

14. D. Philipson, *The Reform Movement in Judaism* (New York, 1931), pp. 195–214, 373; U.S. Department of Commerce, Bureau of the Census, *Historical Statistics of the United States: Colonial Times to 1970* (Washington, D.C., 1975), pp. 155, 172; R. M. Miller, *American Protestantism and Social Issues* (Chapel Hill, 1958), p. 172.

15. *New York Times*, January 10, 1925, p. 15.

16. *New York Times*, September 17, 1926, p. 9.

17. B. K. Hunnicutt, "The Jewish Sabbath Movement," *American Jewish History* 69 (December 1979): 196–225.

18. *New York Times*, February 7, 1924, p. 20. See also the following issues of ILGWA *Journal* 8 (October 8, 1926): 8; 10 (October 5, 1928): 8; 12 (May 1, 1930): 4–5. Dressmakers in New York City worked half-days on Sundays during the Jewish holiday season; see *Journal* 5 (September 21, 1923): 12, and 12 (September 26, 1930). That Jews were interested in time from work for religious reasons, see the following: ILGWA *Journal* 6 (November 14, 1924): 12; 10 (October 5, 1928): 8; 10 (February 3, 1928): 8; *Women's Wear Daily*, February 6, 1919, p. 25, and February 7, 1919, p. 3. See also the following issues: *New York Times*, January 10, 1925, p. 15; January 14, 1925, p. 5; October 16, 1925, p. 22; November 10, 1926, p. 20. And see De Vyver, "Five-Day Week," pp. 223–227.

19. *New York Times*, May 10, 1926, p. 21. See also *Yearbook of Central Conference of American Rabbis* 24 (1924): 51.

20. *New York Times*, January 14, 1925, p. 5. See also *New York Times*, September 17, 1926, p. 9; *American Jewish Year Book* 27 (1925): 26–28.

21. M. C. Cahill, *Shorter Hours: A Study of the Movement Since the Civil War* (New York, 1932), p. 253; NICB, *Five-Day Week in Manufacturing*, p. 28; *American Jewish Year Book* (1925), p. 24.

22. See the following issues: *Advance* 1 (April 6, 1917): 7; 2 (October 11, 1918): 4; 2 (May 31, 1918): 4; 2 (August 1918): 6; 2 (August 16, 1918): 4; 3 (January 24, 1919): 4; 3 (February 7, 1919): 4; 12 (March 11, 1927): 10; 17 (January 2, 1931), 2. See especially *Advance* 21 (April 1935): 10, in which Joseph Schlossberg observed that during the 1920s "working people demanded leisure for participation in the enjoyments of life." But during the Great Depression "a new point" had been realized: that "we work too many hours and we produce too much." See also the following issues of ILGWA, *Journal* 1 (October 11, 1919): 5; 9 (February 3, 1928): 1, 3, 8; 9 (May 1, 1930): 4–5; 14 (September 1932): 12. See also *Women's Wear Daily*, January 10, 16, 24, 25, 29, and February 6, 1919; "The Forty-Four Hour Week," *New Republic* 43 (February 1, 1919): 7–9; *New York Times*, October 28, 1923, p. 17. For criticism of work, see the following issues: *Advance* 2 (October 11, 1918): 4; 2 (May 31, 1918): 4; 2 (August 16, 1918): 1, 4; 2 (September 27, 1918): 4; 3 (February 7, 1919): 4; 12 (April 29, 1929): 7; and *Women's Wear Daily*, January 21, 22, 27, 1919. See also U.S. Department of Labor, Bureau of Labor Statistics, *Bulletins 439, 574* (Washington, D.C., 1927, 1932); J. S. Poyntz, "The Conquest of Leisure," *Justice* 1 (February 15, 1919): 6.

23. ILGWA *Journal* 1 (February 15, 1919): 6.

24. I. Howe, *World of Our Fathers* (New York, 1976), pp. 430–538, *passim*; M. E. Ravage, *An American in the Making* (New York, 1971; originally published 1917), pp. 146–158, 173, 174; I. Howe and K. Libo, *How We Lived: A Documentary History of Immigrant Jews in America 1880–1930* (New York, 1979), pp. 162, 164, 165, 201–204, 279, 280–292, 295.

25. J. Morrison and C. Zabusky, *American Mosaic: The Immigrant Experience in the World of Those Who Lived It* (New York, 1980), p. 14, for the Newman quote. See also E. Hasanovitz, *One of Them: Chapter from a Passionate Autobiography* (New York, 1918), pp. 146, 158–163, 177, 303–305.

26. J. Lynch, "The Shorter Workday: The Complete Argument," *American Federationist* 33 (March 1926): 291; "Shorter Hour Cure for Overproduction," p. 16; *New York Times*, July 18, 1926, sec. 7, p. 6; W. Green, "The Five-Day Week to Balance Production and Consumption," *American Federationist* 33 (October, 1926): 1299; J. Lynch, "Shorter Worker Day Urged as Alleviation of Depression Cycles," *American Labor World*, May 1926, pp. 28–29.

27. Green, "Five-Day Week," pp. 1299, 1300. For Green and Woll's attitudes, see also American Federation of Labor (AFL), *Report of the Proceedings of the 46th Annual Convention* (Washington, D.C., 1926), pp. 195–207. For Hillman's view, see "Attitude of Organized Labor toward the Shorter Work Week," *Monthly Labor Review* 23 (December 1926): 1167–1168; W. Green, "Leisure for Labor," *Magazine of Business* 56 (August 1929): 136–137; Lynch, "Shorter Working Day Urged," pp. 28–29. See also *Monthly Labor Review* 23 (December 1926): 1167–1168.

28. J. L. Wright, "Is the Machine Replacing Men?" *Nation's Business* 15 (September 1927): 79.

29. M. Woll, "Leisure and Labor," *Playground* 19 (1925): 322–323; compare with M. Woll, "Labor and the New Leisure," *Recreation* 27 (1933): 428.

30. Ibid. See also W. Green, "The Five-Day Week," *North American Review*, December 1926, pp. 567–574; *New York Times*, December 9, 1926; W. Green, "Less Working Hours Is Logical," *American Labor World*, November 1926, p. 20; "The Proposed Five-Day Week," *Industry* 108 (October 23, 1926): 1; "The Five Day Week, Facts for Workers," *Labor Bureau Economic News Letter*, November 1926, p. 12; "Labor Now Out for a Five-Day Week," pp. 9–11; "The Five-Day Week in Industry," *Bulletin of the National Association of Building Trades Employers* 4 (August 25, 1926): 1.

31. "Shorter-Hours Cure for Overproduction," p. 16.

32. Ibid. All of these news reports were quoted from *Literary Digest*.

33. AFL, *Proceedings of the 46th Annual Convention*, pp. 195–207; AFL, *Report of the Proceedings of the 47th Annual Convention* (Washington, D.C., 1927), pp. 35, 60–62, 398–401; AFL, *Report of the Proceedings of the 48th Annual Convention* (Washington, D.C., 1928), pp. 43, 44, 187, 188; AFL, *Report of the Proceedings of the 49th Annual Convention* (Washington, D.C., 1929), pp. 46, 161, 387–388.

34. S. Slichter, "Production," *American Federationist* 34 (October 1927): 1176, 1200. Green's comments about shorter hours and production may be found in *American Federationist*, February 1927, p. 146, and March 1927, p. 344. Green talked about shorter hours and unemployment at least once

after 1926. For this exception, see W. Green, "Two Kinds of Unemployment," *American Federationist* 35 (April 1928): 402.

35. "The Unemployment Conference at the Labor College in Philadelphia," *American Federationist* 34 (September 1927): 1050. See also the following issues: *American Federationist* 35 (February 1928): 189; 35 (March 1928): 299; 25 (September 1928): 1109. See also "Report of the Workers' Education Bureau of America to the AF of L on Unemployment," *American Federationist* 35 (December 1928): 1498.

36. J. T. McKelvey, *AFL Attitudes toward Production 1900–1921* (Ithaca, N.Y., 1952), pp. 2–11, 47–49, 64–72, 115.

37. J. C. Lane, "The Five-Day Week Is Now a Vivid Industrial Issue," *New York Times*, October 17, 1926, sec. 9, p. 1.

38. Ibid. See also E. Gluck, "Wage Theories," *American Federationist* 32 (December 1925): 1163; W. Foster and W. Catchings, "More Pay, Less Work," *American Federationist* 33 (January 1926): 35; E. Berman, "Labor and Production," *American Federationist* 33 (August 1926): 964; AFL, *Report of the Proceedings of the 45th Annual Convention* (Washington, D.C., 1925), p. 271. See also AFL, *Proceedings of the 48th Annual Convention*, pp. 43, 44, 182, 188; J. Maloney, "High Productivity Necessitates High Wages," *American Federationist* 33 (April 1926): 570; "Labor Now Out for a Five-Day Week," p. 11; "Prevalence of the Five-Day Week in American Industry," pp. 1153–1169; Green, "Five-Day Week," pp. 566–574; Green, "Leisure for Labor," pp. 136–137; G. Myers, "Once Dreaded Output by Machinery Frees Workers from Long Hours of Toil," *New York Herald Tribune*, October 17, 1926, p. 7. See also the following issues: *New York Times*, October 5, 1926, p. 28; October 10, 1926, p. 1; October 17, 1926, sec. 9, p. 1; January 27, 1927, p. 9. And see Green, "Less Working Hours Is Logical," p. 20.

39. *Monthly Labor Review* 23 (December 1926): 1167. See also C. M. Wright, "Epoch-Making Decisions in the Great American Federation Labor Convention at Detroit," *American Labor World*, 1926, pp. 22–24. And see AFL, *Proceedings of the 46th Annual Convention*; see especially the Report of the Committee on the Shorter Workday, pp. 195–207.

40. Green, "Five-Day Week," p. 1025. In this article unemployment is still mentioned, but the transition to leisure is under way; see also Green, "Leisure for Labor," pp. 136–137.

41. "Editorial," *American Federationist* 34 (November 1927): 1300.

42. "Labor Now Out for a Five-Day Week," pp. 9–11. See also *Monthly Labor Review* 23 (December 1926): 1153–1169; *Magazine of Business* 56 (August 1929): 136–137; *New York Times*, October 17, 1926.

43. Green, "Leisure for Labor," pp. 136–137. See also Green, "Five-Day Week," pp. 567–574; *New York Times*, September 14, 1929. See also Sidney Hillman's statement in "Attitude of Organized Labor toward the Shorter Work Week," *Monthly Labor Review* 23 (December 1926): 1167–1168. For labor's view in general, see Maurer, "Leisure and Labor," pp. 649–655; S. A. Shaw, "Now That Jerry Has Time to Live," *Survey* 52 (September 1, 1924): 568–570; "Leisure Time of Workers," *Playground* 18 (September 1924): 342–347; G. Eastman, "Letter to the Recreation Congress at Atlantic City," *Playground*

16 (December 1922): 409; "Resolution on Community Service Adopted at the American Federation of Labor Convention at Portland," *Playground* 18 (September 1924): 649; "State Education for Adult Workers in Massachusetts," *Monthly Review of Labor Statistics* 17 (November 1928): 975; R. Aiken, "A Laborer's Leisure," *North American Review* 232 (September 1931): 268; Green, "Less Working Hours Is Logical," p. 20; W. Green, *The Five-Day Week: Inevitable* (New York, 1932), passim.

44. *American Federationist* 33 (January 1926) included several articles on the importance of recreation and leisure. See also Editorial, "Recreation Declaration," *American Federationist* 33 (January 1926): 94; W. Green, "Five Day Week in the Building Trades," *American Federationist* 35 (August 1928): 915. The April 1927 issue of the *American Federationist* was devoted to worker education. See also W. Green, "Workers' Education," *American Federationist* 34 (March 1927): 401. Here Green saw worker education leading to "a greater probability of the cultural use of leisure. It is in their leisure that workers find themselves . . . sharing in the common life of the community . . . wider interests . . . and are heirs of knowledge and culture of past generations." See also Woll, "Leisure and Labor," p. 322; "Recreation and the Labor Movement," *Playground* 18 (September 1924): 649; L. Magnusson, "Labor and the Leisure Movement," *Playground* 21 (March 1927): 656; "Utilization of Workers' Leisure Time—Report of the Director of the International Labor Office," *Monthly Labor Review* 31 (September 1930): 593. That labor's interest in leisure existed before 1926, see E. Lies, "Organized Labor and Recreation," *American Federationist* 20 (August 1923): 648.

45. W. Green, "Editorial," *American Federationist* 35 (July 1928): 785.

46. Woll, "Labor and the New Leisure," p. 488; Woll, "Leisure and Labor," p. 322; AFL, *Proceedings of the 46th Annual Convention*, pp. 195–207.

47. AFL, *Proceedings of the 49th Annual Convention*, quotes on p. 46; see also pp. 161, 387–388. Compare the unemployment discussion with AFL, *Report of the Proceedings of the 50th Annual Convention* (Washington, D.C., 1930), pp. 262–266.

48. I. Bernstein, *The Lean Years* (New York, 1960), p. 476.

49. U.S. Department of Commerce, *Historical Statistics of the United States*, pp. 140–145; R. H. Wiebe, *The Search for Order: 1877–1920* (New York, 1967), p. 149; D. Nelson, "Scientific Management and Labor," *Business History Review* 48 (May 1974): 479–481; O. Tead, "Trends in Industrial Psychology," *Annals of the American Academy of Political and Social Science* 149 (May 1930): 110–119; M. L. Putnam, "Improving Employee Relations," *Personnel Journal* 6 (February 1930): 25–32; W. F. Ogburn, "Psychological Basis for Increasing Production," *Annals of the American Academy of Political and Social Sciences* 90 (July 1920): 83–87; J. Dorfman, *The Economic Mind in American Civilization*, 5 vols. (New York, 1949), 4:60; J. W. Kendrick, *Productivity Trends in the United States* (Princeton, 1961), pp. 58–62.

50. W. Foster and W. Catchings, "Business under the Curse of Sisphyus," *World's Work* 52 (September 1926): 503.

51. S. Chase, "Leisure in a Machine Age," *Library Journal* 41 (August 1931):

629–630; S. Chase, "Consumers in Wonderland," *New Republic* 50 (May 2, 1927): 38; S. Chase, "Play," in *Whither Mankind*, ed. C. and M. Beard (New York, 1928), chap. 8 et passim; S. Chase, *Machines and Men* (New York, 1929), passim.

52. D. Rodgers, *The Work Ethic in Industrial America* (Chicago, 1978), pp. 28, 29, 65–124.

53. See chap. 4, note 85.

54. A. S. Link, "What Happened to the Progressive Movement in the 1920's?" *American Historical Review* 64 (July, 1959): 833–851, quote on p. 843.

55. Ibid.

56. Dorfman, *Economic Mind*, 4:107.

Portions of this chapter dealing with John Ryan appeared in B. K. Hunnicutt, "Monsignor John Ryan and the Shorter Hours of Labor," *Catholic Historical Review* 69 (July 1983): 384–402. The author acknowledges, with thanks to Robert Trisco and the *Catholic Historical Review*, permission to include these selections.

57. F. L. Broderick, *Right Reverend New Dealer: John A. Ryan* (New York, 1963), pp. vii, 275–279; A. I. Abell, *American Catholicism and Social Action: A Search for Social Justice, 1965–1950* (Garden City, N.Y., 1960), pp. 172, 173; A. I. Abell, "The Reception of Leo XIII's Labor Encyclical in America, 1891–1919," *Review of Politics* 7 (October, 1945): 464–495; J. F. Cronin, *Catholic Social Principles: The Social Teachings of the Church Applied to American Economic Life* (Milwaukee, 1950), pp. xiv, 618–626; D. J. O'Brien, *American Catholicism and Social Reform: The New Deal Years* (New York, 1968), pp. 120–149; J. F. Cronin and H. W. Flannery, *The Church and the Workingman* (New York, 1965), pp. 7, 141–158; "Right Reverend New Dealer," *Time* 61 (January 11, 1943): 60; E. H. Smith, "Three Score and Ten," *Commonweal* 30 (June 9, 1939): 181–182; Hunnicutt, "Monsignor John Ryan and the Shorter Hours of Labor," pp. 384–402; E. F. Goldman, *Rendezvous with Destiny: A History of American Reform* (New York, 1952), p. 85.

58. P. W. Gearty, *The Economic Thought of Monsignor John A. Ryan* (Washington, D.C., 1953), pp. 38–39, 102–105, 170, 201–253; A. I. Abell, "Origins of Catholic Social Reform in the United States," *Review of Politics* 11 (July 1949): 55–67; Dorfman, *Economic Mind*, 4:107, 3:324; R. Purcell, "John A. Ryan, Prophet of Social Justice," *Studies* (Dublin) 35 (June 1945): 153–174; Broderick, *Right Reverend New Dealer*, pp. 148–151.

59. J. A. Ryan, "The Experts Look at Unemployment: II. A Shorter Work Period," *Commonweal* 10 (October 23, 1929): 636–637.

60. J. A. Ryan, "The Senate Looks at Unemployment: II. Important Facts Which It Failed to See," *Commonweal*, 10 (October 9, 1929): 578–580. See also J. A. Ryan, *Social Doctrine in Action: A Personal History* (New York, 1941), p. 235; J. A. Ryan, *Questions of the Day* (New York, 1931), pp. 241, 242; J. A. Ryan *Can Unemployment Be Ended?* (Washington, D.C., 1940), pp. 3–8.

61. J. A. Ryan, *Declining Liberty and Other Papers* (New York, 1927), pp. 173–178. See also Ryan, "Experts Look at Unemployment," p. 637.

62. J. A. Ryan, *A Better Economic Order* (New York, 1935), p. 23.

63. J. A. Ryan, "Unemployment: Causes and Remedies," *Catholic World* 128 (February 1929): 537–542, quotes on pp. 535, 536; Ryan, *Can Unemployment Be Ended?* pp. 4–8.

64. J. A. Ryan and J. Husslein, *The Church and Labor* (New York, 1920), p. 268; see also pp. ix–xiv, 267–270. J. A. Ryan and J. Husslein, "Economics and Ethics," *National Conference of Catholic Charities Proceedings* 19 (1933): 65–72.

65. Ryan, *Questions of the Day*, pp. 210–217, quote on p. 213. See also Ryan, *Declining Liberty*, pp. 197, 198.

66. Ryan, *Questions of the Day*, p. 242. See also G. G. Higgins, "The Underconsumption Theory in the Writings of Monsignor John A. Ryan" (master's thesis, Catholic University of America, 1942), pp. 19–35; Gearty, *Economic Thought of Ryan*, pp. 185–194; Broderick, *Right Reverend New Dealer*, pp. 33–34, 192–194; J. A. Ryan, "High Wages and Unemployment," *Commonweal* 13 (January 7, 1931): 259–261; Ryan, *Questions of the Day*, p. 213.

67. Ryan, *Social Doctrine in Action*, p. 259; see also Ryan, *Better Economic Order*, p. 65.

68. Ryan, "Experts Look at Unemployment," p. 636.

69. Ryan, *Questions of the Day*, p. 213.

70. Ryan, *Better Economic Order*, pp. 65–66.

71. Ibid.

72. Ryan, "Experts Look at Unemployment," pp. 637–638.

73. Ryan, "High Wages and Unemployment," p. 261.

74. Ryan, *Questions of the Day*, p. 242.

75. Ryan, "High Wages and Unemployment," p. 260; see also Ryan, *Questions of the Day*, p. 240; Ryan, "Experts Look at Unemployment: II. Higher Wages for the Masses," *Commonweal* 10 (October 16, 1929): 612–613. See also Ryan, *Can Unemployment Be Ended?* pp. 4–8, for his views about economic maturity.

76. J. A. Ryan and F. J. Boland, *Catholic Principles of Politics* (New York, 1940), pp. 1–27. For interpretation of how Ryan applied ethics, natural law, and Thomist teachings to economics, see O'Brien, *Catholicism and Social Reform*, pp. 125–138; Gearty, *Economic Thought of Ryan*, pp. 201–241.

77. Ryan and Husslein, *Church and Labor*, pp. 262, 263.

78. Ibid., pp. 260–261.

79. Ryan, *Declining Liberty*, pp. 320–321.

80. Ibid., pp. 322, 323 for quote; see also 324–329.

81. Ibid., p. 322.

82. Ibid., p. 323.

83. Ryan, "High Wages vs. Excessive Capital," *Commonweal* 13 (February 25, 1931): 460–461.

84. *New York Times*, January 10, 1925, p. 15.

85. F. Cohen, "The Blessing of Unemployment," *American Scholar* 2 (1933): 206–207.

86. Ibid., pp. 209, 210.

87. A. H. Silver, "Leisure and the Church," *Playground* 20 (January 1927): 539.

88. Ibid. Portions of the discussion of Jewish Sabbitarianism appeared in B. K. Hunnicutt, "The Jewish Sabbath Movement," *American Jewish History* 69 (December 1979): 196–215, and are used here by the courtesy of the American Jewish Historical Society and Benard Wax, director.

89. B. Eliezer, *Letters of a Jewish Father to His Son* (London, 1928), p. 214.

90. A. H. Silver, *Religion in a Changing World* (New York, 1930), pp. 143–146; see also S. Strauss, "Things Are in the Saddle," *Atlantic Monthly*, November 1924, pp. 577–588; S. Strauss, *American Opportunity* (Boston, 1935), pp. 182–193.

91. C. H. Huestis, "What Shall We Do with Our Leisure?," *Christian Century* 47 (June 18, 1930): 783–785; W. W. Pangburn, "Challenge of Leisure," *Religious Education* 23 (1928): 748–752; G. Johnson, "Use of Leisure Time," *Catholic Action* 14 (1932): 23–24; H. Mongredien, "Leisure," *New-Church Magazine*, April–June 1934, pp. 113–117; W. T. Manning, "The Church and Wholesome Play," *Playground* 20 (January 1927): 537; C. Gilkey, "Recreation and the Church," *Playground* 21 (February 1928): 566; N. E. Richardson, *The Church at Play* (New York, 1922); L. L. Ward, "A Plea for Light Harness," *Catholic World* 127 (1928): 562A.

92. A. N. Marquis, *Who's Who in America 1926–1927* (Chicago, 1927), p. 155; G. Alger, "Effects of Industrialism," *Atlantic* 135 (April 1925): 484–492, quotes on 484, 485.

93. Alger, "Effects of Industrialism," p. 485.

94. Ibid., p. 487.

95. Ibid., p. 492.

96. S. Leacock, *The Unsolved Riddle of Social Justice* (New York, 1920), pp. 23, 24.

97. Ibid., p. 3; see also pp. 34, 66–70.

98. Ibid., p. 82; see also pp. 149, 125–135, 150. See also R. L. Curry, *Stephen Leacock: Humorist and Humanist* (Garden City, N.Y., 1959), pp. 141, 142.

99. Ibid., pp. 125, 126; see also pp. 127–135, 149.

100. "Elihu Root at the Classical League," *New York Times*, February 25, 1923, sec. 2, p. 4; "Editorial," *New York Times*, November 23, 1924, sec. 2, p. 6.

101. A. Lloyd, "Ages of Leisure," *American Journal of Sociology* 28 (September 1922): 160.

102. J. K. Hart, "The Place of Leisure in Life," *Annals* 113 (March 1925): iii; Strauss, "Things Are in the Saddle," p. 577. Other writers dealing with leisure as a way to achieve social reform include Lundburg, *Leisure*, pp. 7, 8; J. Lee, *Play in Education* (New York, 1921), pp. 13, 95–101, 455; A. Dahlberg, *Jobs, Machines, and Capitalism* (New York, 1932), pp. 224–231; H. Braucher, "Play and Social Progress," *Playground* 16 (1922): 103–104.

103. C. Chambers, "Belief in Progress in the Twentieth Century," *Mississippi Valley Historical Review* 43 (December 1956): 405. See also H. F. May, "Shifting Perspectives on the 1020's," *Journal of American History* 43 (December 1966): 406.

104. E. Sapir, "Culture; Genuine and Spurious," *American Journal of Sociology* 29 (January 1924): 401–429.

105. J. T. Adams, *Our Business Civilization* (New York, 1929), p. 17; see also pp. 15–25, 191–196. And see K. Sargent, "Push or Be Pushed," *Forum* 68 (October 1927): 622.

106. Adams, *Our Business Civilization*, p. 17.

107. I. Babbitt, *On Being Creative* (Boston, 1932), p. 229.

108. Ibid., p. 230.

109. I. Babbitt, *Literature and the American College: Essays in Defense of the Humanities* (Los Angeles, 1956), pp. 166–168.

110. Ibid., p. 172.

111. Ibid., p. 169.

112. Ibid., p. 177.

113. H. L. Mencken, "The Library," *American Mercury* 9 (September 1926): 126. See also H. L. Mencken's editorials in *American Mercury* for these issues: 11 (July 1927): 289; 13 (March 1928): 280–282; 14 (August 1927): 408–410. Also see J. W. Krutch, *The Modern Temper* (New York, 1929), p. 26; F. L. Allen, *Only Yesterday* (New York, 1931), p. 188 and, especially, Allen's chapter "The Revolt of the Highbrows"; Adams, *Our Business Civilization*, pp. 191–196; A. Huxley, "Work and Leisure," *Literary Review* 5 (August 30, 1924): 1–2; W. Grimes, "The Curse of Leisure," *Atlantic* 142 (September 1928): 355.

Chapter 4

1. L. A. Finfer, "Leisure as Social Work in the Urban Community: The Progressive Recreation Movement 1890–1920" (Ph.D. dissertation, Michigan State University, 1974), passim; B. K. Hunnicutt, "Playground Reform from 1880–1920" (master's thesis, University of North Carolina, 1972), Intro.

2. Hunnicutt, "Playground Reform," pp. 55–65, 90–95; G. T. W. Patrick, *The Psychology of Relaxation* (Boston, 1916), pp. 5, 263; C. Rainwater, "Socialized Leisure," *Journal of Applied Sociology* 24 (January 1919): 373–388; C. Rainwater, "Play as Collective Behavior," *Journal of Applied Sociology* 8 (1924): 271; C. Rainwater, *The Play Movement in the United States* (Chicago, 1927), pp. 93, 135, 179; L. A. Cremin, *The Transformation of the School: Progressivism in American Education* (New York, 1961), p. ix; "When Everybody Joins the Leisure Class," *World's Work* 46 (October 1923): 571; A. S. Link, "What Happened to the Progressive Movement in the 1920's?" *American Historical Review* 64 (July 1959): 833–851.

3. J. Lee, *Play in Education* (New York, 1921), pp. 13, 95–101, 455; H. Braucher, "Play and Social Progress," *Playground* 16 (1922): 103–104; H. Braucher, "The Machine Revolution," *Playground* 23 (February 1931): 585.

4. L. Gulick, *A Philosophy of Play* (New York, 1920), pp. 23–54; Braucher, "Play and Social Progress," pp. 103–104; F. P. Keppel, "Leisure and Life," *Playground* 21 (1927): 81–83.

5. M. Grodzins, *The American System* (Chicago, 1966), p. 41. See also Rainwater, *Play Movement*, pp. 140–145; Lee, *Play in Education*, pp. 283–285.

6. J. B. Nash, *Spectatoritis* (New York, 1932), p. 4.

7. J. Lee, "Play as an Antidote to Civilization," *Playground* 5 (July 1921): 110–126. "Renaissance of Play," *Survey* 28 (June 1915): 437.

8. H. Braucher, "The Theory of the Economic Value of Waste," *Playground* 23 (February 1931): 473; *New York Times*, January 3, 1922, p. 16.

9. Braucher, "Machine Revolution," p. 585.

10. O. D. Young, "Address before Executives of the General Electric Company," portions reprinted in *Playground* 23 (November 1930): 417. Cf. *supra.*, p. 290.

11. Braucher, "Machine Revolution," p. 585.

12. H. Braucher, "Home and Leisure," *Playground* 23 (March 1931): 641.

13. Braucher, "Play and Social Progress," p. 104.

14. J. Lee "A Critical Look at Recreation as Viewed at the Seventeenth Annual Congress," *Playground* 23 (December 1930): 506.

15. See *Playground* 16 (1922–1923): 11, 409.

16. J. G. Winant, "Leisure and Government," *Playground* 20 (January 1927): 535.

17. *New York Times*, October 17, 1926, sec. 8, p. 4. See also C. Doel, *A Brief History of Parks and Recreation in the United States* (Chicago, 1954), p. 73; President's Research Committee on Social Trends, *Recent Social Trends in the United States*, 2 vols. (New York and London, 1933), 1:958–960.

18. Doel, *History of Parks and Recreation*, pp. 70–85; G. S. Coyle, "Margins of Leisure," *Jewish Center* 5 (1927): 20–24.

19. Letter from Theodore Roosevelt to Calvin Coolidge, April 22, 1924, Calvin Coolidge Presidential Papers, File 1295, National Archives, Washington, D.C.; Doel, *History of Parks and Recreation*, p. 75; "Resolutions Adopted by President's National Conference on Outdoor Recreation," *Playground* 18 (July 1924): 247. This whole issue of *Playground* is devoted to the conference.

20. Press Release, "Statement of the Need of a Nation for Outdoor Recreation," Calvin Coolidge Presidential Papers, File 1295, National Archives, Washington, D.C.

21. "Resolutions Adopted by President's Conference," p. 247.

22. Letter from T. E. Rivers to E. Clark, June 27, 1924, Calvin Coolidge Presidential Papers, File 1295, National Archives, Washington, D.C.; *Playground* 18 (July 1924): 649.

23. "Resolution on Community Service Adopted at the American Federation of Labor Convention at Portland," *Playground* 18 (September 1924): 649; "Recreation and the Labor Movement," *Playground* 18 (September 1924): 649.

24. "Recreation and the Labor Movement," p. 649.

25. "State Education for Adult Workers in Massachusetts," *Monthly Review of Labor Statistics* 27 (November 1928): 975; "Some Major Movements in Adult Education," *School and Society* 25 (May 26, 1927): 276.

26. R. C. Field, "Now That They Have It," *Century* 16 (October 1924): 747. See also R. Aiken, "A Laborer's Leisure," *North American Review* 232 (September 1931): 268; J. H. Maurer, "Leisure and Labor," *Playground* 20 (September 1927): 649–655; G. B. Cutten, *The Threat of Leisure* (New Haven, 1926), pp. 67–73.

27. "The City Worker's Spare Time in the United States," *International Labor Review* 14 (July 1924): 896; "When Everybody Joins the Leisure Class," p. 571.

28. Cremin, *Transformation of the School*, p. 181.

29. Ibid., pp. 179–180. See also L. Morris, *Postscript to Yesterday* (New York, 1947), p. 149. Morris describes the progressives and radicals as tired in the 1920s, wanting "only to be amused." This description is correct for those involved with the leisure issue. But the desire for amusement was less an indication of exhaustion than an expression of a new kind of progress.

30. R. Molloy, "The Problem of the Amateur," *Journal of Adult Education* 2 (October 1930): 422; J. E. Morgan, "The Leisure of Tomorrow," *Journal of the National Education Association* 19 (January 1930): 2; P. Fihe, "Some Observations on Adult Education," *Library Journal* 51 (June 15, 1926): 553; G. Cutten, "Leisure and Education," *Playground* 20 (February 1927): 601–605; J. J. Loftus, "A Program for the Desirable Use of Leisure Time as a Cardinal Objective of the Public Elementary School," *National Education Association; Addresses and Proceedings*, 1928, p. 390; F. D. Bynton, "How We Should Educate for Leisure," *School Executives* 49 (May 7, 1930): 406; E. Lies, *The New Leisure Challenges the Schools* (New York, 1933), pp. 14, 15; E. Wilcox, "The High Cost of Leisure," *North American Review* 224 (April 1927): 304; W. D. Ross, "The Right Use of Leisure as an Objective of Education," *Educational Review*, September 1923, pp. 71–74; "Liberal Education," *New York Times*, September 2, 1929, p. 14; E. Lindeman, "Adult Education: A New Means for Liberals," *New Republic* 54 (February 22, 1928): 26; "Editorial," *New York Times*, June 5, 1924, p. 2; J. M. Dorey, "Leisure for Work," *School and Society* 32 (November 1930): 576; A. Payne, "Education for Leisure as Well as for Vocation," *English Journal* 10 (April 1921): 208; M. C. Winston, "The New Leisure," *Progressive Education* 4 (March 1927): 315–317; M. E. Gibbons, "A Plea for Leisure," *Educational Times* 5 (February 1923): 337, J. W. Hammond, "The Challenge of Growing Leisure," *American Education* 27 (March 1925): 166–167; L. P. Jacks, "Vitalized Leisure," *Journal of the National Education Association* 19 (May 1930): 145; A. B. Brown, "Education for Leisure," *Hibbert Journal* 31 (1933): 440–450; A. E. Brown, "The Leisure Problem," *Hibbert Journal* 28 (1930): 455–464.

31. U. S. Department of the Interior, Office of Education, *Cardinal Principles of Secondary Education*, Bulletin 35 (Washington, D.C., 1918), p. 32. See also W. D. Forman, "The Use Made of Leisure Time by Junior High School Pupils," *Elementary School Journal* 26 (June 1926); E. Goldman, *Rendezvous with Destiny* (New York, 1952), p. 288.

32. Goldman, *Rendezvous with Destiny*, p. 288.

33. Ross, "Right Use of Leisure," pp. 71–74; I. Davidson, "Training in the Right Use of Leisure," *Journal of Rural Education* 3 (March 1924): 298–304; W. M. Davidson, "Leisure and the School," *Playground* 20 (1927): 607–611; R. W. Kelso, "Significance of Educating for Leisure," *American Physical Education Review* 32 (1927): 718–720; J. W. Crabtree, "Leisure: An Energizing Force," *Journal of Arkansas Education* 8 (September 1929): 27; K. L. Woodford, "The Worthy Use of Leisure," *Hawaii Educational Review* 14 (1926): 195–196; E. V. Dobbs, "Training for a Wise Use of Leisure," *Journal of the Florida Edu-*

cational Association 1 (1924): 11–13; M. Ponton, "Education for Leisure Time," *Virginia Journal of Education* 17 (1923): 52–53; E. C. Warriner, "Report of Committee on Best Use of Leisure Time," *Michigan Educational Journal* 1 (January 1924): 347–349; W. H. Johnson, "Education for Leisure," *Chicago Schools Journal* 7 (February 1925): 204–207; W. Pearson, "Possibilities of Leisure Time," *Kansas Teacher* 21 (1925): 14–16.

34. J. Rogers, "Education for Leisure," *National Education Association; Addresses and Proceedings*, 1929, p. 545; A. Schollard, "How the Teacher Is Preparing the Child for a Worthy Use of Leisure Time," *National Education Association; Addresses and Proceedings*, 1926, p. 409; "Training for Leisure," *Playground* 15 (December 1921): 552; "Educational Preparation for the Right Use of Leisure," *New York Times*, September 2, 1929, 14; J. W. Ashbury, "Training for Leisure Time," *Platoon School* 2 (September 1928): 26–30; M. Chapman, "Education for Leisure," *Welfare* 19 (1928): 224–232; "Ruth Pyrtle Announces the National Commission on the Wise Use of Leisure Time," *Journal of the National Education Association* 19 (January 1930): 1; E. L. Thorndike, "The Right Use of Leisure," *National Institute of Social Sciences* 9 (October 1, 1924): 19; E. L. Thorndike, "The Use of Leisure: A Speech Delivered Before Students of the Teachers College of Columbia University," *Playground* 23 (March 1930): 313.

35. "Federal Education Commission Asks the Jersey Convention to Fight Standardization," *New York Times*, November 12, 1929, p. 17.

36. Loftus, "Desirable Use of Leisure Time as a Cardinal Objective of the Public School," p. 390.

37. "Editorial," *New York Times*, June 5, 1924, p. 2.

38. *New York Times*, January 3, 1922, p. 16.

39. "Editorial," *New York Times*, March 25, 1928, sec. 13, 20.

40. H. Suzzallo, "The Use of Leisure," *Journal of the National Education Association* 19 (April 1930): 123.

41. A. H. Reeve, "Leisure and the Home," *Playground* 24 (December 1926): 487.

42. J. M. Dorey, "Leisure and the Home," *Playground* 24 (November 1930): 576.

43. H. T. Bailey, "Leisure Time," *National Education Association; Addresses and Proceedings*, 1923, pp. 925–928.

44. E. Wilcox, "The High Cost of Leisure," *North American Review* 124 (April 1927): 304; Ross, "Right Use of Leisure," pp. 71–74; Morgan, "Leisure of Tomorrow," p. 2; R. S. Lynd and H. M. Lynd, *Middletown* (New York, 1929), p. 74. The Lynds quote a leading Middletown firm's superintendent who claimed that 75 percent of his workforce could be trained in less than a week. The Lynds use this and other examples as indicators of the decreasing value of vocational training.

45. L. P. Jacks, "Vitalized Leisure," *Journal of the National Education Association* 19 (May 1930): 145; A. A. Payne, "Education for Leisure as Well as for Vocation," *English Journal* 10 (April 1921): 208; "Courses in Liberal Education in Milwaukee," *School and Society* 28 (May 19, 1928): 592.

46. Cremin, *Transformation of the School*, p. ix.

47. "When Everybody Joins the Leisure Class," p. 571.

48. H. Elsner, *The Technocrats: Prophets of Automation* (Syracuse, N.Y., 1967), passim; A. Dean, "A Point in View," *Industrial Education* 25 (January 1924): 179.

49. E. Erickson, "Shopwork as Leisure Time Education," *Industrial Education* 30 (March 1929): 336. See also F. A. Adams, "Manual Training and Education for the Use of Leisure," *Industrial Education* 28 (1925): 50.

50. Fihe, "Observations on Adult Education," p. 553.

51. E. C. Lindeman, "Adult Education: A Creative Opportunity," *Library Journal* 50 (May 15, 1925): 445.

52. "Major Movements in Adult Education," p. 278; "What Is Adult Education?" *Review of Reviews* 83 (May 1926): 549.

53. Molloy, "Problem of the Amateur," p. 422. See also Lindeman, "Adult Education," p. 26.

54. W. Roth, "Cure for Spectatoritis," *Journal of Adult Education* 2 (October 1930): 419; E. Lindeman, *The Meaning of Adult Education* (New York, 1926); E. Barker, "Leisure Time," *Journal of Adult Education* 1 (January 1926): 27–35.

55. "Liberal Education," *New York Times*, September 2, 1929, p. 14; "O. D. Young at Dartmouth Alumni," *New York Times*, February 1, 1928, p. 11; W. Trow, "More Dangers of the Doctorate," *Educational Review* 80 (December 1925): 254.

56. Payne, "Education for Leisure as Well as for Vocation," pp. 208, 209.

57. Ibid., p. 210.

58. Ibid., p. 216.

59. Patrick, *Psychology of Relaxation*, p. 5; Cremin, *Transformation of the Schools*, p. 102; R. H. Wiebe, *The Search for Order: 1877–1920* (New York, 1967), p. 169. Here Wiebe says, "If humanitarian progressivism had a central theme, it was the child."

60. Patrick, *Psychology of Relaxation*, p. 29.

61. Ibid., pp. 8–12.

62. E. G. Boring, ed., *History, Psychology, and Science* (New York, 1963), p. 163.

63. Patrick, *Psychology of Relaxation*, pp. 16, 17.

64. Ibid., p. 90.

65. Letter, G. T. W. Patrick to Dean Kay, October 7, 1930, G. T. W. Patrick Collection, University of Iowa, Special Collections.

66. Patrick, *Psychology of Relaxation*, pp. 25–30.

67. Letter, G. T. W. Patrick to Dean Kay, November 24, 1924, G. T. W. Patrick Collection, University of Iowa, Special Collections.

68. Patrick, *Psychology of Relaxation*, p. 50.

69. Ibid., pp. 23, 24.

70. Ibid.

71. Ibid., chap. 5, "The Psychology of Alcohol," and chap. 6, "The Psychology of War."

72. Ibid., pp. 266, 268, 274. Patrick cited Nietzsche, agreeing with him that "physiological vigor is the only enduring ground of human welfare." Letter, Patrick to Kay, October 7, 1930. James had partially developed two of

Patrick's themes in the "gospel of relaxation" and his 1910 essay "The Moral Equivalent of War." Although James had confined himself to muscular and nervous problems in the "gospel of relaxation," concluding that "muscular vigor" would never be "superfluous," since it would always be necessary to "furnish the background of sanity, serenity, and cheerfulness to life, to give moral elasticity to our disposition, to round off the wiry edge of our fretfulness, and make us good-humored and easy of approach," in his 1910 essay concerning war, he touched on the idea that was to inform the leisure debate of the 1920s. Citing "Simon Patten's word" he speculated that "mankind was nursed in pain and fear, and that the transition to a 'pleasure economy' may be fatal to a being wielding no powers of defense against degenerative influences. If we speak of the *fear of emancipation from the fear-regime,* we put the whole situation into a single phrase." Unlike Patrick and Hall, James did not live to see the advent of the American leisure issue and have the opportunity to apply his prophetic concepts to adult play. His influence on men such as Patrick, who were developing play theory in the 1920s, however, was significant. See W. James, "The Gospel of Relaxation," in *Talks to Teachers on Psychology: And to Students on Some of Life's Ideas* (New York, 1900), p. 82. See also W. James, "The Moral Equivalent of War," *McClure's* 74 (August 1910): 112; W. James, *The Principles of Psychology* (New York, 1890), pp. ii, 704; Patrick, *Psychology of Relaxation,* p. 93; Patrick, "The Play of a Nation," *Scientific Monthly* 12 (March 1921): 350–362.

73. Patrick, *Psychology of Relaxation,* pp. 270, 170–171. See also W. Wundt, *Grundriss der Psychologie* (Leipzig, 1913), pp. 360–362, 414; Patrick, *Introduction to Philosophy* (New York, 1924), pp. 324–337.

74. D. Ross, *G. Stanley Hall: The Psychologist as Prophet* (Chicago, 1972), pp. 424–434.

75. G. S. Hall, "Notes on the Psychology of Recreation," *Pedagogical Seminar* 29 (March 1922): 72–99; G. S. Hall, *Life and Confessions of a Psychologist* (New York, 1923), pp. 531–536; G. S. Hall, *Recreations of a Psychologist* (New York, 1920), p. vii.

76. Hall, *Life and Confessions,* p. 536.

77. Hall, "Psychology of Recreation," p. 74.

78. Ibid., p. 72.

79. Ibid., p. 73.

80. Hall, *Recreations of a Psychologist,* p. vii; see also chap. 8, "Notes on Early Memories," passim.

81. Hall, "Psychology of Recreation," p. 98.

82. Ibid.

83. Ibid., p. 99.

84. See note 72.

85. S. Patten, "The Mechanism of Mind," *Annals* 71 (May 1917): 204. See also D. M. Fox, *Discovery of Abundance* (Ithaca, N.Y., 1967), pp. 111, 133.

86. W. F. Ogburn, "The Frequency and Probability of Insanity," *American Journal of Sociology* 34 (March 1929): 822–831.

87. W. F. Ogburn, "Our New Leisure: How Shall We Use It?" *New York Times,* July 7, 1929, sec. 5, p. 3.

88. Cutten, *Threat of Leisure*, p. 9.

89. Ibid., p. 13. During the debate over Prohibition, many advocates of the measure defended their position by reasoning that the newly won leisure would be wasted by overindulgence in alcohol.

90. Ibid., pp. 17, 39, 42.

91. Ibid., p. 43.

92. Ibid., p. 65.

93. Ibid., p. 207. Other writers dealing with the question of instinctual release and compensation through play and leisure include H. Addition, "And What of Leisure," *Journal of Social Hygiene* 16 (1930): 321–334; L. L. Benard, *Instinct: A Study in Social Psychology* (New York, 1924), p. 550; H. S. Curtis, *Education through Play* (New York, 1921), p. 359; H. S. Langfield, *The Aesthetic Attitude* (New York: 1920), p. 287; C. Rainwater, "Play as Collective Behavior," *Journal of Applied Sociology* 8 (1924): 271; E. S. Robinson, "The Compensatory Function of Make-Believe," *Psychological Review* 27 (1920): 429–439; E. S. Robinson, "Play," in *Encyclopedia of Social Science* (New York, 1934), pp. xii, 160–161; J. F. Steiner, *Americans at Play: Recent Trends in Recreation and Leisure Time Activities* (New York, 1933), p. 201; R. Walder, "The Psychoanalytic Theory of Play," *Psychoanalytic Quarterly* 2 (1933): 208–224; P. A. Witty, *A Study of Deviates in Versatility and Sociability of Play Interests* (New York, 1931), p. 57; R. S. Woodworth, *Psychology: A Study of Mental Life* (New York, 1921), p. 580.

94. S. Freud, *The Basic Writings of Sigmund Freud*, trans. and ed. A. A. Brill (New York, 1938), chap. 3, "Three Contributions to the Theory of Sex," pp. 588, 599–602. See also chap. 4, "Wit and Its Relation to the Unconscious," pp. 711–723, and chap. 5, "Totem and Taboo," p. 872. For a more thorough treatment of the topic of sexuality and play, see S. Freud, *Collected Papers*, ed. J. Riviere and J. Strachey, 5 vols. (New York, 1924–1950), 4:14–18, 41, 51, 174–176; S. Freud, *New Introductory Lectures on Psychoanalysis*, trans. W. J. H. Sprott (London, 1933), pp. 106, 114–116.

95. S. Freud, *A General Introduction to Psycho-Analysis*, trans. J. Riviere (New York, 1953), p. 332.

96. S. Freud, *Beyond the Pleasure Principle*, trans. J. Strachey (New York, 1959; originally published in America 1928), pp. 26–28, 32, 46, 76–78.

97. Ibid., p. 37; Freud, "Wit and the Unconscious," pp. 720, 721.

98. S. Freud, *The Future of an Illusion*, trans. W. D. Robson-Scott (London, 1928), pp. 7–15; S. Freud, *Civilization and Its Discontents*, trans. J. Riviere (London, 1930), pp. 34, 86–87, 121, 122, 141, 142.

99. Freud, *Future of an Illusion*, p. 11.

100. Ibid., p. 12.

101. Ibid., pp. 14, 15.

102. Ibid., pp. 17–28.

103. Ibid., p. 21.

104. Ibid., p. 12.

105. H. Marcuse, *Eros and Civilization, A Philosophical Inquiry into Freud* (New York, 1962), pp. 21–25.

106. Freud, *Beyond the Pleasure Principle*, pp. 71–109.

107. S. Ferenczi, "The Sunday Neurosis," in *Leisure and Mental Health: A Psychiatric Viewpoint*, ed. Peter Martin (Washington, D.C., 1967), p. 120; Ferenczi's essay was originally published in 1926.

108. Mrs. T. A. Edison, "Speech," *New York Times*, October 16, 1928, sec. 1, p. 28; D. Mason, "Address at Columbia University," *New York Times*, September 30, 1928, sec. 3, p. 4; C. B. Stendler, "New Ideas for Old: How Freudianism Was Received in the United States from 1900 to 1925," *Journal of Educational Psychology* 38 (April 1947): 193–206. Concern with boredom, although expressed in the 1920s, was at its peak in the depression. See, for example, "Boredom," *Literary Digest* 115 (1933): 26; J. E. Barmack, "Boredom and Other Factors in the Physiology of Mental Effort," *Archives of Psychology* 208 (1937): 1–83; J. N. Hall, "State of Being Bored," *Atlantic* 151 (August 1933): 318–321.

109. G. Adler, ed., *Carl G. Jung Letters* (Princeton, N.J., 1973), pp. 39, 40; Letter to O. Schmitz from C. G. Jung, May 26, 1923.

110. C. G. Jung, *Psychological Types*, trans. H. G. Baynes (New York, 1926), pp. 135–145.

111. F. Schiller, *Essays, Aesthetic and Philosophical* (New Haven, 1954), pp. 74, 75, 76–80, 112, 116, 133–135. That Freud and Jung were familiar with Schiller's ideas about the "play impulse," see Jung, *Psychological Types*, p. 135; Freud, *Beyond the Pleasure Principle*, p. 80; and Freud, *Basic Writings*, p. 193.

112. H. Adams, *The Education of Henry Adams* (Boston, 1918), pp. 451, 495; M. Lyon, *Symbol and Idea in Henry Adams* (Lincoln, 1970), pp. 227, 228. Adams used the terms "random energy" and "surplus energy" interchangeably. He equated both with chaos, which was the "law of nature standing always against order, the dream of man." Even man's "willful striving after meaning and unity contributes one more source of random energy to the pervading chaos." Adams understood this absurd striving as essentially a form of "playing with chaos."

113. H. C. Lehman and P. Witty, *The Psychology of Play Activities* (New York, 1927), p. 13; S. M. Britt and S. Q. Janus, "Toward a Psychology of Human Play," *Journal of Social Psychology* 13 (1941): 351; F. Alexander, *The Psychoanalysis of the Total Personality* (New York, 1929), pp. 14, 9, 12; Freud, *Introduction to Psycho-Analysis*, p. 332; L. C. Birnbaum, "Behaviorism in the 1920's," *American Quarterly* 7 (Spring 1955): 15–30; Thorndike, "Right Use of Leisure," p. 19.

114. H. May, "Shifting Perspectives on the 1920's," *Mississippi Valley Historical Review* 43 (December 1956): 405–408.

115. *Recent Social Trends*, 1:xiii.

116. M. Mead, *Coming of Age in Samoa* (New York, 1950; originally published 1928), pp. 48–65; W. H. R. Rivers, *Social Organization* (New York, 1924), pp. 36–42; C. Wissler, *Man and Culture* (New York, 1923), chaps. 5, 12; A. L. Kroeber, "The Culture-Area and Age-Area Concepts of Clark Wissler," in *Methods in Social Science*, ed. S. A. Rice (Chicago, 1931), pp. 248–265.

117. *Recent Social Trends*, 1:xii.

118. H. Odum to W. F. Ogburn, January 28, 1930, Box 10, Folder 203, Howard Odum Papers, University of North Carolina Library, Chapel Hill.

Hereinafter cited as Odum Papers. In this letter Odum says, "My point of emphasis is . . . that the subject of recreation is one dealing a good deal with the present social structure as well as function and is a fundamental community activity."

119. H. Odum to W. Ogburn, February 18, 1930, Box 10, Folder 205, Odum Papers. Odum suggested that Roscoe Pound be chosen for the committee's recreation study.

120. H. Odum to W. Ogburn, March 22, 1930, Box 10, Folder 212, Odum Papers.

121. W. Ogburn to H. Odum, March 3, 1930, Box 10, Folder 207, Odum Papers.

122. H. Odum to W. Ogburn, March 22, 1930, Box 10, Folder 212, Odum Papers. In this letter Odum insists that the committee's recreation and leisure study be "rigorously supervised by you and to some extent myself . . . so that we could . . . harmonize it with the rest of the studies."

123. J. F. Steiner, "Recreation and Leisure Time Activities," in *Recent Social Trends*, pp. 912, 913.

124. Ibid., pp. 916, 917, 719, 920.

125. Ibid., p. 930.

126. Ibid., pp. 926, 927.

127. Ibid., pp. 933, 934.

128. Ibid., pp. 939, 940, 941.

129. Ibid., p. 949.

130. Ibid., pp. 945, 955, 956, 957.

131. *Recent Social Trends*, p. xiii.

132. Ibid., p. xv.

133. Ibid., pp. xiv, lii.

134. Ibid., p. lxxi.

135. Ibid., p. lxxv.

136. Ibid., p. li.

137. Ibid., p. lii.

138. Lynd and Lynd, *Middletown*, pp. 225, 496, 497.

139. Ibid., pp. 53, 81.

140. Ibid., p. 87.

141. Ibid., p. ii.

142. Ibid., pp. 236, 248.

143. Ibid., p. 251.

144. Ibid., pp. 226, 272, 307, 309.

145. Ibid., p. 80.

146. W. Pangburn, "The Worker's Leisure and His Individuality," *American Journal of Sociology* 27 (January 1922): 433–441.

147. W. Pangburn to H. Hoover, July 27, 1931, Box 212, Herbert Hoover Presidential Papers, Herbert Hoover Presidential Library, West Branch, Iowa.

148. Pangburn, "Worker's Leisure," pp. 436–437.

149. E. A. Ross, "Adult Recreation as a Social Problem, " *American Journal of Sociology* 23 (January 1918): 516–528. Other sociologists dealing with leisure as a way to compensate the individual for natural tendencies, in-

herited nature, or real needs repressed by modern jobs and industrial civilization include C. Rainwater, "Socialized Leisure," *Journal of Applied Sociology* 24 (January 1919): 373–388; Ogburn, "Our New Leisure," p. 3; G. Lundberg, *Leisure: A Suburban Study* (New York, 1934), pp. 9, 19, 21–25; M. Flad, "Leisure Time Activities of Four Hundred Persons," *Sociology and Social Research* 18 (January 1934): 265–274.

150. A. Lloyd, "Ages of Leisure," *American Journal of Sociology* 28 (September 1922): 160. Other sociologists dealing with leisure as a way to a "democratic culture" include Lundberg, *Leisure*, pp. 34–37; E. Todd, "Amateur," in *The Encyclopedia of Social Sciences*, ed. by E. Seligman, 15 vols. (New York, 1933), 2:18–20; C. Aronovici, "Organized Leisure," *American Journal of Sociology* 24 (1919): 382–388; I. Craven, "Leisure," in *The Encyclopedia of Social Sciences*, ed. by E. Seligman, 15 vols. (New York, 1933), 9:402–406; Field, "Now That They Have It," p. 747. See also F. P. Keppell, "The Arts in Social Life," in *Recent Social Trends*, pp. 1003–1008; "Report of the Annual Meeting of the National Institute of Social Sciences," *Playground* 15 (August 1924): 311–312; "Leisure and Culture," *Saturday Review of Literature* 4 (August 13, 1927): 33; Cutten, *Threat of Leisure*, p. 128; Wadsworth, "Training for Leisure, An Aim of Art Education," *School Arts* 29 (November 1929): 131.

151. *The Readers Guide to Periodical Literature*, 35 vol. (New York, 1900–1975), vols. 3–7, under the heading "Leisure." This standard reference provides some indication of the increase in public interest in leisure during the 1920s. In vol. 5, an index of 1919–1921, only 4 entries are listed for articles dealing with leisure. In vol. 7, covering the years 1925–1928 and giving an index of the same 180 reports and periodicals as did vol. 5, over 45 entries are listed. See also L. A. Thompson, "Workers' Leisure: A Selected List of References" *Monthly Labor Review* 24 (November 1928): 508. The best available bibliographies demonstrate the increased attention paid to the subject; see M. Casebier, *An Overview of Leisure* (San Anselmo, Calif., 1963); E. Larrabee and R. Meyerson, *Mass Leisure* (Glencoe, Ill., 1958), pp. 389ff. Larrabee and Meyerson found 51 articles and books having to do with leisure from 1910 to 1919 and over 410 from 1920 to 1929.

152. J. Brack and K. Cowling, "Advertising and the Labour Supply: Workweek and Workyear in U.S. Manufacturing Industries, 1919–76," *Kyklos* 36 (1983): 285–303.

Chapter 5

1. *New York Times*, August 2, 1932, p. 1. See also *New York Times*, March 3, 1931, p. 6. Even before the widespread interest in "new leisure," which surfaced in 1933–1934, the "unemployment or leisure" theme was sounded by prominent people such as Henry Ford; see H. Ford, *Moving Forward* (New York, 1930), pp. 16–88, esp. chap. 5; H. Ford and A. Crowther, "Unemployment or Leisure," *Saturday Evening Post* 203 (August 2, 1930): 19; I. Craven, "Leisure," in *Encyclopedia of Social Sciences* (New York, 1932), pp. 402–406; *New York Times*, July 30, October 2, 1931, August 2, 1932. For business in-

terest in general, see "Spread-Work Plans Gain Ground on the Employment Front," *Business Week* 11 (October 1932); "American Industry and the Five-Day Week, *Congressional Digest*" (1932): 225; L. C. Walker, "The Share-the-Work Movement," *Annals of the American Academy* 165 (January 1933): 13; *New York Times*, March 3, 1931. See also O. F. Williams, Alabama state legislative representative for the Brotherhood of Railroad Trainmen, to H. Black, December 17, 1932; Hugo Black Papers, Library of Congress, Washington, D.C. (Hereinafter, Black Papers.) Williams observed that "'share-the-work' . . . seems to get the unqualified support of all Chamber of Commerce and City officials, also captains of industry," in Alabama.

2. See the following issues: *New York Times*, May 8, 1930, p. 46; November 4, 1930, p. 14; October 10, 1930, p. 39; September 26, 1930, p. 36. See also "Cereals: Six-Hour Day Helps Kellogg Company Do More Work," *Newsweek* 9 (September 1936): 27; "Humanizing Machines—II, Kellogg's Six-Hour Day," *Forum and Century* 96 (1933): 97; "Kellogg Strikes at Unemployment," *Factory and Industrial Management* 80 (December 1930): 1148a–b; "Kellogg Six-Hour Workday Plan Brings Profit and Will Continue," *Business Week*, April 22, 1931, p. 16; "Kellogg Four-Shift Plan Boosts Output and Profit," *Business Week*, April 6, 1932, p. 18; "Forty-Hour Week Established by Standard Oil Company of New Jersey," *Monthly Labor Review* 35 (August 8, 1932): 367; "Six-Hour Shifts Provide More Jobs for Workers," *Business Week*, July 22, 1932, p. 25; "Six-Hour Day: Goodyear Tire and Rubber Company," *Survey* 69 (January 1933): 33; P. M. Mazur, *New Roads to Prosperity: The Crisis and Some Ways Out* (New York, 1931), pp. 175–187. See also National Industrial Conference Board (NICB), "Attitude of 1718 Business Executives toward Soundness of Principle of Spreading Work during Business Depression," in *Shorter Work Periods in Industry* (New York, 1932), p. 38; the NICB reported that 74 percent of those surveyed supported the principle (pp. 33–42).

3. *New York Times*, August 5, 1932, p. 15.

4. *New York Times*, August 14, 1932, p. 1.

5. *New York Times*, August 25, 1932, p. 13.

6. *New York Times*, August 2, 1932, p. 1; Letter to President Hoover from W. S. Gifford, director of the President's Organization on Unemployment Relief (POUR), August 3, 1932, Box 319, 1A, and "Report of the President's Organization on Unemployment Relief" Box 339, both in Herbert Hoover's Presidential Papers, Hoover Library, West Branch, Iowa. (Hereinafter, Hoover Papers.) E. D. Durand to W. C. Garner, 12 March 1931; W. Mitchell to W. C. Garner, member of the President's Emergency Committee for Employment (PECE), March 12, 1931. Mitchell wrote: "I have read your memorandum on the report to the PECE concerning plans for shortening the work day. In all respects I can pronounce [a] favorable opinion, both as to the soundness as a permanent measure, and as to [its] effectiveness." Statement on Spreading Work by the President's Organization on Unemployment Relief, August 1, 1932, Hoover Papers. POUR conducted a survey of 25,000 companies on March 15, 1932, and found that, of 6551 responding, 59 percent used the shorter workweek for work spreading. See the summary in a memorandum prepared by W. C. Garner for PECE, July 8, 1931, Hoover Papers. This is one of the

first suggestions made to President Hoover regarding work sharing. Garner proposed that "it would be sound public policy for practically all enterprises in the United States to shorten hours, with a maintenance of production, to the end that the unemployed be put back to work. . . . The basic hourly rate of wages should not be cut. When and where possible it should be increased. . . . Hours should be shortened proportionate to the number unemployed . . . the idea of laying off hours of time instead of laying off personnel when work slackened." Garner also observed that "independent of one another thousands of employers have been considering it [shorter hours] as a way out of the difficulty." See also "Spread-Work Plans Gain Ground," p. 7; "Spreading-Work Program of President's Conference of August 26, 1932," *Monthly Labor Review* 35 (October 1932): 790–792; "President Hoover's Economy Proposal: Five Day Week Staggered Furlough Plan," *Congressional Digest* 9 (May 1932): 130; W. J. Barrett, "Present Plans for Spreading Employment," *Congressional Digest* 11 (October 1932): 232; "Chemical Industry Approves Six-Hour Day to Spread Work," *Business Week* 9 (October 14, 1931): 7; C. M. Wright, "A Four-Day Week?" *Review of Reviews* 85 (January 1932): 61; J. L. Hammond, "Problem of Leisure," *New Statesman and Nation* 4 (1932): 618–619.

7. *New York Times*, June 30, 1932, p. 2.

8. See the following issues: *New York Times*, July 21, 1932, p. 9; July 22, 1932, p. 14; July 24, 1932, p. 1; July 25, 1932, p. 14; July 28, 1932, p. 2; August 1, 1932, p. 1; August 2, 1932, p. 1; August 28, 1932, p. 1. Early interest in the shorter-hour cure for unemployment in New York State may be seen in *New York Times*, February 8, 1931, p. 5; J. G. Winant, "New Hampshire Plan," *Review of Reviews* 86 (November 1932): 24; O. McKee, Jr. "New Hampshire Does Her Bit," *National Republic* 20 (October 1932): 6.

9. *New York Times*, January 15, 1933, p. 2.

10. *New York Times*, December 9, 1932, p. 2. See also *New York Times*, December 10, 1932, p. 2; "Job Sharing: Five Million Helped by Work-Spreading, Teagle Committee Estimates," *Business Week* 14 (February 1, 1933); "Nation-Wide Drive for the Five-Day Week," *Literary Digest* 115 (1933): 3–4; "Spread-Work Plans Gain Ground," p. 7; "Six-Hour Day," *Business Week* 32 (December 28, 1932): 20; "The Nation-Wide Drive for the Five-Day Week: Topics of the Day," *Literary Digest*, August 13, 1932, p. 114; "Work-Spreading," *Business Week*, November 16, 1932, p. 12; "Work-Spreaders Will Make Jobs Now, Face the Issues Later," *Business Week* 32 (August 3, 1932): 36; Barrett, "Present Plans for Spreading Employment," p. 232.

11. See the following issues: *New York Times*, May 16, 1932, p. 5; May 21, 1932, p. 2; May 26, 1932, p. 27; June 30, 1932, p. 2; September 22, 1932, p. 18; October 5, 1932, p. 16; July 30, 1932, p. 1. See also W. Graf, *Platforms of the Two Great Political Parties: 1932 to 1944* (Washington, D.C., 1944), pp. 336, 354; R. F. Himmelberg, *The Great Depression and American Capitalism* (Boston, 1968), p. 41; Walker, "Share-the-Work Movement," p. 13.

12. See the following issues: *New York Times*, October 7, 1932, p. 38; December 4, 1932, sec. 4, p. 1; January 26, 1933, p. 5. See also "Labor's Ultimatum to Industry: Thirty-Hour week," *Literary Digest* 114 (December 10, 1932): 3–4; "Labor Will Fight," *Business Week* 14–15 (December 14, 1932):

32; "The Labor Army Takes the Field: A Shorter Work Week to Make Jobs, *Literary Digest* 115 (April 15, 1933): 6. See also H. Black to P. A. Redmond, December 23, 1932, Black Papers. There were, of course, scores of letters to Black from labor union leaders and from individuals workers in support of Black's bill. Black described these as "hundreds" of supporting letters. See H. Black to W. H. Hendrix, May 23, 1933, Black Papers; Green to H. Black, April 5, 1933, Black Papers; H. Black to L. Taaffe (mimeographed letter sent to a number of Black's correspondents), January 28, 1933, Black Papers; L. Magnusson, International Labor Organization of the League of Nations, to H. Black, January 9, 1933 (Magnusson regarding international conference on the length of the working day). See also Radio address transcript, WPG and WEVD (1936), C. P. Howard, president of International Typographical union, Charles Howard Papers, University of Wisconsin, Madison; W. Green to H. Hoover, March 12, 1930, Hoover Papers.

13. F. T. Carlton, "Employment and Leisure," *American Federationist 39* (1932): 1256–1260; U.S. Congress, House, Committee on Labor, *Hearings on H.R. 14105*, 72nd Cong., 2nd sess., 1933, pp. 1–23. For a review of the AFL's attitude toward work sharing, see the following issues: *American Federationist* 38 (January 1931): 22; (February 1931): 145; (April 1931): 401; (June 1931): 677; (September 1931): 1056; (December 1931): 1455; 39 (April 1932): 382; (May 1932): 504; (September 1932): 985. For continuous support of the Black–Connery bills, see the following issues: *American Federationist* 40 (January 1933): 13; (February 1933): 179; (April 1933): 347; (May 1933): 458; (November 1933): 1174; 42 (January 1935): 12; (February 1935): 132; 43 (December 1936): 124; 44 (October 1937): 1052; 45 (November 1938): 1176. See also S. Miller, Jr., "Labor and the Challenge of the New Leisure," *Harvard Business Review* 11 (May 1933): 462–667; W. Green, "Leisure for Labor—A New Force Alters our Social Structure," *Magazine of Business* 56 (August 1929): 136–137; H. Black to B. F. Courtright, February 1, 1933, Black Papers; U.S. Congress, House, Committee on Labor, *Thirty-Hour Week Bill; Hearings on H.R. 14105*, 73rd Cong., 1st sess., January 18–30, 1933; U.S. Congress, House, Committee on Labor, *Thirty-Hour Week Bill; Hearings on S. 153 and H.R. 4557*, 73rd Cong., 1st sess., April 25–28, May 1–5, 1933; U.S. Congress, Senate, Committee on Judiciary, *Thirty-Hour Work Week; Hearings on S. 3910, S. 4500, S. 5267 (pt. 1)*, 73rd Cong., 2nd sess., January 5, 6, 10–14, 17–19, 1933); U.S. Congress, Senate, Committee on Judiciary, *Thirty-Hour Work Week; Hearings on S. 5267 (pt. 2)*, 73rd Cong., 2nd sess., January 24–27, 31, February 1–4, 8, 11, 1933; U.S. Congress, House, Committee on Labor, *Thirty-Hour Week Bill; Hearings on H.R. 7202, H.R. 4116, H.R. 8492*, 73rd Cong., 2nd sess., February 8, 9, 15, 16, 19–21, 23, 1934; U.S. Congress, Senate, Committee on Judiciary, *Thirty-Hour Work Week; Hearings on S. 87*, 74th Cong., 1st sess., January 31, February 1, 2, 5–9, 11–16, 1935.

14. See the following issues: *New York Times*, February 12, 1933, p. 3; January 6, 1933, p. 14; January 8, 1933, sec. 4 p. 4; January 12, 1933, p. 2; January 19, 1933, p. 5; January 20, 1933; p. 2. See also U.S. Congress, House, Committee on Labor, *Hearings on H.R. 158 and H.R. 4557*, 73rd Cong., 1st sess., 1933, passim; U.S. Congress, House, Committee on Labor, *Hearings on*

H.R. 7202, H.R. 416, and H.R. 8492, 73rd Cong., 2nd sess., 1934 passim; D.C. Fisher, "The Bright Perilous Face of Leisure," *Journal of Adult Education* 5 (June 1933): 237–243; L. C. Walker, *Distributed Leisure: An Approach to the Problems of Over Production and Under Employment* (New York, 1931), pp. 21–52; A. Pound, "Out of Unemployment into Leisure," *Atlantic Review* 146 (December 1930): 784–792; G. B. Cutten, *Challenge of Leisure* (Columbus, 1933); A. O. Dahlberg, *Jobs, Machines, and Capitalism* (New York, 1932); C. D. Burns, *Leisure in the Modern World* (New York, 1932); W. H. Hamilton, "Challenge of Leisure," *New Republic* 74 (March 1933): 191–192; T. D. Eliot, "Reevaluating Our Leisure in Our Civilization," *Christian Register* 113 (November 1934): 758–759; F. Franklin, "Uses of Leisure," *Saturday Review of Literature* 9 (November 5, 1932): 222; "New Leisure," *Nation* 137 (November 29, 1933): 610–611; W. S. Coffin, "Too Little Culture for Leisure," *American Magazine of Art* 24 (June 1933): 299–300; E. E. Calkins, "Lost Art of Play," *Atlantic Monthly* 153 (April 1933): 438–446; A. B. Brown, "Education for Leisure," *Hibbert Journal* 31 (April 1933): 440–450; M. P. Coleman, "Leisure and the Arts," *Library Journal* 59 (May 1934): 60–61; R. Aiken, "A Laborer's Leisure," *North American Review* 232 (September 1931): 268–273; "New Leisure, Its Significance and Use," *Library Journal* 58 (May 15, 1933): 444; H. A. Overstreet, "Leisure Time and Education Opportunities and Needs," *Recreation* 27 (February 1934): 499–500; A. N. Pack, *The Challenge of Leisure* (New York, 1934); J. Destree, "Popular Arts and Workers' Spare time," *International Labor Review* 27 (1933): 184–206; A. Daniels, "Responsibility of the College in Education for Leisure," *Schools and Society* 41 (May 25, 1935): 706–707; H. S. Dimock, "Can We Educate for Leisure?" *Religious Education* 29 (April 1934): 120–124; J. H. Finley, "What Will We Do with Our Time?" *National Municipal Review* 22 (1933): 416–417; E. E. Hoyt, "The Challenge of the New Leisure," *Journal of Home Economics* (October 1933): 688; E. T. Lies, "Education for Leisure," *National Education Association Journal* 21 (1932): 253–254; E. T. Lies, *The New Leisure Challenges the Schools* (Washington, D.C., 1933); E. T. Lies and R.L. Duffus, *The Arts in American Life* (New York, 1933); L. P. Jacks, "The Coming Leisure," *New Era* 13 (December 1932): 351–353; "Coming: The Age of Leisure," *Literary Digest* 112 (January 16, 1932): 26; B. A. McClenahan, "Preparation for Leisure," *Sociology and Social Research* 18 (1933): 140–149; J. T. Palmer, "New Leisure— Blessing or Curse?" *School Executive* 54 (March 1935): 198–199; W. A. Orton, *America in Search of Culture* (Boston, 1933); W. S. Coffin, "Art and leisure," *Art Digest* 7 (May 1933): 10; W. B. Bizzell, "Learning and Leisure," *School and Society* 39 (January 1934): 65–72; E. E. Calkins, "New Leisure: A Curse or a Blessing?" *Recreation* 26 (April 1934): 22–27; N. M. Butler, "Leisure and Its Uses," *Recreation* 28 (May 1934): 219–222; F. R. Dulles, *America Learns to Play: A History of Popular Recreation 1607–1940* (New York and London, 1940), pp. 365–373; U.S. Congress, Senate, *Hearings on S. 3910, S. 4500, S. 5267,* January 5, 6, 10–14, 17–19, 1933; U.S. Congress, Senate, *Hearings on S. 5267,* January 24–27, 31, February 1–4, 8, 11, 1933; B. Russell, "In Praise of Idleness," *Harper's* 165 (October 1932): 552; B. Russell, "Reduction of Working Hours and the Advantages of Leisure," *Review of Reviews* 82 (1932): 48–54; "Six-Hour Day," pp. 33, 36; M. Woll, "Labor and the New Leisure," *Recre-*

ation 27 (December 1933): 428–431; "Unemployment and the Thirty-Hour Week," *National Education Association Journal* 22 (February 1933): 59; G. Soule, *A Planned Society* (New York, 1932), pp. 257, 258; G. Soule, *The Coming American Revolution* (New York, 1932); C. D. Burns, *Leisure in the Modern World* (New York and London, 1932). Of all the groups responding to shorter hours and the leisure issue in the 1930s, educators were the most active. The newly begun *Education Index* listed 232 articles about leisure in major education periodicals for the period July 1932 to June 1935—see vol 2, pp. 901–903. But this interest declined dramatically as educators turned to work creation after 1934. This decline in evidenced by the same index, vol. 4, p. 948, for July 1941 to June 1944, where only 12 articles are listed for leisure.

15. *Business Week*, February 15, 1933, p. 3.

16. "A.F. of L. Opens War for Its 30-Hour Week," *Newsweek* 1 (July 22, 1933): 6; "Unemployment and Thirty-Hour Week," p. 59; "Six-Hour Day," p. 33; A. J. Lindsay, "Unemployment: The 'Meanwhile' Problem," *Contemporary Review* 143 (June 1933): 687; H. P. Fairchild, "Exit the Gospel of Work," *Harper's* April 1931, pp. 566–573; F. S. Cohen, "The Blessing of Unemployment," *American Scholar* 2 (1933): 203–214; F. H. Allport, "This Coming Era of Leisure," *Harper's* 163 (November 1931): 641–652; "In the Driftway: American Vice of Busyness," *Nation* 132 (January 28, 1931): 98–99; "Coming: The Age of Leisure," p. 26; "Not Less, But More: Thirty-Hour-Week," *Saturday Evening Post* 207 (February 9, 1935): 26; R. Payne, *Why Work: Or the Coming of Leisure* (Boston, 1939); H. A. Overstreet, *A Guide to Civilized Loafing* (New York, 1934); "Machine and Leisure," *Industrial Arts and Vocational Education* 26 (1937): 416–417; "Union Wage and Hour Policies and Employment," *American Economics Review* 30 (June 1940): 290; C. E. Dankert, "Efficiency and Unemployment," *Canadian Forum* 12 (February 1932): 169; Pound, "Out of Unemployment into Leisure," p. 784; H. Braucher, "The Machine Revolution," *Recreation* 24 (February 1931): 585; R. E. Danforth, "Brighter Days Ahead," *Scientific Monthly* 33 (October 1931): 318; "In the Driftway," pp. 98–99; J. D. Rockefeller, Jr., "Leisure," *Recreation* 32 (1938): 201; C. A. Beard, ed., *America Faces the Future* (Boston and New York, 1932), pp. 152, 153; L. M. Gilbreth, "Work and Leisure," in *The Rise of American Civilization*, ed. C. A. Beard and M. R. Beard (New York, 1931), 2:232–252.

17. Green, "Leisure for Labor," pp. 136–137; H. L. Slobodin, "Unemployment or Leisure—Which?" *American Federationist* 37 (October 1930): 1205–1208; W. Green, "Shorter Hours," *American Federationist* 38 (January 1931): 22; Woll, "Labor and the New Leisure," pp. 428–431; L. P. Jacks, "Today's Unemployment and Tomorrow's Leisure," *Recreation* 25 (December 1931): 478; W. Green, "Thirty Hour Week," *American Federationist* 40 (November 1933): 1174; Lindsay, "Unemployment: The 'Meanwhile' Problem," p. 687; H. Ford and A. Crowther, "The Fear of Overproduction," *Saturday Evening Post* 203 (July 12, 1930): 3; Pound, "Out of Unemployment into Leisure," p. 784; S. Chase, *The Economy of Abundance* (New York, 1934), pp. 15–17, 21, see also chaps. 13 and 14 et passim; Letter, J. A. Ryan to H. Black, letter, April 7, 1933, Black Papers.

18. W. Green, "Should America Adopt the Five-Day Week: Pro," *Congres-*

sional Digest 11 (October 1932): 274. Stuart Chase was a strong supporter of 30 hours in 1933–1934. In a letter to E. F. McGrady, legislative representative for the AFL, Chase wrote that "the ravages of technological unemployment are going to be worse and worse. . . . In the event that business recovers, we can expect no decline in the numbers of the technologically unemployed. Thus, both in prosperity and in depression the problem promises to be with us. It is possible to mitigate the evils by reforms, such as unemployment insurance, public works programs, State Government relief, a measure of industrial co-ordination, and so forth. I see no permanent solution, however, except in terms of shorter working hours—allowing society to share in the process of new invention." S. Chase to E. F. McGrady, January 11, 1933, Black Papers. See also H. Black to W. B. Davis, January 30, 1933; H. Black to H. Ayers, editor of the *Anniston Star*, January 27, 1933, Black Papers. With Chase, Black believed that the country would never be able to reemploy its people in the "old working day and week."

19. *New York Times*, April 7, 1933, p. 1; G. Turner, "The New Leisure of the New Deal," *Catholic World* 138 (November 1933): 168; *Newsweek*, April 15, 1933, pp. 8, 21; H. Black to J. H. Hollingsworth, March 8, 1933, Black Papers. Black was optimistic about passage in early March. See also H. Black to R. B. Hogan, April 4, 1933, Black Papers. In April, Black was increasingly hopeful about passage of his bill, writing: "I believe that we will be successful in securing the passage of the measure. . . . At least everything points to this at the present time." For Black's thoughts about the Senate passage of his bill, see H. Black to J. W. McCord, April 10, 1933, H. Black to J. H. Church, May 4, 1933, H. B. to J. F. Suttle, May 6, 1933, Black Papers.

20. Lindley, as quoted in A. M. Schlesinger, *The Coming of the New Deal* (Boston, 1959), p. 95.

21. *New York Times*, April 8, 1933, p. 12.

22. A. Link, *American Epoch* (New York, 1963), pp. 390–395. See also the following issues: *New York Times*, April 8, 1933, p. 2; April 12, 1933, p. 2; April 13, 1933, p. 2; April 14, 1933, p. 1; and *Newsweek* 1 (April 15, 1933): 8.

23. *New York Times*, April 13, 1933, p. 2.

24. *New York Times*, April 14, 1933, p. 18; April 26, 1933, p. 5.

25. *New York Times*, April 13, 1933, p. 2; April 14, 1933, pp. 1, 3; November 17, 1930, p. 1. See also U.S. Congress, House, *Hearings on S. 153 and H.R. 4557*, April 25–28, May 1–5, 1933, pp. 1–24. See also H. Black to F. Perkins, March 29, 1933, Black Papers. This was an invitation to Perkins to appear before the Senate Judiciary Committee. See also her response in F. Perkins to H. Black, March 29, 1933, Black Papers. Perkins wrote that "the aim of the bill is to put an end to overly long hours and to establish hour standards in keeping with the needs of the day." See also Link, *American Epoch*, p. 391.

26. *New York Times*, August 25, 1930, sec. 9, p. 4; November 7, 1930, p. 41.

27. M. C. Cahill, *Shorter Hours: A Study of the Movement Since the Civil War* (New York, 1922), pp. 14–19, 43–46, 156–159, 211; S. Chase, "Leisure in a Machine Age," *Library Journal* 41 (August 1931): 629–632; C. Furnas, *America's Tomorrow, an Informal Excursion into the Era of the Two-Hour Working Day* (New York, 1932); B. Russell, *The Conquest of Happiness* (New York, 1930), passim.

28. *New York Times*, October 5, 1932, pp. 16, 22.

29. F. H. Allport, "This Coming Era of Leisure," *Harpers* 163 (November 1931): 641; Chase, "Leisure in a Machine Age," p. 629; P. T. Frankl, *Machine-Made Leisure* (New York, 1932); C. Beard, *Whither Mankind*, p. 33, and chap. 8.

30. *New York Times*, March 19, 1933, p. 17; "What Price Leisure?" *Business Week* (August 3, 1932): 36; *New York Times*, December 18, 1932, sec. 2, p. 15; "Work-spreaders Will Make Jobs Now," p. 12; "Work-Spreaders Will Have to Spread It Thin," *Business Week*, October 26, 1932, p. 14; *New York Times*, April 2, 1933, p. 12; S. Miller, Jr., "Labor and the Challenge of the New Leisure," *Harvard Business Review* 11 (1933): 462–467.

31. *New York Times*, April 2, 1933, p. 12.

32. See the following issues: *New York Times*, October 14, 1932, p. 3; April 9, 1933, sec. 2, p. 15; April 10, 1933, p. 26. See also National Industrial Conference Board, "Actual Work Periods in 1932," in *Shorter Work Periods in Industry* (New York, 1932), pp. 43–47.

33. *New York Times*, April 8, 1933, p. 12; April 9, 1933, sect. 2, p. 15. See also "Six-hour day: Cornell Crystallizes Some Conclusions on Industry's Attitude," *Business Week* (May 10, 1933): 4.

34. *New York Times*, April 10, 1933, p. 26.

35. See the following issues: *New York Times*, April 2, 1933, p. 12; April 12, 1933, p. 2; April 14, 1933, p. 14; April 15, 1933, p. 2; April 19, 1933, p. 2; April 20, 1933, p. 5; April 29, 1933, p. 25. See also *Newsweek* 1 (April 15, 1933): 8. Typical objections raised by business to Black–Connery may be found in "Resolution Adopted by the Manufacturers Committee of the Mobil Chamber of Commerce," April 11, 1933, Black Papers. See also the flood of letters in April to Black's office from textile, lumber, steel, and canning firms in Alabama opposing the bill. Black Papers, container 160, folders 1 and 2.

36. H. Johnson, *The Blue Eagle from Earth to Egg* (Garden City, N.Y., 1935), p. 205.

37. *New York Times*, April 12, 1933, p. 2; April 15, 1933, p. 2.

38. *New York Times*, April 20, 1933, p. 5.

39. Ibid.

40. *Newsweek* 1 (April 15, 1933): 8.

Chapter 6

1. R. Moley, *After Seven Years* (New York and London, 1939), p. 186.

2. R. F. Himmelberg, *The Origins of the National Recovery Administration: Business, Government and the Trade Association Issue, 1921–1933* (New York, 1976), p. 191. For FDR's and Perkins's support of work sharing in 1932, see *New York Times*, January 26, 1932, p. 46, and August 26, 1932, p. 1.

3. *New York Times* April 10, 1933, p. 26, for Rentschler quote. See also the following issues: *New York Times*, April 6, 1933, p. 5; April 7, 1933, p. 1; April 10, 1933, p. 12; April 16, 1933, p. 1 and sec. 2, p. 13.

A large number of businessmen wrote Black supporting 30 hours; in the early part of 1933, more businessmen were in favor than opposed, if Black's mail is any indication. See, for example, F. Berlinger to H. Black, April 8, 1933; S. Harwood, president of Prodiscon Products, to H. Black, April 20, 1933; H. J. Hubert, president of the Cloquet Commercial Club, Cloquet, Minn., to H. Black, January 10, 1933; M. Goldsmith, president of Armstrong Paint and Varnish Works, to H. Black, December 22, 1932, and January 11, 1933; telegram, G. Hormel, chairman of George Hormel & Company, to H. Black, April 5, 1933, and April 8, 1933; G. Hormel to H. Black, April 17, 1933, and attached letter, H. Black to G. Hormel, undated; all in Black Papers.

Many newspaper editors supported the Black bill, some of whom wrote to Black, sending him their editorials in favor of the bill. See, for example, W. H. Hendrix, editor of the *Wisconsin News*, to H. Black, May 16, 1933. According to Hendrix, all the Hearst papers "have been exceedingly friendly" to the 30-hour bills. See also H. B. Du Bose, publisher of the Birmingham *Daily Mirror*, to H. Black, March 16, 1933, Black Papers.

4. For Filene quote, see *New York Times*, March 23, 1933, p. 33; for Langmuir's plan, see *New York Times*, March 30, 1933, p. 15, and April 2, 1933, sec. 4, p. 4. See also *New York Times*, January 1, 1933, sec. 7, p. 3, and January 6, 1933, p. 18.

5. *New York Times*, April 20, 1933, p. 5.

6. Ibid.

7. See the following issues: *New York Times*, April 21, 1933, p. 8; April 26, 1933, p. 5; April 30, 1933, p. 1.

8. H. G. Moulton, "In Defense of the Longer Work Week," *Annals of the American Academy* 184 (March 1936): 64; H. G. Moulton and M. Leven, "The Thirty-Hour Week," *Scientific Monthly* 40 (March 1935): 257.

9. A. Sachs, "The National Recovery Administration Policies and the Problem of Economic Planning," in *America's Recovery Program*, ed. C. Wilcox, H. Fraser, and P. M. Malin (New York, 1934), p. 107; D. R. Richberg, *My Hero; The Indiscreet Memoirs of an Eventful but Unheroic Life* (New York, 1954), pp. 163–167.

10. R. G. Tugwell, *The Battle for Democracy* (New York, 1935), p. 265.

11. Moley, *After Seven Years*, pp. 186–187.

12. *New York Times*, April 14, 1933, p. 1. See also *New York Times*, April 16, 1933, sec. 4, p. 4, and April 29, 1933, p. 1. For Moley's recollections of the Stark report, see Moley, *After Seven Years*, p. 187.

13. *New York Times*, April 15, 1933, p. 1. See also *New York Times*, April 19, 1933, p. 1.

14. Ibid.

15. *New York Times*, April 20, 1933, p. 5, and April 29, 1933, p. 25.

16. Moley, *After Seven Years*, p. 190. See also the following issues: *New York Times*, April 26, 1933, p. 5; April 19, 1933, p. 2; April 29, 1933, p. 1; April 30, 1933, p. 1.

17. *New York Times*, April 19, 1933, p. 2. For quote, see *New York Times*, April 26, 1933, p. 5. See also U.S. Congress, House, Committee on Labor, *Thirty-Hour Week Bill; Hearings on S. 153 and H.R. 4557*, 73rd Cong., 1st sess., April 25–28, May 1–5, 1933, pp. 1–24, et passim. Black was much more flexi-

ble in his approach than was Connery or the House Labor Committee. Black was willing to compromise and accommodate a wide range of circumstances. See H. Black to L. T. McFadden, April 14, 1933, Black Papers.

18. *New York Times*, April 28, 1933, p. 14.

19. W. Green to H. Black, April 4, 1933, Black Papers; "The Labor Army Takes the Field: A Shorter Work Week to Make Jobs," *Literary Digest* 115 (April 15, 1933): 6.

20. *New York Times*, April 19, 1933, p. 2.

21. *New York Times*, May 2, 1933, p. 1. For the Connery "rebuke," see May 3, 1933, p. 2.

22. *New York Times*, May 3, 1933, p. 2.

23. *New York Times*, May 3, 1933, p. 2.

24. See the following issues: *New York Times*, May 10, 1933, p. 2; May 11, 1933, p. 3; May 12, 1933, p. 1. See also "Labor: Thirty-Hour Week Bill Is Hotly Debated by Congress," *Newsweek* 1 (May 13, 1933): 7. For Black's thoughts about the NIRA as a substitute for his bill, see H. Black to M. L. Cobb, May 17, 1933, Black Papers. Black wrote: "It seems now that my 30 hour bill has been stopped. . . . The President had indicated that he was going to send a message asking for some kind of substitute." See also H. Black to J. C. de Hall, May 19, 1933, Black Papers. Black wrote: "It looks now as if the president's general bill for industrial control, public works, and other purposes will be used as a substitute for my six hour day bill. While I have not had an opportunity of giving this bill . . . through study, I am exceedingly hopeful that the purposes desired may be accomplished." See also H. Black to W. H. Hendrix, May 20, 1933, Black Papers. Black wrote: "You have noticed of course that on account of the sentiment created, the manufacturers and the chamber of commerce saw that something was going through. The president has set up a substitute bill, known as the Control of Industry [*sic*]. I sincerely trust that it may work in such a way as to bring about shorter hours."

25. *New York Times*, May 3, 1933, p. 2, for Green's quote. See also *New York Times*, June 25, 1933, sec. 25, p. 1.

26. *New York Times*, April 28, 1933, p. 14.

27. *New York Times*, May 21, 1933, p. 3, for Harriman quote. See also A. M. Schlesinger, Jr., *The Age of Roosevelt*, vol. 2, *The Coming of the New Deal* (Cambridge, Mass., 1959), pp. 95–98. A. S. Link, *The American Epoch*, (New York, 1963), p. 391.

28. S. I. Rosenman, comp., *The Public Papers and Addresses of Franklin D. Roosevelt*, 5 vols., vol. 2, *The Year of Crisis, 1933* (New York, 1938), p. 202.

29. *New York Times*, June 17, 1933, pp. 1, 2. See also D. R. Richberg, *The Rainbow* (Garden City, N.Y., 1936), pp. 45–54.

30. Rosenman, *Public Papers of FDR*, 2:202.

31. Ibid., pp. 205–206.

32. Ibid. See also Richberg, *Rainbow*, pp. 106–114; F. Perkins, *The Roosevelt I Knew* (New York, 1946), pp. 208–211.

33. Rosenman, *The Public Papers of FDR* 2:246–256; italics added.

34. Ibid., p. 252.

35. Ibid., p. 255.

36. "Chief Features of Major Codes Sent to NIRA in Week Ended July 17," *Newsweek* 1 (July 22, 1933): 23.

37. *Time* 22 (July 24, 1933): 14.

38. *New York Times*, July 15, 1933, p. 5, and July 17, 1933, p. 12. See also "A.F. of L. Opens War for Its 30-Hour Week," *Newsweek* 1 (July 22, 1933): 6.

39. *New York Times*, July 15, 1933, p. 5.

40. *Newsweek* 1 (July 29, 1933): 5. See also Richberg, *Rainbow*, pp. 150–178.

41. H. S. Johnson, *The Blue Eagle from Egg to Earth* (Garden City, N.Y., 1935), pp. 250–276, 439–443.

42. Coincident with the renewal of interest in shorter hours in the administration, the winter of 1933–1934 was the high-water mark in public interest in work reductions. Numerous articles were published about the "new leisure." Administrators of the NRA in New York City called a conference on the wise use of leisure that received national coverage. See "Time for Play," *Collier's*, April 12, 1933, pp. 62, 50; "National Organizations Emphasizing Leisure," *Library Journal* 58 (May 15, 1933): 446; "Nova Et Vetera: The Art of Leisure," *Catholic World* 138 (November 1933): 225; "Organizing Leisure," *Survey* 69 (December 1933): 405; "The New Leisure," *Nation* 137 (November 29, 1933): 3569; "The New Leisure, Its Significance and Use: Forward Looking Men and Women Express Aspects of National Problem and Suggest Ways Out," *Library Journal* 58 (May 15, 1933): 444; "Thirteen Million Hours to While Away," *Literary Digest* 116 (August 26, 1933): 18; E. E. Calkins, "The New Leisure: A Curse or a Blessing?" *Economic Forum* 1 (May 1933): 371–382; G. B. Cutten, *Challenge of Leisure* (Columbus, Ohio, 1933); E. E. Hoyt, "The Challenge of the New Leisure," *Journal of Home Economics*, October 1933, p. 688; G. Turner, "The New Leisure of the New Deal," *Catholic World* 138 (November 1933): 168; R. S. Wallace, "Leisure of the Workless," *Spectator* 150 (June 1933): 635; G. B. Watson, "Families, Education, and the Use of Leisure in the Present Crisis," *Journal of Home Economics* 25 (December 1933): 831; "In the Driftway," *Nation* 138 (January 17, 1934): 73; "Satan Still Finds Work," *Nation* 138 (June 13, 1934): 663; A. Corry, "Leisure and Culture," *Commonweal* 19 (January 12, 1934): 291; H. J. Hobbs, "51 Hours a Week," *Better Homes and Gardens* 12 (January 1934): 24; National Recovery Administration, *Report of the New York Committee on the Use of Leisure Time* (New York, 1934); J. F. Steiner, "Challenge of the New Leisure," *Recreation* 27 (January 1934): 517–522; M. C. Taylor, "The Key to Hidden Mysteries: An Essay on Leisure," *Golden Book* 19 (January 1934): 21; G. B. Watson, "Educator Looks at Work and Leisure," *Recreation* 27 (February 1934): 501–502; P. T. Frankl, *Machine-made Leisure* (New York and London, 1932), pp. 169–178, et passim; A. N. Pack, *The Challenge of Leisure* (New York, 1934); L. Mumford, *Techniques and Civilization* (New York, 1934), pp. 279, 379; M. B. Greenbie, *The Arts of Leisure* (New York and London, 1935); G. Hambidge, *Time to Live: Adventures in the Use of Leisure* (New York and London, 1933); H. A. Overstreet, *A Guide to Civilized Loafing* (New York, 1934), pp. 9–13 and "The Ways of Leisure," pt. 1; "New Jersey Seeks Answer to the Leisure-Time Problem," *American City* 48 (November 1933): 67.

See especially the winter 1933–1934 issues of *Recreation* and the articles by H. Braucher, J. Finley, J. Lee, and reprints from newspapers around the country that responded to the news that the New York WPA division was investigating the problem of the new leisure.

The first historian who recognized the fact that interest in the new leisure was a characteristic of the early depression was F. R. Dulles, *America Learns to Play: A History of Popular Recreation 1607–1940* (New York and London, 1940), pp. 365–373. Dulles accounted for the phenomenon by "the revolutionary transformations wrought by the machine," which no longer "could be ignored." The machine had "not only made leisure possible for the mass of the people, but had imposed it upon them whether they wanted it or not. Boon or Pandora's box of new evils, there could be no escaping it." The depression "dramatized the situation (of inevitable work reduction) as never before"; hence the rise of the new leisure phenomenon.

43. *Time* 22 (August 7, 1933): 12.

44. C. F. Roos, NRA *Economic Planning* (Bloomington, Ind., 1937), pp. 101–153.

45. Ibid.; *New York Times*, February 5, 1934, p. 1. See also the following issues: *New York Times*, October 16, 1933, p. 14; November 18, 1933, p. 17; November 22, 1933, p. 20; April 30, 1934, p. 14.

46. Roos, NRA *Economic Planning*, pp. 101–153, 32; L. C. Marshall, *Hours and Wages Provisions in NRA Codes; A Compilation* (Washington, D.C., 1935), pp. 32–73. See also *Monthly Labor Review* 44 (January 1937): 13–36; U.S. Bureau of Labor Statistics, *Bulletin 616*, pp. 1062–1070.

47. *New York Times*, September 29, 1933, p. 1.

48. See the following issues: *New York Times*, September 10, 1933, sec. 4, p. 4; September 17, 1933, sec. 4, p. 4; September 28, 1933, p. 10; September 29, p. 1 (for quotes); September 30, 1933, p. 4.

49. *New York Times*, October 4, 1933, p. 4, and October 12, 1933, p. 2.

50. See the following issues: *New York Times*, January 7, 1934, p. 29; January 11, 1934, p. 2; January 25, 1934, p. 2.

51. See the following issues: *New York Times*, January 11, 1934; January 18, 1934, pp. 12, 13; January 24, 1934, p. 11; January 25, 1934, p. 5; February 1, 1934, p. 20. See also U.S. Congress, House, Committee on Labor, *Thirty-Hour Week Bill; Hearings on H.R. 7202, H.R. 4116, H.R. 8492*, 73rd Cong., 2nd sess., February 8, 9, 15, 16, 19–21, 23, 1934.

52. *New York Times*, February 10, 1934, p. 12.

53. *New York Times*, February 17, 1934, p. 16.

54. *New York Times*, February 21, 1934, p. 11.

55. U.S. Congress, House, Committee on Labor, *Thirty-Hour Week Bill; Hearings on H.R. 7202, H.R. 4116, H.R. 8492*, pp. 232–245, 280–309, 116–151. Through 1934, Perkins maintained that shorter hours were "necessary for economic balance," although, at the same time, she promoted expansion in employment. See F. Perkins, *People at Work* (New York, 1934), pp. 202–267, quote on p. 241.

56. *New York Times*, February 22, 1934, p. 10.

57. J. G. Frederick, *A Primer of "New Deal" Economics* (New York, 1933), pp. 209–214, 310–315.

58. *New York Times*, August 2, 1934, sec. 2, p. 15. See also the following issues: *New York Times*, March 6, 1934, p. 3; March 7, 1934, p. 1; April 27, 1934, p. 7.

59. *New York Times*, February 5, 1934, p. 1, for McNeir quote.

60. *New York Times*, June 20, 1934, p. 2. See also the following issues: *New York Times*, May 1, 1934, p. 1; May 15, 1934, p. 4; April 16, 1934, p. 6; June 2, 1934, p. 5; July 8, 1934, p. 13; August 26, 1934, sec. 2, p. 15. For labor pressure for 30 hours, see the following issues: *New York Times* September, 1934, p. 6; September 29, 1934, p. 5; October 9, 1934, p. 1. Green, as he did throughout the depression, used the threat of strikes for Connery's 1934 bill; see *New York Times*, June 2, 1934, p. 5.

61. *New York Times*, August 26, 1934, sec. 2, p. 15.

62. *New York Times*, September 26, 1934, and October 14, 1934, p. 18; "Cotton Garment Battle," *Business Week*, December 15, 1934, p. 19.

63. *New York Times*, September 8, 1934, p. 6.

64. *New York Times*, October 9, 1934, p. 1, for quote. See also the following issues: *New York Times*, October 10, 1934, p. 22; October 28, 1934, sec. 8, p. 1; September 4, 1934, p. 6.

65. *New York Times*, October 14, 1934, p. 18.

66. Thinking about shorter hours in the NRA after Johnson's departure was summed up by NRA Director Roos in his book, *NRA Economic Planning*, pp. 122–153; W. P. Mangold, "On the Labor Front: Before and After the Cotton Garment Code—Tempting Employers—The Musicians End a Dictatorship," *New Republic* 81 (January 16, 1935): 276–277; Schlesinger, *Coming of the New Deal*, pp. 159–161.

67. M. Ezekiel, *Jobs for All* (New York, 1939), pp. 186, 187. See also D. Brown, "Helping Labor," in *The Economics of the Recovery Program* (Freeport, N.Y., 1934; reprinted 1968), pp. 69–89.

68. Ezekiel, *Jobs for All*, pp. 218, 219.

69. Ibid., p. 224.

70. Ibid., p. 219, for quote; see also pp. 211–224. See also Schlesinger, *Coming of the New Deal*, pp. 217–222.

71. *New York Times*, October 14, 1934, sec. 4, p. 1.

72. Ibid.

73. *New York Times*, November 22, 1943, p. 20, for Krock quote. See also *New York Times*, October 14, 1943, sec. 4, p. 1; "Washington Notes: Battle of the Session: The 30-Hour Week Bill—Apostle Alfred P. Sloan—Senators on the Spot," *New Republic* 81 (December 16, 1934): 191.

74. Memorandum, F. Frankfurter to FDR, December 28, 1935, in M. Freedman, *Roosevelt and Frankfurter: Their Correspondence 1928–1945* (Boston and Toronto, 1967), pp. 296–297.

75. *New York Times*, November 22, 1934, p. 1.

76. For manufacturing codes, see *New York Times*, November 26, 1934, p. 2. For conference on labor standards, see *New York Times*, December 15, 1934, p. 2. See also *New York Times*, November 23, 1934, p. 18.

77. *New York Times*, December 15, 1934, p. 2. See also *New York Times*, December 13, 1934, p. 14.

78. M. Leven and H. G. Moulton, *America's Capacity to Consume* (Washington, D.C., 1934). The fifth of Leven and Moulton's "fundamental conclusions" was that "we cannot materially shorten the working day and still produce the quantity of goods and services which the American people aspire [*sic*] to consume" (p. 128). See also "Labor's Day," *Business Week*, February 9, 1935, p. 6; "Not Less, But More: Thirty-Hour Week," *Saturday Evening Post* 207 (February 9, 1935): 26; J. T. Flynn, "On the Labor Front," *New Republic* 81 (January 16, 1935): 276. See also Moulton and Leven's ongoing battle to discredit 30 hours in H. G. Moulton and M. Leven, "The Thirty-Hour Week," *Scientific Monthly* 40 (March 1935): 257; H. G. Moulton and M. Leven, *The Thirty-Hour Week* (Washington, D.C., 1935). See also "The Thirty-Hour Week," *Nation* 136 (February 1934): 432; "Wages, Hours—and Recovery," *Business Week*, March 3, 1934, p. 12.

79. *New York Times*, January 4, 1935, p. 15, for quote. See also *New York Times*, January 5, 1935, p. 16, and January 6, 1935, sec. 2, p. 17; H. G. Moulton, "In Defense of the Longer Work Week, *Annals of the American Academy* 184 (March 1936): 64; "Loose Talk on Short Work Week," *Saturday Evening Post* 287 (January 26, 1935): 26; "Thirty Hours Are Not Enough," *Colliers* 95 (February 1935): 54; U.S. Congress, Senate, Committee on Judiciary, *Thirty-Hour Work Week; Hearings on S. 87*, 74th Cong., 1st sess., January 31, February 1, 2, 5–9, 11–16, 1935.

For a negative evaluation similar to Moulton's and the Brookings Institution's, see the National Industrial Conference Board (NICB), *The Thirty-Hour Week* (New York, 1935).

80. *New York Times*, February 3, 1935, p. 18, for quote. See also the following issues: *New York Times*, February 10, 1935, sec. 2, p. 15; February 14, 1935, p. 5; February 16, 1935, p. 2; February 17, 1935, p. 27; February 25, 1935, p. 33; March 4, 1935, p. 2; March 24, 1935, sec. 2, p. 9. See also U.S. Congress, Senate, Committee on Judiciary, *Thirty-Hour Work Week; Hearings on S. 87*; "Politics, Either Way: Thirty-Hour Bill Won't Die Unaided," *Business Week*, February 2, 1935, p. 40.

81. *New York Times*, April 3, 1935, p. 2, for quote. See also the following issues: *New York Times*, April 9, 1935, p. 6; April 13, 1935, p. 14; April 17, 1935, p. 17; N. Carothers, "Would a Thirty-Hour Week Increase Employment? Con," *Congressional Digest* 14 (April 1935): 112; W. Green, "Would a Thirty-Hour Week Increase Employment? Pro," *Congressional Digest* 14 (April 1935): 112.

82. *New York Times*, March 24, 1935, sec. 2, p. 9.

83. *New York Times*, April 5, 1935, p. 3, and April 17, 1935, p. 17, for quotes.

84. *New York Times*, May 2, 1935, p. 22.

85. *New York Times*, May 28, 1935, p. 20, for quote. See also *New York Times*, May 29, 1935, p. 11. Regarding the constitutionality of 30-hour legislation, Black wrote: "My investigation leads me to believe that there is not the slightest constitutional objection on account of the constitutional provision with reference to contracts. The Supreme Court has heretofore passed upon this in a decisive way. . . . It is my belief that the Court would today hold this

bill constitutional. When the hearings have been completed, I shall be glad to send you a copy. They are the most interesting I have ever attended. H. Black to R. B. Chandler of the *Mobil Register*, January 24, 1933, Black Papers. See also H. Black to R. K. Van Zandt, January 11, 1933; H. Black to H. Ayers, editor of the *Anniston Star*, January 27, 1933; J. A. Ryan to H. Black, April 7, 1933; all Black Papers.

86. A. M. Schlesinger, Jr., *Politics of Upheaval*, (Boston, 1960) p. 288.

87. See the following issues: *New York Times*, May 28, 1935, p. 20; May 29, 1935, p. 11; May 30, 1935, pp. 1, 12; June 2, 1935, sec. 2, p. 7.

88. See the following issues: *New York Times*, June 2, 1935, sec. 4, p. 7; June 6, 1935, p. 12 (for quote); June 7, 1935, pp. 1, 16; June 8, 1935, pp. 1, 8; and, especially, June 9, 1935, sec. 4, p. 3.

89. *New York Times*, June 6, 1935, p. 12.

90. *New York Times*, June 15, 1935, p. 1, and June 23, 1935, p. 25; Schlesinger, *Politics of Upheaval*, p. 292.

91. *New York Times*, August 10, 1935, p. 1, and August 13, 1935, pp. 1, 12.

Chapter 7

1. R. Moley, *After Seven Years* (New York and London, 1939), pp. 190–192.

2. A. M. Schlesinger, Jr., *The Coming of the New Deal* (Boston, 1959), pp. 282–296.

3. F. A. Walker, *The Civil Works Administration* (New York, 1979), pp. 31, 39.

4. Schlesinger, *Coming of the New Deal*, pp. 282–296.

5. Ibid., p. 269; R. E. Sherwood, *Roosevelt and Hopkins, An Intimate History*, rev. ed. (New York, 1950), p. 51.

6. See chapter 6. See also Walker, *Civil Works Administration*, p. 18; *New York Times*, January 24, 1934, p. 8.

7. See chapter 6.

8. Schlesinger, *Coming of the New Deal*, p. 227.

9. H. Hopkins, "Federal Emergency Relief," *Vital Speeches* 1 (December 1934): 210–211.

10. *New York Times*, January 5, 1935, p. 2.

11. Ibid.

12. *New York Times*, April 10, 1935, p. 5, and April 18, 1935, p. 1.

13. For J. L. Lewis support of Black–Connery, see *New York Times*, February 3, 1935, p. 3; see also *New York Times*, May 2, 1935, p. 22; H. Millis and R. E. Montgomery, *Organized Labor* (New York, 1945), pp. 201–215; A. M. Schlesinger, Jr., *The Politics of Upheaval* (Cambridge, Mass., 1960), pp. 593, 594.

14. H. Hopkins, "They'd Rather Work," *Collier's* 96 (November 16, 1935), p. 8.

15. Ibid.

16. *New York Times*, August 13, 1935, p. 2, and October 29, 1935, p. 7, col. 5.

17. Schlesinger, *Politics of Upheaval*, p. 349.

18. "How PWA and WPA Projects Differ," *American City* 50 (August 1935): 5; "Facts about Work-Relief; Ickes-Hopkins Dispute," *Business Week*, September 21, 1935, p. 22.

19. H. L. Ickes, "Jobs versus the Dole," *American City* 49 (December 1934): 43.

20. Ibid.

21. Ibid.

22. H. L. Ickes, *Back to Work: The Story of PWA* (New York, 1935), p. 5.

23. *New York Times*, May 12, 1935, sec. 7, p. 1, for quote. See also *New York Times*, January 1, 1935, p. 29, and June 6, 1935, p. 15; Ickes, *Back to Work*, p. 229.

24. *New York Times*, April 23, 1935, p. 17, for Ickes address before the Associated Press luncheon.

25. *New York Times*, May 12, 1935, sec. 7, p. 1.

26. Ibid.

27. Ibid., p. 2.

28. Ibid. See also Ickes, *Back to Work*, pp. 5, 14, 15, 195, 196, 200, 229; "The Cabinet, Helpful Harold," *Time* 26 (December 1935): p. 16; Ickes, "Jobs versus the Dole," p. 43; H. Ickes, "Reading, Ritin' and the Radio," *School and Society* 45 (January 2, 1937): 1–6.

29. *New York Times*, May 17, 1935, p. 2, for quote. See also "Washington Notes," *New Republic* 82 (May 8, 1935): 365; N. Anderson, *The Right to Work* (Westport, Conn., 1938), pp. 41, 93, 105, 106, 125–131.

30. H. L. Hopkins, *Spending to Save: The Complete Story of Relief* (Seattle and London, 1936), pp. 183–184. See also Hopkins, "They'd Rather Work," p. 8.

31. Hopkins, "They'd Rather Work," p. 7.

32. Hopkins, *Spending to Save*, p. 56.

33. U.S. Congress, House, Committee on Labor, *Hearings on H.R. 7202, H.R. 4116, and H.R. 8492*, 73rd Cong., 2nd sess., February 1934, pp. 232–245; *New York Times*, December 19, 1934, p. 21; Hopkins, "They'd Rather Work," pp. 7–10.

34. Hopkins, *Spending to Save*, p. 55; see also *New York Times*, May 17, 1935, p. 2.

35. H. Hopkins, "Employment in America," speech before the Mayor's Conference, Washington, D.C., November 17, 1936, *Vital Speeches* 3 (1936): 103–107; Hopkins, *Spending to Save*, p. 180.

36. H. Hopkins, "Radio Address Given May 8, 1938," *Congressional Digest* 17 (June–July 1938): 177–178.

37. Ibid.

38. "Men at Work," *Time* 32 (July 18, 1938): 9; Hopkins, *Spending to Save*, p. 182; Hopkins, "Employment in America," pp. 103–107; "Mr. Hopkins Puts the Question," *Saturday Evening Post* 210 (July 3, 1937): 22; H. Hopkins, "The Administration's Program for Recovery," *Vital Speeches* 5 (February 24, 1939): p. 335; H. Hopkins, "The WPA Looks Forward," *Survey* 74 (June 1938): 195–198.

39. H. Hopkins and H. Pringle, "How Will They Get through the Winter?" *American Magazine* 118 (December 1934): 16–17.

40. *Congressional Digest*, July 1938, p. 29; Link, *American Epoch*, p. 402.

41. *New York Times*, October 1, 1935, p. 2, for quote. See also the following issues: *New York Times*, April 25, 1935, p. 13; April 18, 1935, p. 1; July 10, 1935, p. 8; July 14, 1935, sec. 4, p. 11.

42. See "Employment Created by Public Works Fund," in *Monthly Labor Review*, December 1933–November 1936: 37: 1512–1521; 38: 207–212, 437–444, 718–725, 968–975, 1232–1239, 1512–1519; 39: 159–167, 478–485, 772–779; 856–860, 1263–1269, 1520–1526; 40: 206–214, 461–469, 792–800, 1049–1057; and, especially, 43: 1150–1152.

43. "America's Vast Synthetic Frontier," *Literary Digest* 118 (August 18, 1934): 9; J. M. Clark, "Cumulative Effects of Changes in Aggregate Spending as Illustrated by Public Works," *American Economic Review* 25 (March 1935): 14–20; S. H. Slichter, "Economics of Public Works," *American Economic Review* 174 (March 1934): 174–185; W. T. Foster, "Planning in a Free Country: Managed Money and Unmanaged Men," *Annals* 162 (July 1932): 49–57; "Public Works the Key to Prosperity and Public Security," *American City* 49 (June 1934): 5; H. M. Olmsted, "Ultimate Economy of Adequate Relief through Public Works," *American City* 49 (September 1934): 86; R. Clapper, "Billions for the Third Economy," *Review of Reviews* 91 (June 1935): 19–22; W. T. Foster, "Bill for Hard Times," *Survey* 25 (April 1936): 200–203; D. C. Coyle, "Financing of Public Works; An Expansionist Point of View," *Annals* 183 (January 1936): 207–211; Recoupment of Public Work Costs," *American City* 52 (March 1937): 5; J. Mitchel, "Jobs for All," *New Republic* 83 (July 10, 1935): 240–242.

44. F. Baerwald, "How Germany Reduced Unemployment," *American Economic Review* 24 (December 1934): 617–630.

45. Link, *American Epoch*, p. 402.

46. Schlesinger, *Politics of Upheaval*, pp. 292–301.

47. Ibid., pp. 292–305; Lippmann quoted by Schlesinger, p. 301.

48. Ibid., p. 301.

49. Ibid., p. 241.

50. *New York Times*, April 18, 1936, p. 21, and May 9, 1936, p. 6; M. S. Eccles, "Monetary Problems of Recovery," *Vital Speeches of the Day* 1 (March 11, 1935): 364–369; S. J. Wolf, "Eccles Would Save Capitalism by Reform," *Literary Digest* 119 (January 5, 1935): 5, 38; "Eccles on Economics," *Time* 33 (January 2, 1939): 9.

51. *New York Times*, March 16, 1937, p. 1, for quote. See also "Federal Reserve: M. S. Eccles, Mormon and Liberal, Succeeds Black as Governor," *Newsweek* 4 (November 17, 1934): 34.

52. *New York Times*, May 31, 1936, secs. 2 and 3, p. 13. For similar views about "idleness reemployed," see R. Tugwell, "How Shall We Pay for All This?" *American Magazine* 116 (December 1933): 11, 13, 87.

53. As pointed out earlier in this chapter, Keynes, with Eccles and Currie, rejected work sharing by 1936. In a revealing passage in *The General*

Theory of Employment (New York, 1936), Keynes remarked on "another school of thought" current in the depression, which "finds the solution of the trade cycle, not in increasing either consumption or investments, but in diminishing the supply of labor seeking employment" (p. 326). He judged this a "premature policy," much less desirable than increased consumption, seeing no reason to "compel" workers to work less. This idea, that increased leisure was an economic disadvantage on its face and not a reasonable contender with more consumption, was new. But it has remained as accepted wisdom. If, as labor had maintained for a century, shorter hours were understood as a form of wealth, freedom, and a basis for progress, Keynesian notions about the advisability of deficit spending, liberal monetary policy, and public works would have been questionable. Creating work was, and remains, an expensive state undertaking. Whether or not it has been more or less costly than additional leisure would have been depends on one's point of view, one's understanding of increased free time as an asset or liability. See also *supra* p. 331, note 93.

54. M. S. Eccles, "Government Spending Is Sound," speech on NBC radio, January 23, 1939, reprinted in *Vital Speeches* 5 (January 23, 1939): 272; Wolf, "Eccles Would Save Capitalism by Reform," p. 5; R. L. Weissman, ed., *The Public Papers of Marriner S. Eccles: Economic Balance and a Balanced Budget* (New York, 1940), pp. 84–85; *New York Times*, March 16, 1937, p. 1; "Federal Reserve: M. S. Eccles Succeeds Black as Governor," p. 34.

55. M. H. Leff, *The Limits of Symbolic Reform: The New Deal and Taxation, 1933–1939* (Cambridge, Mass., 1984), pp. 205–225; *New York Times*, May 15, 1936, p. 6.

56. Eccles, "Government Spending Is Sound," p. 272. See also "Eccles on Economics," *Time* 33 (January 2, 1939): 9.

57. *New York Times*, March 16, 17, 18, 19, 21, 22, 27, 1937; A. E. Burns and D. S. Watson, *Government Spending and Economic Expansion* (Washington, D.C., 1940), pp. 72–86; G. S. Eccles, "What Washington Will Do," in *Pump-Priming Theory of Government Spending*, ed. E. R. Nichols (New York, 1939), pp. 230–342; Schlesinger, *Politics of Upheaval*, p. 334.

58. Eccles, "Government Spending Is Sound," pp. 272–275.

Chapter 8

1. H. S. Pearson, quoted in C. S. Steffler, "A Shorter Work-Week, or a Shorter Work Life?" *Commerce and Finance* 17 (December 1928): 2739–2740.

2. Ibid.

3. Ibid.

4. See the following reports prepared by W. Connery: U.S. Congress, House, Committee on Labor, *Report to Accompany H.R. 8765; To Protect Labor in Its Old Age* (Washington, D.C., 1932); U.S. Congress, House, Committee on Labor, *Report to Accompany H.R. 8641; To Protect Labor in Its Old Age* (Washington, D.C., 1934); U.S. Congress, House, Committee on Labor, *Report to Accompany H.R. 3905; Unemployment Relief* (Washington, D.C., 1933); U.S. Congress, House, Committee on Labor, *Report to Accompany H.R. 2827; Workers' Un-*

employment, Old-Age and Social Insurance (Washington, D.C., 1935). See also U.S. Congress, Senate, Committee on Pensions, *Old Age Pensions; Hearings on S. 3257,* 71st Cong., 3rd sess., February 24, 1931; U.S. Congress, Senate, Committee on Pensions, *Old Age Pensions; Hearings on S. 3037,* 72nd Cong., 1st sess., May 12, 1932; U.S. Congress, House, Committee on Labor, *Old Age Pensions; Hearings on H.R. 1623, H.R. 7050, H.R. 7144, H.R. 7207, H.R. 7556, H.R. 7749, H.R. 7762, H.R. 8350, H.R. 8641, H.R. 9228,* 73rd Cong., 2nd sess., March 1, 2, 7–9, 1934; U.S. Congress, Senate, Committee on Pensions, *Old Age Pensions; Hearings on S. 493,* 73rd Cong., 2nd sess., April 17, 1934; *New York Times,* January 31, 1932, sec. 2, p. 2, and March 27, 1932, p. 18.

5. See the following reports prepared by W. Connery: U.S. Congress, House, Committee on Labor, *Report to Accompany H.R. 4557; To Prevent Interstate Commerce in Industrial Activities in Which Persons Are Employed More Than Five Days a Week or Six Hours a Day* (Washington, D.C., 1933); U.S. Congress, House, Committee on Labor, *Report to Accompany H.R. 14513; To Prevent Interstate Commerce in Industrial Activities in Which Persons Are Employed More Than Five Days a Week or Six Hours a Day* (Washington, D.C., 1933); U.S. Congress, House, Committee on Labor, *Report to Accompany S. 157: Thirty Hour Week Bill* (Washington, D.C., 1933); U.S. Congress, House, Committee on Labor, *Report to Accompany H.R. 8492; Thirty Hour Week for Industry* (Washington, D.C., 1934). See also U.S. Congress, House, *Old Age Pensions: Hearings on H.R. 1623, H.R. 7050, H.R. 7144, H.R. 7207, H.R. 7556, H.R. 7749, H.R. 7762, H.R. 8350, H.R. 8641, H.R. 9228,* March 1, 2, 7–9, 1934; U.S. Congress, House, Committee on Labor, *Report on H.R. 8641, H.R. 998,* 73rd Cong., 2nd sess., March 17, 1934; *New York Times,* March 27, 1932, p. 18.

6. U.S. Congress, Senate, *Old Age Pensions; Hearings on S. 3037,* May 12, 1932; U.S. Congress, Senate, *Old Age Pensions; Hearings on S. 493,* April 17, 1934. As late as December 1934, Black continued to argue the benefits that Social Security would have in helping to reduce unemployment. See H. Black, "Social Security," *Vital Speeches* 1 (January 14, 1935): 249–250. See also U.S. Congress, House, Committee on Labor, *Report 998 on H.R. 8641,* 73rd Cong., 2nd sess., 1934; U.S. Congress, Subcommittee of the Committee on Pensions, *Hearings on S. 3257: A Bill to Encourage and Assist the States in Providing Pensions to the Aged,* report prepared by Thomas Schall, chairman, 71st Cong., 3rd sess., February 24, 1931. The Dill–Connery bills in the 74th Cong., 1st sess., were H.R. 8461 and S. 493.

7. E. E. Witte, *The Development of the Social Security Act: A Memorandum on the History of the Committee on Economic Security and Drafting and Legislative History of the Social Security Act* (Madison, 1962), pp. 49–88, 130, 136n.

8. "Six-Hour-Day to Make Railroad Jobs," *Literary Digest,* 101 (April 20, 1929): 15. See also the following issues: *New York Times,* October 22, 1930, p. 20; October 23, 1930, p. 22; November 13, 1930, p. 12; November 14, 1930, p. 6; November 15, 1930, p. 4; November 16, 1930, p. 28.

9. W. F. McCaleb, *Brotherhood of Railroad Trainmen: With Special Reference to the Life of Alexander F. Whitney* (New York, 1936), pp. 125, 210–212. For an analysis of the seniority system in the railroads, see J. Seodman, *The Brotherhood of Railroad Trainmen* (New York, 1962), pp. 6–11, 35–37.

10. *New York Times*, November 22, 1930, p. 4, and November 23, 1930, p. 1.

11. *New York Times*, November 15, 1930, p. 4.

12. See the following issues: *New York Times*, November 23, 1930, p. 1; December 4, 1930, p. 4; December 16, 1930, p. 3; December 20, 1930, p. 12.

13. W. Graebner, *A History of Retirement: The Meaning and Function of an American Institution* (New Haven, 1980), pp. 170–180. See also W. Graebner, "From Pensions to Social Security: Social Insurance and the Rise of Dependency," in *The Quest for Security: Papers on the Origins and the Future of the American Social Insurance System*, ed. J. N. Schacht (Iowa City, 1982), pp. 35–84; unpublished letter to the author from J. Schacht, University of Iowa, January 18, 1985.

14. McCaleb, *Brotherhood*, p. 207.

15. Graebner, *History of Retirement*, pp. 177–178.

16. *New York Times*, September 27, 1931, p. 1. See also *New York Times*, October 10, 1931, p. 5, and November 22, 1931, p. 21. For employers' intransigence, see *New York Times*, July 28, 1931, p. 30.

17. S. H. Cady, "Railroad Pensions—A Suggested Plan," *Railway Age* 89 (November 15, 1930): 1039–1041; H. E. Jackson, "The Railroad Pension Problem," *Railway Age* 89 (December 6, 1930): 1227–1232. See also the following issues: *New York Times*, January 14, 1932, p. 34; January 19, 1932, p. 7; January 21, 1932, p. 3; January 28, 1932, p. 2; January 29, 1932, p. 1; January 31, 1932, p. 1. And see: *Chicago Tribune*, January 18, 1932, p. 1; January 20, 1932, p. 6; January 22, 1932, p. 1; January 23, 1932, p. 1. For Robertson's transparent denial that the Brotherhoods were divided between work sharing as retirement or as the 6-hour day, see *New York Times* November 20, 1931, p. 19.

18. See the following issues: *New York Times*, January 23, 1932, p. 3; January 31, 1932, p. 1; February 1, 1932, p. 10; March 3, 1932, p. 2. And see: *Chicago Tribune*, December 1, 1932, p. 26; January 24, 1932, p. 3; January 25, 1932, p. 1; January 27, 1932, p. 3; February 1, 1932, p. 1.

19. Graebner, *History of Retirement*, pp. 159–180. For Filbert quote, see *New York Times*, May 9, 1932, p. 16. See also the following issues: *New York Times*, March 6, 1932, p. 2; March 16, 1932, p. 27; May 9, 1932, p. 16; May 12, 1932, p. 30.

20. See *New York Times*, May 25, 1932, p. 13, for Whitney quote. See also the following issues: *New York Times*, July 10, 1932, p. 3; August 3, 1932, p. 23; September 21, 1932, p. 6.

21. Graebner, *History of Retirement*, pp. 156–167, quote on p. 167; U.S. Congress, Senate, Committee on Interstate Commerce, Senate Subcommittee on S. 3892 and S. 4646, *Pensions and Retirements for Employees of Interstate Railroads; Hearings on S. 3892 and S. 4646*, 72nd Cong., 2nd sess., January 11–13, 16–19, 1933, pp. 36–40; U.S. Congress, Senate, Committee on Interstate Commerce, *Retirement Pensions System for Railroad Employees; Hearings on S. 3231*, 73rd Cong., 2nd sess., April 23–26, 1934, pp. 15–17; U.S. Congress, House, Committee on Interstate and Foreign Commerce, *Railroad Employees*

Retirement System; Hearings on H.R. 9596, 73rd Cong., 2nd sess., June 8, 1934, p. 33; *New York Times*, March 3, 1932, p. 2, and May 9, 1932, p. 16.

22. Black's thoughts about the 6-hour railroad bill may be found in H. Black to O. H. Williams, December 23, 1932, Black Papers. See also E. Harris, "Black of Alabama," *Railway Age* 103 (July 31, 1937): 127; Brotherhood of Railroad Trainmen, *Shorter Workday: A Plea in the Public Interest* (Cleveland, 1937), pp. 7, 21, 27–28, 46–48, 53; *BLFE Magazine* 98 (May 1935): 264; *Railway Conductor* 52 (March 1935): 87–88; U.S. Congress, Senate, Committee on Interstate Commerce, Senate Subcommittee on Certain Railroad Labor Legislation, *To Limit Hours of Service for Employees of Carriers Engaged in Interstate and Foreign Commerce; Hearings on S. 1562*, 74th Cong., 1st sess., June 27 and July 3, 8, 1935; "Report on Proposed Six-Hour Day for Railroad Employees," *Monthly Labor Review* 26 (February 1933): 367–369.

23. See *New York Times*, February 16, 1933, p. 21, for Whitney quote. See also U.S. Congress, Senate, Committee on Interstate Commerce, *Six-Hour Day for Employees of Carriers Engaged in Interstate and Foreign Commerce; Hearings on S. 7430 and S. 2519*, 73rd Cong., 2nd sess., March 1, 2, 6, 7, 1934; U.S. Congress, House, Committee on Interstate and Foreign Commerce, *Six-Hour Day for Interstate Carriers; Hearings on H.R. 7430*, 73rd Cong., 2nd sess., March 27–30, 1934; *New York Times*, May 29, 1933, p. 22, and December 14, 1932, p. 3.

Letters from engineers and conductors to H. Black were uniformly in opposition to his and Crosser's 6-hour rail bills, S. 1181 and H. 4597, in early 1933. See, for example, the following, all from Black Papers: A. H. Bourne, general chairman of Brotherhood of Locomotive Engineers, Boston and Albany Railroad, to H. Black, May 9, 1933; P. S. Waite, secretary of Massachusetts Brotherhood of Locomotive Engineers, to H. Black, May 10, 1933; E. A. Lilley, chairman of the New York Brotherhood of Locomotive Engineers, to H. Black, May 11, 1933; T. Gudgel, chairman of the B&O Brotherhood of Railroad Engineers, to H. Black, May 9, 1933; T. T. Beal, general chairman, Brotherhood of Locomotive Engineers, to H. Black, May 9, 1933. In contrast, letters from the porters, dispatchers, and trainmen were supportive. See, for example, the following, all from Black Papers: A. T. Totten, national secretary–treasurer, Brotherhood of Sleeping Car Porters, April 7, 1933; E. B. Curtiss to H. Black, February 1, 1933; J. Thompson to H. Black, May 5, 1933; O. F. Williams, Alabama state legislative representative for the Brotherhood of Railroad Trainmen, to H. Black, December 17, 1932.

24. See *New York Times*, March 6, 1934, p. 3, for Connery's observations. Connery introduced bills for both retirement and 30 hours in the 73rd Congress. See U.S. Congress, House, Committee on Labor, *Report 998* (retirement) and *Report 889* (30 hours). See also U.S. Congress, House, Committee on Labor, *Thirty-Hour Week Bill; Hearings on H.R. 7202, H.R. 4116, H.R. 8492*, 73rd Cong., 2nd sess., February 8, 9, 15, 16, 19–21, 23, 1934; *New York Times*, April 24, 1934, p. 33.

25. For the movement to discharge Crosser's 30-hour rail bills, see the following issues: *New York Times*, April 23, 1934, p. 4; April 25, 1934, p. 8;

April 26, 1934, p. 6; April 28, 1934, p. 8. To follow Crosser's bill's progress, see *New York Times*, May 12, 1934, p. 2 and May 25, 1934, p. 38. For the petition to force a House vote on Connery's 30-hour bill for the NRA codes, see *New York Times*, May 15, 1934, p. 11. See also *Congressional Record*, 73rd Cong., 2nd sess., 1934, pp. 8772–8874, 8890–8893, 9165–9170, 9887–9895; U.S. Congress, House, Committee on Labor, *Report 1763*, 73rd Cong., 2nd sess., May 24, 1934; U.S. Congress, House, *Report 8492*, 73rd Cong., 2nd sess., March 7, 1934; U.S. Congress, House *Resolution 295*, 73rd Cong., 2nd sess. For FDR's announced opposition to Connery's bill, see *New York Times*, April 16, 1934, p. 6. See also *New York Times*, March 3, 1934, p. 6, for Black's railroad hours bill in the Senate.

26. Witte, *Development of Social Security*, pp. 5–10; U.S. Congress, House, *Report 1623*, 73rd Cong., 2nd sess., pp. 204–210; U.S. Congress, House, *Report 1633*, 73rd Cong., 2nd sess., p. 253.

27. W. J. Cohen, *Retirement Policies under Social Security: A Legislative History of Retirement Ages, the Retirement Test and Disability Benefits* (Berkeley, 1957), pp. 17–19, quote on p. 18. See also U.S. Congress, House, *Report 998 on H.R. 8641*. See also U.S. Congress, House, *Hearings on H.R. 1623, H.R. 7050, H.R. 7144, H.R. 7207, H.R. 7556, H.R. 7749, H.R. 7762, H.R. 8350, H.R. 8641, H.R. 9228*. In Advisory Committee on Railroad Employment, *Report*, Box 47, see the file on *Advisory Committee on Railroad Employment; Report of the Committee*, Otso Beyer Papers, Library of Congress, Washington, D.C. See also U.S. Congress, Senate, Committee on Interstate Commerce, Subcommittee, *Retirement Pension System for Railroad Employees: Hearings on S. 3231, a Bill to Provide a Retirement System for Railroad Employees, to Provide Unemployment Relief, and for Other Purposes*, 73rd Cong., 2nd sess., April 23–26, 1934, pp. 154–155, 159–62; *New York Times*, June 21, 1934, p. 35; *Railway Age* 96 (June 23, 1934): 907; G. Martin, *Madam Secretary: Frances Perkins* (Boston, 1976), chaps. 21, 26; Graebner, *History of Retirement*, chap. 6; and Schacht, *Quest for Security*, p. 24.

28. U.S. Congress, Senate, *Report 1166*, 73rd Cong., 2nd sess., pp. 9554. See also the following issues: *New York Times*, June 13, 1934, p. 1; June 14, 1934, p. 1; June 16, 1934, p. 7; June 18, 1934, p. 1; June 19, 1934, pp. 1, 2. See also *Washington Post*, June 22, 1934, pp. 1, 2.

29. See the following issues: *New York Times*, June 15, 1934, p. 21; June 16, 1934, p. 1; July 1, 1934, p. 1; July 2, 1934, p. 16.

30. *New York Times*, July 1, 1934, p. 21.

31. U.S. Congress, House, *Report 1763*, 73rd Cong., 2nd sess., May 24, 1934; see especially Crosser's *Minority Report* to H.R. 1763. See also *New York Times*, April 16, 1934, p. 6, and May 15, 1934, p. 4. For Green's pressure on FDR and threats to strike see, *New York Times* May 1, 1934, p. 1, and June 2, 1934, p. 5.

32. E. E. Pugsley, "Unemployment or Age Insurance—Which?" *Railway Conductor* 52 (February 1935): 43; McCaleb, *Brotherhood*, p. 207; *Signalman's Journal* 15 (June 1934): 124, 127; "Railroad Retirement Pension Act of 1934," *Yale Law Journal* 44 (December 1934): 301–303.

33. Witte, *Development of Social Security*, pp. 5, 7, 165.

34. See the following issues in 1934: *New York Times*, August 11, p. 18; August 12, sec. 2, p. 7; October 11, p. 19; October 25, pp. 1, 41; December 19, p. 31. For the Court's ruling, see *New York Times*, May 7, 1935, p. 1. For the Brotherhoods' renewed 6-hour-day drive, see *New York Times*, January 11, 1935, p. 27; January 13, 1935, p. 27; for quote, see *New York Times*, February 8, 1935, p. 6. For the minor 6-hour-day flare-ups after 1935, see *New York Times*, June 19, 1936, p. 15, and December 30, 1936, p. 29.

35. Graebner, *History of Retirement*, pp. 159–162; E. Harris, "Black of Alabama in Dramatic Drive for 30-Hour Week," *Railway Conductor* 50 (March 1933): 67–68; Brotherhood of Railroad Trainmen, *Shorter Workday*, pp. 7, 21, 27–28, 46–48, 53; *BLFE Magazine*, May 1935, p. 264; *Railway Conductor*, March 1935, pp. 87–88; U.S. Congress, Senate, *To Limit Hours of Service for Employees of Carriers Engaged in Interstate and Foreign Commerce; Hearings on S. 1562*, June 27, July 3, 8, 1935; U.S. Congress, Senate, Committee on Interstate Commerce, Subcommittee on S. 3151, *Retirement System for Employees of Carriers; Hearings on S. 3150, S. 3151, H.R. 8651, H.R. 865, H.R. 7260*, 74th Cong., 1st sess., July 11, 15, 22, 1935; U.S. Congress, House, Committee on Interstate and Foreign Commerce, *Retirement System for Interstate Carriers Employees; Hearings on H.R. 8651*, 74th Cong., 1st sess., August 13, 1935.

36. A. J. Altmeyer, *The Formative Years of Social Security* (Madison, 1966), pp. 39–40.

37. Graebner, "From Pensions to Social Security," pp. 35–84; Graebner, *History of Retirement*, pp. 186–189. Graebner claims that the printed records of the House and Senate hearings on Social Security were "sufficient to support" his revisionist account of the origins of Social Security (ibid., p. 272). The standard historical interpretation, focusing on the security and welfare aspects of Social Security, may be found in A. M. Schlesinger, Jr., *The Age of Roosevelt*, vol. 2, *The Coming of the New Deal* (Cambridge, Mass., 1958), p. 315; W. Leuchtenburg, *Franklin D. Roosevelt and the New Deal: 1932–1940* (New York, 1963), pp. 132–133, 331, 340; J. M. Burns, *Roosevelt: The Lion and the Fox* (New York, 1956), pp. 267, 268; D. Perkins, *The New Age of Franklin Roosevelt: 1932–1945* (Chicago, 1957), pp. 32–33; J. J. Huthmacher, *Senator Robert F. Wagner and the Rise of Urban Liberalism* (New York, 1971), p. 344; C. A. Chambers, *Seedtime of Reform: American Social Service and Social Action, 1918–1933* (Minneapolis, 1963), pp. 181–182, 257, 267; W. A. Achenbaum, *Old Age in the New Land: The American Experience Since 1790* (Baltimore, 1978), pp. 137, 141.

38. Cohen, quoted in Graebner, "From Pensions to Social Security," p. 25.

39. Brown, quoted in ibid., p. 26.

40. Armstrong, quoted in ibid.

41. N. Shock, ed., *Problems of Aging: Transactions of the Fourteenth Conference* (Caldwell, N.J., 1952), pp. 86–87; S. Barkin, "Economic Difficulties of Older Persons," *Personnel Journal* 11 (April 1933): 400; A. Epstein, "The Older Workers," *Annals of the American Academy of Political and Social Science* 154 (March 1931): 31; Altmeyer, *Formative Years of Social Security*, pp. 40, 42; Witte, *Development of Social Security Act*, pp. 100–102, 150; Graebner, *History of Retirement*, pp. 185–186; T. H. Greer, *What Roosevelt Thought: The Social and*

Political Ideas of Franklin D. Roosevelt (East Lansing, 1958), pp. 46–51; L. I. Dublin, "Population Changes and Consumption: A Forecast for Our Industrial Future," *Bulletin of the Taylor Society* 17 (October 1932): 16.

42. See chap. 7.

43. Witte, *Development of Social Security*, pp. 31–38, 64. The CES held formal meetings August 13, October 1, November 9, 16, 27, December 4, 7, 18, 19, 26, January 7, February 15, and March 15. The longest and most important meetings were held December 22 and 23.

44. Ibid., p. 31.

45. Ibid., p. 77; *New York Times*, November 25, 1934, p. 2.

46. Graebner, *History of Retirement*, pp. 185–189; Graebner, "From Pensions to Social Security," p. 27; Witte *Development of Social Security*, p. 28n. See also discussion on pp. 232–235 on the Deane plan.

47. W. J. Cohen, *Retirement Policies under Social Security: A Legislative History of Retirement Ages, the Retirement Test and Disability Benefits* (Berkeley, 1957), pp. 17–19, quote on p. 17.

48. Ibid., p. 18.

49. Ibid., p. 19. Cohen's statement here casts some doubts on Graebner's revisionist account.

50. Ibid., pp. 3, 18, 19, 69–70, and chap. 5.

51. Committee on Economic Security, *Report to the President of the Committee on Economic Security* (Washington, D.C., 1935), p. 3.

52. Ibid., p. 50. The committee concluded that "in placing primary emphasis on employment rather than unemployment compensation, we differ fundamentally from those who see social security as an all-sufficient program" (pp. 49–50).

53. Ibid., pp. 47, 48.

54. Ibid., p. 3.

55. Ibid., pp. 4–10. See also Committee on Economic Security, *Social Security in America: The Factual Background of the Social Security Act as Summarized from Staff Reports to the Committee on Economic Security* (Washington, D.C., 1937), pp. 137–142, chap. 7, et passim.

56. Witte, *Development of Social Security*, p. 79; Witte states that Eliot placed the old age title first because he felt it was the more popular one. See also *New York Times*, January 16, 1935, p. 2, and January 18, 1935, pp. 1, 16, 17, 22.

57. Representatives in the House who wanted to present the bill included Lewis, Ellenbogen, Connery, and Keller. In a conference with FDR and Perkins, Democratic leaders from both houses (Speaker James F. Byrnes, Chairman Doughton of Ways and Means, Representative Lewis, and Senators Wagner, Harrison, and Van Nuys) heard Roosevelt suggest that the bill be introduced in the House by the same members who had offered the bill (i.e., Dill–Connery) in the preceding session. Byrnes told FDR that this was not acceptable to Doughton. Doughton and Lewis then introduced the bill to the House. Witte, *Development of Social Security*, pp. 79, 80; *New York Times*, January 8, 1935, p. 27, and January 12, 1935, p. 1; U.S. Congress, Senate Committee on Finance, *Economic Security Act; Hearings on H.R. 4142, H.R. 4120, H.R. 2827, S. 1130*, 74th Cong., 1st sess., January 22, 24, 25, 28, 30, 31, February

1, 2, 4–9, 11–16, 18–20, 1935, pp. 1138–1140; U.S. Congress, House, Committee on Ways and Means, *Economic Security Act; Hearings on H.R. 3977, H.R. 4142, H.R. 2827, H.R. 4120, H.R. 7120, S. 1130,* 74th Cong., 1st sess., January 21–26, 28–31, February 1, 2, 4–8, 12, 1935.

58. U.S. Congress, House, Committee on Labor, *Unemployment, Old Age and Social Insurance; Hearings on H.R. 2827, H.R. 2859, H.R. 185, H.R. 10,* 74th Cong., 1st sess., February 4–8, 11–15, 1935; *New York Times,* January 12, 1935, p. 1; Witte, *Development of Social Security,* p. 80.

59. *New York Times,* March 16, 1932. Also see A. L. Deane, general president of General Motors Holding Company, testimony concerning the 30-hour bill, in U.S. Congress, House, Committee on Labor, *Thirty-Hour Week Bill; Hearings on H.R. 7202; H.R. 4116, H.R. 8492,* 73rd Congress, 2nd sess., February 8, 9, 15, 16, 19–21, 23, 1934, p. 31.

60. *Congressional Record,* 74th Cong., 1st sess., 1935, vol. 79, pt. 6, quote on p. 6057; see also pp. 6058–6059. See also the following issues: *New York Times* July 5, 1933; July 13, 1934, p. 18; September 30, 1934, p. 30; October 10, 1934, p. 10. Also see Witte, *Development of Social Security,* p. 28; U.S. Congress, House, Ways and Means Committee, *Report 1620,* 73rd Cong., 2nd sess., 1934.

61. A. L. Deane and H. K. Norton, *Investing in Wages; A Plan for Eliminating the Lean Years* (New York, 1932), pp. 68–104, quote on p. 69; "The Deane Plan," *Business Week,* January 6, 1934, p. 22; A. L. Deane, "After NIRA—A Lasting Recovery: The 'Deane Plan' to Sustain Consumption," *Survey Graphic* 22 (October 22, 1933): 512–515; A. L. Deane, "Let's Have Steady Jobs and Stable Markets," *Independent Woman* 14 (January 1935): 5–6; A. L. Deane, *The Deane Plan for Mutual Security* (New York, 1937); A. L. Deane, *Investing in Wages* (New York, 1932); U.S. Congress, House, Ways and Means Committee, *Report 1620,* 73rd Cong., 2nd sess., 1934.

62. *New York Times,* Sept. 30, 1934, p. 33.

63. Ibid.

64. Deane, "Let's Have Steady Jobs," pp. 514–515.

65. *Congressional Record,* 74th Cong., 1st sess., 1935, vol. 79, pt. 6, pp. 6058–6059.

66. Ibid.

67. Witte, *Development of Social Security,* p. 75.

68. Ibid., p. 129.

69. Ibid., pp. 58, 75, 76, 129.

70. *New York Times,* March 9, 1935, p. 8, and January 12, 1935, p. 1.

71. U.S., Congress, House, Committee on Labor, Subcommittee, *Unemployment, Old Age and Social Insurance: Hearings on H.R. 2827, A Bill to Provide for the Establishment of Unemployment, Old Age and Social Insurance and for Other Purposes, H.R. 2859, H.R. 185, and H.R. 10,* 74th Cong., 1st sess., February 4–8, 11–15, 1935; *Congressional Record,* 74th Cong., 1st sess., 1935, vol. 79, pt. 6, p. 5884; U.S. Congress, House, Subcommittee on Labor, *Investigation of Unemployment Caused by Labor-Saving Devices in Industry: Hearings on H.R. 49,* 74th Cong., 2nd sess., February 13, 14, 17, 20, March 2, 1936, 74th Cong., 2nd sess., p. 69.

72. Graebner, *History of Retirement,* p. 193; *Newsweek* 2 (January 26, 1935):

5–6; "The Townsend Plan," *Christian Century* 5 (December 26, 1934): 1643. "Youth for Work—Age for Leisure" was the official Townsend slogan; see A. Holtzman, *The Townsend Movement: A Political Study* (New York, 1963), p. 84; Witte, *Development of Social Security*, p. 99; *Newsweek* 5 (January 5, 1935): 5–6.

73. *Congressional Record*, 74th Cong., 1st sess., 1935, vol. 79, pt. 5, pp. 5537, 5543–5545, 5686–5715, 5773–5795, and pt. 6, pp. 6068–6069. See also U.S. Congress, House, Committee on Labor, *Unemployment, Old Age and Social Insurance; Hearings on H.R. 2827, H.R. 2859, H.R. 185, H.R. 10*, 74th Cong., 1st sess., February 4–8, 11–15, 1935, pp. 181–182.

74. *Congressional Record*, 74th Cong., 1st sess., 1935, vol. 79, pt. 5: Dunn quote on p. 5537, Knutson quote on p. 5543; see also pp. 5544–5545.

75. Ibid., p. 5698.

76. *New York Times*, September 2, 1935, p. 2.

77. Ibid.

78. See *New York Times*, September 1, 1935, sec. 4, p. 11, for Green quote. For labor's continued interest in 30-hour legislation throughout 1934, see the following issues: *New York Times*, June 2, sec. 4, p. 7; June 6, p. 12; June 8, pp. 1, 8; June 9, sec. 4, pp. 3, 9. For labor's building interest in renewing 30-hour legislation after the failure to substitute 30 hours in the Walsh bill, see the following issues in 1935: *New York Times*, September 2, p. 2; September 3, p. 1; September 6, p. 12; September 8, sec. 4, p. 8; October 8, p. 8; October 15, p. 1; October 16, p. 23. See also *New York Times*, June 5, 8, 7, 9, 1935.

79. *New York Times*, October 15, 1935, p. 1.

80. *New York Times*, September 14, 1935, p. 2. For Johnson's activity, see *New York Times*, September 27, 1935, p. 23, and October 12, 1935, p. 18.

81. *New York Times*, October 20, 1935, sec. 3, p. 9; "Cereals: Six-Hour Day Helps Kellogg Company Do More Work," *Newsweek*, January 16, 1937, pp. 9, 27. See also J. M. Carmody to H. Black, December 9, 1935, Black Papers. Carmody, later deputy and then administrator of the REA, supported Black as late as December 1935 when Carmody was still at the National Labor Relations Board. In his letter to Black, Carmody discussed the Kellogg experiment at Battle Creek as an example of how 6 hours could work nationally. See also "Humanizing Machines—II, Kellogg's Six-Hour Day," *Forum and Century* 96 (September 1936): 97; *New York Times*, January 2, 1936, p. 39.

82. See the following issues in 1936: *New York Times*, January 8, p. 14; January 16, p. 2; January 17, p. 12; February 2, p. 1; March 2, p. 4; March 15, p. 24; March 16, p. 1. See also V. Rosewater, "Theory of the Shortened Working Week: Comment," *American Economic Review* 26 (December 1936): 714; H. L. Black, "The Shorter Work Week and Work Day," *Annals* 184 (March 1936): 62.

83. *New York Times*, March 19, 1936, pp. 1, 2, and April 14, 1936, pp. 8, 19.

84. *New York Times*, January 12, 1936, p. 34.

85. *New York Times*, March 19, 1936, p. 2.

86. *New York Times*, April 14, 1936, p. 19.

87. *New York Times*, April 14, 1936, pp. 1, 19.

88. *New York Times*, April 29, 1936, p. 14.

89. *New York Times*, October 17, 1936, p. 1.

90. *New York Times*, April 30, 1936, p. 5.

91. For labor pressure for 30 hours before the election, see the following issues: *New York Times*, September 7, 1936, p. 30; September 8, 1936, p. 11; September 25, 1936, p. 21.

92. *New York Times*, November 28, 1936, p. 1. See also *New York Times*, November 17, 1936, p. 13, and November 27, 1936, p. 2.

93. *New York Times*, January 12, 1937, p. 1, and January 14, 1937, p. 14.

94. *New York Times*, January 12, 1937, p. 13. For Black conference, see *New York Times*, January 22, 1937, pp. 7, 17. For Connery conference, see *New York Times*, January 23, 1937, p. 8. See also J. E. Johnson, ed., *University Debaters' Annual* (New York, 1937), pp. 59–95; "The Shorter Hours Debate," *New Republic* 89 (January 20, 1937): 89, 343. The idealistic rhetoric about the "new leisure" continued to be heard throughout the debates about the Fair Labor Standards Act. See, for example, W. P. Webb, *Divided We Stand: The Crisis of a Frontierless Democracy* (New York and Toronto, 1937), pp. 153, 235.

95. *New York Times*, January 17, 1937, p. 23.

96. See the following issues in 1937: *New York Times*, January 22, p. 7; January 23, p. 8; January 27, p. 1; January 29, p. 1; January 30, p. 1; January 31, sec. 4; p. 3.

97. See the following issues in 1937: *New York Times*, January 24, p. 14; January 27, p. 22; January 28, p. 39; January 29, p. 5; February 2, p. 1.

98. See the following issues in 1937: *New York Times*, January 29, p. 1; February 2, p. 1; February 3, p. 10.

99. Brookings Institution, *The Recovery Problem in the United States* (Washington, D.C., 1936), pp. 517–522, quote on p. 521. For the Brookings Institution view, see also *New York Times*, January 12, 1937, p. 22, and June 13, 1937, sec. 4, p. 6; H. G. Moulton, *Income and Economic Progress* (Washington, D.C., 1935), pp. 1–12. For Eccles's quote, see *New York Times*, March 16, 1937, p. 9.

100. *New York Times*, February 8, 1937, p. 1. See also "A 40-Hour World?" *Business Week*, April 10, 1937, p. 14; and see the following issues in 1937: *New York Times*, April 16, p. 22; April 18, sec. 4, p. 4; April 28, p. 22; May 10, p. 9; May 17, p. 2; May 22, p. 1. For Green's first conference with FDR, see *New York Times*, April 14, 1937, p. 1.

101. *New York Times*, May 22, 1937, p. 1.

102. See the following issues in 1937: *New York Times*, May 23, p. 1; May 23, sec. 4, p. 1; May 24, pp. 1, 7; May 25, pp. 5, 21; May 27, p. 4; May 29, p. 8; May 30, p. 17.

103. *New York Times*, May 24, 1937, p. 1.

104. *New York Times*, May 23, 1937, p. 1.

105. U.S. Congress, Senate, Committee on Education and Labor, and House, Committee on Labor, *Fair Labor Standards Act of 1937*, pt. 1, 75th Cong. 1st sess., June 2–5, 1937; idem, *Fair Labor Standards Act of 1937*, pt. 2, 75th Cong. 1st sess., June 7–9, 11, 14, 15, 1937; idem, *Fair Labor Standards Act of 1937*, pt. 3, 75th Cong. 1st sess., June 21, 22, 1937.

106. *New York Times*, June 4, 1937. See also the following issues: *Time* 30 (May 31, 1937): 8; 30 (June 21, 1937): 17; 30 (August 9, 1937): 8.

107. See the following issues: *New York Times*, June 9, 1937, p. 4; June 10,

1937, p. 14; June 11, 1937; p. 1. See also *Fair Labor Standards Act of 1937*, pt. 1: testimony of R. H. Jackson (Justice Department), pp. 1–10, L. Henderson (WPA), pp. 155–160; F. Perkins, pp. 173–180; W. Green, pp. 211–222. See also *Fair Labor Standards Act of 1937*, pt. 2: testimony of S. Hillman, pp. 943–950; G. Chandler, pp. 866–870; J. E. Edgerton, pp. 760–765; J. Emery, p. 663; N. Sargent, p. 645; J. Ryan, p. 498; J. L. Lewis, pp. 271–275. See also *Fair Labor Standards Act of 1937*, pt. 2: testimony of D. Lewis (R.-Md.), pp. 1105–1108.

108. *Fair Labor Standards Act of 1937*, pt. 2: testimony of J. Ryan, p. 498.

109. U.S. Congress, House, Committee on Labor, *Thirty-Hour Week Bill; Hearings on H.R. 7202; H.R. 4116, H.R. 8492*, 73rd Cong., 2nd sess., February 8, 9, 15, 16, 19–21, 23, 1934, p. 297.

110. See the following issues: *New York Times*, June 16, 1937, p. 23; June 17, 1937, pp. 23, 8; June 20, 1937, sec. 2, p. 5.

111. *New York Times*, January 4, 1938, pp. 1, 25, 26, 27. George Soule and many others remarked on "the powerful movement for shorter working hours in order to increase employment" and the fact that "Congress seemed about to pass the Black bill." But they also noted that the issue raised the question of total wages paid. The linking of hours to wages as a disjunction in the public discussions was the direct result of the political development of Roosevelt's administration. See G. Soule, *The Coming American Revolution* (New York, 1934), pp. 86, 87, 214, 215. The issue of wages was not settled until the passage of the Fair Labor Standards Act. D. Richberg, "Richberg Takes the Stand," *American Magazine* 119 (March 1935): 16, 17, 108–110, is a good example of the ways in which Richberg and others in the administration led the way, defining the "choice" between higher weekly wages and shorter hours. This was also Moulton's contention; see *New York Times*, January 27, 1938, p. 1. Moulton thought that the recession of 1938 was due to a cutback in working hours; see *New York Times*, February 15, 1938, p. 27. In contrast, Black and Connery, along with organized labor, rejected this linkage until forced to accept it in 1938. For example, Black argued that "reflection will also show that those who have opposed reasonable working hours have always taken the position that a reduction would reduce wages. Such has never occurred. I sincerely hope that the working people of this country . . . will not be misled by the groups that have always favored long hours and starvation wages." H. Black to R. L. Weathers, April 14, 1933, Black Papers. Like labor, both Connery and Black reasoned that shorter hours and higher wages were two sides of the same coin; alternatively, long hours and low wages had always and would continue to go together. Hence the reasoning behind the 1938 weekly wage formulation of the Fair Labor Standards act was a defeat for this traditional labor view and a victory for the economists and businessmen around Roosevelt.

112. *New York Times*, January 8, 1938, p. 1.

113. See the following issues: *New York Times*, February 2, 4, 5, 6, 9, 11, 15, 16, 20, 21, 24, 1938; March 1, 2, 3, 26, 1938; May 7, 10, 11, 13, 14, 17, 20, 21, 22, 23, 24, 25, 27, 28, 29, 31, 1938; June 1, 9, 10, 13, 19, 20, 28, 30, 31, 1938.

114. H. S. Commager, "Today's Events in the Light of History: Shorter Hours in the United States," *Senior Scholastic* 36 (May 13, 1940): 7. "Third Year

Finds the Wage Act Finally Reaching Forty-Hour Goal," *Newsweek* 16 (October 28, 1940): 16, 36; "Wages and Hours Law Unchanged," *Senior Scholastic* 36 (May 13, 1940): 36.

115. *New York Times*, April 21, 1938, pp. 1, 17. See also *New York Times*, May 13, 1938, p. 10, and May 25, 1938, p. 5; "G.M. Rehires 35,000," *Business Week*, October 22, 1938; H. W. Dodds, "The Problem of Leisure in an Industrial Age: The Significance of Work," *Vital Speeches of the Day* 4 (August 1938): 619; A. P. Sloane, "Prices, Wages and Hours: More Things for More People," *Vital Speeches of the Day* 5 (November 15, 1938): 36; T. Weed, "Our Great American Sweepstake," *Commonweal* 28 (1938): 69–70; "The State of the Union: The Menace of Leisure," *American Mercury* 48 (December 1939): 477; W. E. Fisher, *Economic Consequences of the Seven-Hour Day and Wage Changes in the Bituminous Coal Industry* (Philadelphia, 1939); E. Lyons, "Menace of Leisure," *American Mercury* 48 (1939): 477–479; A. Walsh, "The Eighty-Hour Week for Executives," *Nation's Business* 27 (July 1939): 80; H. H. Punke, "Labor Laws and Leisure Hours," *Southern Economic Journal* 6 (1939): 185–189.

116. *Time* 30 (December 27, 1937): 9.

117. See p. 184.

118. Schlesinger, *Politics of Upheaval*, pp. 690–692.

Chapter 9

1. R. Tugwell, "Reminiscences," Columbia Oral History Project (1950), p. 6. See also R. Tugwell, *The Industrial Discipline and the Governmental Arts* (New York, 1933).

2. Tugwell, *Industrial Discipline*, p. 7.

3. Ibid., p. 68.

4. Ibid., p. 25.

5. Ibid., pp. 26, 27.

6. Ibid., p. 26.

7. Ibid., p. 28.

8. Ibid., p. 61.

9. Ibid., p. 27.

10. Ibid., p. 62.

11. Ibid., p. 223.

12. Ibid., p. 68.

13. Ibid., p. 35–64.

14. Ibid., pp. 76, 84.

15. Ibid., pp. 91, 94.

16. Ibid., p. 70. V. Rosewater, "Theory of the Shortened Working Week: Comment," *American Economic Review* 26 (December 1936): 714.

17. Tugwell, *Industrial Discipline*, p. 84.

18. Ibid., p. 94.

19. Ibid., p. 114.

20. Ibid., p. 21.

21. Ibid., p. 63.

22. Ibid., p. 223.

23. Ibid., p. 224.

24. Ibid., p. 225.

25. Ibid., pp. 223–224.

26. Tugwell, "Reminiscences," p. 6. See also Tugwell, *Industrial Discipline,* pp. 63, 223–226.

27. Tugwell, *The Battle for Democracy* (New York, 1935), p. 265; see also pp. 7, 78, 84, 90, 256–265, 304–317.

28. Tugwell, "Reminiscences," p. 48; R. Tugwell, "How Shall We Pay for All This?" *American Magazine* 116 (December 1933): 11–12.

29. R. Tugwell, "The Third Economy," *Vital Speeches* 1 (April 22, 1935): 451.

30. Ibid., p. 452.

31. Ibid., p. 453.

32. Ibid., pp. 453–454.

33. For Tugwell's ideas about monetary policies and government spending to "employ the national idleness," see Tugwell, "How Shall We Pay for All This?" pp. 11, 13, 87, 29.

34. Tugwell, "Third Economy," p. 453.

35. R. Tugwell, "The Theory of Occupational Obsolescence," *Political Science Quarterly* 46 (1931): 194.

36. Ibid., p. 196. For other examples of Tugwell's attitude toward share the work, see H. Hill and R. Tugwell, *Our Economic Society and Its Problems* (New York, 1934), pp. 215, 321–322, 531.

37. Tugwell, "Theory of Occupational Obsolescence," p. 227.

38. Tugwell, "Third Economy," p. 454.

39. Ibid.

40. Ibid.

41. Ibid. See also R. Tugwell, "Government in a Changing World," *Review of Reviews* 88 (August 1933): 33–34; R. Tugwell, "Design for Government," *Political Science Quarterly* 47 (September 1933): 321–331; R. Tugwell, "The Progressive Task Today and Tomorrow," *Vital Speeches* 2 (December 1935): 130–135; R. Tugwell and L. Keyserling, *Redirecting Education,* 2 vols. (New York, 1934), 1:50–99; R. Tugwell, *Roosevelt's Revolution: The First Year—A Personal Perspective* (New York, 1977); Hill and Tugwell, *Our Economic Society and Its Problems,* pp. 321–323, 531; R. Tugwell, *Industry's Coming of Age* (New York, 1927), pp. 238, 239, 256–262; J. J. Metz, ed., "The Machine and Leisure," *Industrial Arts and Vocational Education* 26 (December 1937): 416.

42. W. Lippman, "Free Time and Extra Money," *Woman's Home Companion* 57 (April 1930): 31.

43. Ibid.

44. Ibid.

45. Ibid.

46. Ibid., p. 32.

47. Ibid.

48. Ibid.

49. Ibid.

50. Ibid.

51. W. Lippmann, *Interpretations 1933–1935* (New York, 1936), p. 376; see also pp. 374–375.

52. The story of American education deserves a chapter of its own. Because of time and space constraints, it is reduced here to a footnote. The interest in education for leisure at the expense of education for work (vocational education), which educators displayed in the 1920s (see chap. 4), built to a high point in the winter of 1933–1934. This interest is apparent from the mass of publications concerning leisure. The standard reference, D. Carpenter and G. Parker, eds., *Educational Index* (New York, 1929–1941), vol. 2, covering July 1932 to June 1935, shows 232 articles, books, and reports listed under the heading *leisure* (see pp. 901–903); in vol. 4, covering July 1938 to June 1941, only 43 listings are to be found (see p. 941), and by vol. 5, 1941–1944, only 12 were listed (see p. 948). The interest in vocational and career education, as shown by this index, increased somewhat, but the increase was not nearly as dramatic as the fall-off in the number of entries about leisure. For representative articles, see "The Enrichment of Human Life," *Journal of the National Education Association* 19 (February 1930): 64; "Vitalized Commencements and Leisure," *Journal of the National Education Association* 19 (December 1930): 311; A. B. Brown, "The Leisure Problem," *Hibbert Journal* 28 (1930): 455–464; V. K. Brown, "Use of Leisure," *Playground* 23 (1930): 713–714; H. Suzzallo, "The Use of Leisure," *Journal of the National Education Association* 19 (April 1930): 123; E. R. Pyrtle, "Editorial: The Leisure of Tomorrow," *Journal of the National Education Association* 19 (January 1930): L. P. Jacks, "Leisure Time—A Modern Challenge," *Playground* 24 (December 1930): 475; F. W. Kirkham, "The Wise Use of Leisure," *Journal of the National Education Association* 19 (May 1930): 138; L. H. Conrad, "The Worthy Use of Leisure," *Forum* 86 (November 1931): 312; S. Crowther, "Leisure and the Machine: An Interview with Myron C. Taylor," *Saturday Evening Post* 203 (March 28, 1931): 3; W. Pangburn, "Leisure and the Seven Objectives," *Journal of the National Education Association* 20 (April 1931): 20, 121; R. S. Wallace, "Education and Training for Leisure," *Vocational Guidance Magazine* 11 (1931): 28–31; R. S. Wallace, *Education of the Whole Man: A Plea for a New Spirit in Education* (New York, 1931); R. S. Wallace, "Problem of Industrial Leisure," *High School Teacher* 9 (1933): 90; H. Woodbury, "Preparing for Leisure," *Parents Magazine* 8 (January 1933): 11; F. M. Debatin, "Urban University and the New Leisure; with Discussion," in *Association of Urban Universities, Twentieth Annual Meeting* (1933), pp. 66–79; W. G. Moorhead, "Two Committee Reports on Leisure Time," *Journal of Health and Physical Education* 4 (1933): 34–36; L. J. Richardson, "Books and Leisure," *Library Journal* 15 (May 1933): 58, 442.

One of the leading advocates of education for leisure was an Englishman, Lawrence Jacks. He visited the United States several times in the early 1930s and gained national attention. His visits provided one focus for educators interested in the "new leisure," as did his numerous publications, which include L. P. Jacks, *My American Friends* (New York, 1933); L. P. Jacks, *The Confession of an Octogenarian* (New York, 1942); L. P. Jacks, *Education through Recreation* (New York and London, 1932), esp. pp. 1–11, 95–112, 146–155; L. P. Jacks,

Education of the Whole Man (New York and London, 1931), esp. pp. 51–79, 128–141; L. P. Jacks, *Responsibility and Culture* (New Haven, 1925), esp. pp. 25–42; L. P. Jacks, *The Revolt against Mechanism: The Hibbert Lectures* (London, 1933); L. P. Jacks, *Ethical Factors of the Present Crisis* (Baltimore, 1933), esp. pp. 65–77. See also *supra* p. 354, note 14.

The New York NRA's interest in leisure also attracted national attention in 1933–1934, with many educators becoming involved (see chap. 4). See D. I. Cline, *Training for Recreation under the WPA, 1935–37* (Chicago, 1939).

The efforts of the Roosevelt administration to get the schools to focus on work and occupations instead of leisure has been discussed in this chapter. Leon Keyserling and Tugwell were leading advocates of using the schools to teach new work in the "third economy" and transform "useless education" into "functional" career and professional education. This was a development similar to the old vocational education. But there were important differences, having to do with the search for what could be made into work and careers rather than with teaching established work skills. In addition, the National Youth Administration's efforts to find work and teach jobs to teenagers had an impact on America's ideas about what learning and teaching were about. Finally, the creation and reports of the Advisory Committee on Education completed the shift of interest away from education for leisure to education for work. The story of the committee and its struggles over the issues, with leisure advocate members such as Luther Gulick and John Frey contending with work creators Modecai Ezekiel and Frank Porter Graham, are as interesting and compelling as the struggle among American scientists.

Chapter 10

1. G. H. Daniels, *Science in American Society* (New York, 1971), p. 308; see also pp. 309, 319.

2. Ibid., p. 319.

3. R. A. Millikan, "The New Opportunity in Science," *Science* 50 (1919): 285.

4. R. H. Kargon, ed., *The Maturing of American Science* (Washington, D.C., 1974), p. 17.

5. D. Van Tassel and M. G. Hall, eds., *Science and Society in the United States* (Homewood, Ill., 1966), p. 33.

6. Kargon, *Maturing of American Science*, p. 34. See also C. E. Dankert, "Efficiency and Unemployment," *Canadian Forum* 12 (February 1932): 169.

7. "Previews into the Future of Science," *Science* 79 (June 1, 1934): 8–10; L. M. Passano, "Ploughing under the Science Crop," *Science* [N.S.] 81 (July 1935): 46. "Reductions in the Federal Budget for Scientific Work," *Science* 76 (December 16, 1932): 561. "Revolt against Science," *Christian Century* 119 (January 24, 1934): 110–112, D. Ramsey, "Progress and Confusion in Science," *American Mercury* 33 (December 1934): 430–435. J. W. N. Sullivan, "Revolution in Science," *Atlantic* 151 (March 1933): 286–294; H. T. Stetson, "Which Way Science?" *Scientific Monthly* 48 (January 1939): 28–33; "Science

Gives New Motives for Finer and Better Lives," *Science* 33 (May 28, 1938): 216–217; R. C. Tobey, *The American Ideology of National Science, 1919–1930* (Pittsburgh, 1971), pp. 16–18, 185; S. Tschachotin, "Crisis in Scientific Research and the Way Out," *Science* 77 (May 5, 1933): 426–427; H. S. Taylor, "Science and Government," *Scientific Monthly* 36 (May 1933): 463–464; "To Amplify Wealth," *Scientific American* 157 (January 13, 1937): 524–526; H. C. Urey, "Industries without Touch of Science Would Never Be," *Science* 32 (October 30, 1937): 277; E. R. Weidlein, "New Industries for Old," *Scientific Monthly* 39 (December 1934): 547–550; W. R. Whitley, "Accomplishments and the Future of the Physical Sciences," *Science* 84 (September 4, 1936): 211–217.

8. M. Schlesinger, Jr., *The Coming of the New Deal* (Boston, 1959), p. 91.

9. *New York Times*, May 29, 1932, p. 17.

10. A. Dahlberg, *Jobs, Machines, and Capitalism* (New York, 1932), p. ix; see also Preface.

11. Ibid., p. 21.

12. Ibid., pp. xii, xiii.

13. Ibid., p. 100; see also pp. 2, 122.

14. Ibid., p. 233; see also pp. 21–36.

15. Ibid., p. 27.

16. Ibid., p. 36.

17. Ibid.; see also pp. 37–78.

18. Ibid., p. 2.

19. *New York Times*, May 29, 1932, p. 17.

20. Dahlberg, *Jobs, Machines, and Capitalism*, p. 103; see also pp. 99–102.

21. Ibid., p. 99; see also Chap. 3.

22. Ibid., p. 2; see also pp. 76, 238.

23. Ibid., pp. 26–42.

24. Ibid., p. 224; see also Chapter 12.

25. Ibid., p. 225.

26. Ibid., p. 227.

27. Ibid., p. 233.

28. Ibid., p. 242.

29. Ibid., p. 243.

30. Ibid., p. 234.

31. Ibid., p. 235.

32. Ibid., p. 244.

33. U.S. Congress, House, Committee on Labor, *Thirty-Hour Week Bill; Hearings on H.R. 14105*, 73rd Cong., 1st sess., January 18, 19, 20, 23, 24, 25, 26, 27, 30, 1933, p. 268; R. E. Flanders, "Limitations and Possibilities of Economic Planning," *Annals*, July 1932, pp. 352–365.

34. F. Knight, "Review," *Journal of Political Economy* 40 (August 1932): 573.

35. *New York Times*, May 29, 1932, p. 17.

36. *New York Times*, March 25, 1833, p. 6.

37. Schlesinger, *Coming of the New Deal*, p. 91.

38. *New York Times*, April 26, 1933, p. 5.

39. S. Kimball, "The Social Effects of Mass Production," *Science* 77 (January 6, 1933): 1.

40. Ibid.

41. Ibid.

42. "Technology: Definition and Origin," *Nation* 135 (December 28, 1932): 646. See also A. Raymond, *What Is Technocracy?* (New York, 1933), pp. 8–15.

43. C. A. Beard, "America's Capacity," *New Republic* 82 (March 20, 1935): 164. See also C. A. Beard, "Introduction," in G. Laing, *Toward Technocracy* (Los Angeles, 1933).

44. As quoted by H. Elsner, *The Technocrats* (Syracuse, N.Y., 1967), p. 1; reports about the technocrats were made almost daily in the *New York Times* in December and January 1932–1933.

45. For Austin T. Levy's comments on technocracy, see U.S. Congress, House, *Thirty-Hour Week Bill; Hearings on H.R. 14105*, pp. 43ff.; *New York Times*, January 11, 1933, p. 5; L. Cohen to H. Black, January 30, 1933, Black Papers.

46. W. W. Parrish, "What Is Technocracy?" *New Outlook* 161 (November 1932): 17.

47. Quoted in F. L. Allen, "What about Technocracy?" *American Magazine* 115 (March 1933): 123; see also pp. 34–35. W. Parrish, "Technocracy's Question," *New Outlook* 116 (December 1932): 13–17; W. E. Akin, *Technocracy and the American Dream: The Technocratic Movement, 1900–1941* (Berkeley, 1977), p. 62.

48. H. Scott, "Technocracy Smashes the Price System," *Harpers* 166 (January 1933): 132.

49. W. Parrish, "Technocracy's Challenge," *New Outlook* 116 (January 1933): 15–17.

50. H. Scott, "Technocracy Speaks," *Living Age* 343 (December 1932): 297–303.

51. Scott, "Technocracy Smashes the Price System," p. 139; see also pp. 138, 140, 141. See also W. Parrish, *An Outline of Technocracy* (New York, 1933).

52. Allen, "What About Technocracy?" pp. 34–35, 123–125.

53. Scott, "Technocracy Smashes the Price System," pp. 129–142.

54. *New York Times*, January 14, 1933, p. 1. See also E. J. Reed, "The Utopian Society," *Common Sense* 3 (December 1934): 14.

55. Scott, "Technocracy Smashes the Price System," p. 137. See also Scott, "Technocracy Speaks," pp. 297–303.

56. Scott, "Technocracy Smashes the Price System," p. 138. See also H. Scott, "The Imminence of Social Change: The Impact of Technology on a Price System of Production," *National Education Association Addresses and Proceedings* 71 (1933): 564–573; H. Scott, "A Rendezvous with Destiny," *American Engineer* 6 (October 1936): 8–10, 24; H. Scott et al., *Introduction to Technocracy* (New York, 1933); F. L. Ackerman, "Technocrats and the Debt Burden," *New Republic* 74 (May 3, 1933): 337–338; Technocracy, Inc., *Technocracy Study Course* (New York, 1934), pp. 121–156.

57. G. A. Laing, *Toward Technocracy* (Los Angeles, 1933), p. 31.

58. Ibid., p. 33.

59. H. Loeb, *Life in a Technocracy: What It Might Be Like* (New York, 1933), p. 121. See also H. Loeb and Associates, *The Chart of Plenty* (New York, 1935).

60. Scott, "Technocracy Speaks," p. 300. See also monthly issues of *Living Age*, 1933–1935.

61. W. Parrish, "Technocracy's Question," p. 13.

62. Loeb, *Life in a Technocracy*, p. 170.

63. Parrish, "Technocracy's Question," p. 13.

64. Laing, *Toward Technocracy*, p. 56.

65. Loeb, *Life in a Technocracy*, p. 115.

66. F. Arkright, *The ABC of Technocracy* (New York, 1933), p. 70. See also Loeb, *Life in a Technocracy*, pp. 115–116.

67. Laing, *Toward Technocracy*, p. 55.

68. Scott, "Technocracy Smashes the Price System," p. 137.

69. Loeb, *Life in a Technocracy*, p. 114.

70. Ibid., pp. 104–109, chap. 5, et passim.

71. Ibid., p. 104; see also pp. 105, 106.

72. Ibid., p. 106; see also p. 161.

73. Ibid., p. 114.

74. Ibid., p. 115; see also pp. 110–111.

75. Ibid., p. 121.

76. Ibid., pp. 115–126.

77. Ibid., p. 106.

78. Ibid., p. 161.

79. Ibid., p. 164.

80. Ibid., pp. 162–163.

81. Ibid., p. 164.

82. Ibid., pp. 165–166.

83. C. P. Steinmetz, "Science and Religion," *Harpers* 144 (February 1922): 296–302; W. N. Polakov, "The Curse of Work," *Nation* 117 (November 7, 1923): 506; A. Dean, "A Point of View," *Industrial Education Magazine* 25 (January 1924): 179; H. W. Bibber, *Charles Proteus Steinmetz* (Schenectady, 1965); C. P. Steinmetz, "Electricity and Civilization," *Harpers* 144 (January 1922): 227–232; D. Bell, "Technocracy Rides Again In New High-Powered Campaign," *New Leader* 25 (March 14, 1942): 1.

84. B. F. Skinner, *Walden Two* (New York, 1948), p. 84.

85. *New York Times*, January 10, 1933, p. 23.

86. Akin, *Technocracy and the American Dream*, p. 150.

87. "Our Point of View," *Scientific American* 148 (March 1933): 138; "Technocracy—Boon, Blight, or Bunk," *Literary Digest* 114 (December 31, 1932): 5, 6.

88. Kargon, *Maturing of American Science*, p. 34.

89. H. A. Wallace, "The Social Advantages and Disadvantages of the Engineering-Scientific Approach to Civilization," *Science* [N.S.] 79 (January 5, 1934): 1–5; "$16,000,000 Research Program Outlined," *Literary Digest* 118 (December 29, 1934): 18; "Work of the Science Advisory Board," *Science* 80 (December 21, 1934): 582–583; K. T. Compton, "Science Advisory Board," *Science* 78 (October 6, 1933): 78. "Science Advisory Board," *Scientific Monthly* 37 (November 1933); D.C. Jackson, "The Division of Engineering and Industrial Research in the National Research Council," *Science* 77 (May 26, 1933):

500–503; I. Bowman, "Summary Statement of the Work of the National Research Council; 1933–1934," *Science* 80 (October 26, 1934): 368–373. *New York Times*, February 23, 1934, p. 1.

90. Ibid.

91. A. H. Dupree, *Science and the Federal Government* (Cambridge, Mass., 1957), 347–349; Kargon, *Maturing of American Science*, p. 34.

92. *New York Times*, May 29, 1937, p. 19.

93. Kargon, *Maturing of American Science*, pp. 81–95.

94. *New York Times*, February 23, 1934, p. 1. See also *New York Times*, January 28, 1934, sec. 6, p. 6.

95. *New York Times*, February 23, 1934, p. 10.

96. Ibid. See also *New York Times*, February 26, 1934, p. 16.

97. *New York Times*, February 23, 1934, p. 10.

98. Ibid.

99. Ibid.

100. Ibid.

101. There was immediate and strong support for "Science Makes Jobs." See P. G. Agnew, "Harnessing Scientific Discoveries," *Scientific Monthly* 40 (February 1935): 170–173; "Another Century of Progress; American Industry Reveals Its New Products, and Its More Distant Goals," *Business Week*, May 26, 1934, p. 13; R. I. Allen, "Science Versus Unemployment," *Science* 89 (May 26, 1939): 474–479; J. D. Bernal, "If Industry Gave Science a Chance," *Harpers* 170 (February 1935): 257–268; "Financing Research under the New Order," *Literary Digest* 118 (November 3, 1934): 17; C. C. Fernas, "Researchers vs. Salesmen," *American Mercury* 33 (October 1934): 193–197; T. S. Harding, "There Is Research . . . and Research," *Scientific American* 150 (January 1934): 14–16; F. B. Jewett, "Social Effects of Modern Science," *Science* 76 (July 8, 1932): 23–26; W. Kaempffert, "Science Changes Its Mind," *Forum* 90 (August 1933): 104–108; R. A. Millikan, "Science and the World of Tomorrow," *Vital Speeches* 5 (May 1, 1939): 446–447.

102. A. P. Sloan, et al., "Science and Industry in the Coming Century," *Scientific Monthly* 39 (July 1934): 67. See also W. W. Campbell, "The National Academy of Sciences; Address of the President," *Science* 80 [N.S.] (December 14, 1934): 536–537.

103. Sloan, et al., "Science and Industry in the Coming Century, p. 77.

104. Ibid. See also C. F. Kettering, "Industry Research," *Scientific American* 150 (May 1934): 242–243. Kettering, a research director at General Motors, in a speech before a group of scientists and engineers in Chicago, on receiving the Washington Award, noted: "Many people think of scientific research as something to reduce the man hours required to perform any given task. [However, the] "most important factor, and many more times important, . . . is the development of new jobs and new industries."

105. L. M. Passano, "Ploughing under the Science Crop," *Science* [N.S.] 81 (July 1935): 46; "More Science or Less? The Question Arises Again," *Literary Digest* 118 (September 1934): 16; "Does Science Take Jobs or Make Them?" *Literary Digest* 117 (March 10, 1934): 16; *New York Times*, March 24, 1934, p. 12.

106. *New York Times*, December 16, 1934, sec. 6, p. 6. See also *New York Times*, December 14, 1934.

107. *New York Times*, December 16, 1934, sec. 6, p. 6. See also Science Advisory Board, *Report* (Washington, D.C., 1934).

108. K. T. Compton, "Government's Responsibility in Science," *Science* 81 (April 12, 1935): 347–355. K. T. Compton, "Report of the Science Advisory Board on the Proposal of a Recovery Program of Science Progress," *Science* 81 (January 4, 1935): 471–472; H. Ward, "Science and Government; Recommendation of the Science Advisory Board," *New Republic* 84 (September 11, 1934): 126–127, 136; *New York Times*, May 29, 1937, p. 19; W. W. Campbell, "The National Academy of Sciences; Address of the President," *Science* 80 (December 14, 1934): 535–537; Kargon, *Maturing of American Science*, pp. 81–95, 159.

109. Letter from F. D. Roosevelt to Compton, reprinted in "Responsibility of Engineering; with Reply by K. Compton," *Science* 84 (October 30, 1936): 393–394.

110. "Creation of the National Resources Committee," *Monthly Labor Review* 41 (August 1935): 356–357.

111. *Technological Trends and the National Policy*, Report of the Subcommittee on Technology to the National Resources Committee (Washington, D.C., June 1937), p. vii. See also Kargon, *Maturing of American Science*, p. 72.

112. *Technological Trends and the National Policy*, p. viii.

113. D. Weintraub, "Unemployment and Increasing Productivity," in *Technological Trends and the National Policy*, p. 67.

114. Ibid., p. 86; see also pp. 80–83.

115. *New York Times*, May 26, 1935, p. 21.

116. C. W. Pursell, "Science and Government Agencies," in *Science and Society in the United States*, ed. D. Van Tassel and M. G. Hall (Homewood, Ill., 1966), p. 238; H. Hoover et al., "The Scientific Work of the Government of the United States," *Scientific Monthly* 36 (January 1933): 7–34; Kargon, *Maturing of American Science*, pp. 99–100.

117. Kargon, *Maturing of American Science*, p. 99.

118. V. Bush and the Office of Scientific Research and Development, *Science—The Endless Frontier* (Washington, D.C., 1945), p. v–vi. See also Kargon, *Maturing of American Science*, pp. 99, 161.

119. V. Bush and the Office of Scientific Research and Development, *Science—The Endless Frontier*, pp. v–vi.

120. Ibid; see also pp. 1–4, 6, 25–26.

121. Ibid. See also V. Bush, *Endless Horizons* (Washington, D.C., 1946), pp. 40–44, 146–148; G. Wendt, "Science and Leisure," *Science Digest* 7 (March 1940): 3, 97.

Chapter 11

1. Wells's interest in the contest of work and leisure may also be found in H. G. Wells, "The Overflowing Energy of Mankind," in his *The Work, Wealth and Happiness of Mankind* (New York, 1931), 2:751–784. See also H. G. Wells, *The Shape of Things to Come* (New York, 1933), pp. 420–431; H. G. Wells, *Man's Work and Wealth* (Garden City, N.Y., 1931), pp. 620–646. In 1931, he spoke before the Union of Shop Assistants in New York concerning shorter hours and unemployment; see *New York Times*, July 21, 1931.

2. H. G. Wells, *Things to Come* (New York, 1935), pp. 31, 34, 66–70, quote on p. 3; C. Beard, ed., *Whither Mankind* (New York, 1928), Introduction, quote on pp. 11–12. Beard continues: "What is civilization? Implements and devices and practices by which men and women lift themselves above the savage—the whole economic order, the system of leisure built upon it, the improvement of that leisure and all manifestations of religion, beauty, and appreciation. . . . The structure of any civilization is the material fabric that frees mankind . . . forcing continuously the creation of new goods, new processes, and new modes of life." Most reviewers missed Wells's main point. The exception was G. Seldes, "Mr. Wells to the Screen," *Saturday Review of Literature* 13 (November 2, 1935): 11.

The author acknowledges, with thanks, permission to include portions of *Things to Come* and *The Man Who Could Work Miracles* granted by A. P. Watt Ltd. on behalf of the Literary Executors of the Estate of H. G. Wells.

3. Wells, *Things to Come*, p. 95.

4. Ibid., pp. 109–115.

5. Ibid., pp. 121–124.

6. Ibid., pp. 126–127.

7. Ibid., pp. 130–131.

8. Ibid., pp. 132–134.

9. Ibid., p. 155.

10. H. G. Wells, *The Time Machine* (London, 1985; originally published 1895), pp. 60–66.

11. H. G. Wells, *The Man Who Could Work Miracles* (New York, 1936), pp. 3–20.

12. Ibid., pp. 44–47.

13. Ibid., pp. 54, 55.

14. Ibid., pp. 57–60.

15. Ibid., pp. 70–77.

16. Ibid., pp. 78–80.

17. Ibid., pp. 82–104.

18. Ibid., pp. 105–109.

19. Ibid., p. 49.

20. A. M. Okum, ed., *The Battle against Unemployment: An Introduction to a Current Issue of Public Policy* (New York, 1965), pp. vii–viii; A. Rees, "Dimensions of the Unemployment Problem," in *A Symposium on Employment* (Washington, D.C., 1964).

21. E. P. Thompson, "Time, Work-Discipline and Industrial Capitalism," *Past and Present* 38 (December 1967); 56–97, quote on p. 57.

22. U.S. Congress, House, Committee on Education and Labor, Subcommittee on Labor Standards, *Hearings on H.R. 1784: To Revise the Overtime Compensation Requirement of the Fair Labor Standards Act of 1938*, 96th Cong., 1st sess., October 23, 24, 25, 1979. See also *Congressional Record*, 96th Cong., 1st sess., E.5072, October 16, 1979; *Des Moines Register*, October 23, 1979; J. Conyers, "Have a Four-day Workweek? Yes." *American Legion*, April 1980, p. 26. Quote from a personal letter from Conyers to Members of the House of Representatives, photocopy with the author, dated February 15, 1979.

23. See pp. 98–99.

24. S. Linder, *The Harried Leisure Class* (New York, 1970), pp. 77–78; S. de Grazia, *Of Time, Work and Leisure* (New York, 1962), pp. 214–224.

25. J. K. Galbraith, *The Affluent Society* (New York, 1958), pp. 116–123, 259–260, quote on p. 116; H. Marcuse, *Eros and Civilization*, (New York, 1962), Preface and Introduction, quote on p. xi. For a more empirical and less ideological approach, see J. Brack and K. Cowling, "Advertising and Labor Supply: Workweek and Workyear in U.S. Manufacturing Industries, 1919–1976," *Kyklos* 36 (1983): 285–303. Brack and Cowling show that a negative correlation between the amount of advertising and work hours' reduction existed over the whole time period.

26. W. Lippmann, "Free Time and Extra Money," *Woman's Home Companion* 57 (April 1930): 31; E. Fromm, *Escape from Freedom* (New York, 1964), p. 347.

27. J. A. Ryan, "High Wages and Unemployment," *Commonweal* 13 (January 7, 1931): 259–260; J. A. Ryan, *Questions of the Day* (New York, 1931), p. 242. See also B. Hunnicutt, "Monsignor John A. Ryan and the Shorter Hours of Labor: A Forgotten Vision of 'Genuine Progress,'" *Catholic Historical Review* 69 (July 1983): 384–402.

28. Linder, *Harried leisure Class*, pp. 120–139.

29. *C.B.S. Evening News*, June 8, 1987; *New York Times*, June 9, 1987, p. 3.

30. Marcuse, *Eros and Civilization*, p. vii.

INDEX